James Hale Bates

**Notes of Foreign Travel**

James Hale Bates

**Notes of Foreign Travel**

ISBN/EAN: 9783337211905

Printed in Europe, USA, Canada, Australia, Japan

Cover: Foto ©Andreas Hilbeck / pixelio.de

More available books at **www.hansebooks.com**

# NOTES

## OF

# FOREIGN TRAVEL.

BY

J. H. BATES.

NEW YORK:
BURR PRINTING HOUSE,
1891.

# NOTES OF FOREIGN TRAVEL.

*May* 1, 1889.—At last, after so many years, I am about to realize the dream of my life—a visit to lands beyond the sea ; and this cool, bright morning, at half-past six, finds me with wife, daughter Betty and niece Mary on board the huge steamer "City of New York," which at the above hour slowly swings from her moorings into the Hudson at Pier 43, and carefully feels her way down the river and harbor, through the Narrows, into the broad Atlantic.

We leave the city bedecked as never before for the wonderful three days' pageant of the `Centennial Celebration of Washington's Inauguration as President of thirteen United States, now grown to forty-four, with a population increased twentyfold !

The " City of New York," of the Inman Line, now entering on her seventh passage, and her twin sister, the " City of Paris," are the largest steamships now afloat, each being 580 feet long and of 10,000 tons burden. We have state-room No. 5 on the promenade-deck. The first-class passengers number three hundred and sixty-four. We found on the tables in the dining-room many presents of flowers, fruits, wines and delicacies, which the kind thoughts of the donors suggested might relieve the tedium or illness of travel by sea. I think tokens of kindly remembrance are more grateful on the occasions when we are about to absent ourselves from home than at any other time. Specially touching to me were the fine presents from the people in my employ, with the kind words accompanying put into the form of verse and bearing an assurance that each and all would do the best possible in my behalf while absent, with kind wishes so heartily expressed that I must think them sincere.

The ocean is as fully at rest to-day, I should think, as it ever becomes, "dark heaving" only, with the gentlest possible pulsation of its mighty heart.

The North German Lloyd steamer "Trave" left her dock when we did, and although we passed her in the harbor, she has kept in sight, bearing away on a more northerly course, until now, four o'clock P. M., she shows faintly with a veiling banner of smoke far on our larboard, and many miles behind.

I lost the seats I had engaged at table a week ago, because when the steward asked me for what trip I wanted them, I answered the next, and found, when claiming them, that the "next" trip meant the second time the steamer sails from New York, as the "trip" dates from Liverpool. However, good seats were assigned us at a table with Dr. Willoughby Walling and his family of wife and two youthful sons. Dr. Walling is returning to Edinburgh, where he was consul under President Cleveland, and is not likely to be disturbed by the change in the Administration, as he is a friend of President Harrison, and from Indianapolis.

*May 2.*—The sea continues tranquil, but since noon yesterday the sky has been obscured by dull, chilly clouds, with occasional spatters of rain. The warmest wraps are needed on deck to protect from the raw air, and the entire aspect of sky and water is dreary. The face of the deep, away to the horizon's edge, takes on the ashen hue of the sky, and the poet's

> "Old ocean's gray and melancholy waste"

is fully appropriate.

At noon we had made four hundred and eighty-four miles from Sandy Hook, or four hundred and thirty-four miles in twenty-four hours. I saw on the deck a pert English sparrow hopping tamely about. One of the sailors stated that these friendly little creatures often go out with the steamers far to sea, sometimes making the entire passage. It grew more and more chilly in the afternoon, and night came on with a heavy rain, driving everybody under cover of the state-rooms and rather insufficient public sitting-rooms. The rain continued all night.

*May 3.*—At six o'clock in the morning the deafening fog-horn gave token that we were in the remote neighborhood of the Banks of Newfoundland. We have been in fog all day, with some short intervals of open weather, and every half minute the steam-horn screeched terribly enough to wake the Seven Sleepers. The fog is not dense enough at any time to obscure the view within a quarter of a mile of the steamer, nothing at all like what often settles on the East River between New York and Brooklyn. We made four hundred and twenty miles yesterday.

I could not find my sparrow anywhere on deck this morning, and was told that quite likely, as often happens, he had flown too far from the steamer, and could not get back. There is only a moderate swell of the ocean, imparting no more than a slight motion to the huge steamer. After comparatively clearing away, the fog will gather with wonderful celerity, and the dismal fog-horn sounded all night, much to our disturbance, as our rooms are on the promenade-deck, with port-holes open, for it has come off warm. The sea roughened toward night, and the crests of the swells show white with foam all about. Still, the only motion of the steamer is a slow roll, just enough to affect a few of the most sensitive passengers.

*May* 4.—Warm, with very little sea, and the fog quite gone. The run was four hundred and thirty-three miles, so that, under the most favorable circumstances, the steamer is not doing as well as was expected. The machinery is said not to be working well at all points. Now, at 4 P.M., the sun is out almost for the first time since the first half day, and the sky is not all clear from clouds.

I have just seen my little sparrow, or another equally at home, on deck. Life on board is the laziest imaginable. We stroll about or lounge, reading, in the steamer chairs; eat with relish not only the three regular meals at table, but of the many dishes frequently brought about by the cabin-boys. We have on board Senators Sherman and Cameron, with their families; John C. New, Consul-General to London; Thomas, Minister to Sweden, where he married a pretty Norwegian girl, whom he has had home to Portland, Me., on a visit, and is now on his way back; Henry Abbey, the popular theatrical manager, with his family, and a miscellaneous company of the sort one usually meets in travel, including a due proportion of those half-outlandish men and women in looks, dress, and manner, whom one never does see except away from home, but who must needs abide somewhere when on land. We are an epitome of the great world of social existence, twelve hundred miles at sea, in the midst of a loneliness so utter that one feels easily that we alone are left of the human race. Pools on the daily run of the steamer are sold in the smoking-room by a Hebrew auctioneer with a half-horsey look, and the interest taken in them is surprising. The weather continues heavy, with more or less rain, a mild sea and light fogs.

*May* 5, *Sunday.*—No change during the night except increasingly warm, so that wraps are uncomfortable. Divine service in the dining-room at 10 A.M., Captain Lewis reading the prayers and a Boston musical club singing. The noble English service had a peculiar solemnity in mid-ocean, where God's power and man's helplessness are so feelingly contrasted. The run was only three hundred and ninety-two miles, a falling off caused by some injury to one of the propelling screws, disabling it yesterday for some four hours, during which only half speed was made. The outline of a steamer is dimly seen at 3 P. M. on the western horizon, and a little later a full-rigged ship showing spectrally through the mist. The weather is warm, with low clouds all about, giving down frequent drizzles of rain. After dark we watched from the stern the far-streaming line of phosphorescent light in our wake.

*May* 6.—Raining hard in the morning, but about noon the sky cleared, the wind freshened and grew cool, the sea changed its dull hue to the dark blue one associates with it, and heaves in foam-crested swells. A small company of white gulls is noticed hovering with swift wing not far away, although we must be not less than six hundred miles from any land. The run was four hundred and twenty-nine miles.

In the evening a concert took place in the dining-saloon, Senator Sherman presiding. The entertainment would have been thought good anywhere, and yielded something over four hundred dollars.

*May* 7.—All things nearly the same as yesterday. The run was four hundred and thirty-one miles. In the evening, at a meeting over which Senator Sherman presided, a resolution exceedingly complimentary to the steamer, Captain Lewis and all in any way connected with her, was passed. This sort of thing always gets itself managed somehow, and may mean much or little, or nothing at all.

*May* 8.—At half-past one this morning wakened by the fizz of a rocket, and looking out, saw the famous Fastnet Light gleaming through the thin mist like a huge red star, and when I went on deck at four o'clock the wind was fresh, the atmosphere transparent, the blue waves tossing manes of foam, flocks of gulls swirling wildly all about, just such a sea as one imagines guarding the British Isles, and right at hand on our left the precipitous shore of Ireland, its dark rocks forever chafed by the encroaching sea. Above the cliffs all was green and fair and tender in the morning light of May, the east luminous, a church-tower outlined against it from the long crest of a slope, coming down to the steep shore. The first view of the Emerald Isle is enchanting.

At five we were off the entrance to Queenstown Harbor, and slowed up for a perky little tender called the " Flying Squirrel," which came bobbing out to fetch away the Queenstown passengers and mails. But the sea was decided to be too rough, and the steamer worked into the harbor and came to anchor while the transfer took place. Our luggage came ashore with us at the Customs Wharf, where the examination was of the slightest. The only articles dutiable are spirits, tobacco, fire-arms, and dynamite. We took rooms and breakfasted at the Queen's Hotel, and after luncheon rode in a jaunting-car for some distance up the river Lee, then to a point where the broad harbor, formerly known as the Cove of Cork, lay before us in the light of a perfect day. This harbor equals in size and beauty that of New York, is fully land-locked, the ample river Lee coming into it, quite as the Hudson enters New York Bay. Queenstown itself is a small town of little interest. The trains from the interior have brought in hundreds of emigrants to take ship to-morrow for America, who crowd the quays and move along the street fronting them in long procession. They are mostly young men and women, a few of middle age, and fewer still of aged, robust in health, and, as it seemed to me, more pleased than sad at the prospect of leaving a land which promises so little to their future. But surely there must be some fundamental wrong in a country when the very substance and flower of it go into voluntary exile, as the Irish have done and are now doing! Three thousand sailed from this port alone last week.

At half-past three P.M. we took the train for Cork, twelve miles distant, the road following the Lee. The "pleasant waters of the river Lee" flow down to the sea through a charming valley, thickly set with comfortable houses, with now and then the large, handsome residence of the rich citizen, well retired among old trees in full leaf, with lawns of the deepest green. Very much of the land we saw is in grass for pasture, and I have never seen at home such rank, dense herbage and perfect mat of intense green. These small pastures are enclosed in substantial walls of stone, laid in mortar, as indeed are all boundary walls. The larger fields are surrounded by green hedges. Flocks of Southdown sheep grazed contentedly in these, with now and then a herd of comfortable cows. All along the roads the gray boundary walls are overgrown with ivy; on the wide upper surfaces violets and tinted daisies peep from green mosses, and rich grass studded with dandelions hide the lower stones. Everywhere is green luxuriance. Quaint cottages, mostly of stone covered with plaster, with roofs of thatch, and half ivy-clad, appear frequently, blending harmoniously with the landscape, and forming pastoral scenes of peaceful beauty.

We took rooms in the comfortable Hotel Imperial at Cork, and after a good dinner, well served in our private parlor, retired early to sleep on huge bedsteads of solid mahogany, deeply curtained, our first sleep on British soil. I found myself lurching from side to side in my walking for several hours after landing, and steadying myself as when the steamer rolled.

*May* 9.—A rainy day. Ordered a landau, and drove about the town, which lies pleasantly on both sides of the Lee, sloping up from the river, two branches of which unite just below the city. The two parts are connected by nine handsome stone bridges, one of them of great age. The population of Cork is about 80,000, and it has a very considerable export trade. It is well and solidly built, with not much of marked interest to see.

We visited the Cathedral, a modern and not impressive structure of gray stone, with a fine mosaic chancel floor. Went to the little church of St. Ann, in whose belfry hang the bells of Shandon, widely famous for the purity and sweetness of their tones, and thought to be in these respects almost the finest in the world. The church was closed, but at a rear entrance we found a verger, who sent for his daughter, a young person of a fresh and pleasant face, who took us up into the old stone belfry and rang several changes, ending with "There is a Happy Land." The tones of the bells are exquisitely soft and sweet. In the little churchyard is buried, in the plain vault of his family, Rev. Francis Mahony, celebrated as Father Prout, the scholarly and witty priest who died in 1866 in a monastery in Paris. Very tender are his verses to "The Shandon Bells," beginning :

> "With deep affection
> And recollection,
> I often think of
>     Those Shandon bells,
> Whose sounds so wild would,
> In days of childhood,
> Fling round my cradle
>     Their magic spells.
>
> "On this I ponder,
> Where'er I wander,
> And thus grow fonder,
>     Sweet Cork, of thee ;
> With thy bells of Shandon,
> That sound so grand on
> The pleasant waters
>     Of the river Lee."

Returned to the hotel for lunch, and kept our parlor for the rest of the day, for it rained steadily.

*May* 10.—The morning heavy and showery, but at noon clear and bright. Drove out to Blarney Castle, following the Lee up for three miles on its left bank, then turning into the valley of the Coman, a narrow, swift stream, following it some two miles farther. This we cross by a foot-bridge, and are in front of the highest wall of the square stone tower, built from the base of the projecting crag, on which the structure stands. This wall rises to the height of 120 feet, the opposing wall, by reason of its resting on the crag, being little more than half this height. This massive tower rises impressively, in almost perfect preservation, its battlements continuing almost intact. These project over the walls a distance of three feet, and at intervals are spaces opening downward, through which the besieged could look down the face of the walls, not only to see the operations of an assaulting force, but also to hurl down missiles of whatever sort upon it. Indeed, one of these openings is shown where the defenders are said to have poured down molten lead on Cromwell's soldiers. On the inner side of another portion of the projecting battlement, and so three feet from the wall, is a stone representing the traditional Blarney-Stone, the object of earnest osculation to all pilgrims here, by reason of its attributed power of conferring upon those who touch it with the lips an irresistible fascination. To kiss the present Blarney-Stone the devotee lies prone upon his stomach, reaches across the opening of three feet, grasps the upright iron stanchions extending on either side for a support, one with each hand, pulls himself or herself (for one may be sure the gentler sex will not miss this opportunity of replenishing its armories with so fatal a weapon) forward until able, by bending downward nearly two feet, to press the lips upon the lower stone. It is really something of a feat, and ladies generally will require to be held firmly by the ankles while struggling forward.

As I understand the matter, the Blarney-Stone was formerly a huge block of basaltic stone, which stood on the floor of the highest portion of the main tower, and so, easily accessible. The poet Milliken more than a hundred years ago sung of it:

> "There is a stone there
> That whoever kisses,
> Oh! he never misses
> To grow eloquent.
> 'Tis he may clamber
> To a lady's chamber
> Or become a member
> Of Parliament.
>
> \* \* \* \* \* \*
>
> Don't hope to hinder him
> Or to bewilder him;
> Sure he's a pilgrim
> From the Blarney-Stone."

The thick walls are pierced at irregular intervals with loop-holes for archery. The winding stone stairs terminate on frequent landings with recesses where the men-at-arms might collect for concerted action. This fortress was built near the middle of the fifteenth century by Cormac McCarthy, and vividly realizes all one has imagined of the grim strongholds of the bold chieftains of those cruel ages when the strong preyed upon the weak, and men lived for war and rapine. A goodly prospect lay spread before the eyes of the warder as he looked forth from the turrets of this stout castle of Blarney : the gentle valley of the Coman winding amid the gradual hills of either bank to lose itself in the larger and still fairer valley of the Lee, rich in green pastures and delightful groves. The grounds on the banks of the Coman at the castle's foot are laid out with taste, but hardly correspond in particular features with the description of the poet Milliken.

> "The groves of Blarney,
> They look so charming,
> Down by the purlings
>   Of sweet silent brooks,
> All decked by posies
> That spontaneous grow there,
> Planted in order
> In the rocky nooks.
> 'Tis there the daisy
> And the sweet carnation,
> The blooming pink
> And the rose so fair ;
> Likewise the lily
> And the daffodilly,
> All flowers that scent
>   The sweet open air.
>
> \* \* \* \* \* \*
>
> There are statues gracing
> This noble place in,
> All heathen gods
>   And nymphs so fair,
> Bold Neptune, Cæsar,
> And Nebuchadnezzar,
> All standing naked
>   In the open air !"
>
> \* \* \* \* \* \*

Enough remains, however, to remind the visitor of the poet's further description :

> "There gravel walks are
> For recreation,
> And meditation
>   In sweet solitude.

> 'Tis there the lover
> May hear the dove or
> The gentle plover
> In the afternoon."

\* \* \* \* \* \*

The drive to the castle is delightful. In one pasture of not more than six acres were twenty-five cattle grazing the luxuriant turf, and the driver of our landau said it would keep forty head all summer. We passed a field where a number of cows were feeding, and were told they belonged to the landlord, who had seized them for rent and had put them here, waiting a chance to dispose of them. Our driver said this would be hard to do, as no one in Cork would dare buy them, and no shipper would allow them to be sent out of the country with his. Consequently, they have almost no value. The landlord of the greater part of the land hereabouts is Lord Cork, who has no residence here, but lives and spends his money abroad. The annual rent for such pasture as that mentioned above is three pounds per acre.

At 4 P.M. drove to St. Ann's, where I had arranged yesterday with the verger to have his son chime the Shandon bells. We heard half-a-dozen tunes, sitting in our open carriage. The tones floated sweetly down from the old belfry, justifying the praises given these fine old bells. Drove thence along the upper part of the city among the best residences, the most extensive of which is owned by a Mr. Murphy, of a firm of distillers here.

Cork is a handsome, well-built city, amid beautiful surroundings, and has an appearance of fair prosperity. But the wretched appearance of a considerable portion of the population indicates a depth of misery under the surface. There are said to be two thousand paupers in the city and near suburbs cared for by public charity, and whiskey, it is said, will explain seventy-five per cent of the cases. The spring is much in advance of ours. We have had on our table here new potatoes, asparagus, cucumbers, and cauliflowers, grown in the immediate vicinity in the open air.

*May* 11.—Left for Killarney at 12 M, reaching the Lake Hotel there at 4 P.M. by the Great Southwestern Railway, *via* Mallow. To this point the country on either hand is of the same charmingly pastoral character as all we have heretofore seen, but soon after presents a less fertile and cultivated appearance, stony hill-sides, neglected fields and stretches of bog-land alternating with better soil and cultivation. In one dreary tract, made more so by the chill rain which had begun to fall, we noticed, from the carriage windows, the procession of a peasant's funeral, made up of little donkeys attached to the clumsy two-wheel carts used on the farms. There were not less than a dozen of these, each carrying three or four mourners, who sat on them as best they could, the women wrapped up to the ears in large black or red cloaks, a train of grotesque misery.

Our hotel is situated directly on the Lakes of Killarney, or more precisely on Castlelough Bay, opening from Lough Leane, the largest of the three sheets of water which constitute the Lakes of Killarney. The country had improved in appearance as we approached the town of the same name, but there is little intimation of change in its physical conformation, until, on a sudden, we come on the sight of an exceedingly irregular stretch of peaceful water, lying softly in the midst of meadows and many mountains of most agreeable form and variety. The rain is falling chillily, but in a comfortable private parlor, with bedrooms fronting the water, over a good dinner, we wait in patient contentment for a bright to-morrow.

*May 12, Sunday.*—Bright and clear. Walked along the bend of the bay for a mile, and by the payment of a shilling each entered through the lodge-gate to the grounds of Mr. H. A. Herbert, within which are the well-preserved ruins of Muckross Church and Abbey, built in 1343, on the site of a still older church of Franciscan monks. This is said to be the best-preserved ruin in Ireland. The outer and partition walls, chimneys and tower are almost intact, but the roof and floor of the upper or third story are quite wanting. The mullioned east window is perfect and graceful. The abbey is quite separated from the body of the church by a partition wall of stone, and the cloisters, running round three sides of a small court, are in perfect preservation. In the centre of this court is a magnificent yew, of very great age evidently, and said to be of equal date with the structure itself. On the second floor were the living-rooms of the fraternity, the refectory, the store-rooms, the kitchen, with fireplace so enormous that a hermit is said, a hundred years ago, to have made it his abode for eleven years. The abbot's room adjoins the refectory, and through narrow slits of windows he could note the monks as they moved about the cloisters below. The infirmary was also on this floor, and so arranged that through openings in the wall the sick could witness the services in the church adjoining. The structure, under the best circumstances, must have been cheerless to a degree, and I can easily imagine the infirmary crowded with rheumatic brothers. Best not counterfeit, however, for my lord abbot had an exceedingly vile dungeon at his disposal, as we saw, where simulated twinges would soon become real. A royal endowment of land went with the abbey, the fair meadows, rich and broad all about, and noble woodlands, now succeeded by planted trees of oak and beech and ash, throwing their shadows to-day along sward of the deepest green, where a great flock of contented sheep are feeding, much, it maybe, as in the good old days before the Reformation came to harass and suppress. Many a jolly abbot must have ridden his sleek palfrey with "jingling bridle-rein" over the lovely demesne of Muckross Abbey.

After dinner drove to the abbey, past the handsome residence of Mr. Herbert, the owner of many thousand acres, including a good part of the old abbey lands, which, upon its suppression by Elizabeth, was bestowed with an earl's title upon a McCarthy, the last of the line marrying a Herbert, several generations back. But he was badly in debt, and a fair wife becoming faithless, he went to America seven years ago. It was understood here that he was engaged to marry a Baltimore lady, and the tenants had prepared their wedding presents, but finally it came to be said that the lady, not liking the divorce, had withdrawn from the match.

In the preserves through which the road lies we saw many score rabbits, very tame. After crossing by a bridge the narrow channel connecting the lower and middle lakes and skirting a third of the circumference of the latter, we reached the Torc Cascade, formed by a little stream flowing from a basin of water 2200 feet up the side of Margeton, called the Devil's Punch-Bowl. The fall is about 70 feet, and is pretty, but not notably so. From the top of the ravine is a charming view of mountains, lakes and smiling fields.

*May* 13.—Engaged a boat and four stout rowers, and made

a full tour of the lakes, passing twice over their whole length of twelve miles, taking the entire day for it. I cannot describe, even in the most imperfect way, the Lakes of Killarney. They lie among the feet of a score of mountains, winding in and out of their recesses in the most ravishing way, widening here, narrowing there, gemmed with I know not how many islets, green to the water's edge. The mountains have each its peculiar form and character, very much detached, green with vegetation well up toward their crests, and these of a soft brown color, easily becoming purple and violet as the sun touches them through an atmosphere of haze or light mist. Although not impressive by their height to one who has seen their lofty brethren in Mexico and California—the highest, Carrantual of Macgillicuddy's Reeks, rising only to the height of 3400 feet—these mountains still have a sweet majesty of their own, and offer constant and delightful surprises. Nowhere have I seen such delightful variety. Indeed, these lakes and their surroundings surpass anything I had imagined of them, and I have never seen any description at all adequate, nor is any possible. They fulfill the dream of the poet and the imagination of the painter. We had a day of perfect weather, and mark it with a white stone.

We landed on "sweet Innisfallen," an island of some twenty acres, of pleasantly diversified surface, a solid turf of the richest green, studded with noble ash-trees centuries old. The glades are strewn with primroses, violets, cowslips, bluebells, blooming shrubs of many sorts, and the air is tuneful with many birds, the thrush among them. The ruins of a large abbey lie scattered about, said to have been founded in the year 600, but of this I know nothing. But the old churchmen, as well as those of the present time, had a happy faculty of selecting sites for their establishments, and one notices that even the heretical Methodists of our day pick out, with infallible certainty, the most romantic and picturesque spots for their great camp-meetings

We touched at Ross Island, an island only at high water, being connected with the main-land by a narrow isthmus. This is only less interesting in its loveliness than Innisfallen, and has the pretty well-preserved remains of a considerable castle, said to be the last in Munster to surrender to Cromwell. Several old cannon project from a preserved portion of the wall, looking, from their position, more likely to harm the besieged than the besiegers. They seem almost absurdly incongruous, stuck on walls built to protect only from a flight of arrows. One Krupp gun would knock the whole structure, tower and all, into "smithereens" in two hours' time. On Innisfallen is a holly, 15 feet in circumference, said to be the largest in Ireland. The arbutus grows to the size of large trees on this and other of the islands.

Earl Kenmare is lord of the land here, and has a new residence of red sandstone in a great park near the lower lake, reported to have cost him ninety thousand pounds. He is said to be deeply in debt, and living beyond his income.

*May* 14.—We had at breakfast a salmon taken from the lower lake last evening, of delicate flavor. On our return yesterday from the upper lake, at a certain part of the Long Range, a stretch of narrow water separating the middle from the upper lake, we passed a long, detached rock, worn by action of the water into a fancied likeness to the hull of a man-of-war. The captain of our boat, Paddy Lynch, a stout man, middle-aged, serious of visage, but of quick, Hibernian wit, ordered the rowing to cease, saying it was usual here to hold a little talk with Captain Green, and proceeded to execute a colloquy in a loud voice, after the manner of mariners hailing at sea, revealing that bad Captain Green had been to town the day before, and been confessedly drunken. Each sentence was given a pause after it, and one after another repeated by a remarkable echo, in startling distinctness. At another point, opposite Eagle Rock, Paddy awakened an echo repeated seven times, with lessening volume.

Took train at 11.15 for Dublin, *via* Mallow, arriving here at 5.45—distance, one hundred and eighty-six miles. The country passed over is, for the most part, of the same fertile, luxurious character, as nearly all we have seen in this delightful country. One can tire himself with writing superlative phrases in praise of it. Rode over the charming country where the poet Spenser once had a residence, crossing the little river Awbeg, the Mulla of the poet. We are quartered at the Shelburne, in spacious and handsome rooms, looking out on Stephen's Green, a well-kept park of some twenty acres.

*May* 15.—Drove through Phœnix Park, a level pleasure

ground of about eighteen hundred acres. It has handsome parts, but, as a whole, it is not equal to Central Park in New York nor Prospect Park in Brooklyn. Its natural tameness is relieved by clumps of noble oaks, picturesquely placed, with hundreds of deer scattered over the sward. Drove afterward over the city, along the streets of the best residences and those of the best shops. I have seen Sackville Street mentioned as one of the most magnificent in Europe. It is a wide street, with neat shops on both sides, but the architecture is common and bald, and the shops small. The buildings are not more than four stories high anywhere. This street is ennobled by the Nelson Monument, a symmetrical circular shaft rising from the middle of it to the height of 120 feet, with a marble statue of the hero at top, 13 feet high. The whole is majestic, and one feels that it is really worthy of its subject.

After lunch, walked to the Bank of Ireland to draw some money. It is not often that a bank gets into such quarters, this huge granite building with its beautiful Grecian portico having been the House of the Irish Parliament up to the time of the Union. The House of Lords stands exactly as it was left, even to the long table with the chairs about it, where the peers sat. In the portico before the entrance to the bank, two soldiers from a regiment of Highlanders here paced quickly back and forth. Opposite the bank, on College Green, is Trinity College, an enormous pile of buildings, standing about a large quadrangular paved court, with grounds attached of at least forty acres. This land once belonged to All Hallow Priory, a very old foundation, and the college was established as far back as 1320, but had several periods of disaster, until in the time of Elizabeth it received such grants, gifts and endowments as put it into the flourishing condition it continues to hold. It has now twelve hundred students in attendance. The term of study is four years, and one of the professors, who was exceedingly courteous to us, stated that a student could live comfortably in commons and carry on his studies for eighty-six pounds a year. We visited the examination room, the chapel, the commons hall, and the grand library with its arched roof and galleries and rows of marble busts of men famous in science and letters, from Aristotle down. This library, now numbering nearly 250,000 volumes, began in a singular way. The nucleus was formed by the subscriptions of the English Army to commemorate the victory over the Spaniards at Kinsale, and on these shelves rest the rich treasures since accrued. I cannot attempt any enumeration of the rare and beautiful books and manuscripts beyond price, which moved my soul to covetousness, during the all too brief visit. The organ over the entrance to the theatre or examination room is said to have been taken from one of the ships of the Spanish Armada.

Passing a fruit-store, I noticed a barrel of handsome, sound apples from Boston, price twenty shillings. This is cheaper than I bought apples of my grocer at any time last winter, and this dealer said that until lately he had sold them at ten shillings per barrel.

D'Arcy is the name of one of the Norman families cutting a grand figure in this isle for some centuries after the Conquest. Looking out of window this morning, I saw it painted on the side of a poulterer's cart going by. In like manner we have in New York descendants of the high historic names of O'Sullivan, O'Donohue and McCarthy flourishing peaceful whips over the coach horses of Americans who cannot trace a great-grandfather.

*May* 16.—Visited the great brewery of Guinness & Co., covering forty acres on the right bank of the Liffey. They manufacture only porter or brown stout, and send it out only in barrels and half barrels. This they do at present to the extent of twelve thousand hogsheads a day, and can increase the amount to twenty-five thousand hogsheads. They supply the home demand, and export to all parts of the inhabitable globe where the English tongue is spoken. All the processes are on an enormous scale, with the use of all possible appliances. Presenting my card to a liveried attendant at the entrance, we were ushered into a handsome waiting-room until permission could be obtained from some superior, and then placed in charge of a guide, to be shown such part of the processes as I might request. Thorough cleanliness exists everywhere. The brown color is imparted by roasting a certain proportion of the malt to a dark tint. After the hops are added, the fermentation goes on in huge, square tanks, holding fourteen thousand barrels each, and cooled from ice made by steam power on the premises. The fluid is then drawn into vats to ripen. These are huge casks, of which there are two hundred and forty, each holding the inconceivable quantity of eighteen hundred hogsheads. From these the now perfected liquor is conveyed in subterranean pipes nearly a quarter of a mile to a great covered space beside the river, where it is barrelled for shipment. That for home consumption is of lighter body and is allowed to remain in the vats for a month only, while that for export beyond sea is not only heavier, but remains in the vats ripening from a year to eighteen months. In a well-appointed and clean stable I saw two hundred largest sized Clydesdale horses, used in delivering casks of the porter to city buyers.

Visited the Castle of Dublin, the residence of the Lord-Lieutenant of Ireland, now occupied by Lord Londonderry. It is an architecturally mean pile of buildings, standing about a large, open court, chiefly of brick, constructed originally, in the year 1220, for the defence of the town, and early in Elizabeth's reign fitted up as a viceregal residence. We enter the court by a massive gateway and find the housekeeper, a pleasant, middle-aged lady, who shows us the grand staircase, the presence chamber, where receptions are held, the ball-room, the portrait chamber, the private drawing-room, and bowing us out, accepts a shilling with gratitude. These rooms are not impressive, only moderately grand, and the entrance rooms and passages and surroundings are insignificant and gloomy.

Visited St. Patrick's Cathedral, on the site of a church said to have been founded by St. Patrick in person, and declined to taste the water from a well in the north transept, at which he is said to have baptized the natives. The present building was begun in 1190 and added to in 1370. Only the old form and some crypts remain unchanged, for twenty-five years ago Sir Guinness, the brown-stout knight, "restored" it by facing all the outside walls and pretty nearly rebuilding all parts, so that it has little venerableness. In the nave, side by side, lie Swift and Mrs. Hester Johnson, the "Stella" of his verse. He was dean here, and his pulpit stands in the baptistery. At the western door is a queer monument to the wife of Richard Boyle, the great Earl of Cork, wrought in black marble, decorated with wood-carving, gilding and painting, showing the earl and his lady reclining, with their sixteen children about them, seven of whom are demure maidens with long black hair, resembling the Sutherland Sisters, as one of the young people of my party remarked. The inscription sets forth that the "religious wife lieth entombed here with them all, expecting a joyful resurrection." There is also a bust to John Philpot Curran, looking as one might think he was indeed, and a tablet to Samuel Lover, "poet and painter."

Christ Church Cathedral is ancient enough, and would be interesting doubtless had not the distiller, Henry Roe, recently "restored" it out of all odor of old sanctity. The distillers and brewers seem to have pretty much all the money in the country, and well they may, since they furnish the one article of universal consumption. There is in a side aisle a monumental tomb of Strongbow, the first invader of Ireland. He lies on his tomb clothed in mail, and beside him his son, who was killed by his father. Very likely it was done by dividing him just below the waist, for only the upper half is shown in the effigy. History does not state the cause of this impious taking off, but as the doughty warrior is quite minus a nose, perhaps the provocation was that his unfilial offspring bit that member off in a pet.

Dublin presents to the stranger a prosperous appearance—more so, perhaps, than the facts will warrant. It lies pleasantly on both banks of the river Liffey, which, running from west to east, is embanked within the city limits by walls of solid stone masonry with wide quays, which show considerable traffic. The river opens into a broad harbor six miles below, and rises and falls with the tide. The city is well and solidly built of brick and stone, and would be bright except for the smoke from the bituminous coal which has left its grime on the house fronts, and so smutched as to positively disfigure the elaborate façades of the magnificent public buildings. The main streets are wide, well paved with stone, very charming to eyes used to the streets of New York and Brooklyn, and cheerful with a moderate degree of metropolitan life. I have heard the women of Dublin described as beautiful. Those entitled to commendation anywise approaching the significance of that word have kept well out of sight for three days now. It would seem to me that trade must be light from the appearance of the principal streets. It has almost no manufactures. This chief city of Ireland has not quite held its own in population.

This was 254,000 in 1861, 246,000 in 1871, and 249,000 in 1881.

*May* 17.—Took train on the Great Northern Railway at 7.25 A.M. for Belfast, distant one hundred and twelve miles. Reached the Imperial Hotel at 10.30. The whole way is over a most charming country, mostly level, but often diversified with gentle valleys, long-drawn vales and undulating slopes of brightest verdure, such scenery as poets feign, the remote and romantic hills of Antrim always in the background. Far as the eye can reach on either hand, the luxuriant champaign is divided by old stone walls or hedges of yellow furze into little fields of arable and pasture land, four-square, triangular, lozenge, stellar, circular. Often the eye rests on the gray ruins of castle or monastery, picturesquely placed on the brow of some commanding eminence. At Balbriggan peasants were trooping along the roads to a county fair. At Drogheda we crossed the Boyne, and looked up the valley where stout Cromwell breached the walls of the well-defended town, and where, later, William of Orange defeated James II. with bloody slaughter, on through Dunkald and Lurgan and many another historic town; for all these towns and hamlets have traditions and records going back for centuries.

Visited the flax-mills of Mr. Michael Andrews at Ardogne, a surburb of the city, and were freely shown the manufacture of his beautiful linen goods. The weaving is done by handlooms of the simplest sort, almost rude in their construction, in musty old stone rooms on the ground floor of a number of irregular, detached buildings, enclosed in a high stone wall. We were also shown the various patterns and qualities of the finished goods in the store-room, but for prices and goods were referred to Messrs. Murphy & Orr, their sole agents here, of whom we made some purchases, and were then driven over the city for an hour. It is solidly and handsomely built, with wide, well-paved and kept streets, in outward appearance very like several of our best second-rate cities. It has a thrifty, prosperous look, as if there might be less whiskey and more industry than I have remarked elsewhere on this island. It appears, at one view, that the native race has been advantageously grafted with another good stock, or that some difference of religion and mental aptitudes and manners have the ascendency, and we can readily believe that the canny Scotch are at the fore here, and that their sagacity and plucky persistence have created this prosperity. Even the shifty Yankee shrinks before these more rugged and grim Scotch-Irish, who, crossing the Atlantic, take front rank in whatever calling, like those who fill the pews in Dr. Hall's church in New York on Sunday, and make to themselves friends of the mammon of unrighteousness on week days.

*May* 18.—Left for Giant's Causeway, sixty-seven miles by rail to Portrush, then eight miles to the Causeway by electric tramway. The intervening country wears the same delightful aspect I have so vainly attempted to describe, its green mantle extending to the very tip-ends of its northernmost coast in the latitude of Labrador. Near the entrance to the Causeway is a handsome summer hotel, commanding a wide and delightful prospect of land and sea. It is fitted with modern improvements, has electric lights and lawn-tennis grounds, and the manager stated that they have guests, transient and permanent, from all parts of the globe. Hired a boat with two rowers and a guide, and after lunch walked down into a deep craggy cove, quite suitable for a smuggler's landing in the old time, with his cargo of brandy and claret from Bordeaux. We have been favored with excellent weather ever since leaving home, and here our good fortune continued, as the sea lay smooth as a pond, and the tide was at its ebb, enabling us to enter with our boat two huge caverns, worn by the action of the waves on the limestone rock into vaulted chambers, one 300 and the other 600 feet in length. The perfectly formed arches are 60 feet in height, with bands of red and yellow color along the base and up the sides, caused by the presence of iron and sulphur in the rocks. The sea within is of the deepest green ; the least noise deepens to a solemn and almost awful sound. Near by the entrance is a crag so rounded and battlemented into the form of a castle that it is said a stray vessel from the Spanish Armada fired several broadsides into it, in the belief that it was the Castle of Dunluce, five miles down the coast. Beyond is an amphitheatre formed by a perpendicular wall of trap-rock over 300 feet high, set with precise uniformity in a semicircle, fronting the sea. The distance across on the sea line must be at least 1000 feet. All particulars conspire to help the illusion. A row of columns some 80 feet high runs around the top ; below this is a projection, broad and rounded, like an immense bench; then another row of pillars, and so on down to the base, where the water of the cove is enclosed by a circle of black boulder-stones. This is exceedingly impressive. The whole coast here is bold and craggy, and the entire scene one of grandeur.

The Causeway itself is composed of basaltic rocks standing in the form of a promontory of no great extent, and rising out of the sea nowhere more than 20 feet, sloping down from the middle or ridge of the little cape, so that we easily stepped out of our boat on one of them near the outer point. They are said by geologists to have been formed by the cooling of the molten material of which they are composed, the fusion being due to volcanic action. Chemically they are made up of, say, one half of flinty earth, one quarter iron, one quarter clay and lime. Their color is a brownish gray. As the melted mass cooled, it crystallized into these pillars, which stand closely fitted into each other, only the smooth tops, upon which we walked, being visible, except where a mass of them rises above the general level here and there, or at the outer edges they are exposed at the sides. None, perhaps, are more than a foot, or at the most, I should say from those I saw, a foot and a half in diameter. A curious person who counted them states that they number over forty thousand. Almost all have five, six or seven sides; there are three of nine sides and quite a number of four and eight sides. These figures are taken at second hand, of course. It will be understood that the form of the pillars can only be known by noting the lines of cleavage on the upper ends, or tops, as only these are shown, except in the cases mentioned above. Where an entire pillar can be examined, it is found to be smooth, as if polished and formed in sections of, say, one foot long, fitting into each other exactly like the ball and socket joint of an animal. I expected to be disappointed in the Causeway, but, on the contrary, taking it in connection with its surroundings, it exceeded my expectations.

Hired a jaunting-car so as to drive back to Portrush and see Dunluce Castle, a most picturesque ruin, rising from an insulated crag, separated from the main-land by a narrow chasm. The masonry of the walls is so fitted to the irregularity of the crag that crag and castle seem one. It stands 100 feet above the sea, its hoary towers looking out on the broad Atlantic, as they have for centuries. It is washed on all sides by the waves, except at one point, where a wall is built up across the chasm, the top of which, not more than eighteen inches wide, forming the only approach from the structure on the main-land, and, of course, the only way by which it could be assaulted. Its age is not accurately known, but history finds it in possession of the English in the fifteenth century. Many romantic stories are told of it. Walter Scott visited it in 1814, and described it in his diary. The seaward view and along the coast in its neighborhood, this fine spring afternoon, is glorious.

We reached our hotel here in Belfast at 9 P.M., taking the main line of the railway at Coleraine, near the village of Limavaddy, made famous by Thackeray's "Peg of Limavaddy."

*May* 19, *Sunday.*—Warm and pleasant. All attended a Presbyterian church opened in 1827 by Dr. Chalmers. The congregation large, solid and respectable-looking. Services began at 11.30 o'clock. The minister occupied a high pulpit, and the choir sat behind him. There was no organ nor any other musical instrument in sight or in use. The services were quite plain and business-like. After the second psalm had been sung from the metrical version, the preacher delivered a short sermon to the children. This sermon presupposed a sound early training in the essentials, as he dwelt chiefly on the mysterious nature of the Eucharist. Another psalm was sung, and looking at my watch and finding the hour 12.15, I began to congratulate myself that the services were to be brief; but, after a short prayer, the minister gave out another psalm of twenty-two verses, with instructions to sing but sixteen, read another chapter followed by another psalm, then entered on the real work of the day, and gave a sermon evidently sound to the core, then a short prayer, with still another psalm. Besides these psalms there were two hymns coming in somewhere. The psalms were sung in a sing-song sort of way, all the congregation joining with full throats, the choir only giving to the volume of the sound a certain steadiness and ornament. The effect was not unpleasing. One of the stanzas ran as follows:

> " When wicked men arose,
> My adversaries all
> To eat my flesh arose ;
> They stumbled and did fall."

A sturdy folk, these Scotch-Irish, fearing God, loving gain and hating the Pope.

Mr. Jury, the landlord of the Imperial Hotel, has been exceedingly civil to us, furnishing his private landau to take us about town, and after lunch sending his private jaunting-car, with a driver in full livery, to take the two young people and myself to Carrickfergus Castle, ten miles down the spacious harbor, where we went in such dignity of equipage that I might have been taken for a rack-renting, absentee landlord, and fired at from behind a hedge. I was rather disappointed in the castle, which is described as "one of the most complete specimens of ancient Anglo-Norman fortresses in the kingdom." The narrow approach to the entrance is between two high stone walls, and the old portcullis is raised to its place, ready to descend in its grooves of stone. The interior has been modified by the erection of barracks. The cross of St. George floats from the donjon tower, and several figures of the soldiers of a part of a Highland regiment quartered there, lounging on the battlements, gave the exterior quite a look of romance. The famous regiment of the Black Watch, renowned in history and story for more than a hundred years, is stationed now in Belfast. The castle, as it stands at present, is said to have been built in the twelfth century.

Belfast has grown with steady rapidity. Its population in 1821 was 37,000; in 1881, 208,000. The land on which it stands and much of the surrounding country is owned by the Donegal family, descendants of Sir Arthur Chichester, who took it in 1612, and so on back to a grant of the province of Ulster to De Courcy by Henry II. The oldest son of the Prince of Wales is expected here on a visit to-morrow, and the streets are being decorated for his reception. Looking up Donegal Place, the street our hotel is on, I notice one American flag floating in the Irish air. There is a hum of expectation all about; the papers are full of the "visit of royalty;" the newsboys are hawking a pamphlet containing a programme of the ceremonies, to last two days. And this young sprig of royalty is only the grandson of Victoria, with a tough grandmother and a healthy father between him and the throne.

*May* 20.—Visited the Museum, and noted the Irish antiquities with some interest, weapons and utensils of the stone and bronze ages, and a few later ornaments—spearheads, dirks, etc., etc. A lean display, yet Black speaks of it as very fine.

I suppose the truth is, there is not much left, if all objects of the kind remaining in Ireland were brought together. Time and war and rapine and poverty have swept them away.

At 4 P.M. left Belfast by rail for Larne, an hour's ride northward on the coast, where we took the side-wheel steamboat "Princess Beatrice" across the North Channel to Stranraer, at the head of Loch Ryan, this being the shortest sea passage to Scotland, and done in two and a half hours. Thence by rail to Dumfries, seventy-three miles, reaching the King's Arms Hotel at 11 P.M. In Loch Ryan passed the Queen's yacht, having on board Prince Victor on his way to Belfast.

We left Ireland with deep and pleasant impressions.

*May* 21.—Warm and sunny. Hired a pair of horses and wagonette and drove to Ecclefechan, eighteen miles, crossing the Annan, a fine broad river, and over a charming, undulating country of green pastures, meadows and highly cultivated fields, where apparently all the people, men, women and children, were hard at work planting various crops. Drove to the little tavern, Bush's Hotel, and had an excellent lunch. Visited the house where Carlyle was born, a small, two-story stone cottage, built by his father, who was a mason by trade. The only room on the ground floor is the kitchen, and above that the room where he was born, about 14 feet square, and besides, only a bedroom not more than 6 by 9 feet. The cottage is one of a row of similar ones on the south side of a poor street, and connected with the one adjoining it on the east by an arched way. It is a mean, paltry street, with wide, dusty roadway running between low stone cottages, white with plaster, not a green tree or shrub to soften the hot glare of the sun. Just before the street reaches the Carlyle cottage, the sewer of the village, which to that point is covered, flows out into an open way and runs down the middle of the street in front of the cottage, offensive to a degree. The daughter of his favorite sister Jane, the niece who cared for him in his lonely last days in London, married her own cousin, the son of his brother Saunders who went to America, and is now Mrs. Alexander Carlyle, and resides in London. Her father's name was Aitkens. She has bought the cottage here and recently fitted up the larger of the rooms on the second floor with articles of furniture brought from the London house at 24 Cheyne Row, the carpet, the lounge and some chairs from the sitting-room there. His study-chair stands by his study-table, on which rests his student-lamp, with his tobacco-cutter, quite a formidable implement, for cutting "plug," beside his little copper coffee-pot, and the clock from the London kitchen ticks on the wall. One easily imagines the sources of his obfuscating dyspepsia when looking at this apparatus for midnight coffee and nicotine. There are many photographs of himself at various periods and some of Mrs. Carlyle, the dates and some circumstances connected with them being fixed by a note to each in his own hand. It is hard to see how Mrs. Carlyle, judging from these, could have ever been a handsome woman. To be sure, there are none showing her as younger than fifty years, and she was evidently much worn, but the long, strong, nervous face, with its excessively high forehead, is not of a sort associated with beauty of feature. But, as all know, a photograph, while actually reproducing whatever falls upon it, is strangely deceptive by what fails to reach it. A sadly touching one is that of himself—it must have been in his very last days—seated, all shrunken of face and form, with his fair young niece standing beside him. Unlike the rest, this has no inscription from his pen, for the hand which had guided it for so many laborious years would not seem capable of touching it again. From his birthplace, went to his grave in the poor little churchyard of the Presbyterian church, near by. In among the numerous graves, with their plain headstones, is a small space enclosed by a plain, substantial iron fence, with three large, upright stones, his own, of red sandstone, having this simple inscription written by himself:

"*Humilitate.*"
*Here rests Thomas Carlyle, who was born at Ecclefechan,*
*4th Dec., 1795, and died at*
*24 Cheyne Row, Chelsea, London, on Saturday,*
*5th Feb., 1881.*

Lower down is an inscription, in the same brief terms, relating to his brother John. The stone on the right of his is to his father and mother, with a touching epitaph written by him, and the one on the left bears the names of other members of the Carlyle family. There are none of his name now alive in Ecclefechan, and Mrs. Carlyle lies buried in Haddington, near Edinburgh.

We drove back to Dumfries in the beautiful afternoon, along the road he took so often, many times on foot, his mind full of high thoughts and heroic purposes, his heart sad and lonely, sure only of one thing, that he would never do a base deed, that he would fight all forms of vice and false pretence, though it should lead to destitution and the obloquy of men. Grave, stern, grandly poetic soul, with many failings, harsh prejudices and sharp and bitter speech, yet true to the inward voice of conscience and duty!

Carlyle does not seem to be much thought of in Dumfries, nor, it would seem, much cared for in Ecclefechan. Mine hostess of the King's Arms insisted that no person attended his funeral outside the circle of mourners and friends who came up from London with the remains, and here in Dumfries, she said, nobody liked him. Remembering that for many years after he went to London, he insisted on having his clothes made by a Dumfries tailor, I made inquiry after him of a self-contained old burgher, who was said to know very much about everybody, who, after searching himself profoundly for a little, conjectured it must have been old Pattison, and sent his son with me to an ancient shop, where we found "Sartor Resartus" in the person of an offshoot of the earlier Pattison of the Carlyle epoch. My guide, in a shamefaced sort of way, like one engaged in what he thought small business, stated that here was a gentleman to ask if this might be the shop where Mr. Carlyle got his clothes. The younger Pattison, vainly ruminating, asked what Carlyle. "The one they call the philosopher," said my guide. The obliging tailor, having no recollection of his own about the matter, carefully consulted the index to his ledger, still to no purpose, and saying it might be on the old one, drew it forth and went over its index, all in vain. When I had asked him how far back that ledger went and got for reply, 1765, I concluded that Carlyle had not placed his orders there.

But this is pre-eminently the land of Burns, and all along the coast, from the sands of Solway to the Clyde, he reigns lord paramount. Dumfries is the chief town in southwest Scotland, with a population of 17,000. There stands in the square a life-like statue of Burns in white marble. The house where he died in 1796, and where his widow, "My bonny Jean," lived until her death in 1834, is in a narrow and rather poor street, now called Burns Street. It has a respectable front of two stories high, and perhaps 30 feet wide. Hawthorne speaks of the meanness of the surroundings, but when one considers that the town a hundred years ago was poorly built, that the better residences were mingled with the poorer, and that the character of the neighborhood has changed in so long a time, I think that it may be concluded that Burns was housed here in Dumfries in a style above the average. In the churchyard of St. Michael, the Presbyterian church near where he lived, he lies buried in an elaborate and costly tomb of white marble, enclosed in handsome grounds carefully tended. Visitors are admitted on the payment of twopence into an ample room over the vault, where some fifteen years ago the last of his race was placed and the vault finally sealed. The wall of this room, fronting the entrance, is occupied by the beautiful sculpture in white marble of the Genius of Poesy finding Burns at the plough. The figures are largely chiselled in high relief, and the conception and execution are grandly impressive.

The old Globe Hotel is entered through a narrow passage between high stone walls, and there is shown a snug little room on the left of the passage where the poet used to grow cheerful with his convivial comrades. It has an exceedingly cosey look in the half light from the one window looking on the narrow passage, with its wainscoted walls, low ceiling and neat fireplace, and I should not find it difficult, with two or three transatlantic friends I could name, to grow into so comfortable a frame of mind as to excuse the hilarious evenings the bard passed here. The chair he used, of good, solid mahogany, is shown, but kept under lock and key, as is the pretty china punch-bowl, holding near a gallon, with a neat, flowery band about it, an inch below the top. This bowl has been, and is, much sought after, and the old landlady in her time refused a hundred guineas for it, and her son after her, not long ago, five hundred, it is said. In a snug chamber just over this room are two panes of glass, 7 by 9, in the heavy frames of the window, kept with almost equal care, for on them Burns wrote with a diamond these lines, one on each :

"O lovely Polly Stewart,
O charming Polly Stewart,

> There's no a flower that blooms in May
> That's half so fair as thou art.
>
> " Gin a body meet a body
> Coming thro' the grain,
> Gin a body kiss a body,
> The thing's a body's ain."

There are quite a number of objects of interest in and about Dumfries. The New Greyfriars' Church occupies the site of the old castle close by the Greyfriars' Monastery, in the church of which Bruce slew the Red Comyn. Eight miles from the town, on the Solway, is Caerlaverock Castle, an old stronghold of the Maxwells. A mile distant, where the Cluden joins the Nith, is Included Abbey, founded by the Benedictine monks in the twelfth century. Three miles farther up the Cluden is the churchyard of Irongray, in which is the grave of Helen Walker, the original of Jeanie Deans. On the west of the Nith Estuary is Sweetheart Abbey, founded in 1275 by Devorgilla Balloil, and so named because she had her husband's heart buried here in her own tomb.

Left at 8 P.M. for Ayr, by rail, following the windings of the easy flowing Nith, an inconsiderable but pretty stream, its softly curved valley green and fair. We saw plainly on our right—for at this latitude one sees to read at 9 P.M.—the white farm-house of Ellisland, where Burns tried farming to small purpose, on through many a little village, with its low, white cottages, through Mauchline, the maiden home of Jean Armour, where Burns married her, reaching the Station Hotel at 11 P.M.

*May* 22.—The Queen's birthday, so that it was not easy to get a carriage to the Burns cottage, the shops being closed and all forms of business suspended. Drove directly to the cottage where Burns was born in 1759, a one-story stone house, containing just two rooms, each about 12 feet square. In a recess 6 by 4 feet, opening into the kitchen, just large enough to admit a bed, the poet first saw the light, and dim enough it must have been, for it came only through a deep-set window, not a foot square. The rough board dresser, standing on the original stone floor against the wall, between this recess and the oven beside the fireplace, is the only article of furniture remaining in the room, except the spinning-wheel of his mother, but there is no change in the room itself, except that a window has since been let into the front wall. On the other side of the short, narrow passage is the remaining room, now used as a shop for the sale of innumerable articles of ornament, finely made of sycamore or plane-tree wood, with pretty pictures in great numbers on them, illustrating persons and scenes of his poems. I easily touched the ceiling of this most humble kitchen with my hand, but certainly I experienced in it a tenderer feeling mingled of love and reverence than I can possibly do in the stateliest palace in these islands.

> Never rose brighter star from darker cloud,
> Bard of immortal song!
> Thy fame shall ever brighter grow, while Doon·
> Runs murmuring along.

To this low dwelling come from all lands where English speech is used a prodigious multitude of pilgrims. A register is kept, where visitors are asked to enter their names. Many, it is likely, do not comply. For instance, of my party of four, only two did so. Yet, going back, I found by actual estimate only a few short of four thousand names entered during July, 1888. On one page I saw names from Queensland, Nova Scotia, New York and San Francisco. The registering turnstile, through which all who enter the cottage pay twopence for the support of the place, showed something over twenty thousand visitors last year. The cottage was built by Burns' father. There is a handsome hall, founded with Masonic honors on the anniversary of his birth in 1847, attached to the cottage, both owned by the Burns Monument Trustees. In this hall are very numerous mementoes of Burns, many portraits, statuettes, the manuscript of "Tam o' Shanter," the alleged chairs which Tam and Souter Johnny used in life. In one of the glass cases lies a newspaper clipping, containing a a charming little poem to Burns, and signed "An American," which our cicerone said was written by Colonel Robert Ingersoll, who was here not many years ago. A fresh, eager lad, who might be a student, was intently copying it.

A little farther on the highway stands Auld Alloway Kirk the scene of the witches' unholy revel. It is a low stone structure, 43 by 21 feet, roofless now, the eastern end fronting the road, crowned at the peak with a small bell tower, and having the old Gothic window, through the ribs and arches of which Tam, attracted by the blaze streaming from the kirk, saw the witches merrily footing it to the bagpipe of "Auld Nick." The original of Tam o' Shanter was a farmer named Douglas Grahame, living, and now buried at Kirkoswald, thirteen miles from Ayr. Souter Johnny, his "ancient, trusty, drouthy crony," was John Laughlin, a shoemaker of Ayr, who lies buried, with a small, plain stone at his head, in the churchyard of "Auld Alloway." At the time Burns wrote Tam o' Shanter, in 1790, the interior space of the church was unobstructed, but sixty years ago a partition wall was built one third of the distance back from the eastern end, and in the western part there are now several tombs.

We follow the road down to the ancient stone bridge, only a few rods distant, and leaning over the parapet, look down on the softly flowing Doon, here about 60 feet wide, its braes and banks extending up and down in the tender green of spring, dotted with daisies and musical with birds. On a knoll opposite the entrance to the bridge stands, in well-planted and richly cultivated grounds, kept with strict care, an imposing monument to Burns, 60 feet high, a not quite pleasing structure, in which there is an attempt to blend Grecian and Roman architecture, a range of nine Corinthian pillars, surmounted by a dome, built in 1820. It owes its existence to the efforts of the late Sir Alexander Boswell of Auchinloch, a direct descendant, I believe, of Johnson's Boswell. Within the monument is a bust of Burns by the celebrated Scotch sculptor Park, the features of which show more delicacy than any of the great number I have seen. Preserved here are the two volumes of the Bible presented by the poet to Highland Mary, their inscriptions quite legible, and a slender lock of her hair, faded a good deal, but with a slight golden glow still remaining. In a grotto within the grounds are the life-size and striking statues of Tam o' Shanter and Souter Johnny, cut in white marble by Thom. They are seated over their cups, and one feels they might well have been the men here portrayed.

This neighborhood has become a show-place to an almost unpleasant extent, and the good citizens are working Burns' name and fame for all there is in them. The way to the "auld brig" is tormented with whining beggars. A dirty fiddler stood at the very entrance scraping tunes out of his wretched catgut, and on the very "keystane of the brig" stood a hungry creature, fiercely intent on reciting its history. These things jar harshly on the feelings of those who would fain find here the pastoral simplicity of the poet's pictures. The pilgrims to these scenes, attracted by love of Burns, must leave in the city of Ayr, by an easy estimate, in various expenses, more than one hundred thousand dollars annually, an amount increasing year by year. One tenth of it would have assuaged the poet's poverty, lifted him from the black depths of life-long misery, and perhaps have saved him from the wild courses he often ran in his despairing moods.

We drove back to the town by a different road, crossing the Ayr on the new bridge, built to replace the "new brig" of the poem, the old one still standing picturesquely, as the poet predicted it would do. This "auld brig" was builded in the early part of the thirteenth century by two maiden sisters, who devoted their whole fortune to it. It is narrow, "where twa wheelbarrows tremble when they meet," and is only used by foot-passengers. Called at the Tam o' Shanter Inn, the identical little stone tavern where Tam and Johnny sat

" . . . . glorious,
O'er all the ills of life victorious,''

the night of Tam's memorable ride. They show a little wooden cup, or "quaich," now hooped with silver, said to be the one Burns used to drink his usquebaugh from in the poor chamber above. I asked the lad in attendance behind a shabby bar what sort of liquor he supposed Burns drank, who replied with a grin, "Amaist ony he could get." I ordered a toothful of his best put into the cup, and sought to drink it with reverent thoughts. Tam was wise in sticking to his "reaming swats." Had he sat the evening through over this special "John Barleycorn," he would never have tried to cross the bridge.

Ayr is an old, solid seaport town of 20,000 inhabitants, with a good trade in coal. Almost all the coal used in Ireland is from Scotland.

*May* 23.—Left for Glasgow by rail, distant forty miles, one hundred from Dumfries, reaching the Station Hotel at 11 A.M. These station hotels are built and owned by the railroad companies, and are far the best in their appointments, we find. A gentleman at Ayr told me he had been familiar with this coast for many years, and that he never saw the country looking so thoroughly well and handsome as now, vegetation not only here, but in all parts of Scotland, being as forward as is usual in the latter part of June. The weather is regarded by the people as very warm, and the *Edinburgh Scotsman* comments on the great heat of the day before yesterday, when the mercury touched 74°!

Glasgow is the second city in the kingdom, with a population, including the suburbs, of 750,000, solidly built of stone and wearing a look of great prosperity. It has many fine public buildings, but everything is dingy with the smoke from soft coal. Its manufactories are very extensive, its shipping trade enormous, and in ship-building it outranks any city in the world. But the bustling spirit of the modern banishes the romance of the olden time, and there is not much to detain the tourist intent upon the past. The old Salt Market is swept away, the house of good Bailie Nicol Jarvie, standing until lately, is demolished, and the street of the Trongate modernized out of its old fashion.

Took a long drive about the city, visiting the principal points. All shops are closed and all business suspended to keep the Queen's birthday, as was the case in Ayr yesterday. The real day is to-morrow, but it seems that the different towns celebrate it on such near days as they find most convenient.

*May* 24.—Visited the Cathedral, standing on the highest point in the city. It dates from the twelfth century, with portions in the fourteenth. It is 320 feet long, 70 feet wide and 90 feet high; its tower is 220 feet in height. The windows throughout are filled with modern stained glass from Munich, at a cost of one hundred thousand pounds. It ceased to be a cathedral at the era of the Reformation, and the choir is now used as one of the city churches. The most interesting portion is the crypt under the choir, which is really a lower church formed on the sloping ground under a portion of the Cathedral itself. It is supported by sixty-five pillars and lit by forty-one windows. The clustered columns are graceful and symmetrical, with exquisite sculptured capitals and bosses in the groined vaulting, all thoroughly well preserved. Edward Irving, the founder of the sect of Irvingites, and early friend of Carlyle, is buried here. In this crypt, then called the

"Laigh (low) Kirk," Scott placed the scene of Rob Roy's mysterious warning to Francis Osbaldistone. The Cathedral is surrounded by a churchyard, and among the monuments is a memorial tablet to nine persons who suffered martyrdom in 1666 for adhering to the Covenant. A rude stanza in the inscription concludes,

> "They'll know at resurrection day,
> To murder saints was no sweet play."

*May* 25.—Left Glasgow 11 A.M. by rail for Balloch, twenty-one miles, situated on the south or lower end of Loch Lomond. At Dumbarton had a good view of the castle of that name on its steep, rocky hill, 280 feet high. This is one of the four castles secured to Scotland at the time of the Union. Wallace was imprisoned here. Queen Mary, on her way to France to be educated at the French court, embarked here in March, 1548. The town of Dumbarton lies at the mouth of the river Leven, through which Loch Lomond empties its waters into the Clyde. The Leven flows deeply and silently, brimming its level, grassy banks. Smollett, the novelist, was born in this neighborhood in 1721.

At Balloch we take a small side-wheel steamer and proceed the whole length of Loch Lomond, twenty-two miles, to Inversnaid, where coach is taken to cross the ridge between this lake and Loch Katrine. The scenes which successively present themselves to view during the passage up the lake are of exceeding and memorable beauty, and I may not attempt their description. As at Killarney, the effect is produced by a felicitous union of the agreeable and impressive features of natural scenery, each striking in itself and all blending in harmony of form and color, in large and charming variety. At its southern end the Loch is five miles broad, but gradually narrows to a few hundred yards at its northern or upper end. It lies for its entire length between ranges of gradual hills, from which mountain-peaks rise abruptly; it is studded frequently with little islands of beautiful forms and foliage; it is indented with many gentle capes and bold headlands, and pushes itself laughingly into sullen recesses of the mountains and bays of the foot-hills, all its shores and the region, far and near, famous in history, tradition, story and song.

Soon after leaving the pier we pass on the left Glen Fruin,

overhung with the ruins of Bannchara Castle, the residence, in the old time, of the Colquhouns. The name Glen Fruin means sorrow, and here was a sharp battle between the McGregors and the Colquhouns, wherein the latter were terribly defeated. We pass the isle of Inch Murrin, preserved as a deer-park by the Duke of Montrose, who owns the land on both sides the lake for its entire extent, including its islands. On the south end of Inch Murrin are the ruins of Lennox, once a residence of the earl of that name. We pass the isle of Inch Cailliach, on which is the burial-ground of the McGregors. Here on the eastern shore, in the vale of Endrick, is Buchanan House, the chief seat of the Duke of Montrose. He is of the famous old family of that name which figures all along in Scottish history. Farther on, we sail by the mouth of a narrow pass on the east shore, Balmaha, through which the Highlanders used to go down into the lowlands on forays. In advance on our right is Ben Lomond, rising in stately view to the height of 3200 feet, until we reach Inversnaid, where we leave the steamer to go by coach across to Loch Katrine. On the west side of the Loch, here grown narrow, rises Ben Vorlich, 3000 feet, surrounded by many peaks of lesser note, all celebrated in song and story. These Scottish mountains differ from ours in the respect that the various peaks are more distinctly and sharply separated down to their bases, and so present a greater individuality and character. Only the little islands in the Loch and the narrow strip of land between the hills and shore are wooded; the hills themselves have not a single tree or shrub, but are covered to their summits with short grass and heather, the latter now dark, but when in flower in August lying in great purple patches all over the hills. The ride over the divide between Lomond and Katrine is about five miles, the ascent being quite sharp. There is tolerable pasture of short, sweet grass all the way, and we saw many of the Highland sheep, large and handsome, not yet shorn of their heavy fleeces of long, straight, coarse wool. They have black noses and black rings around the eyes, and the hinder part of their shanks is black also.

After descending a little way, the fair water of Loch Katrine gleamed on our sight through its protecting hills. We are now, and have been all day, within the enchanted circle of the great wizard, Walter Scott, whose sway over these mountains is as absolute as that of Burns on the Ayrshire coast. "The Lady of the Lake" will almost serve for a guide-book here, and it is interesting to note the fidelity with which Scott has located his scenes. By a sharp descent we come down to Stronachlacher, a bright hotel on the west shore of the lake, near its head, and after lunching there, step on board the snug little screw-steamer, "Lady of the Lake," and sail down the full length of the lake, nine and one half miles.

If we were not just from Loch Lomond, we would think Katrine the prettiest of all the lakes we have seen. Until we approach the eastern end the shores are not so striking on either hand as those of Lomond. Then the scene becomes of exceeding beauty and grandeur. On the right rises the noble form of Ben Venue, 2400 feet, with its deep vertical gash, called Coirnan-Urisken, a remarkable specimen of the Highland corrie, piled with rocky *débris*, where Scott located the dread Goblin's Cave. Opposite is the cragy peak of Ben A'an, and between, Ellen's Isle, hidden to the water's edge by a luxuriant growth of trees and shrubbery, within the verdant screen of which we may well imagine the open glade with space enough for all the purposes it is required to serve in the poem. The little steamer makes a circuit of the isle, and while it is evident that Malcolm would have no very long swim to reach the shore, nor the fair Ellen be compelled to over-exert herself to guide her "light shallop" to it from the silvery beach where she took on board Snowdoun's knight, still all these distances and conditions are quite sufficient, and the lovers of the poem—and who is not?—need have no fear of lessening their admiration by visiting its scenes.

The city of Glasgow, thirty-six miles distant, takes its supply of water from Loch Katrine, carrying it over its mountainous rim. At the head of the lake we take coach for Aberfoyle, passing through the Trossachs, a mountain defile, through which the Teith, draining Loch Katrine, finds its way to the Forth near Stirling. The Trossachs do not realize my expectations, are only moderately impressive, not equalling in sublimity the "Gulf" below Proctorsville, in the town of Cavendish, Vt. They are really a well-wooded valley, with little of the sternness and grandeur I had presupposed. But there is sufficient to afford material for genius to shape into poetic forms, and with pardonable exaggeration body forth "the Trossachs' rugged jaws." We skirt the southern shore of beautiful little Loch Achray soon after emerging from the pass, of which the aged minstrel Allan took his parting look from the eastern side of Ben Venue.

> "Where shall he find in foreign land
> So lone a lake, so sweet a strand?"

Exquisite is the view on this perfect day as we climb the hilly range separating the valley of the Teith from that of the Forth, Ben Ledi in the background, with softer slopes and gentle glens and narrow green fringes of pasture and meadow, extending far down to Loch Vennachar, with a dim view of the Brig of Turk, the meadow of Coilantogle Ford and Lanrick Mead. An hour's winding in and out, up and down the ridge, always grass-grown, brings us in full view of the broad valley of the Forth, and we descend sharply from the shoulder of Craigmore on the old clachan of Aberfoyle at the foot of the comb and on the north bank of the Forth, here of small size. A modern hotel stands on the site of the old inn celebrated in "Rob Roy" as the scene of the encounter between Francis Osbaldistone and the Highlander, where honest Bailie Nicol Jarvie intervened so effectually with his red-hot poker, as is duly shown on the swinging signboard and in pictures on the cover of the wine list of this Bailie Nicol Jarvie Hotel, where we dined, waiting for the train to Stirling.

After dinner strolled out to an old stone bridge over the Forth, and not many times hereafter can we hope to look upon a more enchanting scene than lay extended up its valley to the west. The sun was nearing its setting, flooding the crest of Ben Lomond and all the lesser heights about him with purple light, and touching with peculiar softness the broad, verdant meadows of the tranquil, winding stream, the whole vista refined and withdrawn into the unreal domain of fairyland by the violet flush half screening the outlines of hills bordering the long-drawn vale on either hand.

Took train at 7.30 P.M. for Stirling, and after a ride of an hour are gathered, at the close of another day worthy of marking with a white stone, within the portals of the Golden Lion, whose gilded effigy crouches above it, wearing that grim smile attributed in heraldry to the king of beasts. At 9.30 one easily reads a book by daylight.

*May 26, Sunday.*—My family attended services in the "Free Church," while I strolled up the steep streets of the old town, standing on the sloping side of the crag on whose abrupt edge the castle towers 340 feet above the wide valley of the Forth, here greatly broadened, having received the waters of the Teith some miles above.

We passed yesterday, but did not visit, the Lake of Monteith, with its Isle of Rest—Inchmahone—on which are the remains of the monastic pile where Princess Mary, afterward Queen of Scots, was conveyed after the battle of Pinkie, to seclude her from the "rough wooing" of Henry VIII. in behalf of his son Edward, and where she lived some time with her four Marys—Mary Beaton, Mary Seaton, Mary Livingston and Mary Fleming. I took the walk called the Back Walk, which winds entirely round the castle half way up the crag on which it rests, made with a deal of labor by excavating the abrupt sides of the crag. The view up the luxuriant valley of the Forth is exceedingly beautiful. On the south side, far below, lies the "King's Garden," with its turfy embankments. In the centre is a raised octagonal space, flat at top, where the monarch, James V., and his courtiers engaged in the amusement of the Round Table, which perhaps consisted in personating the fabulous King Arthur and his court. Alleys, banks and all are covered with rich turf. This garden is said to have been restored early in this century from a plan of the original found in the castle, and as often as its outlines become effaced they are renewed by the town authorities.

After dinner at four o'clock, served at that early hour, as the housekeeper said, to give all a Sunday rest—we are now among the grim descendants of the Covenanters—I took the young people on the same walk I had made in the morning. A detachment of the Salvation Army has greatly infested these narrow, steep streets since last evening, and with red banner, and with wilder and fuller-throated tunes than I have heretofore heard, are almost picturesque. But they seem to get as little attention here as at home.

*May 27.*—Engaged a landau and pair for a full day. Had an excellent, well-informed driver. Rode up the steep street leading to the entrance of the castle, alighted, passed the sentinel, and engaged for guide, as requested, an army pensioner, who did not look over fifty, although he stated he had served forty-five years. The castle covers a large area, and its various buildings are now used for military purposes, and but few rooms are open to the public. The most interesting exterior is that of the palace built by James V., its walls rich with sculpture. Entrance is given to what is called the Douglas Room, a small, low chamber, some ten feet from the ground, where James II. stabbed William, Earl of Douglas, in a fit of passion, in 1452, because he would not consent to submit to his authority. This room adjoins a still smaller one, from the window of which the body of the murdered earl was thrown. It had been supposed that he was buried where he fell, and in 1797 some masons, making an excavation there, found a human skeleton, believed to be that of the Douglas. Queen Victoria has filled the little window above the spot with illuminated glass, containing the Douglas arms, a bleeding heart. From that part of the ramparts styled the "Queen's Look-out," since Queen Victoria visited the castle, is a most magnificent view, including that part of the valley of the Forth we traversed from Aberfoyle and still farther westward, taking in the vale of Monteith, and bounded by Ben Lomond to the extreme left ; then, rising in due order to the right, Ben Venue, Ben A'an, Ben Ledi, the cone of Ben Vorlich, Uamvar, the Ochil Hills to the north and east and the Campsie Hills to the south ; Sanchieburn, where James III. was defeated by his insurgent nobles in 1488, the house near by still standing where he was assassinated the day after the battle ; to the north the field of Stirling, where Wallace gained his first victory over the English in 1297, and farther on, the upland slope of Sheriff Muir, the scene of the battle between the Earl of Mar for the Pretender and the English forces under the Duke of Argyle, in 1715. On a rough piece of ground on the crag, but outside the castle walls, still stands the "Beheading Stone," where many a noble and fair head fell under the headsman's axe. Underneath the wall on the northeast of the castle, a very narrow passage, walled high on both sides, leads steeply down to the level, called from old time Ballangeich, which James II. was wont to take when going out in disguise for purposes of business or gallantry.

As all know, this castle of Stirling has played a most important part in Scottish history from the earliest time. It is said that the date of its building and its earliest history are unknown, because Cromwell carried away its records, and when he sent them back at a later period, they were lost at sea. It was a fortress in 1124, and was taken by Edward I. of England in 1304. It withstood siege for three months, and as there were no cannon then, the king called on all knights to join his large army, and it was found necessary to bring from London Tower all the besieging implements then known. One of these, called the "Wolf," effected a breach, the castle was taken and held by the English ten years, and so important was it considered that Edward II. brought a great army to maintain it, and in the end was defeated by Bruce under its walls at Bannockburn. It became a royal residence with the accession of the house of Stuart to the Scottish throne. James II. and James V. were born here, and the latter crowned here, and James VI. and his son Henry were baptized here. These are trite facts, old and musty, but they are rehabilitated in new flesh as one looks upon the scenes themselves with living eye. They bring back to me the time when in the wilds of the new West I pored over the "Tales of a Grandfather," and dreamed of the plumed Wallace and the Black Douglas.

In a steep, narrow street near the castle stands a fine house called Argyle's Lodging, now used as a hospital, with pinnacled round-towers and finely decorated windows. It belonged to William Alexander, the poet, created Earl of Stirling by Charles I., the same who obtained the grant of Nova Scotia. In 1640 it came to the Argyle family, whose arms are sculptured over the doors and windows. It was the headquarters of John, Duke of Argyle, during the rebellion of 1715.

An exceedingly interesting front of an unfinished house, with its sculptured doors and windows and numerous grotesque gargoyles, in an adjoining street near by, is the one called "Mar's Work," begun by the Earl of Mar and left unfinished; for, having plotted the death of Queen Mary, he lost his head at Stirling in 1572. Before the castle entrance stands a statue of Robert Bruce, of heroic size, erected in 1877, its face turned toward Bannockburn, whither we also went directly. A little burn runs winding through a slightly undulating stretch of plain, with no memorial of the foughten field except a rock almost buried in the earth called the "Bore Stone," in the top of which is a jagged, circular hole, in which the royal standard is said to have been set. This stone is now covered with an iron grating to save it from relic-hunters. A mile away is an eminence called "Gillies Hill," behind which Bruce had stationed his camp-followers, who, showing themselves at a critical moment, threw the English into a panic, and gave the Scotch the victory. On the way our driver pointed to a snug suburban residence, where he said General Grant lunched with the Provost when he visited Stirling.

Drove back to the northeast of the town to the ruins of Cambus-Kenneth Abbey, founded in 1147 by David I., and said to be one of the richest in Scotland, whereof only the square massive Norman tower remains. Here the Lady of the Lake was left by her father, the Douglas, when he went to Stirling to make his peace with the king. On a crag rising from the plain, just as that of Stirling does, but to the greater height of 560 feet, the sides clothed with sylvan verdure, is a recently erected monument to Wallace, 220 feet high, in the form of a baronial tower, most unpleasing to my eyes. Wallace's sword is kept here—a huge blade over six feet long, well adapted to lopping off heads, which was the steady employment of all heroes in the good old days. We crossed the Forth on the old bridge of Stirling, in perfect preservation, though built in the fifteenth century, and for a long time the only bridge over the Forth or Tay, and so the only gate between the north and south of Scotland. Archbishop Hamilton was hanged on this bridge for his share in the murder of the regent Moray in 1570, from which we conclude that masons did good work in those early times, and archbishops engaged in murders and got "stretched" for them—sometimes.

After lunch drove to Doune to visit the castle there, eight miles from Stirling, crossing the Forth and going through the beautiful grounds of Blair Drummond, a seat of G. Stirling Home Drummond Moray, Esq., enriched with magnificent oaks and beeches standing singly in the miles of park, and casting a vast circumference of shade on the velvet sward. We cross a noble bridge over the Teith, built in 1535 by Robert Spital, tailor to the Most Noble Princess Margaret, the queen of James IV., as an inscription on the parapet declares, where the worthy tailor, with the heart of nine, boldly chiselled his arms, a pair of scissors *en saltier*.

Half a mile below, on a peninsula formed by the union of the

Ardoch Burn with the Teith, stands the majestic ruin of the old castle of Doune, with its two square towers, turrets, and high embattled walls, its spiral staircase, dungeons, and battlements, from which exquisite views are obtained up the Teith, whose slender waters glide softly between high banks dusky with the shades of low, overhanging trees, and verdant with flower-strown turf. The court-yard is 100 feet square, and in the centre is the old draw-well, 60 feet deep, which supplied the inmates with water, cold and sparkling, of which we drank. The site of the well was discovered only a few years ago, and it was recurbed to the depth of 40 feet, the curbing below that depth being in good condition. At the bottom was found the old oaken windlass, well preserved, and now shown in one of the upper rooms. The castle has long been the property of the Moray family, and lately two of the rooms have been restored in good taste. One of these is the dining-room, on the second story of one of the quadrangles, and a fine old massive hall it was and is. The kitchen has a famous fireplace, 15 feet across the front, where a whole ox could easily have been roasted, with an enormous chimney, still black with the fires that roared up its throat centuries ago. The castle dates back to the time of James I., 1436, who occupied it. It is supposed that Scott's Knight of Snowdoun, James Fitz-James, slept here the night before he set out for the chase, and the castle also figures in Scott's novel of "Waverley." John Home, the author of the play "Douglas," was taken prisoner at the battle of Falkirk by the Royalists and confined here, and the room is shown from the window of which he let himself down by tying his bedclothes together—some 60 feet, I should say. The custodian of the castle is a certain James Dunbar, formerly of the 79th Cameron Highlanders, and possessed of a gift of gab exceeding anything ever known, I am sure, in that windy vein. He has written a book on the castle, bound in wooden covers made from the Hangman's Tree, once standing just outside the walls. Noticing that it seemed less in volume than his talk would certainly be, I purchased a copy, and hurried away to the quaint and pretty village of Dunblane, on our way back to Stirling, to see the Cathedral there, said to rival in the beauty of its proportions that of Melrose Abbey, and to be one of the few specimens of Gothic architecture which to a great extent escaped the destruction of the Reformation period. There is a beautiful little window in the western gable in the shape of a forest-leaf, and the doorway and the arches of the clerestory are exquisitely formed and shafted, and filled with foliated work. It dates back to 1100. The carved and canopied stalls of oak, black with age, are still preserved in the choir, now used for Presbyterian worship. There, too, lie side by side the effigies of the Earl and Countess of Strathearn, as they have lain since 1271, something the worse for wear, time or man having bereft the fair countess of her head, and nipped away the nose of her stout liege. Noses seem to be lacking always from these effigies; and they carried them so high in air, too, when in the flesh!

We cross the river Allan, a little stream rising in the Ochil Hills, and joining the Forth just below. The village, Bridge of Allan, has fame as a health resort from its sheltered position, but chiefly from some mineral springs. Rode entirely round the castle on a level with the plain. Perched on this beetling crag at such a dizzy height, commanding in wide sweep as fair scenes as I have looked upon, this castle of Stirling fulfils my ideal. The castle rock is greenstone trap, the same formation as the Palisades of the Hudson. Dined at the Golden Lion, and left at 9 P.M. for Edinburgh, thirty-six miles distant, and are well cared for at the Royal Hotel, where we found awaiting us our heavy luggage, which had come forward directly from Glasgow on Saturday.

*May* 28.—We could not have desired better weather than we have enjoyed ever since landing at Queenstown. With the exception of one rainy day at Cork, we have had no foul weather to hinder or even incommode us. Experienced friends insisted we were a month too early for the Highlands, and that we should be frozen and drenched, and that the fogs and mists would hide everything from us, and fields and trees be bare. In fact, we have needed only light wraps—linen dusters would have suited better than mackintoshes—not a day of mist or fog, the whole land smiling in the flowery verdure of forest, meadow and hill. This morning there is rain, but in a cosey private parlor with a bay-window, giving a view up and down Prince Street and across the fair borders of the ravine separating the old from the new town, of the stately buildings crowning the opposite ridge, of the imposing monument to Walter Scott just at the left, and the classical buildings of the

Museum and National Gallery on the right, and with just a glimmer of fire on the hearth and a fresh budget of letters from home, we pass a cheerful morning, despite a shifting mist, which does its best to screen us in.

After luncheon, the clouds having lifted, we engaged the much-to-be-commended Frazer, with his "best horse in Edinburgh," and a snug little landau to take us for a general view of the city; and a fair city it is too, with its wide and regular streets, its handsome and solid houses, its frequent bits of parks, well kept and enriched with fine monuments and statues. Many of these small parks are circular, and the streets and houses about them conform. The night did not become fully dark until nearly eleven o'clock, and happening to awake at two in the morning, I found it daylight.

*May* 29.—Frazer came up and took us to drive across the ravine—in the lower part of which run railway-tracks—up into the old town and into High Street, which extends steeply down in a straight line from the castle to Holyrood Palace, but taking along its course the names of Castle Hill, Lawnmarket, High Street, Netherbo, and the famous Canongate. Many old houses still stand in a dilapidated state on this street, once occupied by rank and fashion in the days of the Stuarts. Beginning at the castle, that nearest to it was the mansion of the Duke of Gordon, still bearing his carved ducal coronet, and having in its gable a cannon-ball said to have been shot from the castle in 1745. Just below the esplanade to the left is a lane leading to the house of the poet, Allan Ramsay, author of the "Gentle Shepherd," who died here in 1758. Passing along down on the right is the General Assembly Hall of the Church of Scotland, which held its first annual session in 1560. May is the month, and it is now holding daily meetings in this handsome Gothic building, with its tapering spire of 241 feet. The Queen is represented at these meetings by a peer appointed for the purpose, who is styled the Lord High Commissioner, and occupies a seat in what is called the throne gallery. A little farther down on the north side of the street, here called the Lawnmarket, is James' Court, where David Hume lived and Boswell, who brought Johnson here before they set out for their tour to the Hebrides in 1773. Near this is Lady Stair's Close, named after Elizabeth, Dowager Countess of Stair, whose singular history forms the groundwork of Scott's story of "My Aunt Margaret's Mirror." Over the doorway is the inscription, "Fear the Lord and depart from evil ; 1622." The Close adjoining, called Baxter's, contains the lodging first occupied by Burns when here in 1786. Then we reach, still in High Street, St. Giles' Cathedral, or the old Parish Church of Edinburgh, named for St. Giles, the patron saint of the city. This we do not visit to-day. At the northwest corner of it once stood the Old Tolbooth jail—the Heart of Midlothian—made world-famous by Scott's novel of that name. The site is indicated by the figure of a heart in the causeway. In the little square here was once a churchyard, where John Knox lies buried, his grave marked by a small stone near the equestrian statue of Charles II., and inscribed "J. K., 1572." This statue of Charles is in lead, and erected at the expense of the city in 1680. He is shown in Roman garb, but the weak, sinister face shows poorly above the dignified toga. On the east of the little square stands the old original Market-Cross, a shaft topped by the heraldic unicorn on a restored base, the latter the gift of the Hon. W. E. Gladstone, four years since. The old Parliament House on the square we do not visit to-day, nor the Advocate's Library connected with it. Visited John Knox's house a little way down, protruding itself into the street. This is the manse where he lived from 1559 to his death in 1572 while minister of Edinburgh, and an exceedingly pleasant and quaintly interesting old house it is, with its odd little rooms, handsome old oaken panels, tiled fireplaces and many relics. There is a little pent-house thrust out over the street with a window looking up it, where he might stand and preach to the crowd below. Above the entrance-door is the inscription in Old English letters and the spelling of the time,

" Lofe.God.aboune.al.and.yohr.nechtbohr.as.yiself,"

and under the window a rude effigy pointing to the name of God carved on a stone above in Greek, Latin and English. A little below two new streets come in, made to open up the dense mass of old buildings here. On one of these was replaced Trinity College Church, which before stood lower down and in the way of the modern improvements. This church was founded in 1462 by Mary of Gueldres, wife of James II. The stones were numbered in taking them down, so that it is exactly restored. Here begins the Canongate, a narrow street going down to the palace of Holyrood. Many of the ancient nobility had their residences on either side of it down to the palace. A notable one is Moray House, on the south side, the mansion of the Earl of Moray, built in 1618 by Mary, Countess of Home, eldest daughter of Lord Dudley. On her death in 1645, goes the record, it fell to one of her daughters, Margaret, Countess of Moray, and so became the property of the Moray family, and remained in the same until 1835. Oliver Cromwell occupied it the first time he visited Edinburgh, both before and after the battle of Dunbar, 1648–50, when he established friendly relations with the Covenanters, and it is said the design of beheading Charles I. was first considered within its walls. Soon after the marriage of the Marquis of Lorne with Lady Mary Stuart, Lord Moray's eldest daughter, took place here, and it is related that the wedding party witnessed from the balcony the Marquis of Montrose being led to execution. Near the Moray House is 13 John Street, where Lord Monboddo and the fair Miss Burnet lived. Burns often visited here while in Edinburgh, and her early death inspired one of his most feeling poems. At No. 10 lived James Ballantyne, Scott's publisher—at least he printed the Waverley novels. Smollett lived near by. Still farther down stands the Canongate Tolbooth, erected in the reign of James VI., an exceedingly interesting exterior. We did not visit the Canongate Church to-day. But time fails to notice all the houses of interest on this famous old street. Near the foot on the north side is the ancient hostelry of the White Horse, one of the oldest of the Edinburgh taverns. Opposite is the Abbey Court House, and two lines of darker stone in the pavement mark limits within which a debtor could not be molested by his creditors—a sort of handy Canada.

We are now at the open space before Holyrood Palace, dating as it is now mainly from 1670. It was originally a convent, as the name abbey implies, and dates back to the early part of the twelfth century, when King David I. founded and endowed the Church of the Holy Rood. After a time, of which the records are not complete, other buildings were added for a royal residence. The tower and high-roofed buildings, containing what are now called Queen Mary's apartments, were built by James V., as an inscription on them shows. All the abbey except the church was burned by the English in 1544. The whole of the palace, except the double tower and the building adjoining containing Queen Mary's apartments, was again burned at the close of the civil war. Charles II. built the present palace in the form of a quadrangle, with a piazza running all around the inner court, a bare space covered with gravel. This building does not much interest me.

In one of the sides of the square is the Picture Gallery, the largest apartment of the palace, and the only one in the modern portion shown to visitors, the other rooms all around the court being occupied by the apartments and offices of one sort and another pertaining to a royal residence. This Picture Gallery is 120 feet long, and on its plain walls are hung, say, one hundred portraits of Scottish kings, from Fergus I. to James VII., all painted by one artist, De Witt, 1685. The earlier ones, of course, have little or no value as portraits, but have, I should say, considerable merit as paintings, and the faces are stamped with much individuality. Specially interesting are those of Mary Queen of Scots and Charles II., the latter strikingly expressing the essential meanness of his character. A long table is set in this room to-day, and now for several days during the session of the General Assembly, to which the present Lord High Commissioner, Earl Hopetoun, daily invites a considerable number of the delegates for dinner. His lordship and suite were just going forth in much state from the palace as we entered, in two coaches and four, guided by a postilion in scarlet jacket and white breeches on the nigh horse of each pair, enveloped in a whirl of cavalry and preceded some paces in advance by two troopers with carbines held at "ready." In this hall the sixteen members of the peerage of Scotland are elected for each Parliament by the Scottish peers themselves, as provided by the Treaty of Union. Here, too, Prince Charles Edward gave the ball described in "Waverley." Queen Mary's apartments, in the original portion of the palace, are much in the same state as when she last used them. In the audience chamber, a room about twenty feet square, stands the bed of Charles I., on which Prince Charlie slept in 1745. From this opens Queen Mary's bedroom, about fifteen feet square, with her bed and many articles of her furniture and toilet. Here is her Venetian mirror, said to be one of the first brought to Scotland, which was wont to reflect her fair face, keeping its beauty through her life of suffering; her work-box, with its cover wrought in silken figures by her own fair fingers, and a touching memento in a little willow baby basket—work in willow being then new and rare and highly prized—covered with faded, tattered blue silk, sent to her by Queen Elizabeth for the use of the little James, who succeeded her on the throne of England. A narrow door opens through the thick wall to a little private supper-room, not ten feet square, into which her husband, Darnley, with several armed attendants, burst on the evening she sat at table with several of her maids of honor and Rizzio. They came up from Darnley's rooms below by a secret passage opening into the adjoining bedroom. Our guide's version of the murder is somewhat different from the current one. It is that they at once proceeded to stab him; that Mary rushed past them into the bedroom, Darnley following and placing himself before her while the armed band were dispatching Rizzio with repeated stabs; and when she would have gone back to intercede for him, drew his dagger and said, "Madam, if you stir a foot I will cut you into collops"—a statement well calculated to keep almost any woman quiet. They dragged his bleeding body through the audience-chamber and left it at the head of the stairs leading to the court below, where, on the authority of our guide, it lay all night. The guide relates, what I think is not to be found elsewhere, that in the morning Mary "was quite annoyed" at finding the body there, and ordered the dark old oaken partition put up, which now parts off a portion of the audience-chamber nearest the stairs, so as to shut out the hateful spot. Our guide, too, quite mocks at the notion of a stain of blood on the clean, worn floor, and he is correct in this, for there is no such spot, as may well be supposed. It was a picturesque tragedy: the low-browed little room hung with tapestry from the looms of France; the fair faces, the rich robes, the jewels sparkling in the full light of the chandeliers, the conspirators filing up the narrow winding staircase, pale Ruthven foremost, clad in complete steel, the sudden terror, the quick dagger-thrust, the shower of succeeding blows—thirty-six stabs in all—the cries of the women, the proud and compassionate anger of the insulted queen.

The Chapel Royal is a fragment of the ancient abbey of Holyrood House, adjoining one side of the quadrangle, dating back to 1128, now in ruins by the tooth of time and the religious frenzy of the Reformers. There is a roofless nave with beautifully carved doorway. There are a few tombs of noble families on the northern side, and it is a circumstance of interest to us that we look on a grave newly dug to receive the body of the Earl of Caithness, who died here suddenly last Saturday at the age of thirty, and will be interred here an hour hence—the last burial, it is said, that will be permitted in Holyrood. He is the fifteenth earl of the name, was never married, and the title now goes to a descendant of the eleventh earl. By will he has left his estates to a college friend, on condition that he takes the family name of Sinclair. As we were about to leave the palace, we were motioned back behind a half-drawn curtain, shutting the corridor we were in from the main entrance, by a flustered lackey in red livery, whose manner indicated some tremendous portent impending, and looking out, saw a fellow-mortal in a long black robe holding in both hands a mace with a gold head as big as his own, who stood facing the entrance, through which marched, in high fig of scarlet and gold, my Lord Hopetoun, a well enough looking, youngish man, returning from the opening of the General Assembly in all the pomp with which we saw him set out two hours before. Several functionaries, bareheaded and powdered, some in dresses marking their offices, all the significance of which I am ignorant, walked close about him, as if to see that the order of the universe gets no detriment this day. I suppose it tickles the dull imaginations of these grim old Scotch Presbyterians, whose ancestors brought their Church through from the militant to the triumphant condition, to have the semblance of royalty attending upon their assemblies, with all its feathers on. In the royal vault in the chapel are buried, among others of note, David II., James II., James V. and Magdalen, his queen; Henry, Lord Darnley.

Although I have noted our visit to Knox's house as occurring before that to the palace, in point of fact it immediately followed, and from the window at which the Reformer was wont to stand and preach we saw the funeral of the Earl of Caithness descending the steep street from St. Giles to Holyrood, with much sad pomp and circumstance. Six black horses plumed and caparisoned in sable drew a huge hearse in which lay open to view the oaken coffin, followed by his piper, with his pipes draped, and the house steward, both on foot, and after, a train of carriages, the foremost conveying the male relations and friends who acted as pall-bearers. There were no ladies in the train.

After luncheon visited the National Museum of Antiquities in the Royal Institution near the National Gallery, both buildings in the classical style with Grecian porticos, a favorite style here, practised largely by the architect Playfair. The collection seemed to me of exceeding interest. There has been no catalogue for twelve years now. I can attempt almost no description of the contents. There is the " Maiden," the ancient Scotch beheading machine, consisting of a wide blade sliding up and down in grooves and loaded with a stone to give it needed force. The victim stooped over and rested his neck on the bed of the framework, some three and one half feet from the ground. Many noble and fair heads have been shorn away by this fatal axe. There are several forms of the "Thumbikins" or thumb-screws, the pain from the application of which the matron who has the Knox house in charge says is "awfully bitter and goes to the heart." Also the "Branks," an iron head-dress with a projection to thrust in over the tongue as a punishment for arrant scolds, and an iron band with chains and fetters to fasten about the body and secure the victim to the stake for burning. Here is the blue ribbon worn by Prince Charles as a Knight of the Garter in 1745, and a ring given him at parting by Flora Macdonald, and an exceedingly interesting collection of Scottish weapons during many centuries.

*May* 30.—Visited the castle, standing on a precipitous crag of basalt 300 feet above the valley below, and occupying almost eight acres of irregular ground. Most of the buildings are modern and plain and greatly detract from the effect of the view from below, but enough remains of walls and the older structures to render the whole extremely grand and picturesque from whatever point it is viewed. I cannot undertake its history, which begins authentically when in 617 Edwin, King of Northumbria built a fortress on this rock, at the foot of which sprang up Edwin's Burgh. It is accessible only on the eastern side. We approach by an esplanade, cross a drawbridge over a moat which must have been a dry one, as there could not have been a supply of water, pass through the old portcullis-gate, underneath the ancient State Prison in the

"Argyle Tower," where the Marquis of Argyle and many adherents of the Stuarts were confined before their execution, and note the barred window of the little room where the brave marquis passed his last night, the old sally-port leading to the town below, St. Margaret's Chapel, the oldest of all the buildings, to the Crown Room, where we are shown the insignia of Scottish royalty, the regalia, called also the "Honors of Scotland," consisting of crown, sceptre and the sword of state.

The history of these crown jewels is interesting, and is told at length by Sir Walter Scott. I can only say here that they were lost from the knowledge of men from 1707 to 1818, when commissioners were appointed to search for them, Scott being one. They were found in the very room where they are now shown, this room having remained closely shut and neglected during this hundred years. The two massive doors, one of iron and one of oak, were forced, as was the great oaken chest, the only article of furniture in the chamber, and to the great joy of the people gathered below, who raised a shout as the news of it spread, all the articles were found safe and sound. They are of exquisite form and workmanship. With them was found the mace of the Lord Treasurer, wrought of solid silver. There is also shown a ruby ring set round with diamonds, the coronation ring of Charles I., a large, fine ruby; also a golden collar of the Order of the Garter, presented to James VI. by Queen Elizabeth on his being created a Knight of the Garter, a fine piece of workmanship. The beautiful sword of state was presented to James IV. by Pope Julius II. in 1507.

Adjoining this room, but reached by another entrance from the court, is Queen Mary's Room, where she gave birth to James VI., commemorated by the initials H. and M. and the date 1566 over the doorway. This room has its original ceiling, with the initials J. R. and M. R. wrought in the panels. There is a portrait of Mary of inexpressible sweetness and beauty and tenderness, a copy of the one in the Bodleian Library at Oxford, the origin of which I would like to know. There is still another of a bolder and more coquettish air painted by Furino about 1562, when she was Dauphiness, and presented by her to Cardinal Lorraine. In this her hair is a dark rich auburn. Adjoining is a little room from the window of which it is said the infant James was let down in a basket to be conveyed to Stirling for greater security. On the bomb battery is the big gun, Mons Meg, now mounted on a carriage, and it seems to me a very creditable cannon to have been made in 1476, so soon after the discovery of gunpowder. It is 13 feet long, 20 inches in diameter and weighs five tons. It was forged at Mons, Belgium, of long bars of malleable iron held together by bands of the same, these bands being continuous, welded perfectly, and the bore smooth and solid. James IV. used it at the siege of Dumbarton in 1489 and at that of Norham Castle in 1497. It burst near the powder-chamber when firing a salute in honor of the Duke of York in 1682. It was drawn about on a wooden carriage by an immense number of horses, and could not be elevated or depressed, and the surface is so rough that it could not be sighted. The balls were huge round stones, several of which are lying near by having been picked up in those parts of the country where this unwieldy monster deployed its horrors to the consternation of bowmen, spearmen and harnessed knights as its huge boulders lumbered along their ranks.

After luncheon the intelligent Frazer took us for a drive in his comfortable landau to Calton Hill, 355 feet high, at the east end of the New Town, where is the Royal Observatory. A time ball-signal here on a flag-staff atop of the ungainly Nelson Monument fires a gun from the castle every day at 1 P.M. A fine view of the city is obtained here. Thence to Arthur's Seat which rises up directly from Holyrood 800 feet. An excellent road called the "Queen's Drive" goes entirely round the upper portion of the hill and commands a wide and beautiful prospect, embracing the smoky city, the estuary of the Forth, the mountains all about and many a fair field and valley and pleasant wood. We pass the ruins of a little chapel on the hill-side—that of St. Anthony—once connected with a hermit's cell, below which is a pure and abundant fountain dedicated to that saint. These are alluded to in the old ballad,

> " Now Arthur's Seat shall be my bed,
> Saint Anton's well shall be my drink,
> Since my true love's forsaken me."

Near by on our road is Muschett's Cairn, a pile of stones marking the spot where Jeanie Deans held the interview with her sister Effie's lover in Scott's "Heart of Midlothian." A portion of the road is overhung by a range of porphyritic greenstone columns of a pentagonal form, from 50 to 60 feet high, called "Samson's Ribs," a part of Salisbury Crags, at the foot of which was Scott's favorite walk. At the foot of Arthur's Seat to the southeast lie Duddingston Loch and village. The house where Prince Charles Stuart slept the night before the battle of Prestonpans is pointed out, and the red-tiled roof of the cottage of Jeanie Deans' father. On the wall of a little church in the village near the entrance hangs an adjustable ring suspended by a chain the height of a man's neck, used to fasten an offender by that member—a sort of stock called the "Jougs." About a mile south, the road running across a charming bit of country, is Craigmillar Castle, nobly situated and well preserved, dating from 1374. It was a favorite residence of Queen Mary, and no wonder, for from the battlements are views fit for a queen's eye by sea and land. It is much more commodious and with more abundant living-rooms than we have seen in any other castle, and seems to have been a sort of strongly fortified summer residence. Mary lay sick here, it is said, on the night Darnley was killed by the explosion in a near suburb of the city, called Kirk o' Field, a spot now occupied by the University.

*May* 31.—The *Morning Leader* here has a long article on the late Earl of Caithness, whose funeral we witnessed yesterday, headed "Caithness—a Lapsed Earldom. Thrilling Story of the Centuries;" and as it illustrates well the past of this country, and throws light on the history of those who fill the high places, I feel an interest in recording the facts of the case, and quoting from this article at some length :

"Tragedy and romance mingled strangely round the ceremony of the sealing of the tomb at Holyrood, wherein on Wednesday were deposited the remains of the Earl of Caithness. It was the symbol of four hundred years of history completed. Yea, more, it seems to have signified that the last of the many conspicuous Scotchmen destined to rest within the precincts of the venerable Chapel of Holyrood had taken his appointed place, and the dust of the dead within these tombs will remain undisturbed till the last syllable of recorded time.

"According to the Domesday Book, the estates of the Earl of Caithness in Caithness-shire extend to 14,460 acres, and the rental is £4478. Stagenhoe Park, the property in Hertfordshire belonging to the family, extends to 613 acres, of which the rental is £973.

"The earldom of Caithness is of very great antiquity—some chroniclers say it is the oldest in Scotland—and has been held by different families. It was one of the titles of the ancient Vikings, or sea kings. In the ancient sagas and the Danish records mention is made of Dungaldus, Earl or Jarl of Caithness, as far back as 875. It is undisputed that the early earls were also Earls of Orkney. Harold, Earl of Caithness and Orkney, was a good and faithful servant of William the Lion till 1196, when he broke out into rebellion, and after defeat by the troops of his royal master, was confined in a turret of Roxburgh Castle till his irate sovereign's wrath was appeased, after which the prisoner was set at liberty. His restless and rebellious spirit, however, soon got him into further trouble; and after murdering John, Bishop of Caithness, he had the compunction (if he felt any) of seeing his son Torpin's eyes put out, the latter having become a hostage to the king for his father's fidelity. In 1231 John, Earl of Caithness, was murdered in his own house by his servants, in retaliation for his connivance at the burning by an angry mob of another Caithness bishop—Bishop Adam, a tithe-exacting ecclesiastic who had made himself obnoxious to the people. The succession to the earldom about this time is involved in perplexity, and little that is authentic is known, but it appears that John, Earl of Caithness, was one of the Scottish nobles to whom Edward addressed a letter proposing the marriage of his son to Margaret of Norway, the young Queen of Scotland. He was also one of the peers who made default when Baliol held his first Parliament at Scone, February 10th, 1282–93.

"The title was next possessed by a branch of the royal family of Stuart, Prince David, Earl-Palatine of Strathearn, eldest son of King Robert II., having been by his father created Earl of Caithness early in his reign. On the attainder of Lord Brechin, afterward Lord Caithness, for the execrable murder of his nephew, James I., in 1437, the earldom was forfeited and annexed to the crown. A Sir George de Crichton, who had acquired the favor of King James II., and who had obtained several large grants of land from that monarch about 1450, was the next inheritor of the title, but on his death in 1455 the title became extinct, and the large estates appear to have reverted to the Crown.

" This brings the narrative to the date of the accession of the St. Clair or Sinclair family, for in the year mentioned (1455) James II. conferred the earldom on William Sinclair, third Earl of Orkney, Lord High Chancellor of Scotland, in compensation, so the charter bears, for a claim of right he and his heirs had to the lordship of Niddesdale. From this earl the branch of the family that recently enjoyed the title was remotely descended. William Sinclair, the second earl of this race, was killed with his royal master, James IV., at the battle of Flodden Field, in 1513. The succession of John Sinclair, the third earl, marks the beginning of that series of feuds and quarrels with the neighboring earls of Sutherland, in the course of which no form of baseness and cruelty on the part of the Sinclairs seems to have been too gross to be resorted to. The prosperity of the earldom reached its climax under George, the fourth earl, to whom the descent of Mr. James Augustus Sinclair, the Aberdeen banker, who is heir-presumptive to the title, remotely traces back. This fourth earl was a cruel and avaricious nobleman, who scrupled not at the commission of the greatest crimes for the attainment of his purpose. In company with a neighboring chief, Donald Mackay, he took possession of the bishop's lands during the absence of the latter in banishment in England, levied the rents and pocketed them. Following up this barefaced robbery by more aggressive measures, Mackay possessed himself of Skibo, one of the bishop's palaces, while the noble lord, the instigator of this outrage, installed himself in the Castle of Strabister, another episcopal residence, which he fortified. In 1555 he was committed by the Queen Regent, then sojourning at Inverness, to the prisons of Inverness, Aberdeen and Edinburgh successively, for refusing to bring his countrymen with him to the court, then sitting at Inverness. Oddly enough, we find this gentleman serving on the jury on the trial of the Earl of Bothwell for the murder of Darnley. But the foregoing were mild offences compared with what was to come. His hatred to John, Earl of Sutherland, was notorious and intense ; and, to gratify his thirst for revenge, he conceived the diabolical purpose of poisoning the earl and countess. His plan matured, he got his cousin, Isobel Sinclair, a relation also of the Sutherland family, to do the dirty work; and by her means the noble earl and his lady were done to death by eating poisoned food prepared for their supper at Helmsdale in 1567, their only son and heir, Alexander Gordon, making a very narrow escape, not having returned from a hunting expedition in time to join his father and mother at supper. To free himself from the imputation of being concerned in the murder he punished some of the Earl of Sutherland's most faithful servants under the color of avenging his death. Isobel Sinclair, the guilty instrument of this arch villainy, was soon after apprehended by the murdered earl's friends, tried in Edinburgh and condemned, and during the time of her incarceration previous to her death in prison, on the day fixed for her execution she uttered the most dreadful imprecations on the Earl of Caithness for having incited her to the horrid act. No crime, however bold, daunted the heart of the tyrant. He had the effrontery, in order to get the young Earl of Sutherland into his hands, to carry him into Caithness, and though he was only fifteen years old, forced him to marry Lady Barbara Sinclair, his daughter, then thirty-two years of age. Divorce put an end to this unhappy *liaison*, the lady continuing a connection with her paramour, Mackay of Far, an ally of her father's. In the mean time, the Earl of Caithness had fixed his residence at Dunrobin, in Sutherlandshire, the seat of his minor son-in-law, whom he treated with great indignity, and burned all the papers belonging to the house of Sutherland on which he could lay his hands. He expelled many ancient families from Sutherland, put several of the inhabitants to death, and burned others, after disabling them in their person by new and unheard-of modes of torture, and stripping them of all their possessions. He even entertained the design of destroying the Earl of Sutherland himself, and marrying William Sinclair, his own second son, to Lady Margaret Gordon, the eldest sister of the Earl of Sutherland; but the latter, being apprised in time of his designs, succeeded in escaping from Dunrobin Castle. The bloodthirsty earl in revenge burned the Cathedral of Dornoch, and reduced the town, in which a band of followers of the Sutherland family had taken refuge. His eldest son, John, Master of Caithness, who carried out this expedition, accepted three hostages from the defenders that they would depart out of Sutherland within three months, but the earl, his father, refused to ratify the conditions, and basely beheaded the hostages.

"This long-drawn-out tale of ferocious cruelty reached a climax in the punishment meted out to the earl's own son. The Master of Caithness, having incurred the suspicion and displeasure of his father for not having, when he found the opportunity, extirpated the whole of the inhabitants of Dornoch, was flung into a dark dungeon beneath the castle, where for seven years he dragged out a wretched existence. His keepers, David and Ingram Sinclair, relatives of his own, determining at last to destroy him, kept him for some time without food. They then gave him a large mass of salted beef, and, withholding all drink from him, left him to die of raging thirst. This inhuman earl died in Edinburgh in September, 1582, and his body was buried in St. Giles', where, *mirabile dictu*, a monument was erected to his memory. His heart was cased in lead and placed in the Sinclair's aisle in the church of Wick, where his murdered son was interred. The decline of the earldom commenced through the improvidence of this man's grandson and successor, George, the fifth earl. In the time of his great-grandson, George, sixth earl, the estates had become so burdened with debt that he sold them in 1672 to his principal creditor, Lord Glenorchy, and by him and his successors all that remained of the family possessions were disposed of, many of the wadsets with which the earldom was burdened having become purchasers of the several lands possessed by them. Of the fifth or, as he was termed, 'the wicked Earl,' the compass of the article permits us only to say that he amply maintained the unenviable reputation earned by his grandfather. With the assistance of a professional blackleg, one Arthur Smith, who was condemned to death for counterfeiting the coin of the realm, he filled Caithness, Orkney, Sutherland and Ross with base money, the illegal workshop being situated in a retired spot under the rock of Castle Sinclair, to which there was a secret passage from the earl's bedchamber. For his share in this crime the earl was apprehended, but received the sham punishment of a pardon on promising, forsooth, to remain at peace with his hereditary foes the Earls of Sutherland. About the same time 'the wicked Earl' distinguished himself by assaulting Lord George

Gordon in the High Street of Edinburgh ; and not long after he added to his laurels by surrendering a cousin, John, Lord Maxwell, whom he professed to befriend, and whom, on that footing, he lured to Castle Sinclair. Lord Maxwell, who was under hiding for the murder of Sir John Johnstone, was afterward, in May, 1613, beheaded at the Cross of Edinburgh. With the death at the age of seventy-eight of this lawless bandit, the careers of the Earls of Caithness became much less eventful.

"On the death of John, the eleventh earl, a major of the 78th Foot (wounded in the groin by a musket-ball in America while reconnoitring with Sir Henry Clinton at the siege of Charlestown), the title went to a very distant branch of the family, Sir James Sinclair of Mey, the ninth in lineal descent from George Sinclair of Mey, third and younger son of the fourth earl. This Sir James Sinclair had two sons, and it is from the second son, Robert Sinclair of Durran, that Mr. James Augustus Sinclair is descended, his father having been Lieutenant-Colonel John Sutherland Sinclair, R.A., born in 1778."

If the records of the titled families of these islands whose names stand in the Domesday Book should be brought to the light from their dusty hiding-places, how many would be found likewise stained with blood and foul with many a deed of cruelty and shame?

Attended morning session of the General Assembly of the Church of Scotland in the hall built for its use, and one of the worst in its acoustic properties I was ever in. The Lord High Commissioner came to the hall in the flamboyant style I described a few pages back and occupied a seat on a raised throne railed off at one end with a private entrance, his purse-bearer one side in powder and scarlet with a big red bag holding papers of one sort and another which he produced and put back without apparent purpose ; on the other his chaplain in gown and single eyeglass, flushed with good living, and a step behind two pages in red coats and powdered hair, an aid with more gold braid on his chest than it could well hold, a big gilt mace hanging at one side from the crimson canopy of the throne. His lordship took no part whatever in the proceedings which were guided by the Moderator seated just below him at the head of a long table, about which the leading lights of the Church clustered. The delegates occupied the central portion of the hall and seemed a solid, heavy sort of men, almost all wearing full beards. I should say that, compared with a similar body in our country, they looked less intellectual and more sensible. They did business in a straightforward, dull way, speaking briefly and to the purpose on the subjects before them. There was less Scottish peculiarity of speech than I expected, but their fashion of clipping words and the faults of the hall made it difficult to catch the full purport of any speaker's remarks, even when we were seated not far away. Admission is by tickets, which I had procured, but our seats were so poor that I went out and was referred to the "agent," of whom I asked more desirable sittings. He said he could do nothing as the part allotted to spectators was crowded, but on my stating that we were from America, said there was a reserved portion of the hall where we could go at one shilling each. I bought four tickets and we were shown to better seats. Think of the General Assembly of the Presbyterian Church in the United States reserving a part of their place of convocation and selling tickets to it !

P.M. visited the National Picture Gallery, where we saw many pictures by the leading Scotch artists of the last hundred years, as well as instances of the famous artists of many lands and times, including Van Dyck, Greuze, Salvator Rosa, Cuyp, Titian, Murillo, Valasquez, Rubens, Rembrandt, Watteau, Jordaens, Teniers, Jan Steen, and other masters, constituting by far the best gallery I have seen. They gave me the liveliest pleasure, but I am almost new to the best works of this delightful art and like an humble disciple will wait until I have more experience before giving my feelings expression.

Our life here is very agreeable. We have a parlor where our meals are served, with good sleeping-rooms connecting, with fine views from our windows, all our wishes when indoors noiselessly attended by a waiter specially assigned to us and we gather about our table after a day's sight-seeing quite as at home. Prince Street extends in nearly a straight line for a mile from east to west, built up only on one side, is terraced in front in pleasure grounds down to the bottom of the deep ravine, beyond which rise grandly the buildings on the opposite side. Near at hand on the upper

terrace rises the majestic monument of Walter Scott to the
height of 200 feet, in form of a Gothic spire, with arches like
those in Melrose Abbey. Under the central canopy is a
marble statue of Scott in a sitting posture, his dog Maida
beside him. This monument was completed in 1844, at a cost
of sixteen thousand pounds. Along the same stretch of
terrace are bronze statues of Livingston, Professor Wilson
(Christopher North), and several other celebrities.

*June* 1.—Driven by Frazer to Rosslyn seven and a half
miles, over a fine road—macadamized, as all the roads are
hereabout—with charming views on either hand, rounded and
woody Corstorphine to the west, nearer and farther southward, the long uneven line of the Pentland Hills, and stretching far along to the east and southeast the sad range of Lammermoor. Rosslyn Chapel is a poem in stone, unfinished, only
the choir being completed. All parts are exquisitely carved, no
pattern being introduced, but done as if pious hearts had patiently wrought their tender and gentle fancies with reverent hands
into imperishable forms. Vaulted ceiling, columns, arches
and panellings, all exposed parts, indeed, of the interior are
ornamented with leaf and flower in bewildering variety and
exuberance, affording the eye new pleasures at every turn.
All this finds its fullest expression in the "Prentice's Pillar,"
of which tradition relates that the master builder, being
unable to execute it from the designs he had in hand, went
to Rome to study there, and on his return, finding it completed by an apprentice, mad with envy, smote him dead
with his mallet. Most fair stands this chapel in an enclosed
field of richest verdure, and not to be forgotten.

We lunched near by, and made the walk of two miles down
the wild and rocky glen of the Esk to Hawthornden, passing
at first through the court of Rosslyn Castle quite in ruins,
but with a portion of the wall standing on the side of the
deep ravine through which the muddy Esk flows in its narrow
bed, and impressive as one looks up from below. In the space
once enclosed by the castle walls stands an enormous yew said
to be six hundred years old and still vigorous. The castle stands
not far from the chapel, and these, with large lands all about,
are the property of the present Earl of Rosslyn, descended
from the family of that name. The glen is savagely picturesque, but not more so than the "Gorge" of the Black River

in Cavendish, Vt. A foot-path leads down by the water, and following it we at length cross a bridge, to enter on the domain of Sir James Drummond of Hawthornden, a direct descendant of the poet Drummond, Shakespere's friend, whom Ben Jonson walked up from London to visit. A portion of the old house remains, and succeeding owners have added portions, making a picturesque mansion in an imposing situation on a bold rock descending precipitously to the stream nearly a hundred feet below. There is a curious arched passage cut through the solid rock just below the house, extending a hundred feet, and broadening into a chamber of say ten feet square, with recesses of nearly the same size on either hand, one called Bruce's bedroom, the other, which has quite a well-cut set of bookcases in the rock on one side, his library, the tradition being that Bruce once took refuge here. A villainous sword is shown here under an iron screen, said to be his. One cannot believe all he hears. But here are these strange subterranean chambers, and a well in a recess cut down at least twenty feet into the toughest sort of rock. A huge plane-tree stands near the house, said to be the one under which Jonson and Drummond sat in "conversation." It is an enormous tree, and flourishing as if good for another hundred years.

I should say that when we entered Lord Rosslyn's chapel I paid a shilling apiece for my party of four, and a like sum when we entered the grounds of Sir Drummond. Gentle blood here does not despise the "siller." I understand the Esk does not much increase in volume before joining its south branch. If not, it is hard to see where "Ford there was none" in the time of Young Lochinvar. 'Tis easy to see he might have waded his horse across anywhere. Swimming is more poetical, but Scott generally, I find, makes all things conformable, taking a good deal of pains to do so; witness his showing by actual trial that James Fitz-James could have ridden in one day from Coilantogle Ford to Stirling.

Frazer met us at the lodge-gate, and we drove to Dalkeith House, the seat of the Duke of Buccleuch and Queensbury, passing through the little village of Lasswade, where Scott passed some happy years of his early life, as he has written. Melville Castle, the seat of Viscount Melville, is near by. Dalkeith House stands in a large park with noble trees, singly and in clumps, over a far-spreading and luxuriant greensward.

The house, or palace, is a large stone building, not specially grand or attractive in its exterior, but within containing pictures, china, and cabinets worth a king's ransom. I think the contents of the duke's drawing-room would bring at public sale in New York half a million dollars. We were freely shown all parts of this most interesting palace by a dignified matron, to whom I offered a shilling on our departure with a shamefacedness quite uncalled for.

We have found almost no American news in the local papers at points we have visited, and I have found mostly a report about an inch long, day after day, of a game of chess, as the only item thought worthy of telegraphing from our side of the water. But as we drive into town to-night we see posted in the windows of the little shops where newspapers are sold freshly printed and written placards announcing "Appalling Accident in America," and eagerly buying an evening newspaper at my hotel, find a long telegram from New York giving the first known particulars of the dreadful flood which devastated the Conemaugh Valley below Pittsburgh, a horror which I fear, from the nature of the accident, will prove even more distressing than the first reports indicate.

*June 2, Sunday.*—Attended morning service at St. Giles', the most ancient church in the city, although its renovated exterior does not indicate it. The well-known publisher, the late Dr. William Chambers, made judicious alterations almost wholly at his own expense, which have restored it to its pre-Reformation state. The old spire has never been disturbed. Its history is of national interest, but I must pass it over. Here the National League and Covenant was sworn to and subscribed in 1643. In 1636 the attempt to introduce the new "service-book" of Charles I. led to Jenny Geddis throwing her stool at the head of the dean, thereby intimating that she was too sensitive in her religious nature and too refined and cultivated of intellect to tolerate any service smacking of papacy. She confounded "collect" with "colic," but distinctions were not nice then, nor forms of speech, and this uncomfortable female has a brass tablet to her memory. The church was crowded. The Lord High Commissioner came in his accustomed state and occupied a high stall against one of the walls, and after he had bowed thrice to the congregation we were at liberty to transfer our attention from this reflection of regal grandeur to the King of kings. The provost and bailies of the city entered in a body in powdered wigs, preceded by halberdiers and followed by the judges in their wigs and gowns. A silver mace was hung behind the preacher's chair after he entered the pulpit, and removed by a verger in red facings just before he vacated it. The prayers were read, and the service altogether was more ceremonious than that of the High Church Episcopalians at home. The grandeur of the whole service—for it had a certain grandeur in this massive church, high-roofed and many-pillared, with its broad arches and stained windows—was heightened by a heavy thunder-storm, whose solemn reverberations rolled heavily through nave and choir and chapel.

After lunch Dr. Walling called, and we walked for two hours through the old parts of the city, traversing the Canongate, Grass Market and Cowgate, and many obscure wynds and closes. These are now the most squalid portions of the city, and many poor wretches showed themselves on the streets and at the windows, but we can easily match anything I have seen so far in several parts of New York. A mist came on while we were out, "a fine specimen of a right Scotch mist," the doctor said, which dampened my clothing and carried a chill with it. It is common here, and we have not had a clear morning since our arrival, but mostly it scatters as quickly as it comes.

*June* 3.—Rained all the morning, but the people pay little attention to it, carrying umbrellas, and further protected by water-proof outer garments, manufactured here in many kinds and colors, of fine finish and excellence. I should say, from what I see and hear, that the climate is for the most part sombre and dull, though never very hot or very cold. The morning papers have two columns of telegraphic despatches from New York about the fearful freshet. Passed the P.M. selecting photographs of scenes visited in Scotland.

*June* 4.—Left on 9.30 train for Loch Leven, crossing the Firth of Forth by a ferry—five miles—to Burntisland, thence on by rail through Kirkcaldy, where Carlyle and Irving once taught separate schools. Near Dysart are the ruins of an exceedingly old castle known as Macduff's Castle. Forty-three miles from Edinburgh Kinross is reached, only twenty-seven miles by turnpike on the direct highway to Perth, seventeen miles farther on. Are driven through its old and crooked streets to an old and comfortable inn, where we dine well, the famous Loch Leven trout figuring on the bill of fare. Hired a boat and rowed to the island, half a mile from the shore, on which stands Loch Leven Castle, now a ruin, but with enough remaining to give a good idea of what it was once. The donjon stands almost entire, as well as the walls enclosing the court-yard of 150 feet square; and the southeast tower, containing the apartments in which Queen Mary was kept a prisoner by the Confederated Lords in 1567 for a year, when she made her escape, is also well preserved. An ancient elm, called "Queen Mary's Tree," stands in the deserted court-yard, now overgrown with luxuriant grass, while all about the solid walls are festooned with wild ivy. Here, as in all these old ruins, there are no traces of woodwork remaining. Not much wood was ever used, but floors and doors are always lacking unless restored by later hands. All buildings, old and new, are of stone. I have not seen any sort of a wooden structure since we landed at Queenstown. Brick is used considerably in the larger towns of Ireland, but both there and in Scotland every sort of habitation and improvement for man's use is of the most durable materials, except the poorest cottages or huts, and they are of earth and plaster. What surprises me in these old ruins is the tenacity of the mortar. It outlasts the stone, and in cases I have noticed where a fissure or break has taken place, it is the rock and not the mortar which has yielded. This castle of Loch Leven dates back beyond authentic history, and is attributed to Congal, King of the Picts. All the stone used in its construction was brought from the main-land nowhere nearer than half a mile. The story of Mary's escape is told by Scott, and is full of romance. The lake is oval in shape, nearly four miles long by about two wide, a charming sheet of water set among tranquil hills—Benarty, Lomond, Cleish, Ochil—with peaceful meadows at their feet. There are about seventy acres of the island on which the castle stands, and a still larger one named St. Serf, where are the ruins of the very ancient Priory of Port Mary, which figures in Scott's "Abbot."

We have so far met very few tourists from home, being here too early in the season for the annual stream, but these are arriving at the Royal in daily increasing numbers. A curious specimen, presuming me to be an American, began a conversation this evening in the smoking-room, and advised me by all means to go to London, where he had just passed four days, having come on to Edinburgh by last night's train. He said I would find it an "orderly" city, and that if I felt as much interest in historical subjects as he himself, I should by no means omit seeing Madame Tussaud's Wax Works, they give so much information, although he confessed he should not have recognized the effigy of General Grant except by the label.

*June* 5.—Frazer drove me slowly through the Canongate and Cowgate streets of the old town, to deepen the impression I have of them, the most interesting parts of all the city to me. Arranged for a coach to drive from here up through England by a route I have marked out.

*June* 6.—Visited the Advocates' Library, housed in dim alcoves of a long arched hall, nowise comparable to Trinity in Dublin. There are present here a boyish letter of Charles I. to his father and one from Queen Mary to her mother, both distinctly legible; also a copy of the first Bible printed from stereotyped plates. The library adjoins the courts of law, connected by a long, fine hall, adorned with portraits and statues of eminent judges and advocates. This seems to be a hall of consultation, and a dozen or so of lawyers were walking up and down, singly and in couples, wearing black robes and queer powdered wigs, giving them, especially the younger ones, a bizarre appearance. We have passed ten very pleasant days in Edinburgh, and leave it with fond regret. It is a stately and beautiful city.

*June* 7.—Left the Royal on our hired coach to go as far as Stratford-on-Avon or London, or, if sooner tired of it, to dismiss it at any intermediate point. It is the form of a coach called here a drag, having a closed coach-body, with seats inside for four, and on the roof for ten, besides those for coachman and groom. I sent direct to London all superfluous luggage, putting hand-bags, wraps, etc., inside, and one steamer trunk on the roof. We set out with considerable *éclat* and bowled along the streets of the city, through the suburbs, and entered on the fine old-time stage road to London at the rate of ten miles an hour. Twelve miles to the south we strike the Lammermoor Hills, and traverse them for the most part along a glen beside the Heriot, a clear, bright stream, tributary to the Tweed, and in some part of its course one of the sources of the water-supply of Edinburgh, gathered in a reservoir some twenty-five miles distant from the city. The scenery all along is charming, with wide prospects from the roof of the coach, the motion exhilarating, and all is life and enjoyment in our little party of four, when the nigh wheeler, after "striking" badly, seemed stunned, and pulling up short, staggered and reeled as if to fall. After a moment's rest he seemed to revive, and we went on again to Stowe, some three miles farther, and twenty-seven from Edinburgh. Here we lunched and baited, and a half hour later, as we drew near Galashiels on the Gala River, our invalid wheeler again showed heavy pain ; coachman and groom sprung to him, had him out of harness in a trice, left him in charge of the groom, put one of the leaders in his place, and on we sped to Melrose, seven miles away, but shining with somewhat diminished splendor. Put up at the Abbey Hotel, immediately connected with Melrose Abbey by a door into the grounds, and had rooms assigned us which looked directly through the nave to the fine eastern window of the chancel. We went at once into the abbey and wandered among its ruins until dusk, and later sat long, looking from our windows on the beautiful eastern window, revealed in the full light of the rising moon.

"Slender shafts of shapely stone,
By foliaged tracery combined."

Melrose Abbey, now a grand and beautiful ruin, was founded by David I. in 1136 as a monastery for the Cistercians, and dedicated to St. Mary. Edward I. of England destroyed it, and Robert Bruce rebuilt it in the early part of the fourteenth century in the late Gothic style with elaborate magnificence, as the ruined church, the only portion remaining, abundantly testifies. The nave and central tower are much destroyed ; only a small part of the roof remains over the south transept ; but the grace of the slender and lofty pillars, with their rich capitals, the harmonious proportions, and chiefly the symmetrical tracery of the windows, and the association of all with the tender and glowing poetry of Scott, make of this ruin a memorable object. Among the tombs is one containing the heart of Robert Bruce, and another with a bizarre effigy, called the grave of the wizard, Michael Scot. William Douglas, " the dark knight of Liddesdale," and James

II., earl of that name, with others of that family, are buried here. In the grass-grown choir beneath the broken central tower stands a section of a fallen column on which, our guide informed us, Scott used to sit for hours at a time in meditation. The church was of goodly size, the nave even now some 250 feet long and the transept 130 feet.

Before retiring my coachman came to say that the groom had just come from Galashiels, that the sick horse had dropped down dead all of a sudden in the stable, that he had himself telegraphed to Edinburgh for another horse, which would be here ready to start at 9 A.M. to-morrow. He is the same coachman, George Punton, who drove Mr. Carnegie and his party of twelve, including Mr. Blaine and his two daughters, last summer from London to the north of Scotland, a short, stoutish, fresh, cheerful man of thirty-five, self-possessed, resourceful, and handling four horses as if they were one. He is in the employ of Scott, Croall & Sons, Job and Postmasters—so their card reads—of whom I hire my coach at a fixed sum per day. This firm own and work in various ways sixteen hundred horses, keeping their lives insured. The farrier at Galashiels reports that the horse we lost yesterday died of heart disease.

*June* 8.—At 9 A.M. George is at the door fresh and smiling with a stout wheeler to fill the gap made yesterday, but the becoming uniformity of our four dappled grays is broken by the new-comer in his soberer suit of dark bay. However, he looks stanch and true, and we take the road from the narrow, crooked streets of Melrose, in the market square of which stands an old stone cross with the date 1642, to Abbotsford, three miles west, over a charming country, with the Eildon Hills—the Tremontium of the Romans—on our left close at hand, the highest of the three peaks rising 1385 feet. The famed wizard, Michael Scot, whose tomb and bizarre effigy we saw in the abbey, is reputed to have formed these three peaks by cleaving apart the one rounded dome erewhile standing there. But a greater magician of the family has cast a mightier spell over all this region, and here we are at Abbotsford, where the *open sesame* of a shilling apiece admits us to such rooms as are open to visitors. These are shown by a civil custodian, and consist of Sir Walter's study, library, drawing-room, armory and entrance hall, shown in the order given above. Everything in these rooms is pretty much as Scott left it, and they are crowded with objects of exceeding interest, which I can undertake only to barely mention in small part. In the study are his writing-table and ample leathern chair, which stands as if waiting for him, with books and pictures, one of these, a portrait of Rob Roy, covering the walls. A small turret-room opens from this, which Scott was wont to call "Speak-a-bit," alluding to its convenience for a *tête-à-tête*, where is kept the bronze cast of his head taken after death, showing the strong features composed and calm. The carved panelling of this little room is said to have belonged to a bedstead used by Queen Mary at Jedburgh during her visit and dangerous illness there in 1566.

The library, a handsome room 40 by 15 feet, with a ceiling richly carved in oak, copied mostly from the roof of Rosslyn Chapel, contains about twenty thousand volumes standing orderly on their shelves, mostly in handsome bindings, the upper ranges being reached from a light iron gallery extending round. The marble bust done in 1820 by Chantry has the place of honor, and conveys an expression of more humor than in the copies I have seen. There is also a full-length portrait of Scott's eldest son, the second Sir Walter, in the uniform of the 15th Hussars, a tall, slender young man—he died young—with no resemblance to his father. There are the miniatures of Scott and Mademoiselle Charpentier, afterward Lady Scott (these are the pictures they exchanged before marriage), and a score of most interesting historical articles. The mother-of-pearl cross which Queen Mary last pressed to her lips is here.

The drawing-room is a large well-proportioned room hung with Chinese paper, and contains many interesting paintings, including a water-color sketch of Sophia Scott (afterward Mrs. Lockhart), one of Anne Scott in fancy dress, a portrait of Scott's mother, and one of Scott himself by Sir Henry Raeburn, painted in 1809, representing him at full length, seated, with his greyhound Percy at his feet, and the valley of the Yarrow for a background. There is an "awesome" portrait of the head of Mary Queen of Scots after decapitation, with the signature of the painter, Amyas Cawood, dated February 9th, 1587, the day after her execution, a picture to haunt one with its stony features of ashen pallor.

The armory bristles with all sorts of weapons, offensive and defensive, admirably disposed, and, like all the objects here, in excellent condition. Here are a sword given to the great Marquis of Montrose by Charles I., and Rob Roy's gun, a handsome long Spanish-barrelled piece with his initials, R. M. C., Robert McGregor Campbell, the latter name assumed by him in compliment to the Argyle family; also his broadsword with Andrew Ferrara blade and basket-hilt, and long Highland dirk with blade of the same maker.

The entrance hall in like manner is filled with armor of all ages and countries. Here are the original keys of "The Heart of Midlothian," or Old Tolbooth of Edinburgh. There are two fine *cap-a-pie* suits of polished steel tilting armor, glorious to see. The last suit of clothes Scott wore lies well preserved in a glass case, including a singularly high and wide-brimmed white hat. I noticed the shoe, whose outlines indicate a small, shapely foot.

Abbotsford is built of a light cheerful stone, with considerable ornament of one kind and another in its ambitious architecture, and is really a fine residence, but one has a feeling that somehow it is not altogether what the builder intended, as if he had been compelled to stay his hand before having all to his mind. No doubt he tried for too much, and enslaved himself to meet the demands on him. The situation, too, is on the level bank of the river, sloping upward in its rear, so that it is shut out of view until one comes right upon it. But the broad brown Tweed flows swiftly with murmuring song close below the windows of the cheerful alcoves of his goodly library; no fairer fields may be than those sloping southward to the sun on the opposing bank far up and down the valley; a deep serenity is over all, and one can feel how dear to the master's heart Abbotsford must have become. The place is now owned by the Hon. Mrs. Maxwell Scott, Sir Walter's great-granddaughter, the daughter of a daughter of Lockhart. The custodian informed me that about six thousand persons visited Abbotsford last season. About twenty thousand visited Burns' birthplace during the same time.

We drove back through Melrose to Dryburgh Abbey, five miles, that we might see where Scott lies buried. We climb Bemerside Hill, whose summit commands a glorious view of the Tweed Valley and all the fertile space southward to the blue line of the Cheviots. It is said that here Sir Walter always reined up his horse to admire the scene. Dryburgh Abbey was founded in 1150 by Hugh de Moreville, Lord of Lauderdale and Constable of Scotland. The Tweed sweeps round the well-wooded knoll on which it stands. In 1322 Edward II., returning from his unsuccessful invasion of Scotland burned the monastery which then underwent repairs. At the Reformation it passed into a temporal lordship, as was the fate of such institutions, and is now owned by the Earl of Buchan. It is much in ruins but specially interesting by reason of the considerably well-preserved remains of so much of the monastic buildings, including the refectory, the abbot's parlor and the wine and almonry cellars. There is a St. Catharine's window in this part of the ruin, 10 feet in diameter, much overgrown with ivy, and high up the same wall climb rose-vines gay with flowers against the hoary stones taken from the same quarry as those of Melrose Abbey. In the grounds stands a yew of great size, said to have been planted soon after the foundation of the abbey. The most beautiful and interesting part of the ruin is that of the north transept, called St. Mary's Aisle. Here Sir Walter Scott was buried on the 26th of October, 1832, in the tomb of his maternal ancestors, the Haliburtons of Newmains, at one time owners of the abbey. His wife lies beside him. She died in 1823. On the other side is the tomb of his oldest son, and at his feet that of his son-in-law, Lockhart. No others of his family are buried here. All is fair and peaceful around this tender and venerable spot, cheered by the various songs of many tuneful birds, a spot, fitting for the final rest of a weary and gifted soul, who has vastly added to the innocent and high enjoyment of his kind, leaving a name the world will not willingly let die.

Crossing the Tweed by a foot-bridge we rejoined our coach and sped merrily on for twelve miles over the same fair and fertile country we find all along to the ancient Border town of Jedburgh, the county town of Roxburghshire, situated in the pretty valley of the Jed. It was a "royal burgh" seven hundred years ago, and the chief town of the middle marches. The citizens in the old days were famous for their skill in handling a peculiar partisan called the "Jethart Staff." Their war-cry was "Jethart's here," and their coat-of-arms a mounted trooper charging. The proverb of "Jethart justice,"

"Where in the morn men hang and draw,
And sit in judgment after,"

appears to have taken its rise from some instances of summary justice executed on the Border marauders, says Black. The population of the town is now about 3500, chiefly well built in modern houses, some few of the old buildings still remaining; among these a long two-story house with the Scottish coat-of-arms chiselled on one of the walls, where Queen Mary is said to have lain dangerously sick for several weeks after her visit to Bothwell at Hermitage Castle, not far away.

But Jedburgh has its lion in the favorite form of a ruined abbey dating back to near the middle of the twelfth century, and built by that father of so many in this kind, David I., for a society of Augustine friars from France. There is a fine Norman west door, a flamboyant St. Catharine's window, and a graceful display of pillars and arches in the nave. The triforium and clerestory are in excellent preservation, and show the Norman mingled with the Gothic in an interesting manner. The tower is in perfect condition, 100 feet high, and I was simple enough to be persuaded into going to its top by the narrow winding stairs usual in these structures of the uncomfortable old times, and have registered a vow never again to elevate my two hundred pounds avoirdupois to any such altitude by a similar process.

Our inn here is the Spread Eagle, a gilt effigy of the same surmounting the door, not the "fierce gray bird with bending beak" of Uncle Sam, but a most tame dunghill creature with double head and supine tail flattened on the wall, humiliating for the free-born American to look upon. But here under its feeble wings we are doomed to stay over the more than Puritan Scottish Sabbath.

*June 9, Sunday.*—A sour, rainy, chilly day, so that a melancholy fire in our dingy private parlor in this mouldy old house agreed well with the state of nature outside. Finished reading Froude's "Two Chiefs of Dunboy," an exceedingly interesting book as illustrating the state of things in Ireland something over a century ago. In the afternoon walked in the churchyard by the abbey, noticing on the stones names often appearing in the histories and stories of the old Border times—Turnbull, Allan, Elliott, Graham, Hilson,

Chisholm, Fenwick, Rutherford, Douglas, Grahamslaw, Cranstoun, Borthwick, Laidlaw.

*June* 10.—Fine, cool, bracing morning. Took the road at 10 A.M. for Newcastle, fifty-six miles, to be done in easy stages of two days. Followed the narrow and picturesque valley of the Jed some seven miles, then bore away more to the south straight upon the long, wide range of the Cheviot Hills. These are a series of low hills, or rather an irregular succession of broken ranges, with innumerable small peaks and domes, woodless, grassy to the top, rising out of a high moor tufted with wild grass and stretching away indefinitely in all directions, with no outcropping of rock of any sort—at least until the southern slope of the plateau is reached. On the crest of almost the last ridge to the south is the dividing line between the two countries, and we pass from Scotland into England at a good round trot, and for the first time are on right English soil. All about us, on hill-sides, in valleys, on broad stretches of moor, are thousands of sheep—for the whole region is pasture—watched by shepherds whose solitary huts rise infrequent, the work being mostly done by dogs of the collie breed, whose movements we watched with lively interest. Each shepherd was accompanied by at least two of these, and at a quiet intimation conveyed by voice or gesture they headed the flock in any required direction, closed it up or opened it out or separated it into as many parts as was wanted, without a moment's indecision. George, our Scotch coachman, says he has himself seen the collie go into a large herd of cattle pasturing in common and bring out those of his master as handily and more speedily than a man could do.

After driving twenty-six miles to Otterbourne, we are still on the southern slope of one of the ranges of the Cheviot. We purposed stopping at the little tavern here, but found all good space taken by a party of young folk from Newcastle on their Whitsuntide holidays:

> "The Otterbourne's a bonnie burn,
> 'Tis pleasant there to be ;
> But there is nought at Otterbourne
> To feed my men and me."

Therefore we drove back four miles to the Redesdale Arms, Horsley, where we are in just such a snug, clean, quiet country inn as I have read about and longed for since boyhood, and in our private parlor I am closing the day with these imperfect notes of it, a lump of coal flickering in the high grate, two tall candles in high, silver-gilt stands on my table, half-a-dozen small cases of stuffed birds on the low walls, solid mahogany furniture, an old mirror, and exceeding peace. Such a broad, free view we had after dinner, just two hours ago, the still water of the Redes winding below us, with its narrow valley above, growing dusky in the slant rays of sunset!

*June* 11.—Clear and cool. Had the best breakfast since leaving home—brook trout from the stream near by, savory ham, excellent coffee with rich cream, toothsome bread, all good and well served, and at a cost of unwonted moderation. We shall have a kindly memory of the Redesdale Arms, into which we fell by accident. We were on the road at 9 A.M., with much such scenery as yesterday, now on a lower level; hills sharp and gradual, long stretches of moor and fen, pretty valleys, high pastures with multitudinous sheep, abundance of small game, rabbits, grouse, partridges, plover, and many sorts of birds. I saw the starling for the first time and the meadow-lark, although I had been asking for a sight of the latter ever since we landed in Ireland. This morning George said, pointing with his whip, "A lark," and a small brown bird rose toward the sun with a continuous, wavering song, clear and sweet, ever mounting higher, until the tiny form, lost to sight in the sun's effulgence, seemed to dissolve in melody.

Lunched and baited at the Highland Inn, whose sign of a Highland piper, looking as if he had come out of bonny Scotland with Prince Charlie in '45 and got badly "left," very fairly indicated the entertainment for man and beast. But it could have been worse, and it sustained us well for the ten remaining miles, when we entered the smoky, bustling town of Newcastle-on-the-Tyne, and drew to their doors a fair share of its 150,000 inhabitants as we rattled up to the Station Hotel. There is little here we care for, and we are here only because it is in our way. The town lies on the left bank of the Tyne, nine miles from its mouth in the midst of an extensive coalfield, and is probably the chief coal-exporting city of the world. The old church of St. Nicholas has a striking lantern-tower resembling that of St. Giles' in Edinburgh. The keep of the castle, the only part remaining, dates from 1170, and is 85 feet high—to the top of the turret, 107 feet—with walls 12 to 18 feet thick. There is a bridge over the Tyne designed by Robert Stephenson, and above its roadway, another for railways, both solid, and doing excellent service. The upper level is 112 feet above the water, and on the top of one end is a locomotive built by George Stephenson, " Stephenson's No. 1 Engine."

*June* 12.—At 9 A.M. left for Durham, fourteen miles. Passed through Chester-le-Street, the only place of interest on the route, an old town of 6000 population. It was the seat of the Bishop of Bernecia from 883 to 995. Saw near at hand on the left, Lumley Castle, the seat of the Earl of Scarborough. At 11 A.M. pulled up at the portals of the County Hotel, Durham, another good instance of an English inn. And I desire to put on grateful record my relish of such a mug of ale as one encounters but few times in his mortal pilgrimage. Strengthened thereby with the adjunct of an excellent lunch, I took my little party by a pleasant walk along the Wear to the Cathedral, which stands proudly on a high tongue of land around which the river forms a loop. Deeply impressive to me is this massive pile, with its square Norman central tower of 214 feet in height, its walls 70 feet high, its length 510 feet, its width across the transepts 170 feet, across the nave, 80 feet. But these figures give no idea of the effect of mingled awe and admiration with which one gazes from the western end through the pillared nave and rich choir, and still beyond over the reredos to the great rose-window over the "Nine Altars." The huge piers and pillars supporting the arches on which the triforium rests, the clerestory above, and still farther away the heavily groined roof, all parts complete and variously representing in form and ornament the changing phases of what are styled the Romanesque and Gothic, almost oppress the senses, like the near presence of some majestic and awful object in nature.

I shall attempt no description of this great Cathedral, reckoned as one among the six finest in England. I do not believe any description of cathedrals can convey an adequate impression. They may be felt, not described. Nor shall I dwell upon its history, which begins when Bishop Williams, the second bishop after the Norman Conquest, completed the choir in 1093. The work went on through four centuries, and some changes, called "renovations," mostly for the worse, have occurred since. It is dedicated to St. Andrew, and has been specially honored by the presence of the bones of St. Cuthbert, which are supposed to rest behind the reredos in a spot of peculiar distinction. Great must have been the odor of his sanctity, for the monks of Lindisfarne, fearful that the Danes would covet his bones, brought them here and bestowed them in a church completed in 990, succeeded by the present Cathedral, because this spot is better fitted for defence. Out of deference to his saintly abhorrence of woman as a suggester of evil thoughts, it is said, the Lady's Chapel is set in the unusual position of the west end, and some twenty-five feet from the western door is a blue stone cross in the pavement of the nave, beyond which no woman must venture in the old days. Pretended personal articles and memorials of the fine old saint are shown to such an extent in cases in the library that one might fancy himself among the relics in a Mexican cathedral rather than in a Reformed Protestant church.

I was much interested in the monastic buildings formerly occupied by the Benedictine monks in connection with the Cathedral. These are well preserved, and the huge kitchen, still used as such, with its conical roof and larders and high windows; the long hall of the dormitory, with its oaken roof black with centuries; the comfortable refectory; the ample cloisters, with their "carrels" or recesses for study, call back the old days, and the imagination easily peoples these stout habitations with buxom monks, wearing the days of their life away in animal content, caring little what befell, so that the venison pasty was hot and toothsome and the ale clear and foaming in the tankard. By-the-bye, I wonder if the beer I have this day commended is brewed after the recipe left by the good monks for the benefit of the inhabitants of quaint Durham for all time?

For centuries the bishops of Durham were earls of Northumberland as well, and most princely was their state of independent sway over the Palatinate of Durham. They occupied the castle on the other side of the Palace Green, dating back to William the Conqueror, rebuilt and altered since, and now since 1833 occupied by Durham University, the lofty keep being used by the students as dormitories. There is in one part a fine carved staircase of oak black with age, leading to a series of apartments used as living and sleeping rooms by certain judges of the courts and professors of the University. One of these, an ancient hall about 40 feet in length by 25 wide and 20 high, with its huge handsome fireplace, built four centuries ago, in which a good fire was burning, window recesses the thickness of the wall—not less than 12 feet—heavy oaken wainscoting with carved oak ceiling, and rich old mahogany furniture, was a delight to me. It is used by the professors, who come up here for their dessert after they have dined in hall below with the students. If I might not be Bishop of Durham, I think the next thing I should choose would be to serve as a professor here, and sitting in the mellow light of this quaint room, with a cobwebbed bottle or so to give a smack to the old jokes over the walnuts, wear the hours away.

*June* 13.—The sweet Cathedral bells were chiming the first quarter after 9 A.M. as George gave rein to his freshened horses through the ancient city of Durham, and we entered on the level highway in the direction of York, sixty-eight miles southward. The road is macadamized, and ever since we left Edinburgh smooth and firm as the driveways in Prospect Park. Lunched at the King's Head, in the town of Darlington, important only for its manufactures of woollens and carpets. The luncheon was excellent, and in an hour we were on the road again, and at 4 P.M. are snugly within the portals of a second Golden Lion at North Allerton, having encountered the first in Stirling. This is a market town half way between Durham and York, and our inn was of consequence in the old coaching days. The main street is over 100 feet wide, paved with cobble-stones from the front line of the little houses slantwise down to the centre, leaving there a level road-bed, say 20 feet wide.

Our ride to-day has been over a fair rolling country, cultivated into greater fertility as we advance southward. The arable lands are prepared for crops with great pains, the heavy soil being worked to thorough mellowness, tilled fields, meadows and pastures are separated by verdant hedges, on whose line stand single trees not unfrequently, so that the wide prospect on either hand offers a most agreeable variety. Here and there rise the red-tiled roofs of low cottages scattered over the landscape, with now and then a stately mansion half hidden among trees. We dash through the single street of many a quaint village, drawing to the cottage-doors stout little children whose flaxen hair and blue eyes declare their Saxon descent. The white plastered walls are green with ivy and flushed with clambering roses, now in full bloom, contented cattle browse in the rich pastures or lie in the shadow of broad beeches, oaks and elms, and over all is the air of an exceeding and enduring tranquillity. The day has been almost cloudless, but the sun does not shine with the fierce glare of our June at home, but as if his rays passed through some medium which partially abstracts their fervor. The songs of many birds went with us all along, the thrush, hedge-sparrow, and, chiefest, the meadow-lark, who rained his melody down from the upper air, like faint tones from the Celestial City.

How many times have I yearned to ride over some interesting part of England on the top of a coach, and now the fact exceeds the anticipation! The Englishman seeks to hide his home life, and the first thing he undertakes in building is a high wall of stone or brick to shut out even the prying eyes of passers-by. But from the vantage of our coach-top we overlook his insufficient defences, and get views of the pretty swards and flower-beds and gardens and orchards hidden behind these churlish barriers. I should say, from what little I have seen of the Briton, that his nature is a good deal like his home, rough and repellent on the outside, but sunny and cheerful once you are allowed inside. We crossed the Tees, a few miles below Durham, and noted the plain on our left just before reaching North Allerton, where the battle of the Standard was fought between the English and Scotch in 1138.

*June* 14.—On our way again, all in good condition at 9 A.M., lunching at the York, a poorish tavern in the little village of Easingwold, and reaching the welcome of the Black Swan in York at 4 P.M., where we are made comfortable in clean, old-fashioned rooms. Found mail awaiting us, and eagerly devoured the news from home. Our ride to-day has been almost a repetition of that of yesterday, except that the country is more level, stretching away, indeed, like a Western prairie, only far on our left lay the blue range of the Appleton Hills. York is a very ancient city, the Eboracum of the Romans, who made it their principal city of Britain during their long occupancy of five hundred years. It was founded, so go the records, by Julius Agricola, made Governor of

Britain by Vespasian, A.D. 78. The Emperor Hadrian took up his residence here A.D. 120, and it became a luxurious Roman capital. The Sixth Legion accompanied the emperor and continued here nearly three hundred years. Severus came here about 207 in his old age and died in 210, was cremated, and his inurned ashes taken to Rome for burial. In 304 Constantius Chlorus, Emperor of the West, came to Britain and took up his residence here, where he died two years later, when his son, Constantine the Great, was here proclaimed emperor. When the Romans withdrew from Britain in 420, the city, left to its fate, was sacked by the barbarian Scots and Picts, but despite all calamities still continued to hold its importance through all the changing fortunes of English history. During the Wars of the Roses, Richard Plantagenet, Duke of York, fell at the battle of Wakefield, 1460, and his head, crowned with a paper diadem, was, by order of Queen Margaret, stuck on a pole over Micklegate Bar, one of the city gates—

"Off with his head and set it on York Gate,
So York may overlook the town of York."

And so through all the centuries this has continued to be almost the chief city in historical interest in the kingdom. It has now settled down into a prosaic city of some 60,000 inhabitants, and while for the most part wearing a modern look, has many characteristics of the past. It is a walled city ; and after dinner we walked on the top for a considerable portion of the circuit, the whole being two and three quarter miles, and complete, except in those few places where necessary improvements for extending the city outside are going on. These walls are about 18 feet high and 4 feet thick, with an outer crenellated parapet, and rounded into towers a few feet higher at short and regular intervals. There are eight entrances or gates, called "bars," in the circumference. These consist of square towers built over a circular arch, with embattled turrets at the angles. They had an outer gate with a massy chain across, then a portcullis, and then a heavy inside gate. In several of the gates these are still preserved. When a portion of the walls gives way it is restored at the expense of the city, and these are used as promenades. These walls are ancient, going back to the time of Edward

II., and in Henry III.'s time a patent was granted, empowering the levy of a toll on goods coming for sale in York, to be applied to the support of the walls and fortifications.

At sunset strolled out and looked at the glory and pride of York, its Cathedral. It requires more than one look to realize the vast size of this structure. It is cruciform, with an extreme length from east to west of 524 feet, height of 100 feet, 104 feet wide across the nave and 224 feet across the transepts. The two western towers are 201 feet and the central tower 216 feet high. The satisfaction of the first glance is somewhat lessened by a certain blotchy appearance caused by patches of the façades peeling off and showing the white of the magnesian limestone of which the Cathedral is constructed. These ragged spots contrast unpleasantly with the surface, darkened by time, which is slowly consuming the lavish ornaments of the exterior, and even weakening the strength of the very walls, so that a considerable force of masons is constantly at work repairing damages.

*June* 15.—Hired a hack and drove about the city, noting many quaint old houses with overhanging upper stories, and rejoiced in one of these dated 1579, with its carved gables, its projecting windows, its exposed frame of heavy timbers filled with yellow-tinted plaster. Also drove entirely round the circuit of the walls, visiting the several gates; then a picturesque, ivy-clad manor house, built by Henry VIII., now a school for the blind; then into the Philosophical Society's Gardens, in which stand the picturesque ruins of St. Mary's Abbey and what is called the Multangular Tower, consisting of ten sides, determined to be a Roman work of the third century. It is capped by several layers of stone of mediæval date. It is in perfect preservation, and formed one of the angle-towers of the walls of Roman York. Visited in the same gardens an old timber and plaster building, supposed to have been the hospitium of the abbey. In the upper room—the old refectory—the Yorkshire Philosophical Society has a museum of antiquities, mostly Roman, consisting of stone coffins, altars, tessellated pavements, coins, lamps, tiles, vases, urns, articles of Roman use and ornament in great variety. Almost all these were found here in excavating for the site of the great railway station, said, by the way, to be the longest in the world—800 feet. Startling it was to see the abundant, rich, dark auburn hair of a Roman lady taken from her coffin of stone, still fastened with two pins of polished jet. It might, so lively is the look of it, have been shorn away in its glossy pride but yesterday. From another coffin came a fillet of gold which had rounded the brow of a woman buried therein, and in her mouth a small Roman coin—the denarius. Was this Charon's fee for her ferriage over the Styx, and did he, in the press of business that day, neglect to take it; or did pity or admiration of her beauty move his churlish spirit; or, sad to think, has her shade never crossed, but is still wandering, wailingly, on the hither shore, because he will have no denarius, but his obolus only? Well, here is the coin, waiting, waiting.

Passed most of the P.M. in the Cathedral. Entered by the door in the south transept and felt disappointed. Whether the ponderous majesty of Durham Cathedral still overshadowed my mind, or whether this was not my cathedral day, or whether the circumstances were untoward, I could not realize the impression which should come from the first view of so vast an interior. The noble heights, the broad spaces, the clustered columns, the harmonious and pure ornaments, wrought by the pious skill of centuries—all these indeed moved me deeply, but something was wanting. The plague of all places of interest here is the professional guide, from whom it is so difficult to escape. Here it is one of the vergers, who was in the act of collecting a drove of visitors to show them the choir and other parts of the Cathedral kept under lock and key and only exhibited on payment of sixpence. I tried to arrange with him to be shown about later, but this could not be, as no other party can be allowed to-day. So we paid each his toll as we filed through a narrow gate leading to the south aisle and were conducted through the beautiful lady's room, the treasury, the chapter-room and choir, unable in reverent silence to consider these beautiful things, the mind being distracted and worried by the hard, quick, monotonous description in a set order of just what the guide sees proper to call one's attention to. For instance, taking a straddling attitude before the glorious eastern window and playing with his watch-chain, he proceeds something in this fashion: "This window may justly be called the wonder of the world, not only for masonry but for glazing. You will ob serve that there are one hundred and seventeen portions, and so much of the Holy Writ is taken up thereby that you see at a glance a'moast the whole history of the Bible. Of the Scripture characters the following are the principal : the Creation, *the* Temptation, *the* Tower of Babel, patriarchs *and* Moses *and* David, including Revelation. This window is 77 feet high, 32 broad and divided *into* two hundred compartments about a yard square. John Thornton of Coventry was the glazier, and he begun A.D. 1405 for four shillings a week and must have it done inside of three years. The pay looks small, but *you* must remember," fixing his cold eye on me, as if I were about to forget, " that a penny then would come near buying a whole sheep and a shilling a whole beef." This could not hinder me, however, from admiring the beautiful Chapter-House, octagonal in form, 63 feet in diameter and 67 feet high. Large windows of stained glass dating back to 1350 fill seven of the sides, and the whole circumference below the windows is taken up with forty-four canopied stone stalls for the dignitaries composing the chapter. These canopies are richly ornamented, and at the lower termination of each is a small head exquisitely carven. Some of these are sweet female faces, beaming in saintliness, while next one of them perhaps is the head of a sensual monk leering at her—all sorts of grotesque features being wrought in this holy place as if in mockery and satire of its ministers. How does it happen such imagery has place here and in the corbels and gargoyles of the exterior and in many another place all about these old churches ? Was religion in those centuries only half in earnest ? Was piety mingled in a half impious way with all manner of carnal pursuits and pleasures ? We are shown the statue of an archbishop here with a violin on his breast, in position to play, and are told that he was a wild boy who ran away from home with his fiddle, turned pirate, and after many adventures through many years, returned to York, became archbishop, and here he stands in stone, fiddle and all.

When the building of this Cathedral, as it now stands, was begun in 1215, as funds were wanting, the archbishop of that time, Walter de Grey, a thorough worldling, granted indulgences to those who would contribute, as did the then pope ; also to aid the work a former archbishop was canonized and a fame established for him as a miracle-worker of peculiar force, and in consequence great contributions were made by those flocking to his shrine.

I cannot undertake to give an account of this great Cathedral. It was founded by King Edwin, the first Saxon king of Northumbria, in 627, and in the crypt we saw a piece of Saxon wall in what is styled herring-bone masonry, this being all that remains of the first structure dedicated to St. Peter. It was built and rebuilt, added to and altered from that time on, the building as it now stands having been begun in 1215 and completed in 1472, different parts being done by different hands ; so that, as the Norman style was undergoing changes through all these years, almost all good forms of English ecclesiastical architecture find their expression here.

*June 16, Sunday.*—Attended morning service in the Cathedral, the magnificent choir of which is fitted up with pews, the entrance to it being through a small arched door in the richly ornamented stone organ-screen. This is 25 feet in height, and in its fifteen niches are statues of the kings of England arranged in order from William I. to Henry VI., who was on the throne when this work was done. Most impressive on entering is the view of the lofty roof, the groined arches, the clustered columns and, most of all, the great east window. This choir by itself occupies the space of a very large church. The seats are well filled this morning, as the ordination of some forty priests and deacons by the Archbishop, who is the Primate of England, takes place. The fifty-two oaken stalls on the sides are filled this morning with high-colored Yorkshire maidens and matrons in spring hats, and frocks, showing prettily under the dark carven canopies. But I could take no interest in the ceremonial, having no eyes or thoughts for anything but the wonderful windows with their old stained glass. These are the special glory of this minster, the original glazing existing here, it is said, to a greater extent than in any other church in England. Such marvellous purples and blues and yellows and grays combined with such cunning skill and infinite patience into harmonious and perfect forms ! Wherein lies the vast difference between these rich colors and the effects produced now by even the best modern artists ? Is the art of staining glass as it was done five hundred years ago here in England a lost art, or has time mellowed these tints through centuries of storm and sun, even as it mellows and deepens the color of all things in nature and in art too, not always with benefit? In the north transept are five beautiful lancet windows, each one 54 feet high and 5½ feet wide. These are called "the Five Sisters," from having been presented to the minster by five sisters, who each wrought with her own hands the embroidered patterns for the stained-glass devices. They form the subject of Dickens' story of the "Five Sisters of York," in "Nicholas Nickleby."

I discovered this morning why I felt disappointed in my first view of the interior yesterday, in comparison with that of Durham. The organ stands above the rood-screen, so as to shut out the view of the east window and really to separate the nave from the choir and destroy the effect of the great distance from the extreme west to the east—a considerable defect as it seems to me. At Durham the organ consists of two parts, one on each side of the choir, and the view to the east window not being obstructed, from the west to the east end is for that reason more impressive, although the nave of the York Minster is forty feet longer than that of Durham. The greatness of the parts grows on the mind like Niagara. But it is idle, at least for me, to attempt to describe these marvels of man's hand.

Attended evening service, but had little good in the charity sermon—able and disposed for nothing but studying the windows. The sinking sun set them ablaze with emeralds, turquoises, sapphires, rubies and diamonds and made every pane a flashing glory. When the sun withdrew his shining, little jets of gas glimmered far up, circling the capitals of the lofty pillars; the gorgeous hues died slowly out, Michael sheathed his flaming sword, his bright squadrons folded their lustrous wings, the roses faded, and the ineffable glory of these windows passed into darkness, in all likelihood never to be rekindled before eyes of mine. *Vale* venerable minster and may the couplet inscribed over the door of the Chapter-House in Saxon letters continue to stand for many an age:

"*Ut Rosa flos florum
Sic est Domus ista Domorum.*"

I intended to note that in the vestry of the Cathedral, formerly called the Treasury, we were shown in an old oaken cupboard, among other curious things, the horn of Ulphus, a great carved drinking-horn of ivory. Ulphus was a Saxon prince, who, finding his two sons on the point of quarrelling over their inheritance, came to York with his horn and kneeling before the altar in the minster, filled it with red wine and devoutly quaffing it—a swingeing draught it was too—gave all his lands and rents to God ; and the Cathedral to this day holds a very considerable property, by the evidence of this horn. In the wall of the south aisle of the choir is a tablet to the memory of Jane Hodson, wife of Dr. Hodson, Chancellor of the Cathedral, who died in 1636 in giving birth to her twenty-fourth child, she herself being in her thirty-eighth year. If one may judge from the troops of children everywhere, Yorkshire matrons are emulous of the patient continuance in well-doing exhibited by this fruitful dame of other days.

The curfew bell is still tolled in York at eight o'clock in the evening from the steeple of St. Michael, a small ancient church ; and at 6 A.M. every morning except Sundays, after this bell strikes the hour it is tolled a certain number of times and then struck once for each day of the month already passed, a sum of money having been bequeathed for that purpose by a traveller who, having lost his way in the neighboring wood in the olden time, located himself by hearing this bell strike six.

*June* 17.—George came to the door smiling at 9 A.M., his horses in good fettle, coach and harness burnished, and we rolled in good form out of this exceedingly interesting old city, stopping long enough in front of a section of the ancient wall to have our equipage photographed, as a token of our coaching experience, and proceeded to Leeds, twenty-six miles distant, passing through several small villages of no especial note, unless one might be Boston Spa, reputed to have a healing spring, of which we saw nothing. Lunched at the poorest wayside inn we have yet fallen on, in the poor little hamlet of Wetherby, it being conveniently situated half way, and at 4 P.M. had ample solace at the excellent Queen's Hotel in smoky Leeds, a manufacturing town of 300,000 souls and as like Pittsburg as need be. Not often does the sun penetrate the hovering cloud of factory smoke belched from its thousand chimneys.

To-day has been the warmest we have felt since landing at

Queenstown, and man and beast seem to suffer and feel it as very hot, but it does not so affect us. As I have said before, the sun's rays are dulled by some property of the atmosphere, so that we miss the sultry glare and fierce heat of our summer skies at home. The country continues of the same attractive sort I have tried to so little purpose to describe. Fields of white clover studded with wild, flaring red poppies are frequent. The hawthorn hedges all along are sweet with wild roses, and if not "white with May" are "red with June." From the rose-clad cottages of the straggling villages the children pour out to see the passage of our coach and salute us with robust cheers, while their elders heed the phenomenon more stoically. I seem now and then, however, to notice an old man in these villages bring his rheumatic limbs into position with stiff celerity, his dull features kindling somewhat into a pleased expression, as if the now unusual spectacle of a four-in-hand had called back to his failing memory the old times before the railways had superseded the coaches which ran their regular trips on these highways, making twelve miles an hour, with hourly change of horses, and so doing a hundred miles in the daylight of each day on the through line from York to London if, as a handbill I saw in York, dated 1707, states, "God permits." All is changed now; the roads are still kept in perfect condition, as if the traffic were likely to return any day, the ample stables of stone are in every village and the inns too; but how fallen from their state, when the horn of the guard announced to the jolly landlord coachful after coachful of hungry and thirsty guests and the great carts which then moved all merchandise from point to point crowded his noisy court-yard. Then huge roasts smoked on the table and the ale frothed and 'twas merry all along these old roads.

*June* 18.—Left Leeds in good condition for Sheffield, distant by highway thirty-two miles. The scenery grows more diversified soon after leaving Leeds and presents an agreeable variety of hill and dale, and the immediate neighborhood of Sheffield is picturesque and lovely. Twelve miles from Leeds we passed through Wakefield, where on a bridge over the Calder is a chantry, an interesting fourteenth-century relic of a demolished church. Lunched at Barnsley, six miles farther on, and found the Victoria Hotel at Sheffield an excellent one, as are all the railway hotels where we have put up. Sheffield is another Leeds, only more so, grimy all over, a huge workshop, of nearly 300,000 inhabitants, overhung with a pall of dun smoke from hundreds of tall chimneys. Its reputation for cutlery is of old, there is a guild, the Cutlers' Company, incorporated in 1624, and the office of Master Cutler is the highest dignity of the city. For miles before reaching the city we meet miners by the hundreds, returning to their cottages from the mines, black as negroes, and for the last three days have encountered along the road an increasing number of wretched tramps begging their way. We meet vans of showmen of all sorts, many handsomely painted, with little stove-pipes protruding from the roofs, smoking along, and clean lace curtains drawn back with red ribbons at the little windows—such carts as Dr. Marigold was wont to go about in.

*June* 19.—Had an uninteresting drive of eighteen miles to Clay Cross, half way to Derby. The whole way to Chesterfield is lined with shabby factory villages, made hideous by great hills of slag and refuse from the smoking factories, spoiling a fair rural country in the way which has so wrung the artistic soul of Mr. Ruskin. At Chesterfield is a large and ancient parish church, whose tall, fluted, pointed spire is curiously twisted and bent to an angle of some fifteen degrees. The local legend is that Satan gave it a twist in a mad freak, but a more prosaic explanation is that the woodwork within the leaden outside has yielded to the action of time. Lunched at Clay Cross and rode to Derby, thirty-six miles from Sheffield. For three miles the road runs on a narrow ridge dividing the landscape, which stretches away in the most enchanting manner on either hand. Indeed, the whole way this afternoon is over as fine a country as we have traversed, but our satisfaction has been lessened by the cloud of dust made by the coach and borne along with it by a following wind. There has been no rain now for many days, and the country, while not suffering, is yet quite dry. We find growing all crops usual to our farmers in the Western States, except Indian corn, and all look well. Haying is just beginning, while wheat will certainly not be ready to harvest before the latter part of July. Large fields of turnips and beans are seen and all field crops are tended with great care. Very much of the last year's wheat all along the road is yet in the stack, being held for better prices. In many cases more than one year's crop is standing in the stack, which would be ruinous to the grain at home, but they make such solid stacks, almost works of art, and shelter them so perfectly with water-proof covers of thatch, sloping like roofs, that I imagine the grain keeps almost as well as in barns ; still, there must be some waste and deterioration by such keeping, and the loss of interest on the value must be added.

At 5.30 P.M. reached the St. James', a comfortable inn at Derby, a well-looking town of some 90,000 inhabitants. It lies on the full-flowing Derwent, and is the county-town of Derbyshire. It was presented by William the Conqueror to his natural son, Peveril of the Peak, whose castle, once dominating the town, has entirely disappeared. It marks the most southerly point reached by Charles Stuart and his Highlanders in the march to London he tried to make in 1745. The Midland Railway Company have works here covering two hundred and fifty acres, employing ten thousand men, most of whom I should say we met pouring out of their shops after working hours—a sturdy, well-looking body of workmen. The only building of interest to us is All Saints' Church, whose tower, 170 feet high, of the sixteenth century, is very handsome.

*June* 20.—Got off in good form at 9.30 A.M. for Lichfield, twenty-three miles, without stopping except once to give the horses each a half pail of water. George does not water his team during an eighteen or twenty-mile drive, saying "the best way is to keep water off them, for they get sickened with it." Whether there is anything in this vague maxim more than the senseless jargon of a groom I cannot say, but true it is that our four-in-hand are making their long steady drive in admirable condition. Half way lies Burton-on-Trent, where are the prodigious breweries of Bass and Allsop, the former covering one hundred and thirty acres of ground and employing two thousand men, the latter fifteen hundred. They send their ales out in casks, and whoever chooses buys and bottles them with such name on the labels as he pleases. We get both as good in New York as I find them here. We have not passed over a richer or handsomer country than to-day. Haying is going on, and I should say the crop, so far as I see it, is yielding from two and one half to three tons per acre, and wheat oats and barley promise well. The weather is warm and dry and we had some annoyance from dust. We have had fine strawberries now for several days, large and sweet.

Reached the George Hotel, Lichfield, at 1.30 P.M., and found a batch of letters from home. No ill news, save particulars of the terrible catastrophe in the Conemaugh Valley. After luncheon visited the Cathedral, exceeding graceful and beautiful, dating from about 1250 and two hundred years building. It is of reddish sandstone, has borne the weather well, and wears a fresh, warm look. It is 408 feet long, 65 feet wide, and across the transepts 149 feet; height, 60 feet; central steeple, 260 feet; those of west end 190 feet. But these cold, dull figures convey no notion of the harmony and grace of the west façade, or the symmetrical lightness of nave and choir. The early English and later decorated styles are well shown here side by side. I can in nowise put on paper anything which will hereafter recall the picture in my mind tonight of this exquisite church, which surpasses in certain essential features of beauty any one I have yet seen. The choir-stalls are modern, exquisitely carved and all done by Thomas Evans, of Elliston, a brother of George Eliot. The apse is polygonal, with glorious stained glass, three hundred and fifty years old, brought from a convent in Liege. Fine, too, is the Chapter-House, octagonal, with a ribbed roof supported by a central arch. Above is the Diocesan Library, where I specially noted with rankling envy an illuminated manuscript of Chaucer's "Canterbury Tales," done about 1400, and a Saxon copy of the Gospels (St. Chad's Gospels), not later than 700, easily worth its weight in gold; also a copy of South's Sermons belonging to Dr. Johnson, the margins of the leaves all the way through being marked in an uncouth way with various signs, evidently having significance to him. The Cathedral is dedicated to St. Chad, the patron saint of Lichfield, of some 8000 souls—a city because of its Cathedral, while Leeds, lacking that ornament, with its population of over 300,000 is only a town.

Dr. Johnson was born here in a house still standing in good preservation fronting the market square, with a bill of sale in the window. It is a wide three-story house of stuccoed brick, and shows well now even in this well-built town, and when the

Doctor first saw the light in it, must have ranked among the best houses. A huge and not quite pleasing statue of him stands in the square just in front of the house, representing him seated, intent upon a folio volume in his hand. The features in this effigy and in the bust in the Cathedral are lighter and finer than in the engravings I have been used to see of him. Went into the Three Crowns Inn, the house next his birthplace, where he entertained Boswell when they visited Lichfield together in 1776; and here it was that the "sage" after a "comfortable supper" gave expression to his encomium of his townspeople, that they "are the most sober, decent people in England, are the genteelest in proportion to their wealth, and speak the purest English." How easy it is to speak well of our neighbors after supper, and take most of it back next morning! Was shown into a comfortable room to the rear of the bar, where the landlady said the Doctor used to sit, and she had the nerve to point out a chair which she said he used. And why not? I sat down in it in full faith and partook of a "light collation" in the form of a glass of Lichfield brewed ale, not very good, but I called to mind that the Doctor was not particular in his eating and drinking and so fared very well. The George Hotel, where we remain until to-morrow, is said to be the scene of Farquhar's "Beaux Stratagem."

*June* 21.—Left Lichfield at 10 A.M. for Coventry, twenty-eight miles distant, and tried to lunch at the Swan in Foleshill, probably the dirtiest village tavern in all this land. But the country all along our road to-day is most fair and fertile and the whole drive delightful. Before reaching Coventry we remind ourselves that hereabouts are the localities where George Eliot passed her early years, and that on the Foleshill road, some five miles to the north of Coventry, stands the house where she lived with her father before his death. Not knowing just how far we might be from this house and having found that those one meets on the road never, by any chance, know anything of the neighborhood where they live, outside the radius of five miles at the most, I got down at the post-office in the rustic village of Meriden and inquired of the middle-aged postmistress if she knew anything of the house where Mr. Evans, the father of George Eliot, lived. With her was a young lady of some twenty years, quite a bright, intelligent-looking girl, and neither one had ever heard of George Eliot and knew nothing about the place I wanted ; yet, as we found after reaching Coventry, it could not have been more than a mile away. Arbury Farm and Griff, where she passed the first twenty years of her life, are between Coventry and Nuneaton, some ten miles to the north.

Coventry is an ancient city of some 45,000 inhabitants, where the old and new are blended in a pleasant way, the modern buildings being of a good sort and the old ones quaint and interesting. The streets are mostly narrow, crooked and winding, and every once in a while one comes on a timbered house overhanging the street, venerable with its three hundred years. We are well received at the Queen's, an exceedingly comfortable hotel, and engaging a landau, visit the sights of the town, which Falstaff was ashamed to march through with his ragged regiment, and where, according to the legend versified but not verified by Tennyson, Lady Godiva won the freedom of the city from her nice husband, in the eleventh century, by fulfilling what he thought an impossible condition which he had imposed. As the condition was that she should ride naked through the town on horseback in broad daylight, it did seem unlikely this lady would comply; but she did make the ride, " clothed on with chastity" and a full head of long hair, all the citizens shutting themselves up in their houses save " Peeping Tom," who is shown high up on a corner house in a red collar, green sleeves and blue cap, a sorry spectacle for all virtuous folk to hiss at. But my lord was as good as his word and set the city free in these words : " I Lurichi for the love of thee doe make Coventrie tol-free," and it is to be hoped never suggested to his lady such an act of self-sacrifice again.

St. Michael's Church, built of red sandstone, is a noble building with a beautiful spire 300 feet high—and I mean all that is implied in the word beautiful when a spire is spoken of, *me judice* ; Trinity Church also has a fine spire, 237 feet high ; and these with that of the old Greyfriars Monastery make " the three tall spires" of Coventry. Very interesting to me also is St. Mary's Guildhall, a piece of municipal architecture of the fourteenth century, with the great kitchen and the mayoress' parlor, and chiefly for its great hall with a large window of old glass at one end and pointed narrow ones high up on the sides, the oaken roof with carved beams, its tapestry, its suits of Cromwellian armor and a carved oak seat used by Henry VI. when holding parliament here, which, could I set it down in the hall of 64 Remsen Street, I would make the occasion of a festival and ask a houseful of friends to come and see and admire and envy me the possession of. This is the hall described by George Eliot—who attended school here—as the scene of Hetty's trial in her novel of "Adam Bede."

Drove to Rosehill, "Ivy Cottage," close to the city, where Mr. and Mrs. Bray lived, the long friends of George Eliot, where she often visited. Mrs. Bray is still living, over eighty years old, but hale and hearty. Her husband, at one time a prosperous manufacturer of ribbons, failed in business and Mrs. Bray subsists on the income of one hundred pounds per annum provided by George Eliot. After dinner I walked about the streets for an hour, going into the court-yard of Bablake Hospital, built in the sixteenth century, well preserved and pleasing, and Ford's Hospital, of the same period, equally so.

I like Coventry; its situation is pleasant and it wears a cheerful look. George remarked as we approached it that it had a "squandered" look, by which I found that he meant it covered a good deal of ground. We have here as good strawberries as I ever ate, big and luscious.

*June* 22.—Drove to Kenilworth, five miles, over a charming country. The castle here is a ruin, but a noble one, well indicating its former magnificence. There was a castle here from very early times and it played all along an important part in English history. By the marriage of Blanche, daughter of Henry of Lancaster, to John of Gaunt, son of Edward III., and soon after created Duke of Lancaster, it became greatly enlarged and enriched, as the fine remains of the banqueting hall he built still attest. At his death Richard II. seized it from his cousin, Henry Bolingbroke, who recovered it when he became king as Henry IV. Henry VIII. repaired it largely, and Elizabeth, early in her reign, gave it to Robert Dudley, son of John Dudley, Duke of Northumberland, whom she created Earl of Leicester. He expended a prodigious sum upon it, and in July, 1575, entertained Queen Elizabeth here in the magnificent style described by Scott in the notes to his novel of "Kenilworth," which moving tale has thrown a glamour over all the scene. The Earl of Leicester left Kenilworth by his will to his brother Ambrose, Earl of Warwick, for his life ; next to Sir Robert Dudley, Knight, his son by Lady Douglas Sheffield, daughter of Lord Howard of Effingham, whom Leicester had secretly married but never owned as his wife, having in her lifetime married the Lady Lettice, Countess of Essex. Sir Robert could not or rather was not allowed to establish his legitimacy, and by a series of sharp practices Charles I. acquired it. Then came Cromwell and his Puritans and ruined it, as they did most of the venerable buildings throughout the kingdom ; then the Restoration, when the lands and ruins of Kenilworth were granted to a Hyde, and by marriage of a female descendant they passed to Thomas Villiers, Baron Hyde, afterward Earl of Clarendon, one of whose descendants with that title still owns them ; and a liberal gentleman must he be, protecting the ruins by constant repairs in excellent taste, as it seems to me, and freely admitting all the world to roam about at pleasure for threepence a head.

Drove on to Warwick through a most lovely and fertile country, getting glimpses of Wootton Court and farther on of Guy's Cliff, the charming home of Miss Bertie Percy, and "put up" for lunch at the Warwick Arms, clean and good. This is a quaint old town situated on high ground near the Avon. Drove to the Hospital of Robert Dudley, Earl of Leicester, an exceedingly interesting pile of old buildings in timber and plaster established by Lord Dudley for "twelve poor brothers" in 1571, although the buildings themselves are said to be considerably older. The quadrangle is very picturesque, and in the various rooms are many rare and curious relics of armor and furniture, one being a Saxon chair said to be one thousand years old, and a rich bit of embroidery by Amy Robsart. The Spanish chestnut beams of the old dining-room look perfectly fresh. The endowment is sufficient to have kept here in comfort now for three hundred and fifty years twelve worthy indigent persons chosen from the neighborhood, with certain conditions. They wear always when abroad a livery of a handsome blue broadcloth gown with a silver badge of a bear and a ragged staff, Lord Leicester's crest. The badges, all but one, are those worn by the first brethren, whose names with the date 1571 are engraved on the back. The pensioner who showed us about said he had been here forty-four years and still looked a tough old boy with a good deal of wear in him. A man might be much worse off than a poor brother here and I do not pity them.

Thence to Warwick Castle, standing on a commanding height, about whose base the Avon winds. The view from a bridge just below the walls and a nearer one from the site of an old mill up to the dizzy summits of the towers and along the stretch of the lofty walls are most impressive and realize one's ideal of a feudal castle. The avenue leading to the outer court is cut through solid rock, and we come into the beautiful inner court with its velvety turf through a double gateway between the "Cæsar Tower" and "Guy's," the latter 128 feet high. Cæsar's Tower is the oldest portion, nearly 150 feet high, and dates almost back to the Norman Conquest. The interior of the castle is shown in part to visitors on payment of one shilling, and I wish to say once for all that I think it a most handsome and generous thing for the gentlemen owning the priceless treasures of these old hereditary homes to open them to the public and to have in charge, as in this instance, courteous and well-informed servitors to point out and explain the rare objects which crowd the great rooms. I can give no idea of the treasures of armor and pictures in the great entrance hall, 60 feet long, 40 feet wide, 39 high. It is said that there is no such private collection of armor in Europe. The model of a horse is completely covered with the defensive armor Scott so loves to describe and on it a knight armed *cap-a-pie* in a magnificent suit of plate-armor. The guide told a curious incident of these. In a fire in this room in 1871 some of the armor became much injured and the defensive armor of this horse was replaced with a suit obtained by the present earl's agent, after much search, in Germany. When it was being put in place and the rider mounted it was found by private marks on the suits that they were originally intended for each other. The state-rooms, thrown open as we saw them, disclose a vista over 300 feet long and are filled with amazing treasures of pictures, cabinets, furniture, china, etc. There are, for instance, sixteen portraits by Van Dyck, including his "Charles I. ;" nine by Rubens, including his full-length portrait of Ignatius Loyola, and a pair of lions, said to be the only picture of animals he ever painted ; Raphael's "Assumption of the Virgin," Godfrey Kneller's "Queen Anne," Holbein's "Henry VIII. and Anne Boleyn," Teniers' "Card-Players," and a multitude of others. There is in one of the rooms a mask of Cromwell's face taken soon after death, which fully justifies the worst his enemies have said of his appearance, with its long square chin, massive jaws, coarse wide mouth, huge ugly nose, and low, bony, retreating forehead, like an African's—the face of a coarse bigot.

The celebrated Warwick vase, found in Hadrian's Villa at Tivoli, stands in a place of honor in the conservatory fronting the castle and is shown and described *ad nauseam* by a wearisome *commissionaire* until one wishes him drowned in the huge sculptured marble bowl of it.

These magnificent treasures are the accumulations of centuries by the great family of the Grevilles, the first of whom, born in 1554, was a cousin of Sir Philip Sidney, with whom he was educated. The present Earl, George Guy Greville, was born 1818. He has been very ill here for some weeks now, and has just gone to London, and has afforded us an entertainment I shall not soon forget.

The Church of St. Mary here has a fine chapel, Beauchamp—pronounced here Beecham—with fine old windows and carved oak seats, a rich and handsome monument to its builder, Richard Beauchamp, Earl of Warwick, who died in 1464. There is another to the favorite of Queen Elizabeth, the Earl of Leicester, who entertained her so famously at Kenilworth. He lies here clad in armor, his wife the Countess Lettice beside him in her robes of a peeress—both comfortable effigies and looking better content with each other than they were supposed to be in life. An inscription by the countess, who survived him, states that "his most sorrowful wife, through a sense of conjugal love and fidelity, hath put up this monument to the best and dearest of husbands !" What lies are told by very nice people—on tombstones !

Drove to Stratford-on-Avon and have very pleasant rooms at the Red Horse, with a bay-window in our sitting-room. The country between here and Warwick is most fertile and charming, and we can hardly hope for a more agreeable ride than this has been in the cool of the cloudy afternoon amid sights and sounds of a June landscape, sweet as famed Arcadia. As we approach Stratford, we follow the southern boundary-wall of Charlecote Park, fair to see from our coach-top, with its verdant lawns spotted with numerous deer, and have a good view of the old red brick Elizabethan house, still occupied by a descendant and namesake of the Lucy family. When Shakespere was a youth here the story is that he was brought up before Sir Hugh Lucy for deer-stealing and that he afterward took his revenge by making him the "Justice Shallow" whom Falstaff visited on his way to Shrewsbury. A likely enough tradition: why not? Stratford is a clean, pretty town of some 8000 inhabitants, with wide streets and substantial modern buildings mingled with quaint old timber and plaster houses of two and three centuries ago. Its business seems to be chiefly Shakespere and all departments seem working successfully.

*June 23, Sunday.*—Our hotel has the room where Washington Irving wrote his paper on Stratford-on-Avon. The chair he sat in is kept locked in a glass cupboard, and the poker he used to stir the fire while meditating is done up in a worsted case. Attended morning service at the Church of the Holy Trinity—Shakespere's church—a much handsomer, larger and more imposing building than I had supposed. It dates back to the fifteenth century, has a lofty spire and is charmingly situated directly on the Avon among fine old trees, an avenue of overarching limes leading to the west entrance being specially noticeable. The services were held in the nave. Some changes are going on in the interior, so that a scaffolding shut off the choir. The congregation was large, decent, dull and homely. There is no access to the chancel on Sunday; so after service we strolled through the grassy churchyard and returned by the site of New Place, the house Shakespere bought when he retired from London and where he lived until his death. The house, one of the finest in town after he had altered it over to suit him, was razed to the ground in 1759 by the Rev. Francis Gastrell, who had come into possession of it in 1753, because he was compelled to pay the monthly assessments for the maintenance of the poor of Stratford. He disposed of the materials and left the town for good. Three years before he had cut down the mulberry-tree behind the house planted by the poet's own hand, then remarkably large and fine, because he was troubled by visitors desirous of seeing it. For these impious deeds may dogs dishonor the grave where his body lies ; may his spirit, harder than adamant, be condemned to wander until it relent and soften, in a hot and thirsty land where no shade is, its weeping eyes tortured with the far-away sight of an unattainable mulberry-tree, with its phantom whisperings of cooling shadow ever in its ears ; may—

With the house Shakespere bought about one hundred and twenty-five acres of land extending in orchard and meadow down to the Avon, on the greater part of which are now well-built streets. But a portion nearest the site of the house in the rear is now a public garden, and the spot where the house stood and the house next it, together with the Birthplace, were purchased in 1847 with funds raised by public subscription, and are under the control of trustees. This garden is open on Sundays only from 2 to 6 P.M., and after an early dinner we strolled there. By chance the custodian of the New Place, a genial-looking matron, was walking in the grounds, and although visitors are not admitted on Sunday, she kindly noticed us near the gate separating the grounds from the public garden, came forward and admitted us to the ample corner lot where the house once stood. The space is say 60 by 150 feet, covered with greensward, nicely tended, and surrounded by a handsome iron railing. The outlines of the foundations of the outer walls are preserved by enclosing the space of their thickness in lines of brickwork level with the ground, the depressed space within showing pieces of the old stone broken and lying loose. The old well which supplied the house with drinking-water stood in the cellar and is now curbed and overgrown with ivy. We drank from it and found it clear and cold. The remains of the bay-window are pointed out where he sat when he wrote "The Tempest." A little back of this is a flourishing mulberry-tree, a scion of the old one. We were shown into the adjoining house which connected with Shakespere's and was occupied in his time by Mr. Nash, whose son afterward married Shakespere's grand-daughter Elizabeth, daughter of Mrs. Hall. Within the Nash house are shown many articles in some way connected with the great poet. What struck me most was the "shuffle-board," a long table from the Falcon Tavern on the opposite corner, where he used to drop in for a game.

Strolled in the pleasant gardens connected with the Memorial Buildings lying along the Avon. These buildings include a pretty theatre and a handsome library, including many editions of Shakespere's plays and many interesting portraits of actors, the interiors being much better than the external appearance of the structures gives promise of. All these were paid for by subscriptions, and handsome mention should be made of the statue of Shakespere with the striking figures of Falstaff, Lady Macbeth, Hamlet and Prince Henry at its base, the gift of Lord Ronald Levison Gower.

*June* 24.—Our coach returns to Edinburgh this morning, leaving us to get to London as best we may. We are sorry to part with it. We have lived two happy weeks on the top of it. George is a good fellow and capital coachman. We have not met the slightest mishap since the first day out, when one horse fell dead of heart disease, and not any rain to drive us inside. It could not have been better. Nor should the guard, "Alec," be passed over without a good word, sitting stiff as a ramrod all day long, his face burned to peeling—we are all well tanned for that matter—attentive, civil, prompt, just what we would have him. They both seemed sorry to leave us. We should have kept on to Oxford as intended, but could not get rooms there this week as I had hoped to do.

Directly after breakfast went to the church and straight into the chancel, on the north side of which is Shakespere's grave. The flat slab over it contains nothing but the verse invoking a curse on whoever shall disturb the bones of the sleeper below. On his right hand and filling the space between his grave and the wall is the grave of Anne Hathaway, his wife, who survived him nearly eight years ; on his left hand lie the remains of Thomas Nash, who married his granddaughter Elizabeth ; next, Dr. Hall, and on his left his wife Susannah, Shakespere's eldest daughter. These graves are within the sanctuary, reached by two steps up from the pavement of the nave. I should certainly say the slabs over them are not the original ones but others, recut later. They are in the most honorable and sacred part of the church, and with the bust in its position of honor on the north wall just above these graves, sufficiently attest the high social position held by the families of Shakespere and Hall. The well-known bust executed soon after his death by Gerard Johnson interested me greatly. It was ordered and put in place by the

Halls. Dr. Hall was a physician of good standing, an author of repute, of excellent social position, and it is a very reasonable supposition that the bust, executed and put in place at so considerable an expense, would be as good a likeness as could be had, certainly that it would be satisfactory to his near relatives. The bust was cut from a fine sandstone and the features painted to resemble life—the cheeks florid, the eyes a light hazel, the hair and beard auburn. Malone in 1793 had the whole whitewashed, but many years ago this was removed by a chemical process bringing the original colors to view. The face is strong and handsome, indicating a large, vigorous physique well nourished, a joyous, open nature, while the dome of the forehead, the broad brow and the large, full eyes in their capacious cavities, betoken a sensitive and ample soul. The bust is certainly authentic and genuine. I am not aware that so much can surely be said of any other portrait or effigy of any sort claiming to be a likeness.

From the church we went to the house known as the Birthplace. This house has undergone many changes and restorations, so that one cannot feel much certainty about the apartments. The plan of the house is pretty certainly the same, and it all looks ancient enough to be the poet's birthplace. The timber framework is no doubt the same and the recent restoration aimed to reproduce the house as it stood in 1564. The room where he is supposed to have been born is shown, and about the different rooms are many interesting articles, more or less authentic, associated with him. Most interesting to me is the so-called "Stratford portrait," carefully kept in an iron safe hung up against the wall, the doors of which are kept swung open during the day, to allow its being seen. This shows the poet in the same dress as the bust in the church. This portrait is a very interesting one, and while the expression of the features varies from that of the bust, there is, on the whole, a striking resemblance. It belonged to the Clopton family. Sir Hugh Clopton built the house about the year 1530, which Shakespere bought when he returned to Stratford to live, also the fine bridge over the Avon, and he and other members of the family lie buried in the church. Nothing is more likely than that this family should have been on intimate terms with Shakespere, have admired his genius and have possessed a portrait of him.

This is, of course, an exceedingly interesting spot, but the mechanical garrulity of the attendants and the busy stir of a throng of sight-seers of all ages go far to quench such glow of sentiment as might naturally warm one's fancy shut up alone in the quaint old walls. There is a considerable garden attached where for a long time such flowers as Shakespere mentions in his plays were cultivated, but this pleasing practice has been discontinued.

Drove to Shottery, one mile from town. Here is Anne Hathaway's cottage standing as it did when Shakespere came here a-courting and even more interesting as an old house than the Birthplace, because of its perfect preservation in its condition of three hundred years ago. The family room with its small lead-glazed window-panes and the deep-sunk chimney with seats inside is unchanged from the time when the boy Shakespere sat here beside the "fair Anne Hathaway," some eight years older than himself, he being eighteen. By the way, a curious question has arisen as to whether Anne, who survived her husband seven years, was married a second time. The entry in the parish register stands just as below :

["1623 : *Mrs. Shakespere*,
Aug. 8. : *Anna Uxor Richardi James*."]

This entry, although included in brackets, probably means two different persons buried on the same day, for the inscription on her stone is this : " Here lyeth interred the body of Anne, wife of William Shakespere, who dpted this life the 5th day of Aug., 1623, being of the age of 67 years ;" still the entry is unusual and careless in either case. The old lady having care of the cottage is a descendant of the Hathaways—a Mrs. Baker. The garden in front is now blooming with old-fashioned flowers, from which the kindly old woman culled us each a nosegay.

Noticed in town a handsome old half-timbered house where John Harvard, founder of Harvard College, married his wife. It bears the date 1596. Looked into the quaint old building where the grammar-school founded by Edward VI. is still maintained. The master politely showed us the room where Shakespere attended school as a boy—his desk is shown at the Birthplace—and the small ancient hall where very likely he was wont to see the players in their visits to Stratford.

*June* 25.—Went to the church and again carefully looked at

the bust. My previous favorable impressions are confirmed. Walked through the still churchyard on close-shaven turf of deepest green, studded with great roses flaming with June, to the eastern end of the church separated from the poet's grave only by the chancel-wall, and looked across the brimming Avon, lingering here without noise, upon a broad meadow odorous with its freshly cut grass. Beyond, still other smooth, fertile fields, then gentle swells of rich and quiet landscape—a picture of joyous tranquillity. Just then from the untedded swaths of meadow-grass rose first one lark, then another, both mounting skyward on waves of their own song. Other tuneful birds were not wanting in tree and hedge, and all nature seemed interfused with the cheerful spirit of the Master Soul of all the world of men.

Left at twelve noon by rail for London, passing through Banbury, Oxford, Reading, with many a fair view along the slender stream of the upper Thames, and at 4 P.M. reached our rooms at the Metropole, engaged with difficulty by a friend on the spot, who informs me he never knew London so full as now.

*June* 26.—Took a hansom and made several calls. These hansoms furnish a very quick, cheap and comfortable way of getting about. The magnitude and ponderosity of this enormous city oppress me and I feel quite helpless to struggle with it. Hired a landau with driver in livery—a handsome turnout—for regular use during our stay here. P.M. drove about the city and at the fashionable hour, 5.30 to 7, in Hyde Park—a crowded scene of wealth and luxury in dress and equipage. Received calls from friends in the evening.

*June* 27.—Passed the morning with family in shopping; evening to see "Macbeth" at the Lyceum Theatre. Had stall-seats corresponding to the parquette-seats at home. These run in unbroken rows across the full width of the theatre, and are reached by narrow and not very pleasant passages along the first tier, from which stairs go down to their level. The auditorium is of about the size of the best New York theatres, with rich, unobtrusive ornamentation. I never saw any play so superbly mounted nor so poor a Macbeth as Mr. Irving.

*June* 28.—Drove down to Chelsea to see the house where Carlyle lived so long and where he died. The number is 24 Cheyne Row, changed from No. 5. There is a bust of him on the front wall, and the present owner, Mrs. Cottrell, is an old friend. It is an English basement house, say twenty feet wide and three stories high, with a deep garden in the rear. He died in the second-story front room, a good-sized, pleasant apartment. The street is not less than thirty feet wide, and, while humble, is not mean nor specially unpleasant. It abuts on the Thames embankment, which has been improved along here since his time, I believe. Crossed the Thames by the Albert Suspension Bridge, and drove along Battersea Park—finely laid out and admirably kept—and returned by the Vauxhall Bridge.

*June* 29.—Drove to Spurgeon's church, on the Surrey side, to get passes for morning service to-morrow. It is in a poorish neighborhood, much like that of Atlantic Avenue and the streets south of it in Brooklyn. Returned by London Bridge, on which the traffic is enormous. Passed all the morning until one o'clock in Westminster Abbey. I shall attempt no description of this great minster, where those whom England has held in most reverence and love for a thousand years lie buried or have the honor of a bust or tablet or some form of lasting remembrance. There are costly monuments to a good many nobodies, and men, women and children one would not expect to find honored here, while so many names one readily recalls are overlooked, but the vast abbey is the worthy home of much of the world's departed greatness. The structure, as a whole, does not impress me with the solemn awe of Durham or York Cathedrals, but neither of these approach the richness of many of the different parts, and the tracery of the roof is beautiful, beyond anything we have seen. In the Baptistery I had a little shock at seeing half way up the lofty wall a long brass tablet bearing the inscription,

"*D.D. Georgius Gulielmus Childs, Civis Americanus ;*"

for when I left my native land this eminent Philadelphia philanthropist was heartily above ground, and from his habits of total abstinence from all forms of vicious indulgence, likely to continue so for many good years to come, let us hope. But I soon recalled that having much in common and greatly sympathizing with those tender and sensitive souls, George Herbert and William Cowper, he has filled two windows above his name with stained glass in their honor, and sought to veil his part in the beautiful work by using the dead language of the ancient Romans in the modest inscription. There is a good bust of Longfellow in a good place, and I was pleased to notice a fresh white rose on his breast, put there, it may be, by the loving hand of one of his own countrywomen. Dickens' plain slab is above his grave in the very best part of the Poets' Corner, while the handsome busts of Thackeray and Macaulay are rather overshadowed by the fine full-length statue of Addison, a little behind which they stand.

In the evening witnessed a performance of "Lohengrin" at Covent Garden, the Royal Italian Opera House. Had stall-seats, one guinea each. This opera house is not quite so large as the New York Academy of Music in Fourteenth Street, and is comfortable, but plain. There are four tiers of boxes running entirely round it. Full dress is *de rigueur*, and the show of bare arms and necks, both in stalls and boxes, quite imposing and a little startling; but we are working toward the same at home. There were many fine toilets and a rich show of diamonds, but I should say that neither the house itself nor audience nor the performance at all surpassed what our own Metropolitan can show in a good season. The exclusion of ladies' hats—this is done at the Lyceum Theatre also—gives a handsome drawing-room appearance to the auditorium, saying nothing of the comfort and convenience of the spectators, and we might well imitate this excellent fashion. At the rising of the curtain scarcely a box was occupied, nor were they filled until the second act was well begun.

*June* 30, *Sunday.*—Drove over Blackfriars Bridge to the Surrey side to hear the famous Mr. Spurgeon preach. I was furnished with little envelope tickets on which was printed a request that the holder would put into them a contribution for the work of the church. These admitted us at the entrance for pew-holders, so that we were not compelled to wait outside until these were seated, but were shown into good seats well forward in the vast, plain building, which easily accommodates five thousand, and can, under stress, hold seven thousand. Pretty nearly the former number were present this morning. Two wide galleries run entirely round the deep hall, well lighted and ventilated. At the end opposite the entrances is a raised platform some six feet high, railed about and occupied by a miscellaneous thirty or so of young and old men, among whom I noticed one reporter and a precentor who sought to lead the congregational singing—there is no organ or other instrument of music. Six feet above this, on a level with the first gallery, is a smaller semicircular platform, railed in and reached on each side by a flight of steps from the ground floor and also from the level of the gallery behind it, and furnished with a little table and chair.

Precisely at eleven o'clock there walked heavily, limping a little as it seemed, down from the inclined plane of the lower gallery a short, stoutish, solid man with much the appearance of a substantial farmer, and took his seat in the chair on the upper platform. Mr. Spurgeon has a softer face than his portraits show; still his features are somewhat coarse and dull, his forehead is low, his eyes full, his iron-gray hair thick on his head, with full brown whiskers a little streaked with gray, cut rather close, open a little on the chin, without mustache. His stubby hands are red and look as if he used them in labor, and his physique and manner suggest Mr. Beecher, although his face to-day neither showed the animal force of Mr. Beecher's when at rest nor its spiritual exaltation when wrought upon by the fire of the inner spirit. But anything like resemblance ceases here. Spurgeon's voice is an admirable one, both soft and strong, and perfectly under his control. Some years ago I read a volume of his sermons and tried to see wherein lies the secret of his power. That will be found in the man himself, for his personal magnetism is extraordinary and of the same kind I sometimes felt in hearing, in the new West, those spiritual pioneers put into those rough fields by the Methodist Church known as presiding elders, so-called, who with plain and forcible natural gifts trained by constant contact with natural men in the deep forests and on the broad prairies, where God seems most present, were able to move the heart beyond the arts of the most accomplished orators. So with Spurgeon, whose city life seems to have had no effect on his mind or person, as he steps into his pulpit a natural man with God's message, as if he had received it direct in the desert and could not rest until he had come forth and declared it. He sinks himself and in plainest speech utters it from the heart of him, not without a certain force of high imagination, almost always belonging to such men. He is a powerful man far beyond what I had understood, and has none of the tricks of manner or speech usual with popular preachers. The vast audience was greatly moved and swayed by him, and while I do not hold the faith he professes, I do declare that I far prefer his methods and gospel to the mediæval ceremonies and perfunctory worship we have attended in the great churches of the Established Church since we came to this country. May he live long and prosper!

*July* 1.—Passed the morning in the National Gallery and saw great store of great pictures by masters of the Italian, Flemish and Dutch schools, leaving the others for a future visit. Here for the first time do I see at their best the famous painters whose works hand them down to fame in all time. How well deserving, as it seems to me, they are—Fra Angelico, Leonardo da Vinci, del Sarto, Dolci, Raphael, Correggio, Pellegrino, Tintoretto, Paul Veronese, Salvator Rosa, Titian, Velasquez, Van Dyck and so many more, but chiefest, thou, great Rembrandt!

Evening drove in Hyde Park, and am more and more impressed with the display of wealth and magnificence made here in this heart of the world. A single one of the equipages here would attract attention in any one of our great parks, and there are literally thousands like the best of ours rolling along in an endless tide. It is hard, when mingled in it, to believe that there can be want and misery anywhere in the world, so profuse and prodigal is the show of wealth and pomp. We managed to cut quite a respectable figure in our hired landau, with a well-stepping pair of handsome bays and coachman in brave livery, with the regulation purple cheeks.

*July* 2, 3, 4, 5, 6.—These days include one "event," the regattas or rowing matches at Henley, thirty-five miles up the Thames, for which we left London by rail at 5 P.M. on Tuesday. We were met at Henley Station by a London friend, through whose thoughtful kindness and the exceeding hospitality of his family we were enabled to witness the whole three days' pageant in the most agreeable circumstances. We were driven to the mansion of Lord Camoys, which, with three thousand acres of the estate, is rented by our host for a summer residence, during a term of years. Just such a house I have always desired to visit. Parts of it are more than five hundred years old. It is of brick, the main part having a front of at least 100 feet, with two wings of half that length, and at the end of one of them an old chapel of stone, with windows of stained glass, where a priest of the Roman Catholic Church daily officiates, the Camoys family being of that faith. Within are intricate arched passages leading into all sorts of quaint rooms with high-arched windows, a honey-comb of entanglements, where it is easy and pleasant to become lost and most natural to meet any description of ghosts, especially as the walls are hung with ancestral portraits running back for centuries, and of a diversity able to supply any species of ghost, from a turbaned warrior, glaring fiercely out of his frame from behind a pair of tremendous mustachios, to the peach-tinted maiden in her teens, with arched eyebrows and decorous curls, smiling now for these hundred years in a fadeless frock of white. There is a secret door and passage from one of the sleeping-rooms, said to lead by a subterranean way to a neighboring wood, useful in the troublous times of the Pretender, when arms were hidden here and robed priests came and went stealthily on unlawful errands. There are a large, fine library stored with books gathered during many centuries, a drawing-room of admirable proportions, altogether a house to see, to feel and to remember. We were four of sixteen guests, all cared for—such is the admirable domestic management in this great house—as if each were the only one.

Next morning all driven five miles to the "house-boat" of mine host, at Henley. This is a flat-bottomed boat some fifty feet long, with a well-appointed cabin and caboose, with a flat roof over all, railed about and furnished with seats, shaded with awnings, decorated with flags and flowers, where sixty people can have comfortable stations, looking on the river from a height of fifteen feet. Similar boats to the "Ione" were moored side by side, nearly touching each other close to the shore on one side of the Thames, here flowing with a scarcely perceptible current some thirty rods wide, forming a fine rowing course of a mile and a half, staked off midway in the stream and pretty well in straight line. Here for fifty years the Henley regattas have been rowed during three days, when thousands of the better sort of people come to assist in forming an aquatic pageant. There was a rowing match nearly every half hour from 12 noon to 7 P.M. The scene on the river during all these hours was of the brightest and most animating description. We have nothing at home at all similar. Probably there were on the course during the intervals of the races not less than a thousand craft of all sorts, ranging from steam and electric launches down to the canoe, moving slowly up and down, laden chiefly with ladies in charming summer toilets, the fair-complexioned, plump girls reclining in easy abandon on cushions of rich-colored cloths, forming the most charming pictures. All was a continually moving pageant full of life and color, an aquatic pomp noiseless and brilliant in a setting of green and shady shores, with softly rounded hills behind, all rich with the luxury of an English midsummer. The good-nature, self-possession, and courtesy shown by the occupants of the crowded, constantly colliding boats was pleasant to see. All was joy and sunshine, and I was surprised to see how fully the steady English folk can give themselves up to prolonged holiday. Nothing could exceed the pains taken by our entertainers to make all agreeable for their guests. Excellent refreshments were served at frequent intervals, good wines flowed freely, and, notably, the strawberries grown on the grounds of one of the family and gathered each morning for the occasion were not easily to be surpassed in size and flavor.

We dined, breakfasted and slept in the great Elizabethan house, reaching it at a late hour, and driving down to Henley each morning. On the night of the third day, Friday, all the house-boats were illuminated with thousands of colored lights, and hundreds of boats were moving up and down, carrying Chinese lanterns, and far as the eye could see the right bank of the river shone like the city of a dream, a vision of fairy-land. We glided up and down in the midst of this dreamlike pageant in an electric launch, moving without noise or jar, as if by magic, in the midst of excellent fireworks from the "Ione" and most of the other house-boats. The "Ione" alone was hung with six hundred colored lights.

We reached the hospitable mansion of our friends at midnight, on this last day, after three days of great enjoyment. We bade adieu to our most kind hostess, and returned to London and the Metropole by the 11 A.M. train on Saturday.

*July* 7, 8, 9.—Have done little in these days but *nibble* a bit at the rind of this huge cheese of a city, postponing any serious doing until we return to it for a longer time. Have passed another half day in the National Gallery, chiefly among the fresh, pure and clear paintings of the British school. Such beautiful, natural landscapes of Constable, a scene by Morland, any number of Gainsboroughs, many by Sir Joshua Reynolds, *such* dogs by Landseer, and a whole roomful of Turner's romantic canvases, magical as dreams—many, too, by Hogarth. Hired a courier for the Continent, Girado Frattini, sometime of Milan.

*July* 10.—Called on Mr. Lincoln, our Minister to the Court of St. James, to whom I had letters. He is a plain, unpretending gentleman, in his manner quite American, but not, as I could see, with any look, expression or feature of his great father. He seems a man of sense, and the two or three speeches he has been obliged to make here on public occasions have shown much of the tact and happy knack of saying the right thing on the spot so marked in his two immediate predecessors.

*July* 11.—Passed the day making calls and shopping with family. Drove down to 24 Cheyne Row to get a photograph of Carlyle with his faithful niece who cared for his last days with such affection standing beside him, partly promised me when we called before, but Mrs. Cottrell had not been able to procure me one. The little house again struck me as not uncomfortable or unpleasant and the neighborhood not at all mean.

We were at the Tower yesterday. The several towers or masses of buildings, enclosed by a massive wall and, with the ample open spaces, occupying some thirteen acres, have become so modernized as not to make a very serious impression as a fortress and prison where, during the dark and bloody centuries of early English history, so much transpired of a sort to touch and sadden the mind. The moat is dry, broad paved driveways lead into the courts thronged with groups of sightseers and bustling with various activity and signs of modern life, so that one experiences little emotion on being informed in broad daylight that at the foot of a certain staircase the bodies of the murdered princes were supposed to have been buried, there being no token whatever of such an event ; nor can one—at least I could not—grow sad in spirit over certain flat stones forming a pavement in a sunny court with inscriptions in most cases illegible from wear and dust, the sun shining down hotly on them and a busy throng of holiday people moving about, where certain illustrious dust of victims of old-time tyranny is supposed to lie. But the show of ancient armor is very fine and in marvellous quantity and perfection. The regalia, too, is interesting. In Queen Victoria's crown is a huge ruby which burned in the casque of Henry V. on the field of Agincourt. On the whole, I was disappointed in the Tower.

*July* 12.—Left London at 11 A.M. for Brussels *via* Dover and Calais by the Southeastern Railway. Our way to Dover, seventy-three miles, lay through the fair county of Kent, fertile, well cultivated, rich in promising fields of hops and many orchards. Reached Dover at 1 P.M., and thought of Shakespere's "Lear" as the train swept along the base of the white, chalky cliffs beside the Channel. Our good luck in weather still attended us, for the sea was smooth as a pond, and we reached Calais in just one hour, in all comfort, on a new, large, well-arranged boat, the "Calais-Douvre." Lunched in the Calais Station restaurant, and took train at 2 P.M. Frattini showed tact in procuring us a coupé or forward end of a carriage with a glass front, all to ourselves, and this with no extra cost except a small fee to the guard. The roads are not so smooth as the English nor the carriages as good. These are mounted on higher wheels, much as ours are. After leaving Calais we crossed for a long way a low, level country. At twenty-six miles we reach St. Omer, with 20,000 inhabitants; at sixty-six miles, Lille, 188,000 inhabitants, the chief town of the French Department of the North. Tall chimneys everywhere indicate its importance as a manufacturing town. 'Tis here Lisle thread is largely made. The Picture Gallery is said to be one of the largest in France, embracing eight hundred and fifty pictures, many of them by the best artists. Eleven miles farther on we reach the Belgian frontier at Blandain and have our luggage inspected at the customhouse there—inspection a mere form. At sixteen miles is Tournai, with 36,000 population, very ancient and the most important in the province of Hainault, very pleasantly situated on the Schelde. Like the most of these border towns it has a checkered history, belonging first to one and then to another of the greater neighboring powers, but in 1728, by the Treaty of Aix-la-Chapelle, it was set back to the Netherlands. We pass on through Ath, thirty-five miles from Lille, through

Enghien, fifty miles, Hal, fifty-three miles—a famous resort of pilgrims to the wonder-working image of the Virgin in the Church of Nôtre Dame—and reach Brussels, sixty-eight miles from Lille and one hundred and thirty-four from Calais, at 8 P.M., and are very comfortably established in the charming Hotel Bellevue in the upper part of the town near the Park.

At Enghien we passed from the province of Hainault into that of Brabant; and our whole ride this P.M. has been through a country naturally fertile, but rendered many times more so by such minute, patient and thorough cultivation as I have never seen or hardly thought possible. Imagine a vast plain stretching away indefinitely, with no greater irregularities of surface than an occasional knoll never attaining the dignity of a hill, or rising beyond a series of long, low undulations, all this surface compelled to yield the utmost possible of an exceeding variety of crops in little space—wheat, oats, barley, beans, beets, potatoes, etc., all in the same small field, so that the whole face of the country presents the appearance of a vast garden. Especially as we draw near Brussels every inch of land is made to produce something.

It is now the season of the wheat harvest, and in a bit of triangular land among green crops I saw in one case two and in another one little shock of wheat carefully set up. All crops are looking excellently well, as they must under such cultivation. Such abounding fertility, such fecundity of nature would of itself form a delightful picture; but when amid fields where green bits of pasture and meadow thick with red and white clover and varied crops also richly green, and yellow wheat fields as yet untouched or set thick with long, slender shocks and round stooks of sheaves, are many trim farm-houses, yellow-roofed, with low walls of brown, yellow, white and even blue, and dainty villages among trim trees, out of which rises the church-belfry, all these not at distant intervals, but in constant succession, the wide scene becomes of amazing beauty. On spots of vantage gray windmills, often high-stilted, fling out huge vans, sixty feet long, looming against the blue sky, at rest or lazily revolving in the light breeze of to-day, and over all is tranquillity and peace. The elms rise tall and slim from constant trimming, in graceful rows along the canals and the boundaries of the little farms, with willows dwarfed by cutting off the tops, and

Lombardy poplars—not growing in the scraggy, funereal way we see them at home, but fully and gracefully, branched low down, green and thrifty.

The Belgian provinces we traversed to-day sustain the prodigious numbers of more than eight hundred to the square mile. I fancied I saw a more complete cultivation and thrift from the time we crossed the frontier from France, though much struck with both before. This little kingdom of Belgium is only one hundred and seventy-nine miles long by one hundred and ten miles wide, but its population in 1886 was 5,900,000, of whom about two and one half millions are Flemings of Teutonic origin and two millions Walloons, partly of Celtic origin, more enterprising as well as more excitable than the phlegmatic Flemings. Belgium is a thoroughly Roman Catholic country, there being only some 1500 Protestants with 3000 Jews in its population. It became independent of Holland by a revolution in 1830, and a national congress summoned by the provisional government called to the throne in 1831 Leopold of Saxe-Coburg, whose son, Leopold II., is the present king. Charlotte, the widow of Maximilian, the ill-starred Emperor of Mexico, is his sister.

*July* 13.—Here we are in Brussels, a well-built, handsome city of 175,000 inhabitants, and if its ten suburbs are reckoned, more than double that number. The streets of the upper town rebuilt after a great fire in 1731, are wide and paved with square granite blocks; the private dwellings—mostly of brick covered with stucco and painted white—are handsome and fine, and the public buildings, both for the use of the State and city governments, really magnificent and far beyond anything we pretend to in any city at home. The new Palais de Justice is said to be the largest architectural work of this century, and is a wonderful structure. It is almost square at the base, is 590 feet long by 560 wide, and occupies a greater area than the Church of St. Peter's at Rome. The dome is 320 feet high in the interior, which contains twenty-seven large court-rooms, two hundred and forty-five other apartments and eight open courts. The gilded cross on the top is 400 feet above the pavement. Imagine this mighty mass of stone, richly wrought in its principal parts and adorned with many statues, and the cost of ten million dollars of our money seems almost preposterous when one thinks that that amount of money expended by the city authorities of New York would not build one wing of it.

In the beautiful Hotel de Ville, completed in the middle of the fifteenth century, containing the rooms used by the Common Council, are costly paintings and tapestry, the ceiling-painting by Victor Janssens representing the gods on Olympus, the figure of Cupid turning toward the spectator its face and bended bow in whatever position he may stand. This is an orderly city, so these gorgeous rooms are in perfect condition; the city fathers have not stolen the pictures and tapestry nor disfigured them nor the beautiful carved oak with boot-heels or tobacco. Charming old rooms, these.

The king has a huge palace here, occupying the full space of a New York block, and a summer residence at Laeken, a near suburb, with a great tract of good land, where we drove about on the royal farm, parts of which with a park are open to the public, who are made content by thus sharing in a mild way the advantages they bestow on their rulers. No subject is so poor that he has not an interest in his sovereign and can feel proud and important in proportion to the grandeur of his state, no matter how much he himself is stripped in helping to maintain it. So these Belgians, numbering not quite 6,000,000 souls, make fine provision for a good-sized royal family and furnish them palaces and parks and all the etceteras of the most powerful monarchs. But they seem able to do it with their wonderfully patient energy and thrift, and who will begrudge them their pleasure in it?

Passed the morning in the beautiful halls of the Palais des Beaux Arts among the paintings there, many poorish and many of a high order. As we are near Antwerp, the home and special field of Rubens' prolific pencil, his work abounds here, this gallery containing at least a dozen by him, the magnificent "Adoration of the Magi" among them. He has a large piece illustrated with all his wealth of color, so horribly repulsive that one sickens at the sight of it. It was painted for the Church of the Jesuits at Ghent, and is called the "Martyrdom of St. Livinus." The executioner has torn out the tongue of his victim with pincers and is offering it to a dog standing by. The taste of Rubens in choosing his subjects often seems to me of a debased sort. I cannot dwell in my poor hurried notes on the satisfaction we found in the works of masters who were only names to me three months ago—Claude Lorraine, Tintoretto, Paul Veronese, Guido Reni, Van Oost, the Teniers—many examples—the Ruysdaels, Maes, Jan Steen, the Brueghels, Frans Hals, Hobbema, Van Dyck, Adrian van Ostade, Van der Weyde, Memling, Quentin Matsys and a long list of lesser but bright names.

*July* 14, *Sunday*.—This is the Feast of St. Michael, the patron saint of Brussels, and there are special exercises at the Cathedral of St. Gudule and a pretty procession of school-children in white dresses and veils. The finest of all the numerous squares in the city is the Grande Place, in the centre of the lower town, where the noble Hotel de Ville stands, and all about it the old guild-houses. Great events in the history of Belgium have transpired here; among them the execution, in the spring of 1568, of twenty-five of the nobles of the Netherlands by order of the Duke of Alva, including Counts Egmont and Horn, to whom fine statues have been erected. The Porte de Hal, at the south extremity of the lower town, is all that remains of the old fortifications, built in 1381, and during the Belgian Reign of Terror the Bastile of Alva. It is a huge square structure with three vaulted chambers, one above the other. Notable, too, is the palace of the Duc d'Arenberg, once the residence of Count Egmont, with its beautiful gardens. So, too, the market squares for flowers, fruits and vegetables, all brought in from the country round in little carts drawn by stout, intelligent, well-looking dogs in harness with collars, sometimes in pairs, oftener single. So, too, the new Exchange, the Bank and many another magnificent building in such number, with fine private residences, as make this the handsomest city we have yet seen. Everywhere is order and cleanliness and the shops are filled with fine goods in every kind.

We visited a shop where lace is made and saw old and young workers bending unremittingly over their delicate and exacting work. The worn, sad face of a woman of seventy years impressed me, low bent, her spectacled eyes within six inches of the cushion on which an exquisite flower in lace was growing under her worn fingers. She had so wrought, the woman in charge told me, since she was a child, and her pay when fully expert was two francs per day. "Is there any provision for such as she when quite unable to work longer?" I inquired. The only answer was an indescribable shrug expressing more clearly than words could do that such workers must take their chances with all other old and infirm creatures in this teeming hive of industry, where little girls go about the streets and older ones stand in doorways knitting stockings, all human creatures careful and busy at some task.

Our rooms in the Hotel Bellevue look out on the Place Royale, on the left of which stands the Church of St. Jacques sur Caudenberg with a handsome portico of the Corinthian order, with noble statues and a warm fresco on the tympanum by Portaels representing the Virgin comforting the afflicted. In front is the equestrian statue of Godfrey de Bouillon, the hero of the First Crusade, said to be the finest modern Belgian work of the kind, erected in 1848 on the spot where the hero in 1079 is said to have exhorted the Flemings to the Crusade. He sits with majestic face, grasping with right hand the banner of the Cross. Near by is a charming park, originally the garden of the Dukes of Brabant, laid out and tended with great skill and care and set thickly with pleasing sculptures.

Back of the Hotel de Ville stands one of the curiosities of Brussels, a diminutive bronze figure called the Manikin Fountain, a great favorite among the lower classes and always dressed in gala costume on great occasions. This being a festal day he wears a court costume of velvet of the fashion of two hundred years ago. He has changed his colors with the different changes of government during the last one hundred and fifty years and now possesses eight different suits. He has a valet appointed by the civic authorities to attend on him at a salary of two hundred francs per annum, and some years ago an old lady left him a legacy of one thousand florins. In 1817 he was carried away from the scene of his aqueous activity by some sacrilegious hand, and great was the popular rejoicing at his discovery and restoration, the loss being felt as a public calamity—an odd illustration of the extent a fantastic notion will take hold of an intelligent, industrial community.

*July* 15.—Drove in a landau to the battle-field of Waterloo, ten miles from the city. Passed through a part of the Bois de la Cambre on the southeast side of the city, made into a fine park from a part of the Forêt de Soignes, said to be much like the Bois de Boulogne of Paris. There is a driveway of square granite blocks quite to the battle-ground. The village of Waterloo is a long single street, chiefly of connected farm-houses, whence issued droves of stout children with great flaxen heads, to turn summersaults and beg beside the carriage. Went directly to the Château of Hougomont, passing through the little village of Mont Saint-Jean. This château, as it is called, is a strong brick house with numerous out-buildings, all enclosed by a heavy brick wall some eight feet high, which also surrounds an orchard of say four acres—really a strong defence against anything but artillery. It was just in front of the lines of the allied forces and was pierced, walls and all, with loop-holes the day before the battle and occupied by the Coldstream Guards and some German riflemen, partly protected by the small cannon in the main line of the Allies behind. The French assaulted it at the beginning of the decisive battle of the 18th, but so stout and determined was the resistance of its handful of brave defenders that although during the day some twelve thousand men were hurled against it— nearly one-fifth of the entire French force—it was not taken. The buildings still stand in good preservation, showing the marks of bullets, and within the court-yard stands the battered brick tower over the old well into which some two hundred bodies of the ghastly dead were thrust.

Lunched at a little tavern near the field, then walked to the Mound of the Belgian Lion, an artificial pyramidal mound thrown up on the spot where the Prince of Orange was wounded on that day. The lion, weighing twenty-eight tons, was cast from captured French cannon. Climbed up the steps leading to the summit, whence the undulating country lay before me like a map, and with the aid of an old Frenchman who has made a business of laying out the plan of battle for so many years that he seems fully to believe in its genuineness, tried to get an idea of the general disposition of the respective forces and to comprehend the changing fortunes of the day. It seemed to me on the spot that I had pretty well done so, but when I had shaken myself down the long flight of steps, I ceased to feel certain of anything about it except what I had well known before, that this was one of the famous battles of the world, and that when all conjecturing is done with as to what the result might have been had this or that gone differently, we who trust in a Providence who orders the affairs of nations believe that by the very nature of His laws a limit is set to human ambition and endeavor, whereby the hour had come for the overthrow of Napoleon Bonaparte, the gigantic enemy of the human race. The fair fields, once ghastly with corpses, now wave with harvests, with no traces of the tempest which laid them waste, unless the red poppies showing among the yellow wheat like stains of blood have caught their hue from the ensanguined stream which filled these furrows seventy-four years ago. A little bird has built its nest in the jaws of the great lion on the mound, the cheerful voice of the peasant is heard, land and sky are full of peace.

*July* 16.—Left this fair city and the capital Hotel Bellevue at 11 A.M. for Ghent, where we arrived by rail at the Hotel Royal in the Place d'Armes, and drove about the city, noting well the belfry rising near the Cathedral with its great bell Roland, bearing an inscription in Flemish the translation of which is, "My name is Roland: when I am rung hastily, then there is a fire; when I resound in peals there is a storm in Flanders." Many a storm has it announced in these turbulent and much-tried lands, calling to arms the stout burghers in the tall houses of these narrow streets and waking with affright the peasants far out on the level fields. The gifted Theodore Tilton, whose star went out in darkness before the midday of his life, took this bell for his theme in a stirring poem at the beginning of our civil war, calling the country to arms. How well I remember his showing me the manuscript just after it was written and how when printed it rung through all the North like a battle-cry! The lofty square bell-tower supporting the chime, of which Roland is one of the oldest and heaviest bells, was begun in 1183; work was suspended on it in 1339 and it was only carried up two-thirds of the intended height. The tower is 270 feet high with a spire added some fifty years ago, reaching altogether to 375 feet.

Visited the Cathedral of St. Bavon, plain on the outside, but rich within. The crypt was consecrated in 941 and the whole completed in 1300. The last chapter of the Knights of the Golden Fleece was held here by Philip II. in 1559 and the walls of the nave bear their names and armorial bearings.

There is a fine pulpit by Delvaux, half oak, half marble, representing Time and Truth in allegory, and handsome carved mahogany choir-stalls. There are four enormous copper candlesticks some ten feet high before the choir, which once stood in St. Paul's, London, and were sold by Cromwell during the Protectorate. There are many good pictures, too; but the glory of the church is the "Adoration of the Immaculate Lamb," by Jan and Hubert van Eyck, two brothers—Hubert, the elder, born 1366, and Jan, the younger, in 1381. Hubert was believed to have invented oil painting. While it is now said by the best authorities that he did not do this, still he carried the use of oil as a medium so far in his wonderful coloring that what was believed has good grounds. The famous picture in the Cathedral here is in its chief parts the work of Hubert, the remaining of Jan. It is an altar-piece, consisting originally of twelve sections, but the wings, excepting the figures of Adam and Eve, which are at Brussels, are in the gallery of Berlin. I see, for my part, in this renowned picture great power and beauty, but am not able to see in it so much as great critics do—the more is the pity for me, no doubt. But I shall honestly adhere in all these things to saying what I think and not what others have said. To me the picture is pleasing and high, but not great except when it is considered that he, in a time when art was low, began that noble work of revival which blossomed into the splendor of a century later. Give the Van Eycks high praise certainly for their lofty conceptions and beautiful execution. This picture has a history worth noting. Philip II. tried to get hold of it, but had to be satisfied with a copy. In 1566 it was barely saved from the Puritanical Reformers and in 1641 it had a narrow escape from burning. In 1794 it was taken to Paris and only the central pictures were replaced, the wings, by ignorance or fraud, having been sold to a dealer from whom they were bought by the Museum of Berlin for four hundred and ten thousand francs. The two wings with Adam and Eve were kept concealed here as unsuitable for a church until 1861, when they were removed to the Museum at Brussels, where we saw them, and queer figures of our common parents they are. Lucky for her male descendants that Eve did not freely transmit to her daughters her corporeal characteristics as shown by the good brothers Van Eyck. The missing wings are replaced with copies by a clever artist named Coxie. The verger who showed us about and opened the doors covering this renowned picture with reverent and tender hands is a singular-looking man, and the like of him is not possible, I think, in our country. Such short legs, dwarfing his height, while all the rest of him is of good size, his big Flemish face, whose features, taken singly, are coarse and ugly, yet are harmonized and pleasing from an habitual composure of them into a cheerful and kind expression, a voice of gentle goodness and uniform politeness of tone, and a manner in all he did conforming to these, made of him a picture to be laid away in connection with the memory of the treasures he shows with such affectionate care that his acceptance of the expected gratuity did not belittle him.

In the same square is the Hotel de Ville, said to be the most beautiful piece of Gothic architecture in Belgium. It dates back to 1518. In the Marché du Vendredi, surrounded by antiquated buildings, is a statue to Jacques van Artevelde, and a stout and tough demagogue he seems, with a look something like our own Ben Butler. In a corner of this square is a huge cannon called "Mad Meg," dating from the fourteenth century, a sister in size and shape to the "Mons Meg" in the court-yard of Edinburgh Castle. We did not visit any picture galleries here, not understanding them to be of especial merit, and being something weary of pictures, wanted a little rest before seeing the more important ones of more famous galleries elsewhere.

Drove in the afternoon to a huge convent, or rather village of conventual houses on the northeast side of the town, called the "Beguinages," from St. Begga. It is really a little town enclosed by walls and moats with streets, squares, gates, eighteen convents and a church, forming a curious and picturesque whole. The houses are small two-storied Gothic brick structures, the wall, running all along their fronts, being pierced for little doors numbered and having the names of the saint to whom each is dedicated painted on them. These institutions were founded in 1234 and have been spared through all the destructive changes of the centuries. The objects aimed at are a religious life, works of charity and the honorable self-support of women of all ranks. At present nearly a thousand women occupy the convents and separate dwellings. They make lace, which is sold at a house near the entrance.

Ghent is the capital of East Flanders with nearly 150,000 population, and has always been an important city, but is losing its consequence since the separation of Belgium from Holland, and presents a dull but comfortable and pleasing appearance, with considerable manufacturing of cotton goods, the raw material coming increasingly from British India.

Left for Bruges at 5 P.M. by rail and arrived at the Hotel de Flandre in forty-five minutes. Dined and took a long carriage ride about the city, which for mediæval picturesqueness and quaintness surpasses anything we have yet seen. Five hundred years ago it was one of the renowned cities of the world and the mart where the East and West brought their divers products for sale and exchange. Venice, Genoa, Constantinople and the English cities brought here their richest stuffs, and it held this supremacy almost up to the sixteenth century, when its decline began, and now out of its population reduced to 50,000, one-quarter are said to be paupers. One effect is that the city stands as the refluent tide of mediæval prosperity left it, no changes being called for to meet the demands of modern trade. So we passed along narrow winding streets of high narrow houses with deeply notched gables, projecting windows, steep roofs and walls whose original colors of white and gray and blue and red have become toned by time into hues softer and richer than painter may spread on canvas, through public squares where the grass shoots up between the stones and the clatter of a pair of sabots awakens prolonged echoes, over which dominate the lofty structures of centuries ago, such as the Tour des Halles, or Belfry, with its sweet chime of bells, now one hundred and fifty years old, Au Lion de Flandre, the Cranenburg, the Hotel de Ville, dating back to 1376, the Maison de l'Ancien Greffe, the Palais de Justice, and fifty more, each a joy to the lovers of the old in architecture.

*July* 17.—Visited the Cathedral of St. Sauveur with pictures by P. Pourbus, Jacob van Oost, Seghers, De Crayer and Francken—all excellent these. Then to the Church of Nôtre Dame, where is a statue of the Virgin and Child by Michael Angelo, a marble group of life size and extreme beauty. The French carried it to Paris during the Revolution, and the refined Horace Walpole is said to have offered thirty thousand florins for it. There are also two sumptuous tombs in a side chapel here of sculptured brass with life-size effigies recumbent on them of Charles the Bold, Duke of Burgundy, and his daughter Mary, wife of the Emperor Maximilian, wrought by the famous artists Beckere and Jongelincx in the sixteenth century. Beautiful they are. Near at hand is the Hospital of St. John, upward of five centuries old, where the sick are tended by Sisters of Charity. It contains two hundred and forty beds, and in the quaint prescription-room two sisters with pleasing, intelligent features in great black bonnets faced with white, were preparing remedies from huge jugs and bottles, and all sorts of quaint vials and packages ranged on shelves all about. But what the world comes here mainly to see are the pictures by Memling, who lived and worked and died here in 1495, and for thirty years or more painted small pictures of sacred subjects of such perfect workmanship that a magnifying-glass in enlarging them only reveals their beauties the more. Sweet-faced saints look out from his canvases in a way to touch the heart. The Châsse of St. Ursula, a reliquary of Gothic design standing on a rotatory pedestal in the centre of the room, is said to be his finest work. There are five of his pictures here in all.

Such mellow quaintness of color and form along the canals as we drove about, such sweet, clear tones from the many belfries! I shall not soon forget thee, ancient and stately Flemish town! I must not forget to mention the richly ornamented little church of St. Basile, commonly called Chapelle de Saint-Sang, dating from 1150. Its name comes from some drops of the blood of the Saviour said to have been brought from the Holy Land in 1149 by Theodoric of Alsace, Count of Flanders, who deposited them here, where they are exhibited every Friday. N.B.—Do the priests who have the care of this imposition and the higher church authorities, who of course order and sanction its exhibition, really believe in this? Who can tell? I saw in a suite of rooms the regular yearly records of the city ranged on shelves, running back to 1235! In the Palais de Justice is a noble chimney-piece, filling up almost the entire side of the room, done in 1529 by Guyot de Beaugrant to celebrate the battle of Pavia and Peace of Cambrai—wonderfully fine.

Left Bruges for Antwerp at 4.30, arriving at 7 P.M., passing through Malines, where we had a very good view of the tower of the Cathedral of St. Rombold, dating back to 1312, never completed, but now 324 feet high with a clock whose face is 49 feet in diameter. This cathedral was mostly built with money raised from pilgrims who flocked here during the fourteenth and fifteenth centuries to buy the indulgences issued by Pope Nicholas V.

Frattini had secured us good rooms in the Hotel St. Antoine.

*July* 18.—Unless I make myself a slave to this flimsy journal, which I cannot do, I must be content with the merest jottings and only touch on a few things. I hoped, by the sight of a somewhat full record of what we see abroad, to help my memory in the years to come, if haply I shall be spared to live these months over again in retrospect, but objects of interest so press that I cannot. The great cathedrals we visit are my despair and I have ceased to attempt any description of these reverent piles, where pious souls, inspired and glowing, wrought in "sad sincerity" these marvels of ages not to be renewed. They can be felt, not described. So one feels when gazing on the tower of the Cathedral of Nôtre Dame here, rising like the fabric of a dream 400 feet into the air, delicate as a spider's web and so beautiful in its workmanship that Napoleon well might compare it to a piece of Mechlin lace. We went directly there in the morning to see Rubens' masterpiece, "The Descent from the Cross." I have never been so moved by any work of human art. I could not, I am not ashamed to say it, hold back my tears at sight of the bloodless Christ, whose relaxed limbs and pallid face showed how great the agony had been, with what inexpressible suffering the strong and noble form had at last yielded up the ghost. And then the afflicted mother benumbed with woe, and Mary Magdalene clasping his wounded feet with eager love, as if she would not even yet think him dead—these, and all the accessories, so harmonious, so contributing without one detracting element, to perfect the sad scene, show the marvellous power of the painter's art beyond anything I had thought possible. In all Rubens' pictures I have seen before this one—and I have already seen many—there is something to detract from the effect, coarseness of sentiment often and huge unnatural limbs, but in this great picture nothing of these disturbs the mind from realizing the awful impressiveness of the scene. The picture has winged sides showing the Salutation and the Presentation in the Temple. Into these Rubens has introduced, as he often did, the portraits of his first wife and daughter. On the other side of the altar is his hardly less famous " Elevation of the Cross," full of life, with a noble figure of Christ, but the canvas is overcharged with figures whose limbs are abnormally distended with brawn. The high-altar piece is also his: an " Assumption," wonderfully fine. There is also fine stained glass of 1615 and a noble pulpit carved in wood, of the seventeenth century, by Van der Voort. In the Cathedral tower is a chime of ninety-nine bells, the smallest only fifteen inches in circumference, the largest, cast in 1507, weighing eight tons. Near the principal door of the Cathedral is an old well with a canopy of wrought iron done by Quentin Matsys, buried in 1529 near the entrance to the tower, exceedingly graceful.

The handsome Hotel de Ville has a fine chimney-piece from the old Abbey of Tongerloo, representing the marriage of Cana.

The Museum of Paintings has some seven hundred pictures, many of them gathered from the suppressed monasteries and churches of the city, including nearly a score by Rubens. Notable among these are his " Baptism of Christ," " Christ Crucified between the Two Thieves" (" *Le Coup de Lance*")— a wonderful picture—" Adoration of the Magi" (" *Christ à la Paille*"), " The Doubting Thomas," " St. Theresa Interceding for Souls in Purgatory," and " Holy Family" (" *La Vierge au Perroquet*"), exceedingly fine, and so on. Fine too are very many of the works of Schut, Jordaens, Maes, de Vos, Rembrandt, Hals, Jan Steen, Van Dyck (including his " Christ on the Cross"), D. Teniers the younger, Quentin Matsys, Jan van Eyck, Roger van der Weyde and many others. Curious to see the many good pictures marked in the excellent catalogue, " onbekennen"—artist unknown.

In 1718 the old Jesuit Church of St. Charles Borromée was burned. This was planned by Rubens and he furnished for it thirty-nine pictures, all of which were consumed except three large altar-pieces, now in the Belvedere Gallery at Vienna.

The new Bourse is a large space covered with glass and surrounded by a double arcade, held up by sixty-eight columns, opening toward the centre in Moorish-Gothic arches, a very curious business-place.

The Church of St. Jacques, finished in 1656, is exceedingly rich and sumptuous in its monuments and ornaments. Among the richest of the many private chapels of the wealthiest and most distinguished families of Antwerp is that of Rubens in the choir at the back of the high altar. This beautiful Gothic chapel was designed by him. The altar-piece, a "Holy Family," is among his most beautiful works. All the faces are said to be family portraits. He sleeps between his two wives under the chapel floor, where he was laid to rest at the age of sixty-four in 1640. There are many fine pictures in this rich church, and beautiful stained glass of 1626.

Quite near the Royal Palace stands Rubens' house, large and richly decorated, built from his own designs, showing well that he was a prosperous man of affairs.

The National Bank Building, of massive and rich architecture, covers an enormous space—as large as one-half a full block in Brooklyn.

Passed all of one morning in an exceedingly interesting place, the Musée Plantin-Moretus, the house of the famous printer, Christopher Plantin, who set up his printing-office in Antwerp in 1555, and since 1579 almost to the present day business has been carried on by Plantin at first, then by the family of his son-in-law, Moretus. Since 1800 the printing-office was only used at intervals until 1875, when the building with all its antique furniture, tapestry, paintings (ninety portraits, including fourteen by Rubens and two by Van Dyck), and all other collections were bought by the city of Antwerp. The whole, as the guide-book to which I am indebted for the above inventory well remarks, "now presents a unique picture of the dwelling and contiguous business-premises of a Flemish patrician at the end of the sixteenth century." The almost monastic building surrounds a large court and consists of a long series of delightful old rooms, oak-panelled, with the quaintest little windows. There is the printing-office with the hand-presses, cumbersome but good, standing as if ready for work to-morrow, the proof-readers' room with copy lying about, the proprietor's office with its gilt leathern hangings, the type-room with old matrices, the composing-room with various type arranged in cabinets as is practised now. There are rooms containing the finely cut wood type, including great initial letters once used so much in books, and copper plates with impressions from them, and many original designs—some by Rubens—for title-pages. There are rooms with first copies of early books and a library of those published by the house. There is a type-foundry too, and beautiful living-rooms with the furniture, and rare old china, brasses, etc., of this wealthy family during many generations, all in perfect order and goodly to look upon. How different the recluse and dignified air of this old place from the swift maelstrom of giddy activity of the hand-to-mouth work of the modern printer! In a frame on the wall of the publisher's business-room, tacked on with big brass-headed nails and covered with glass as if put there yesterday, is a well-printed list of books forbidden by the Holy Inquisition to be bought, sold or read—an "Index Expurgatorius" issued by the court of that infamous institution and approved by the Duke of Alva when the Spaniards held this city.

From the reading of this it was natural enough to visit the Steen, once forming a part of the Castle of Antwerp, the seat of the Spanish Inquisition, now a museum of antiquities of no great interest. But with candle in hand one goes down into dungeons where many a sturdy Flemish Protestant went, never to return more. At the foot of the dark stairway, going down from the Judgment Room on the first floor, is a large circular opening which may be closed, as now it is, by a trap-door, and when the condemned, whose sentence had been rendered to him in ambiguous words, had been ordered down the dark stairs, he dropped into the deep pit below. Our candle showed us a vaulted room of stone, circular in shape, into which the condemned felt the water slowly rising about him, with a pump at hand, by which his most active exertions just sufficed to keep the water at a standstill, then felt it gain on him as his strength failed, until, inch by inch, it filled the room. In the old world then, as in the new, in the Netherlands as in Mexico, the traces of the Spaniard are the same, bloody and cruel.

Although Antwerp is sixty miles from the sea, the difference between high and low tide in the Schelde is anywhere from 12 to 25 feet.

In the Church of St. Andrew, dating from 1514, is a wonderful pulpit carved from wood by Van Geel and Van Hool, representing St. Peter and St. Andrew in a boat on the sea, called by the Saviour. All the figures are life-size. In the Church of St. Paul is a fine Rubens, "Scourging of Christ," and delightful wood-carvings of the choir-stalls and confessionals, beside the doors of which are life-size figures of the apostles and saints. In the court on the south side of the church and rising high on an artificial mound, styled Mt. Calvary, are winding ways up to the top, on which all along are statues of saints, angels, prophets, patriarchs, in great numbers—a curious and rather striking exhibition. At one side in a recess behind great iron bars is a representation of Purgatory, with plaster faces painted in all forms of suffering expression, wrapped in red flames.

I greatly enjoy looking at the beautiful Cathedral tower. Last evening at sunset it pierced the blue of the sky flecked with small bright clouds, seeming to lift its summit above them, and lower down many swallows whirled about it in wide circles, the liquid notes of the bells chiming the hours dropping softly down from the lofty height.

Passed half an hour again in the Cathedral this morning before Rubens' " Descent from the Cross." In the square in front stands his statue in bronze, fair to see. It shows a large frame clothed with abundant flesh, such as he loved to wrap his mortals in—and immortals too, for that matter—his face full, clear and handsome. In the joyful exuberance of his fancy, the depth of his invention, the richness of his colors, he seems to me to resemble Shakespere. He painted more than one thousand pictures, throwing them off with a free hand.

Even beyond Bruges was this city of Antwerp grand and opulent three hundred years ago, but under the Spanish régime its population, numbering 125,000 in 1568, had dwindled in 1589 to 55,000, and following the Treaty of Munster in 1648, by which no sea-going vessel was permitted to ascend the Schelde to Antwerp, it shrunk to 40,000. Still worse, in 1830 it was bombarded by the Dutch, who, in their turn, were besieged by the French in 1832 and the city frightfully laid waste. But its natural advantages as a distributing point are so great that it quickly rallied, and when in 1863 the navigation of the Schelde was made free, it came forward with a bound, and now has a population, including its suburbs, of 240,000, with a commerce increasing in a ratio beyond any city in Europe. It is, too, one of the strongest fortresses on this side of the water, made so by modern earthworks. It has not remaining so many of the traces of the old times as Bruges. We drove to the docks, which include an area of some two hundred and fifty acres. The quays of solid stone lead to the several basins where ships from all parts of the world lie, each in its own dock of stone.

I saw a curious thing in the Museum yesterday. In one of the saloons—there are a number of copyists at work in all the galleries we visit—there was an easel standing before a picture —"Card-Players," by the younger Teniers, if I mistake not— with an unfinished copy on it, which I glanced at and thought fully as good as any others, when what was my surprise to see a bright-looking little man drop into a chair before it, and slipping his feet from his loose shoes, lift one leg to his hat and remove it by taking hold of the edge of the brim with his big and next toe and placing it on the floor in a perfectly easy and careless way. I then noticed that he had no arms and that his toes were bare. He proceeded in the handiest way—if such a word may be used of the feet—to open some vials of colors, mix them to suit, took his palette with the toes of his left foot, adjusted his stick, seized his brush between the big and next toe of his right foot and went to work with as much ease and skill as another. Frattini said he had a commission to make the copy on which he was working for three hundred dollars and that his work is well thought of; also that he shaves himself, ties his cravat and does his toilet otherwise, all with his toes. Speaking of this phenomenon to Mr. Stewart, our Consul here, that gentleman informed me that he not only knew this case, but also another in a gallery in some German city.

*July* 19.—After three interesting days here left for The Hague at 3.30 P.M., and reached comfortable rooms at the Hotel Bellevue there at 6.30, a railway ride of three hours. At Roosendaal, twenty-three miles from Antwerp, we underwent the Dutch Custom-House, which threatened to be formidable, as many squatty officials with much gilt braid on them rushed out with much jargon and gesture and compelled all the train into the big examining-room by one entrance, guarded so that no return was possible until the word was given, but really it proved quite mild, as not a single box or bag was opened, I believe. Passed through busy Rotterdam with its 200,000 inhabitants and thronged canals, Delfshaven, Schiedam, the source of "Schnapps," "Hollands" and "Geneva," so called from the jenever or juniper-berry with which it is flavored, of which it is noted there are over two hundred distilleries, also that some thirty thousand pigs are annually fattened from their refuse; through Delft and Ryswyk, where the great peace between England, France, Holland, Germany and Spain was concluded in 1697.

The country we passed through in Holland is so wet, notwithstanding the numerous canals and ditches, that field crops are not cultivated at all to the extent hitherto noticed, but instead are miles and miles of good pasture land, on which thousands of fine Dutch cattle are feeding, big handsome creatures, mostly white with large patches and bands of black. Lofty picturesque windmills are seen everywhere. I counted twenty in sight at once from the car-windows. On the canals great, burly, awkward brown boats with all sorts of queer cargoes and clumsy, lumbering tackle are towed along sluggishly by men or horses, sometimes moving creepingly by the use of a tall, mahogany-colored sail, with broad-backed boatmen, in wide hats, puffing short pipes. There are no fences by the road-sides or dividing the fields any more than in Belgium, only hedges and more frequently lines of trees, which are everywhere cultivated with great care and often set in double rows, forming avenues along the canals. These are in many places higher than the country they traverse, and the water is pumped up into them by the windmills out of the ditches intersecting every acre of the land, one would think.

Just before reaching Dordrecht we crossed an arm of the sea called the Hollandsch Diep on a bridge seven-eighths of a mile long, formed by fourteen iron arches, each of 110 yards span and 15 feet above the level of the highest tide, with swing bridges for the passage of large vessels. Thirteen stone buttresses support the bridge, each 50 feet long by 10 wide. The foundation of three of these is 50 feet below low-water mark. The cost was about two and one half million dollars. Fares are low on the railways here and in Belgium, but the practice of charging well for every pound of luggage brings the cost to about the same as our roads at home.

The Hague is a pleasant, well-built town of 140,000 souls and has a prosperous and rather high-toned look, owing to the residence of the court and other high functionaries, home and foreign. It has a modern look and the public buildings are not specially imposing nor interesting. Most so are the old Hall of the Knights, the Town Hall, the Groote Kerk and the Mauritshuis built by Prince John Maurice of Nassau in 1679, wherein is now a celebrated picture gallery of three hundred paintings. Jan Steen, Terburg, David Teniers the Younger, Gerard Dou, Adrian van Ostade and Adrian van de Velde are seen at their best here, with fine landscapes by the Ruysdaels. Rubens and Van Dyck also each have several excellent pictures here and Wouverman half a dozen, said to be among his best, and fine they are. There is a beautiful "Madonna" by Murillo. There is a "Susanna" by Rembrandt, greatly praised, but not pleasing to me although I recognize the greatness of the style, because of the ugliness of the form portrayed. It is said that his wife Saskia stood for the model. If so he could easily have chosen better elsewhere. His "Presentation in the Temple" is here, but I did not become greatly interested in it; but did greatly in his "School of Anatomy," a large painting showing a group about a corpse, listening to the celebrated Dr. Nicolaus Tulp as he explains the anatomy of the arm. Wonderful is this picture with its strong faces and striking accessories. An ornament of the collection is Paul Potter's "Bull," famous the world over and justly so. The whole canvas—peasant, cow, sheep and bull—is alive—the bull is almost flesh and blood. Potter painted this picture at the age of twenty-two. There are two others here, also by him, one fine, very fine, a landscape with cows and pigs. Altogether a fine collection of pictures.

We had admission to a small collection in the private residence of Baron Steengracht, say a hundred in all, hung in his drawing-rooms, all of a high order, comprising choice examples by Gérôme, Willems, Horace Vernet, Winterhalter, Meissonier, Bouguereau, Blees, Koekkoek, Rubens ("Drunken Bacchus"), Cuyp, Jordaens, Paul Potter ("Three Cows"), J. Ruysdael, A. van Ostade, Teniers the Younger, Jan Steen, Hobbema, Gerard Dou, and Rembrandt's "Bathsheba after her Bath," called one of his finest, but not liked by me for the same reason as I give in the case of his "Susanna."

There are many pleasant squares in the town, and in front of the Royal Palace on one of these is a fine statue of William I. of Orange.

We drove out to Delft, five miles, and saw the beautiful marble monument to William of Orange, the Silent, in Nieuwe Kerk, and the Prinsenhof Palace, where he lived and was assassinated in 1584. In the Oude Kerk lie Admiral Tromp, who defeated the English fleet under Admiral Blake and hoisted a broom to his masthead afterward to signify that he had swept the sea, and Admiral Piet Hein, who in 1628 captured the Spanish " silver fleet " with a freight valued at twelve million florins, nearly five million dollars. Both have monuments where they lie, well carved in marble, short in the legs, but stout of heart. The road to Delft ran along a great canal, the water in it and in all the many others —we crossed scores and scores of them—full of algæ and looking dirty, as it really is, and smelling vilely. I should say a good country for quinine. And such huge windmills, two and three stories high all along!

Our pleasant rooms at the good Hotel Bellevue look across a canal into a well-kept lawn where is a great herd of deer, the fringe of a noble park with finer trees than I have seen anywhere except in a few places in England, great beeches and elms and horse-chestnuts. I walked here on Sunday afternoon. Thousands of decent, orderly people were moving about slowly in the grand avenues, quietly conversing or listening to the music of an excellent band. Here and there were clean little carts with the brightest of brass cans, from which milk was sold, the only fluid visible. Hardy little infantry soldiers were frequent, being off duty, with their sweethearts holding by the sleeve of their ill-fitting jackets; ditto in the cavalry service, with hot fur shakos a mile too big for their round heads, and terrible, long spurs to their heels.

We made a visit to Scheveningen, a watering-place on the sea, three miles from The Hague. There is a good beach enough, a big hotel, a good many shops and boarding-houses, plenty of sand, bathing-machines, innumerable wicker-covered chairs crowding the shore and looking in the distance like cones of yellow sand, some bathers, many people moving up and down, happy children with toy shovels, and all the marks of a seaside place, but nothing peculiar, and inferior to our Coney Island, in the location, the accommodations and the various life.

In a corner of the park I have spoken of, a little out from the city, is the Huis ten Bosch, meaning, in the easier American tongue, the "House in the Wood," a royal villa erected by the widow of Prince Frederick Henry of Orange, who died in 1647. The late Queen, first wife of the present King William III., was a friend to Motley, and he resided here some time while writing his "Rise of the Dutch Republic." His portrait hangs in one of the rooms. Let no one come here without visiting this house, in whose stately and beautiful rooms are such treasures of hangings, furniture, mural paintings, frescoes, cabinets, vases and many more precious things, such as one is not likely to meet many times, wherever he may wander.

*July* 23.—At 4.30 P.M. left The Hague for Amsterdam, arriving at 6 P.M. and finding most excellent quarters at the handsome Brack's Doelen Hotel. Indeed, the size and sumptuosity of our parlor rather disturbed me for fear of the cost, but Frattini, whose previous letter had secured all this splendor, explained that the cost would be only the ordinary charge for simply good rooms ; so we bestow ourselves without scruple, taking the risk of being thought to belong to some one of the many ranks of nobility in which these small kingdoms do so much abound. The country we came over from The Hague is nowhere more than two feet above the surface of the water in the small canals and ditches which interlace the whole face of it like the veins and arteries of the human hand. In a great many places there are miles and miles not six inches above the water. The great canals into which the water is lifted from this intricate system are anywhere from ten to fifteen feet above the level of the land. The country is in great part in pasture, supporting immense herds of Dutch cattle, with frequent fields of wheat, oats, beans, every foot being carefully cultivated. At one point I counted twenty-nine windmills from the car-windows. It has been a good deal rainy since we came into the Netherlands, and the farmers seem to be troubled by it in securing their wheat and hay.

Amsterdam is an old city, numbering now nearly 400,000 inhabitants, and is the commercial capital of Holland, lying at the influx of the Amstel, one of the mouths of the Rhine, into an arm of the Zuyder Zee.  Although the number of ships that enter its excellent harbor is only about one-third that of Antwerp, it is the chief mart for the colonial produce of the Dutch colonies and one of the first commercial cities of Europe. The city lies in the form of a semicircle and is divided into ninety islands by the "Grachten" or canals, crossed by some three hundred bridges. The water in these canals is about three feet deep, with almost the same depth of mud below. This is dredged out and the water frequently renewed by an arm of the North Sea Canal, so that the canals in and about the city look cleaner and smell less offensively than those of The Hague or Antwerp. The nature of the soil is such that no structure can be erected without driving piles to sustain it down through the upper strata of loam and fine sand into the firm sand below. All the houses are so founded. The Exchange rests on 3469 and the Royal Palace on 13,000 such piles. The vast system of the city canals is connected with the large and commodious harbor, and this with the North Sea Canal leading to the sea-coast, fifteen miles away.

The streets are narrow for the most part, except where they border on the canals, and the houses high and narrow, rising often in five or six stories, of exceedingly various and quaint styles of architecture, the greater number with lofty gables curved in and then rounding out again, presenting the appearance of an open loop. Near the top projects the end of a beam covered by a little roof with a hook on the under side for attaching a pulley. Bricks, thin, dark and fine, are the principal material used in the houses, and a firm gray sandstone in many of the more important public buildings. The streets are well kept and quiet, as there are very few carriages, and the business traffic is chiefly by water. Indeed, pedestrians freely walk in the driveways of the streets and slowly make way for a passing carriage, the driver of which must regulate his pace according to the free or crowded condition of the thoroughfares. The numerous shops look bright and well filled with good wares of every sort, and the people seem contented and well-looking, though not comparable in their personal appearance with those of Brussels or Antwerp, the men, and especially the women, seen abroad in the former city being better formed and handsomer in face than any I have seen on the Continent.

The Hebrew element is large here, comprising some 30,000

German and 3500 Portuguese Jews, who come to the front apparently with the ingenious activity characteristic of the race in whatever land it gets a foothold. The large trade in diamonds and the cutting of them is quite in their hands; indeed, we hardly visit a shop for articles we take an interest in without finding the proprietor a suave and polished Hebrew, and if not honest, a Yankee on a brief visit is not likely to discover it.

The number of specially fine public buildings is not great, but the whole city is well built, and in the endless variety of detail giving the houses an individuality, so that scarcely any two are just alike, it presents a series of pictures constantly fresh and new and charming. I greatly admire these strange, quaint houses. A considerable number of them lean out of the perpendicular by reason of the sinking of some part of their artificial foundations, but this, even when it has gone to a considerable extent, does not seem to affect their stability. Except in the case of quite well-to-do families, the citizens seem to live over their shops and places of business of whatever kind, where they have large and commodious premises.

The Royal Palace is a large and massive structure, once a town hall, but presented to King Louis Napoleon as a residence in 1808. In contains fine halls and its tower is crowned with a gilded ship. The great Central Railway Station is an instance of what a great architect can do to make an imposing and handsome structure devoted to common and prosaic uses. But the crowning glory of the city is its government museum, called Ryks Museum, covering nearly three acres of ground and including, besides one of the finest picture galleries we have seen, containing over fifteen hundred pictures of old and modern masters, collections in all fields of the history, arts and sciences of the Netherlands. These are housed in three hundred and thirty rooms, spacious, highly ornamented and finely lighted. The word magnificent is not too strong to apply to this noble building built by the government, wherein it is proposed to place all the great paintings of the kingdom, and only the natural reluctance of towns like The Hague, Haarlem, and indeed all others (for gems of art are scattered through them all) prevents. But here are the best works of the Dutch artists whose names I have already had occasion to mention so often heretofore, and as this is

Rembrandt's home, so here we find several of his best pictures, and notably his " Night Watch," his largest and most celebrated work, 11 by 14 feet. It represents Captain Frans Banning Cocq's company of arquebusiers emerging from their guild-house, whose lofty vaulted hall is lighted only by windows above, so that many figures are in partial twilight, while the faces and forms in the foreground are shown in an atmosphere of light, mellow, wonderful, and all the canvas stirs with the most energetic and picturesque life. The room where this picture is shown is called the Rembrandt Room, and while his spirit does not pervade this city as that of Rubens does Antwerp, the tokens of him are frequent, and his statue stands in a little square called by his name, where are stately trees and many flowers and benches where the citizens sit and smoke and meditate. 'Tis a handsome statue in bronze, showing a handsome man in Flemish dress, with a face earnest, thoughtful and a certain deep, half sad look like that Dante wears. Indeed, in the homely and repulsive subjects he often chooses for his pencil and the mystical mingled with the realistic tones and colors he used, he seems to me not unlike the great Italian poet.

I hired a little steam-launch one morning, which we took just beside our hotel, and we threaded our way among the canals into the river Y, passing under a great many bridges, so that the little smoke-stack had to be constantly lowered and raised—a process the stolid mariner attending on it took as quite a matter of course—and where this estuary issues from the Zuyder Zee were raised to the level of its surface, a height of three feet, by a lock which protects the system of city canals from overflow. Two hours' quite smart steaming on the broad inland sea brought us to the objective point of the trip, the little island of Marken, which rises just above the level of the sea and has been from time immemorial the abode of a race of fishermen who with their families are the sole occupants, who intermarry and have for centuries held strictly to their old habits, manners and costumes. The dreary little island consists of say a hundred acres, intersected everywhere by narrow canals, and contains something over a thousand inhabitants, who subsist entirely by fishing. I counted one hundred and twenty of their stout, brown, lumbering boats, each with a tall, strong mast, a little pennon flying atop, drawn up on the beach in double rows in the most perfect order. They hold themselves aloof from the outside world, are proud, and jealous of strangers, who, as a rule, are not made welcome, and I engaged a man to go with us who, by many visits, has ingratiated himself with them, learned their ways, and now makes a business of getting visitors the privilege of landing, and to some extent visiting them in their homes. The men wear little caps, loose blue blouses, huge baggy trowsers, ending at the knee, long, coarse woollen stockings and wooden sabots, and are strong, bold, independent-looking men. The women wear caps of white lace, jackets embroidered in gay colors, blue petticoats puffing out enormously at the hips, and sabots like the men. The children until seven years of age are dressed alike in long gowns, with embroidered caps, and with their hair banged in front are of undistinguishable sex except by a circular bit of different colored cloth in the crown of the caps of the boys. At the age of seven the boys assume the *toga virilis* and go at once into the full costume of the men. We saw a sturdy, flaxen-pated little fellow who had put on his only a few days before, in which he strutted about quite at home in his enormous breeks, and our conductor pointed to the heavy silver clasp which fastened his blouse at the neck and explained that all the men wore these of such value that should any poor fellow become drowned and his body be found by strangers, the value of this jewel would pay for his burial in some spot of earth—a sad and touching indication, I thought, of the perilous life they lead.

A smart shower was falling as we threaded our way along the dismal and slippery path leading from the landing to the nearest of the little villages, when a small cracked bell in the little tower of the only poor little church on the island began to toll in the dismalest way, and we saw a long, straggling procession of these picturesque people coming from another village, and were aware of its funereal character by the slow, measured pace and the clanging bell, and as it came nearer, by a boat towed along on one of the ditch-like canals, a coffin resting in it on low trestles and several women about it bowing their heads on their knees. I have never seen so mournful a funeral as this, which passed directly by us as we managed to stand aside on the insecure soil to give it room, in attitudes of respectful sympathy, and noticing with interest the brown, manly faces and strange costumes. They have one huge common tomb in a low mound, where the coffins of the dead are placed together since a great inundation a century ago swept the island and washed the dead from their graves and out to sea. All parts of the island are subject to overflow, except the few somewhat higher spots where the three or four villages are placed. They raise no crops but grass and maintain no domestic animals save some half-dozen cows to supply a little milk, all other food coming from the main-land—fish of course excepted, which with potatoes and bread form the chief part of their food. And yet in the little houses—they are more than huts—of these fisher folks are certain treasures of old Delftware, brass and pewter, carved oaken furniture, old clocks and old silver work, which would make a collector green with envy, nor can they be had of these poor people for love or money. They treasure them from age to age, from generation to generation, handing them down as precious home-treasures to be sacredly kept along with the embroidered wedding and gala dresses, which lie carefully bestowed in old cabinets for hundreds of years. Only in the last extremity, when the pressure of distress can no longer be endured and other relief is despaired of, does any owner of these precious heirlooms part with enough to prolong life. And so they remain here as in the two houses we visited, the two little rooms of each actually made noble by rows of these precious articles kept in these mean surroundings with the utmost care and pride. There would seem to be no reason for apprehending an extinction of this peculiar people, as the island swarms with children, who kept us eager company in our tour and struggled for the small coins and cakes dealt out by our conductor, with a clamorous vigor promising well for their length of days.

We steamed across to Monnikendam, a quaint, dull town on the main-land, then down a sluggish canal to Broek, so picturesque and clean that a dirty sidewalk would have been refreshing, and visited a farm-house where Edam cheese is made, with such wonderful neatness in all the arrangements that one would hardly suspect the tiled stalls for the cows to be used by four-footed tenants. Thence back to Amsterdam by the old North Holland Canal, some ten feet higher in many places than the country on either side, a country level, green with rich pastures bordered with trees, and thousands of sleek, tranquil cattle feeding, windmills all along the horizon, little villages and great farm-houses with huge pyramidal red roofs, making such a picture in the soft light of sinking day as will not easily be effaced from my memory.

There is scarcely anything left of national costumes or peculiarities of dress anywhere in the Netherlands. In Belgium we saw nothing distinctive in that way, and in Holland only now and then a rich head-dress of lace, with plates of gold in front of the ears and great gold pins standing high up like horns on some matron of the old-fashioned sort, and becoming it seemed too, giving a kind of dignity to the wearer. But ready-made clothing is reducing all nationalities to a dreary uniformity of ugliness, and the people in the streets of Brussels, Antwerp and Amsterdam might, so far as appearance goes, have bought their clothing in Rochester. Only the sabot holds its own astonishingly well when one considers what an inflexible wooden trough it is, and its use is quite common among the poorer people. It is interesting to see how well they manage them, and the children run and leap in them with a freedom and ease one would not think possible.

On Sunday I strolled along the streets well filled with neatly dressed people sauntering soberly about in a contented sort of way, and as well fed, housed and clad as the people of our own cities ; and this is true of all the cities, big and little, we have visited here. There may be depths of misery somewhere, but nothing apparent indicates it either in town or country. I noticed nearly one half the shops were open, but very few customers inside.

Holland has a population of about four and one half millions, three-fifths of which is Protestant. Long may these prosperous and, to the eye of the traveller, happy people of the snug little kingdoms of the Netherlands continue so, kept from foreign harm by the jealousy of the surrounding nations, and so left to pursue, as they are successfully doing, all the arts of peace.

*July 29, Monday.*—Left the goodly city of Amsterdam, where I would gladly have lingered a month at least, at 9 A.M. for Berlin, where we arrived at 10.30 P.M. the same day and found good rooms at the Hotel Kaiserhof, secured in advance by the attentive Frattini. We had a comfortable compartment to ourselves all our journey, and a warm dinner handed in at one station, the trays, with ingeniously arranged dishes, being taken off at the next. As far as Utrecht the country continues at the same low level of pasture land, sustaining thousands of fine cattle on grass, which is not renewed for ages, and only invigorated by the manure of stock spread broadcast on the land, forty acres of which keep in excellent condition sixty head of the large Dutch cattle. All that part of Holland we have visited is in the Rhine delta, and the land was deposited by that river in the long past and is a rich alluvium at top. I have not seen a stone in Holland big enough to throw at a dog, unless brought into it, as is all the enormous amount used in constructing their docks and dikes and other great public works. After leaving Utrecht, however, the face of the country is somewhat more elevated, the moisture in the soil less, and good field crops succeed one another all along.

At Emmerich we take the customs examination, and the only piece of my luggage examined was a hand-bag holding some forty-five cigars, for which a polite German official mulcted me in the sum of one and three-quarter marks—about forty-three cents of the coin bearing the image of the American eagle. I smiled on him benignly, as I had in an unopened trunk another full box. We crossed fertile and well-tilled Westphalia, all along snug brick farm-houses with red roofs of curved tiles, many pretty villages and charming views among the hills, for we were in quite a high and dry region there, though the general face of the country is level ; on through Hanover—entitled to whatever credit may belong to it for giving birth to the first of the English Georges ; on through a land less fertile, with a soil growing more sandy ; still on in the growing darkness until the long rows of distant gas-jets give token of a great city near, and we roll into the commodious railway depot of Berlin, the capital of the great and mighty German Empire.

I find this city of Berlin to be handsome, even magnificent. It is comparatively modern, and under the fostering care of Frederick William, the "Great Elector," its population in 1685 was only 20,000. Under Frederick the Great, who nourished it in all ways and lavished money on its architecture, it had increased at the time of his death in 1786 to 145,000, and from 200,000 in 1819 it grew to 330,000 in 1840, and now, as the capital of Prussia, the residence of the Emperor of Germany, centrally situated in the empire, with large commerce through its extensive railway system and navigable rivers, extensive manufactures and important money market, it has reached a population of 1,300,000 and ranks as the third city in Europe. Its situation is not interesting, on a level, sandy plain, with the dull river Spree flowing through it, a location not unlike Chicago with Lake Michigan omitted, and, like that city, brought forward by the steady application of intelligent human energy, and enjoying in addition the affectionate fostering of a long line of rulers. The whole look of the city is modern, and there is not much that is picturesque about it, not even a cathedral or town-hall. But the eye rests with pleasure on broad, regular streets, well paved in granite and asphalt, lined with lofty, solid and architecturally fine buildings of stone or stuccoed brick, squares adorned with statues and refreshed with fountains, shops rich with the finest goods in all kinds, and abounding marks of opulence on every hand.

I am rather disappointed in the famed "Unter den Linden," a street 200 feet wide and a mile long, planted on each side with an avenue of trees, from the Brandenburg Gate to the statue of Frederick the Great. The old linden-trees seem to have come to grief, most likely through the severity of the weather, for the wind must come in bitingly, in the wintertime, through these wide streets from the broad plain round about, and their places are filled with young, smallish trees of several sorts, as elms, horse-chestnuts, and not many of a new race of lindens. Its width, too, gives it a rather dreary look, with rows of plain chairs and benches strung along under the trees, and this bareness is not relieved by the lively movement of handsome equipages up and down, such as we are used to in our larger American cities, where nearly all well to-do citizens keep carriages, as does not seem to be at all the case in any continental city we have seen so far. But several palaces border it—the plain ancient one of old "Kaiser William," where at one of the corner windows on the lower floor he loved to station himself down to his last days, at precisely ten in the morning, to see his favorite guards march by; the late Emperor Frederick's and the royal palace of the present Emperor William, now absent on an excursion to Norway, so that we visited the great rooms of state in it, and putting on felt shoes so as not to mar the oak floors, traversed some fourteen very rich rooms with good pictures, much gilding and some fine effects in decoration. The ballroom and royal chapel are quite impressive in those respects. The reigning family is Protestant of course, and it struck me oddly that a massive crucifix stood on the altar, with one great wax taper burning before it.

The finest building in the city is the "Old Museum," so called, opposite the Royal Palace, built in 1824 by the famous architect Schinkel, who did a great deal of good work here in his time. This is in the Greek style with an Ionic portico of nineteen columns, and we saw many good pictures there, and among the antiquities the very interesting friezes from the altar of Zeus on the Acropolis of Pergamus, found and excavated by the engineer Herr Humann in 1879, supposed to have been erected by Eumenes II. 180 B.C., in honor of his victory over the Gauls there. Most parts of these are thoroughly well preserved, fresh, full of life and rich in fancy and fine execution. The usually trusty Baedeker says there are no other antique remains so good on such a scale. At the entrance is Kiss' Amazon.

We drove out to Charlottenburg, passing through one of the five arches of the Brandenburg Gate, the central one of which is guarded by sentinels, so that none but royalty may pass there. Our road took us through the very handsome public park of the Thiergarten, containing six hundred acres ornamented with fine avenues of large trees, miniature lakes, grassy lawns, natural forests, many statues—an admirable park and one of the best we have seen. The Royal Palace at Charlottenburg was built for Sophia Charlotte, wife of the first Frederick, in 1699, and we wandered through the gorgeous rooms of it opening into each other in a vista of 500 feet. In one apartment is a fine show of old china of all the factories then known, artistically arranged, quite covering the walls, and said to be in the same arrangement as when the good Charlotte left all these vanities to lie down in dust, as royal heads must do at last, and the good Emperor Frederick did sadly not many months ago at Potsdam, stopping here a few weeks on his way thither. A gloomy, damp, close-smelling sort of a place, this Royal Palace of Charlottenburg, despite its magnificence. We passed a whole day among the remains, traces and tokens of the Great Frederick, a character in whom I have always been interested.

In the Hohenzollern Museum in the Monbijou Château are a great number of reminiscences of him and his time. There is a wax model of his face after death, singularly striking, showing every lineament of his strong face and every line of each feature with startling distinctness, his clothing from childhood to death, including a uniform and little musket in which he underwent the severe drilling to which his martinet of a father subjected him, his flute and the manuscripts of his musical compositions, and his horse, Condé, cream-colored, and life-like in its state trappings. Interesting, too, are the relics of his father, Frederick William I., including his turning-lathe, the table of his "Tobacco College," with a great array of the long clay pipes used, and the large, comfortable, high-backed, rudely painted wooden chairs in which he and his councillors used to sit far into the night in a cloud of smoke, drinking deeply, with much horse-play and quarrelling, as Carlyle so graphically describes in his life of Frederick the Great, one of the wonderfulest books in the world. There are also many good portraits and busts of characters of that time, old tapestry and furniture, cabinets, porcelain, table services of kings and electors, including a series of tankards going far back

Visited Potsdam, sixteen miles southwest from the city, well situated on an island in the Havel, with some 50,000 inhabitants, where the Great Frederick erected many buildings and pretty much made the interesting place what it is, and where he loved to reside. Crossing the bridge from the station to the town, we come at once upon the palace with the famous lime-tree, its trunk covered now with metal, but in good foliage and bearing itself sturdily, where petitioners used to take position and wait for Frederick the Great to appear. This palace was built in 1660, but took its present form under Frederick in 1750. His rooms are kept as he used them, and fine rooms they are, done by the artists he brought from France, their ceilings rich in fresco and abundant gilding on walls and doors in the revived classic fashion of the time. Here are his writing-desk, convenient and roomy, his music-stand, and snug library with shelves on one side filled with French books handsomely bound. Among them is a full set of Voltaire's works bound in red morocco, with many marks of reference rising from the gilt upper edges, just as Frederick placed them. This library is separated from his bedroom only by a heavy silver balustrade, and adjoining it is a charming little cabinet with double doors and a cheerful outlook from its one window, and a round table in the centre, the central part of which could be readily let down into the kitchen below and returned without any servants being present, where he entertained confidentially, quite free from all espionage.

We entered the vault under the pulpit of the plain Garrison Church where lie the remains of the Great Frederick in a chest of lead as they were placed at his funeral, and beside him, the only other occupant of the little vaulted room, those of his redoubtable father, still and peaceful enough now in this plain case of black marble. Several dried wreaths of bay rested on the coffin of the Great Frederick, and taking a fresh red rose from the jacket of one of the young ladies of my party, I placed it among them. The grizzled and stiff old soldier who had admitted us smiled grimly, and handed me with hesitating carefulness a leaf from a wreath of bay placed there in 1813 by the Czar Alexander of Russia, and we emerged musingly, soon to find ourselves in the fair and famous park of Sans Souci, laid out by French gardeners under Frederick's care, in imitation of Versailles. There are innumerable statues, single and in groups, along the broad avenues, and in the centre a fountain rising to the height of 112 feet, and falling into a basin more than a hundred feet in diameter. From this scene of cultivated sylvan beauty a broad flight of steps intersects six terraces leading up 66 feet to the palace of San Souci. These terraces are prettily cultivated in turf and flowers, and on their sunny steep sides grapes ripen on trellises, and I noticed dwarf trees of apples and pears in huge earthen pots, laden with ripening fruit of more than average size. At the east end of the upper terrace the greyhounds and chargers of the Great Frederick are buried, and near a statue of Flora is a favorite spot where he used to say he would like at last to lie—" *Quand je serai là, je serai sans souci.*" The long palace of one story was built for him in 1745 and he lived there almost constantly, and his rooms are still kept as they were in his life. They are handsome rooms, and show the occupant to have been a man of cultivated and luxurious tastes. His portrait by Pesne in his fifty-sixth year is said to be the only one for which he ever sat. The features are the same as in the death-mask, and as shown in the majestic statue in front of the Royal Palace in Berlin. Here also is a small library, chiefly of the French classics, and some fine paintings by Pesne, Watteau, Lancret and others, and a few ancient busts on the walls. A small white marble clock is shown which he used to wind up himself, said to have stopped at the precise moment of his death, 2.20 P.M., August 17th, 1786. In the west wing is the unaltered room in which William IV. died, and another is shown as the one occupied by Voltaire.

Not far from the palace, on the way to the Orangery, I noticed the old wooden windmill, whose owner refused to sell it to the great king. We climbed a flight of broad steps to look at the façade of the Orangery, a structure in the Florentine style, 330 yards in length, completed some forty years since, imposing and fine with its many statues, but I cannot dwell upon it nor the garden of tropical plants adjoining, nor the Palace of Friedrichskron a mile away, founded by the Great Frederick in 1763 after the Seven Years' War, and completed at a cost of four hundred and fifty thousand pounds. We noticed its handsome façade of 375 feet, and its noble dome rising among the lofty trees of the surrounding park, but did not seek to enter as we might have done, in the absence of its occupant, the Empress Victoria. Her husband, the Emperor Frederick, died here a little more than a year ago. In fact, we have "supped full" of palaces in the last few days, and are glad to get back later in the day into the quiet of our rooms at the Kaiserhof and dine in the covered court under electric lights, amid much gilding and marble and fresco, attended by a civil waiter with English nearly as good as that of Frattini, whose manner mildly rebukes my enthusiasm over what we have seen since falling under his care, as he requests me from time to time to wait until we shall reach Italy, and then, etc., etc.

I neglected to say that the sandy, level parade-ground overlooked by the windows of the old palace in Potsdam, where the father of Frederick the Great used to drill his big grenadiers, still serves as a parade-ground, and in his rooms in the

Sans Souci Palace are shown the perpendicular graduated scale by which he used to measure the recruits for his gigantic guards, and a long row of stout canes wherewith he used to belabor all sorts and conditions of people, his own family included.

In riding and walking about this city of Berlin, I am more and more impressed with the solidity, prosperity and magnificence of it. In a general way too, the cities on this side of the Atlantic are growing and prospering in a manner not so much behind those of our own country. The apathy of feudalism, the inertness of the old traditional life feels the quickening of the modern spirit, and progress is rapid and thorough almost everywhere we visit—at least so it seems to me. To illustrate the growth of population, take the city of Hanover, once the sleepy capital of the kingdom of that name, the cradle of the Georges of England and now the capital of a Prussian province. In 1837 its population was only 27,000; to-day it is 160,000.

*August* 2.—Left Berlin for Dresden at 8 A.M., arriving at the latter city at 11.20. The route by rail is one hundred and five miles over a sandy, unfertile plain, with few farm-houses in sight and the scantiest crops, in spite of a good deal of labor expended on the land. We passed not more than half a dozen small villages in all the distance. Find excellent quarters in the Hotel Bellevue, close beside the river Elbe, overlooked by a pleasant terrace, where one can partake of the good rolls and coffee one finds almost everywhere on the Continent.

Dresden is the capital of the kingdom of Saxony, where its sovereigns have resided since 1485, and, like almost all towns we have so far visited on the Continent, has been greatly rebuilt, and enlarged during the present century in rapid growth until it now numbers 245,000 souls. It lies on both sides of the Elbe, here about 300 yards wide, artificially made so from a width above and below the town of say 150 yards. There is a picturesque old bridge always in view from the hotel terrace, connecting the old and new parts of the city, lively with much passenger traffic on the tramway and sidewalks. This bridge, resting on sixteen fine arches and one-quarter of a mile long, was built in the thirteenth century. The valley of the Elbe here is pleasant, with low ranges of hills in plain sight; but I do not find the environs of Dresden so attractive as the reports of travellers usually make them. It is well built, and in view of our hotel is an imposing opera house, the Hoftheater, in the Renaissance style, by Gottfried Semper, opened in 1878, and called one of the finest in Europe, covering an area of over 5000 square yards, ornamented with statues and richly decorated by eminent artists. On the same square rises the Palace, a large, dull structure with the highest tower in the city, 331 feet. In a room or series of rooms on the ground floor, called the Green Vault, is a wonderfully fine collection of curiosities, including the jewels of the reigning family, of exceeding value, with a great number of fine diamonds, among them one of green color weighing five and one half ounces, set as a hat-clasp. There are many large pieces in gold of the work of the earlier German goldsmiths, ivory carvings, including one of ninety-two figures, cut out of a single piece, representing the "Fall of the Angels," Limoges enamels, and an endless number of rare and costly objects in silver, brass, tortoise-shell, crystal and the various precious stones, on which an incredible amount of labor has been expended by famous artists, making this, it is said, one of the most valuable collections of these curious things to be found anywhere. One wonders how the rulers of this small state come to possess all these treasures, and is obliged to look on them as accumulations made during those centuries when the divine right of kings stood for much more than it does now, and the strong hand to take went with the desire to possess, and the means to buy were wrung from abject subjects with no one to withstand or gainsay.

The Roman Catholic Court Church is also on our square built in what is called the "baroque style," by which I understand a commingling of various styles so as to produce a sort of harmonious and not unpleasing effect. This church dates from 1737 and has some sixty statues of saints on the parapets and at the entrances. We attended mass there Sunday morning, as the music is notable, and listened with pleasure to the magnificent baritone voice of the officiating priest intoning the prayers and the soprano in the choir, the only female voice, Frattini says, to be heard in any Catholic church in Europe. But the old kings of Saxony were Protestant, and it will be recalled that stout Ernest of Saxony was one of Luther's stanchest friends and supporters, and possibly this pure female voice rising from the braided melody of the numerous choir is a lingering reminiscence of those days when old bands of church practice and custom were relaxed and women mingled in the worship of God more openly than under the Romish forms.

But the crowning attraction of Dresden is its Picture Gallery, housed in an ample and handsome museum designed by the architect Semper, completed in 1854, and ranking as one of the finest collections of pictures in the world. I cannot dwell at length on the many choice examples of the various schools of painting shown here. Here are the " Sacrifice of Abraham," by Andrea del Sarto ; " The Madonna Enthroned," " Madonna with St. Sebastian," " The Holy Night," " The Madonna and St. George," all by Correggio ; " The Tribute Money" and portrait of his daughter Lavinia, by Titian ; masterpieces of Paul Veronese, Tintoretto, Velasquez, Murillo, Claude Lorraine, Watteau, Nicolas Poussin, Rubens, Van Dyck, Rembrandt—his portrait of his wife, Saskia, portrait of himself with her on his knee, " Samson's Riddle," " Manoah's Sacrifice" —Gerard Dou, Paul Potter, Wouverman, and the long list of Flemish, Dutch and German painters whose works I have seen and partly noted elsewhere. Here are Dürer's " Crucifixion," Holbein's portrait of Morett the English goldsmith, two most charming pictures by Angelica Kauffmann and two by Heinrich Hofmann, " The Child Jesus in the Temple" and the " Woman Taken in Adultery before Christ," worthy to rank, as it seems to me, with the works of the great masters. But what can I say of the exceeding glory of the " Sistine Madonna," by Raphael, hanging in a quiet and almost sacred room, the only picture there, whither visitors come from the connecting halls where they have chattered and criticised straying carelessly and noisily, to uncover their heads as in a holy place and softly and with no words to gaze long and tenderly on this divine apparition ? Who can do so unmoved ? There stands the Virgin Mother blessed above all women, holding to her breast the infant Redeemer, the beauty of her face faintly shadowed by the awful mystery whose full import she cannot yet have comprehended. What unfathomable depths in those tender, luminous eyes, what saintly beauty in all those Oriental features ! What composure of maternity in them touched with something of shy virginity, of modest pride, of vague jealous fear, of happy awe! No wonder the world comes to admire and reverence and worship. And what a wonderful thing it is that the brain and heart and hand of man can with a few earthy pigments create so glorious an image, looking as if ready to step down to earth with throbbing heart and lips informed with human speech!

We drove across the old bridge through the new town and by a long, rising road, passed in the suburbs the picturesque house looking down on the river, where Schiller lived for a time with his friend Körner, author of the "Song of the Sword," and crossed the Elbe, on our way back to town, by an awkward ferry-boat, which did its work handily enough, and passed through the small but pretty Brühl Terrace, well kept and enriched with frequent statues of famous men.

I was wakened one morning here by the shrill notes of some not at all musical wind instrument, and looking out of the window saw a group of soldiers collected at the foot of a long iron ladder running up the lofty side of the opera house, being drilled in evolutions on it as firemen and regulating their movements by the notes of the aforesaid instrument in the mouth of the officer in charge. Three men mounted the ladder at a time, some distance apart, with a common and measured step, so deliberate as to be almost amusingly solemn, and fastening with simultaneous motions a strap each wore round the waist by a hook to a rung of the ladder, let go their hands and accustomed themselves to using them freely and to bend backward from the waist so as to be at liberty to expend their force in any action required in the exigencies of a fire. They then descended in the same uniform manner, and others took their places. All these movements were made with automatic precision.

The royal manufactory of the famous Dresden porcelains is at Meissen, fourteen miles from here. This was founded in 1710, when the chemist Böttger discovered how to make "china." We visited the show and sales rooms of the company in the city, and saw most beautiful productions—vases, plaques, figures, etc. The most expensive of their dinner sets of one hundred and twenty-four pieces in stock cost three hundred and fifty dollars here. Sets of higher cost are only made to order and easily run into the thousands. The paternal government of Uncle Sam claps a duty of sixty per cent on these wares in order that some New Jersey potterie may experiment, as they have been doing for fifty years. Without this enormous duty, the manager said sadly, they would do a large business with America.

Our hotel here is the best we have found since the Bellevue in Brussels, and very pleasant it is to sit under the striped awning swung over the terrace of tessellated marble, festooned at the sides with clambering vines, the brown Elbe with its lazy boats just below, the gray old many-arched bridge near by on the right, and on the opposite shore the dull red roofs of ancient houses with queer windows in them, so arched in tiles that a pair of them look like eyes staring unwinkingly at you. Here we order our meals served at one of the many little tables and rest dreamily.

*August 6.*—Left Dresden for Frankfort at 8.30 A.M. and arrived there at 9.45 P.M. Rooms at the Hotel d'Angleterre on the Rossmarkt, the small but principal square of the city. We changed cars at Leipsic at 10.45, the intermediate country between that city and Dresden being flat, the soil light and sandy, but well cultivated. At Halle we cross the river Saale, a muddy water, here some thirty feet wide, and farther on pass along the larger of the two Mansfeld lakes, the only salt water in Germany. Twenty-four miles from Halle is Eisleben, the birthplace of Luther in 1483. The house in which he was born and another in which he died here in 1546 are both standing. There are silver-mines near here employing over two thousand men. The face of the country grows more interesting as we advance, and at Wallhausen begins a beautiful and fertile region lying along the river Helme, a small brown stream. Many peaceful villages are passed, the most considerable being Nordhausen on the southern slope of the Harz Mountains, Heiligenstadt on the little river Leine, and Eichenberg. Thence down the valley of the Werra to Witzenhausen, with charming scenery all along, changing trains again at Cassel on the Fulda, once the capital of the Electorate of Hessen and now the seat of the government of the Prussian province of Hesse-Nassau. In the centre of the Friedrichs-Platz stands the statue of the Landgrave Frederick II., who furnished the English during our war for Independence with twelve thousand of his subjects, the hated Hessians, for twenty-two million dollars, nearly two thousand dollars per head.

These poor wretches, torn from their homes and leaving their bones to whiten in an alien land beyond the sea and their memory to the continuing execration of a great nation, had no interest whatever in the war they were engaged in, and were sold bodily to fill the treasury of a petty prince. The world moves, however, and a like act could not possibly occur again in any part of the civilized world.

The station-masters on the German roads are gorgeous in the extreme. The first one I noticed chanced to be a man of a somewhat warlike carriage and mien, and for a moment when considering him I really took him to be a personage of high military rank. His blue double-breasted coat with great gilt buttons and black velvet cuffs, these and the collar faced with a heavy gilt braid, a sort of incipient epaulette sprouting from a big gilt button on each shoulder, a red cap also heavily gilded in the band, and dark broadcloth trousers with a red stripe down the leg constituted him a warrior in appearance fit to figure in one of Wouverman's battle-pieces. And to think that his mission is to come out when the train approaches, stare sternly at the passengers for a space, and then pull a bell to announce the time for leaving!

A most picturesque town is Marburg, with its red-roofed houses, climbing in semicircular tiers up a precipitous hill about the castle at the top, an imposing, well-preserved structure where in 1520 Luther, Zwingli and Melanchthon with other Reformers held a conference to try and come to an agreement upon the nature of the Eucharist, which failed because of Luther's holding fast to the exact words, "*Hoc est corpus meum*," which he wrote in large letters on the table. There is a prosperous university here founded in 1527, attended by a thousand students. Frattini pointed out one of these at the station with a long purple scar on his left cheek, got by the slash of a sword in a duel, and still another, out of the four to be seen in red caps, with a similar mark of foolish courage. The students are said to be very proud of these scars, and exaggerate them by irritation during their healing. From the level at the foot of the hill rise the towers of the Church of St. Elizabeth, pure and noble, to the height of 310 feet.

We follow the fertile valley of the Lahn, with old villages of timber-framed houses filled in with brick, and half a dozen ruined castles frowning darkly from the heights on either side in the advancing twilight, through Friedberg, once a free imperial city, with its well-preserved, handsome watch-tower, 165 feet high, and at last, slackening speed in a maze of many-colored lights, come to a stand in the huge new Central Railway Station of Frankfort-on-the-Main. This important city with its 154,000 inhabitants lies on the right bank of the Main in a spacious plain, with the Taunus range of hills all about. Down to 1866 it was one of the free towns of the German Confederation and the seat of the Diet, but now belongs to Prussia. Although an old city, its antiquity is being rapidly modernized away, and at the rate changes are going on, not only here but everywhere else in fact, the relics of the mediæval ages in a very few years will be largely swept away. In the square before our hotel is a fine monument to Gutenberg, designed by Launitz and erected in 1858. It represents himself, Faust and Schöffer of life size. On the pedestal are portrait heads of fourteen famous printers, among them Caxton. We visited the house of Goethe's father, where the poet was born August 28th, 1749, a large, comfortable mansion, probably among the best of the city at the time it was built. It contains many memorials of his family and himself, among these many busts and portraits, remarkable for their unlikeness to one another.

Very interesting is the Römerberg market-place, the picturesque old buildings around which are mostly unchanged. Among them the Römer, built in 1405, with its three lofty gables and broad, pointed doorways, and halls where the electors used to choose the emperor and where he dined with them afterward, after showing himself to the people from the balcony. The lofty dining-hall is hung with portraits of the emperors, from Charlemagne down, presented by German princes, art and other associations and private persons—a gallery of imposing portraits, as like their subjects, it may be presumed, as the sculptured heads of the English kings in the minster at York.

Until the present century no Jew was permitted to enter this square, and the Judengasse or Jews' Street, where the people of that enterprising nationality were compelled to reside, was closed at night and during Sundays, a precaution which does not seem to have hindered them from driving a good business in the daytime, for here, midway of the old Jews'

Street, now handsomely rebuilt and christened Börne-Strasse, stands at No. 148, as it stood a hundred years ago, the well-looking residence of the founder of the Rothschild family. Their present place of business is near by on the corner, a huge, dull, silent-looking house of massive stone.

The opera house is very imposing. We went to a little museum called the Ariadneum, and saw the group of Ariadne on the panther by Dannecker, the Stuttgart sculptor, so well known in America from the little Parian copies of it. It is shown in a small circular room, the light excluded except from above, whence it falls through a flesh-colored curtain upon the beautiful figure as it slowly revolves on its pedestal to meet the eye of the spectator.

There is an old bridge of red sandstone over the Main, built in 1342. Near by the statue of Charlemagne in a recess of the parapet half way over, is a very old figure of Christ on an iron cross surmounted by a cock, the image of the one with which the architect paid his vow to sacrifice to the devil the first living creature crossing the bridge.

*August* 7.—At 3.30 P.M. by rail to Homburg, that naughty old watering-place, fourteen miles north of Frankfort, and found shelter in the crowded Four Seasons, this being the height of the fashionable season. This little town of 8500 inhabitants is charmingly situated on a low spur of the Taunus Mountains, which projects itself into a wide, fertile valley, the higher ranges of the same hills lying three miles distant, and culminating in the Great Feldberg, 2900 feet high. Some ten to twelve thousand visitors come here annually to enjoy the diversions and drink the water of half a dozen springs of saline and chalybeate properties, and I should judge, from the taste and the account of them by Fr. Hoeber, M.D., "Sanitary Councillor to H.M. the King of Prussia"—a fair pamphlet in which I invested one mark and eighty pfenning—quite the same as half a dozen which might be selected out of the some thirty now gushing at Saratoga. These springs are situated in the midst of prettily wooded grounds, and in their long, shaded avenues, during the hours when the waters are taken from seven to nine in the morning, a great multitude of people of both sexes and all ages and conditions of physical being promenade about, waiting the time for a second or third glass from some prescribed spring or attending upon the complete digestion of the regular allowance to the accompaniment of a good band.

There are agreeable walks into the neighboring country for the more hardy and adventurous visitors and an extensive tennis lawn rimmed round with stately and flourishing forest-trees, specially affected by the younger people, who, scattered prettily about on the rich turf, display their graceful skill to each other and to the groups of comfortable older people seated in stuffed willow chairs under great gaudy umbrellas. There is very little driving, and nothing of the fine show of equipages we see at Saratoga. All is quiet and orderly, with no appearance of the brilliant wickedness we read about in books written twenty years ago. But the gaming-tables here then attracted male and female adventurers from all Europe, and fortunes were lost and made—chiefly lost—on the green cloth spread in the gorgeous halls of Mons. Blanc, whose prosperity was blighted some seventeen years ago by the fiat of the government, which closed his establishment. This gentleman gracefully yielded and presented the building and fair grounds adjoining to the town, and these now form the Cursaal, and his costly apartments are used as dancing-hall, concert, reading-rooms, etc. On the north side, fronting the grounds, extends a wide, light piazza for some 300 feet, with a few broad steps leading down to a wide terrace of equal length, from which is easy descent to the grounds themselves. The piazza is set with little tables, where light refreshments may be ordered ; the terrace-floor is of smooth, firm earth strown thick with fine sand, and here all the world comes in the evening to promenade back and forth in the full electric light, the ladies in handsome costumes looking their best, the younger ones under the eyes of observant parents or chaperones, willing to captivate and not unwilling to be captivated in turn. One sees a pretty face or figure now and then— one where in a like gathering in America he would see ten. It cannot be said that the German maidens here are well-favored. There are many solid, fresh-looking English families, with a sprinkling of Americans, the latter quite at home and bearing themselves with easy nonchalance, as if Homburg were the most natural place in the world for them. Many stylish, self-possessed German officers saunter by in handsome uniforms, the bright metal scabbards of their long, trailing swords leaving a line in the sandy terrace as they pass. By ten o'clock the excellent band has finished its programme, the company melts away into the numerous hotels and more numerous pensions, and the mild dissipation is ended.

We made a long drive to the Saalburg, said to be the remains of the walls of a Roman castle built about the year 70 A.D. to protect the Germanic provinces Rome had conquered from the incursions of other German tribes. These ruins are on the lower summit of the line of the Taunus range, 1300 feet above the sea-level, and look to the unpracticed eye like a row of stone-walled cellars from which the houses over them had been removed—very prosaic memorials of old Rome, if such they be. The widow of the late Emperor Frederick has a castellated residence near the town in spacious grounds, and is at present residing here. Everything indicates that Homburg is a healthful, as it certainly is a pleasant and cheerful resort.

*August* 10.—Left for Frankfort at 10 A.M., and at 11 took train there for Strassburg, arriving at 5.30 P.M. to find pleasant rooms at the Hotel Ville de Paris. Seventeen miles from Frankfort we reach Darmstadt, the capital of the Grand Duchy of Hessen, a bright-looking town of 54,000 souls. Here begins the Bergstrasse, an old road made by the Romans and continued in repair and use, which skirts the rounded hills of the Odenwald range for twenty-seven miles to Heidelberg. The railway lies parallel to this road, the slopes of the Odenwald fresh with vines and fruit-trees and frequent ruins of castles and towers on the left and a wide expanse of cultivated plain on the right. These towers, perched on high commanding points, were in the middle ages the nests of robber barons and lawless knights, whence they swooped down on the defenceless ; and I made for our solace, as we went along at the slow German rate of about twenty-five miles an hour, many a picture of timid merchants with long trains of sumpter-horses laden with rich stuffs, toilfully wending northward, with many an anxious glance at these frowning keeps, momently expecting, and not in vain, to hear the blast of the warder's horn, sharply on the lookout for their approach. Then the hot mounting in the court-yard, the clang of steel, the resounding drawbridge as the marauding band rides clattering over it, the noonday sun glancing from helm and lance, the swift attack, the pillage, the pale trader left penniless, fortunate if his life be spared, the gay return to the mountain fastness with the rich booty, and the wild carouse at night by the red glare of flaming torches, lighting up the warlike furnishing of the great hall. These are things of the past, but the gray strongholds stand along the Odenwald, memorials of those fierce and bloody centuries when war and rapine were the vocation of the strong, and society knew but two classes, the oppressor and the oppressed.

I hoped that in old Strassburg we should find mediæval architecture and unusual and strange customs, manners and costumes. The first thing I noticed on emerging from the station was a tramcar of the latest fashion pulled by a pair of solid horses on an excellent track along a modern street paved with square granite blocks, a line of hackney landaus, and pedestrians in easy garments, the like of which are shown in the windows of the Bowery clothing-stores. Still, the march of innovation has spared many a strange old building in out-of-the-way streets crooked and narrow, as if shrinking together and seeking to hide themselves. A feature new to me appears in these old houses; enormously high and steep roofs mostly with four ranges of queer dormer-windows in them. But one would hardly find Strassburg attractive enough to warrant a visit except for its cathedral, and this will amply repay any pains. I have given up the description of these noblest of man's works in dumb despair. This was three hundred years building, a stretch of time extending from the twelfth to the fifteenth centuries, during which time the Romanesque style passed by gradations into the pure Gothic, so that the various parts show examples of all styles. Many famous architects gave their lives to the work in turn, among them Erwin von Steinbach, a rare soul, to whom is due the glorious west façade with three richly carved portals, said to be among the finest Gothic works in the world, and the great rose-window above them, exquisite as the flower it is named after, with its wonderful old glass. The entire façade, including the Gothic Three Portals, is wrought in delicate tracery, and ornamented with hundreds of sculptured figures and imposing statues. From it rises the single tower to the dizzy height of 465 feet, 30 feet higher than the dome of St. Peter's in Rome. It is of delicate open work and the distant summit is airy and almost bodiless, like the fabric of a dream. The interior with its broad central aisle is harmonious and impressive, altogether a thing of beauty. The material is chiefly a red sandstone which resists the tooth of time so well, that the exterior shows few marks of age, and the injuries done by the bombarding Germans in 1870 have been carefully repaired.

In the south transept is the famous clock built by Schwilgué, a Strassburg clockmaker, in 1838-42, to replace an older one constructed in 1571, which was in use down to 1789. The beautifully painted case of the old one is all that was used in the new. It exhibits itself at noon every day, and on Sunday we attended the manifestations. Precisely at twelve o'clock a figure of Death strikes the hour on a bell in his left hand with a hammer in his right, and as he begins, an image of a genius turns the hour-glass he is holding; before the image of Christ higher up the twelve apostles pass in order bowing before Him while He waves them a benediction, and a cock on His right, looking like life, flaps his wings and crows three times in the most natural manner. The quarters are struck in turn by four images: the first of Childhood, the second of Youth, the third of Manhood and the fourth of Old Age. Each day its symbolic deity moves out of a niche, Apollo for Sunday, Diana for Monday, and so on. I bought a thin pamphlet of a handsome and much-begilt verger with a long staff of office, and have read with interest what this wonderful piece of mechanism is capable of, and will say in brief that it exhibits a perpetual calendar with the variable feasts, an orrery after the Copernican system, showing the phases of the moon, the eclipses of the sun and moon calculated for all time, a celestial globe with the precession of the equinoxes, and so on, the whole regulating itself and fitting its motions to those of the seasons—altogether a wonder of a clock.

In the Protestant Church of St. Thomas, which dates back to 1273, is a magnificent and strikingly original monument erected to Marshal Saxe, the victor of Fontenoy, done by Pigalle at the order of Louis XV. of France. It was finished in 1776, after twenty years of labor. Very impressive is the manly figure of the Marshal as he steps fearlessly forward to the open coffin to which the half-shrouded figure of Death is beckoning him, while an agonizing female typifying France, strives to detain him, and Hercules leaning mournfully on his club, looks helplessly on. The figures are of heroic size, and the whole is startlingly realistic.

Noticed a huge stork's nest on the broad capstone of a stack of chimneys rising from a lofty roof. It is said that formerly great numbers of these birds inhabited the roofs in this manner, but the bombardment in 1870 frightened them away.

This city has long had a reputation for its *pâté de foie gras*, which it continues to prepare and export in great quantity. Frattini says that to obtain the enormous livers of which two fill one of the cans sold in the shops, the geese are nailed by the feet to the floor of a warm room and stuffed with food to the point where the enlarged livers threaten suffocation and then killed. I did not verify this statement.

Strassburg, with its 100,000 inhabitants, is the capital of Alsace and Lorraine, the seat of the governor and administration of that province, the headquarters of the 15th Corps of the German Army and the see of a Roman Catholic bishop. It is situated on the river Ill two miles from the Rhine, and is connected with the latter by a canal. Louis XIV. seized it in 1681, without the shadow of a cause in a time of peace, having before annexed to France the rest of Alsace, and time brought its revenge in 1870, when Germany with a strong arm took it back. It has always been looked on as a place of great strategical importance and kept heavily fortified. It withstood a siege by the Germans in 1870 for thirty days, during which the citadel and other works erected by the great engineer Vauban in 1682 were destroyed by the bombs of the besiegers, and many parts of the town, including the Cathedral, suffered greatly. But all damages have been repaired and a great system of earthworks established all around the town, extending out for some five miles. As there are twenty-five thousand soldiers stationed here, they are to be met everywhere, as in all the German cities we visit, hearty, vigorous young men, looking well used to labor, marching, drilling, and strolling about the streets.

*August* 12.—At 8 A.M. left Strassburg by rail and a few miles out, at Offenburg, changed to a train on the Schwarzwald Railway, running directly across the mountainous region known as the Black Forest, named so probably from the dark masses of pine which closely clothe all the hills and valleys of this extensive tract. We enter upon the mountains by the fertile valley of the bright little stream called Kinzig, rounded mountains sloping gently down to it, on one of which, vine-clad, rises the Château of Ortenberg, overlooking a village of the same name. At Gengenbach, six and one half miles away, we have risen 580 feet, and note the fine old Benedictine Abbey there. At Hausach the road leaves the valley of the Kinzig and ascends the picturesque valley of the Gutach, a clear little stream, babbling like the New England brooks, and at Hornberg, twenty-seven miles from Offenburgow, on the level plain, we have risen 1265 feet. All about are charming pictures capped by a château on a precipitous hill. At Triberg, eight miles farther on, in the heart of the Black Forest, we are 2000 feet above the sea, and at St. Georgen, ten miles away, 2660, winding up the heights in loops and zigzags—so that often we see a stretch of the road in a parallel line below us—over lofty viaducts and through twenty-six tunnels in eighteen miles. The highest point reached is at Sommerau, 2730 feet, the watershed of the Rhine and Danube, where we emerge through a tunnel of 1852 yards, the whole constituting a wonderful feat of engineering, reminding one of the Colorado Division of the Union Pacific and Denver and Rio Grande railways.

At St. Georgen we enter the valley of the Brigach, a little mountain stream which, running twenty miles, unites at Donaueschingen with the Brege, a like stream, and forms the great Danube, which, after traversing western Germany, discharges its enormous volume of water into the Black Sea, 1872 miles away as the river runs. We cross the plateau and descend the gradually sloping side of the mountain range to Donaueschingen, thence along the flat and marshy line of the Danube, giving, like a dull boy, little indication of the greatness before it. At Singen we turn southward to Schaffhausen and reach the excellent Hotel Schweizerhof at Newhausen at 3 P.M., and are met and served by brown, healthy maidens in picturesque Swiss costumes.

A great many beautiful scenes passed under our eyes during the passage of the Black Forest, heightened by the strange and quaint character of the construction of the dwellings, both in the villages and country-side, all along the way. Deep in the green recesses of the hills and along the narrow valleys and on the mountain-sides stand long, one-story weather-browned wooden houses with steep thatched roofs twice as high as themselves and balconied gables hooded by the drooping projection of the roof. Often, especially in the little villages, these houses are of two stories, with a wide, open balcony running all along the sides. Many were the ruined castles and châteaux perched on high among the mountains. Nigh a score of these we saw during the day, and very notable among them, as we skirt the Hohgau, are those of Hohensinger and Hohentwiel, frowning from the summit of lofty, detached volcanic cones, well-nigh inaccessible to man and impregnable before the use of gunpowder. The latter stronghold is famous in German song and story.

At Neuhausen, in full view of the balcony of our rooms at the hotel, are the famous Falls of the Rhine. The river above—the water of the deepest green—is something over 500 feet wide and descends in three almost continuous leaps some 60 feet, broken into the whitest foam, with a deep roar not so heavy as to be disagreeable to the ear. It is usual to count the swift but not striking rapids above as a part of the falls, and call the whole 100 feet. Although not great compared with several in our country, these are considered among the finest in Europe, and taken in connection with the charming surroundings, the Falls of the Rhine are to be greatly commended, and I do hereby commend them. Every evening a strong electric light is thrown upon them, and they are lit up by many Bengal lights, red and green and blue, along the sides and from the craggy peak rising in the middle of the stream. The effect is beautiful, and noticeable in the bills of the guests, where each one is charged a mark toward the expense of the exhibition, and cheap enough, as any one will admit who has seen the fairy effect upon the foamy green of the waters and the old gray turreted walls of the Schloss Munoth on the high bank opposite the garden of the Hotel Schweizerhof. May they flow and foam and murmur many a year, and the good hotel stand facing them as now.

*August* 13.—Were driven in a comfortable omnibus something over a mile up to Schaffhausen, where at 10 A.M. we took a little steamboat up the Rhine to Constance. Schaffhausen is the capital of the Swiss canton of the same name, has nearly 12,000 inhabitants and is quaint and picturesque, words I find myself often using for the want of better in my slender vocabulary. In the Cathedral hangs a big bell cast in 1486, with a Latin inscription, "*Vivos voco: mortuos plango: fulgura frango.*" The Castle of Munot has almost the finest roundtower I have seen, with a conical projecting cap.

The squat captain of our little boat has, I think, the most remarkable nose ever bestowed on man. It resembles an enormous toad in a high state of inflammation applied to his face back up, a nose corrugated, carbuncled, Bardolphian, lustrous, wonderful! The late Dr. Valentine Mott would have begged of its owner the favor of removing it without charge. The crew in uniforms do not hold themselves better than the passengers, but condescend to occupy the choicest positions under the awning, and smoke and enjoy themselves, the captain looking on, probably to see that the passengers do not insult them. At one landing a jovial person with a green apron got aboard, and a smart shower falling, he took position under the awning and entertained the crew, who gathered about, with waggish stories, which caused prodigious laughter and quite hindered any one from giving attention to anything else.

We steamed up against the stiff current of the beautiful Rhine, the northern bank on our left rising into gentle hills covered with vines lying warmly to the sun, the southern into woody stretches and cultivated fields. Wise and solemn storks sat here and there on the trees by the shore and would not stir for all the noise made to frighten them. Old gray and brown villages repose sleepily on either side, often the time-stained walls of the street next the water being washed by the current.

At Stein is a Rathhaus charming to see, and on a hill near Berlingen rises a château built by Eugene Beauharnais, son of the Empress Josephine by her first husband, and a little farther on a residence of his sister, Hortense, the mother of Napoleon III., and now owned by the ex-Empress Eugenie. The river has widened before this point is reached into the broad Untersee, but narrows again as we pass Gottlieben, in the château of which Huss and Jerome of Prague were confined before their execution.

Landed at the pier in Constance at 1.30 P.M. and found excellent apartments ready at the Konstanzer Hof, charmingly situated where the river emerges from the lake. Constance —Konstanz—is a very old city, and formerly much more prosperous than now. A population of 40,000 has dwindled away during the last three centuries to 14,000. It was a free town until 1548, but became subject to Austria after the Reformation, and in 1805 became a part of Baden, so that it is now a German city. It is agreeably situated on the Rhine at the northwest extremity of Lake Constance, which stretches away before it for forty miles, with a width of some seven miles. It is really a huge basin of the waters of the Rhine. So far as we can see, the shores are gently sloping, with a pleasant diversity of wood and cultivated fields, but to the eastward would be seen, did the weather permit, the chain of the Appenzell Alps with their snow-clad peak of the Sentis, all shut from us in our two days here by banks of sullen clouds. The Cathedral dates from 1052, but has been rebuilt, and its open spire of light gray sandstone is quite modern. It has at the western portal doors of oak beautifully carved by Haider in 1470, and exquisite wrought-iron screens before several of the chapels. A stone is pointed out in the nave where Huss is said to have stood when he received his death sentence, and in the Kaufhaus or Town Hall is the great Council Chamber where the conclave of cardinals met in 1414. The massive oak pillars supporting the roof still stand, and the form and structure are unchanged, but it has lately been wainscoted anew and decorated with frescoes illustrating the history of the town. West of the city and outside the walls as it then was is the spot where Jerome of Prague and Huss were burned in 1416, marked by a great boulder with inscriptions.

We were served at dinner with a very good fish something like our sea-bass, called felchen, and, as I was informed, peculiar to the lake.

*August* 15.—Left for Zurich by rail at 10 A.M. Although the distance is only seventy-six miles, we were three and a half hours making it. We followed the Rhine back on the route we came as far as Stein, reviewing the points of interest along its banks and again admiring specially the well-preserved Castle of Hohenklingen, dominating the valley from a lofty point opposite Stein. Turning to the left at this point we cross the Thur over a fine bridge 148 feet high, change cars at Winterthur, and half an hour later are at the charmingly situated Hotel Baur au Lac, whose well-kept gardens run down to the narrow lake of Zurich, stretching away southeast for twenty-five miles, its waters of a pale green hue. The country we passed over to-day is about 1500 feet above the sea-level, and presents in its vegetation an appearance very like upper New England. The same kinds of crops are grown, with wayside weeds and flowers mostly the same. I noticed a little patch of Indian corn doing as well as could be expected among strangers and in an alien soil, where, I fear me, it is more mocked at than respected. What do the benighted people of this Continent know of the supreme satisfaction of boiled corn on the ear, succotash and fried mush? Cows are worked in harness singly and in pairs, the draught being on a stuffed band of leather applied just below the horns. They work contentedly and easily, with moderate loads, and look in good condition. All along, wherever we have been on the Continent, women work in the fields in numbers, I should say, equal to the men, but this may be especially the case in the time of harvest. The tools used seemed to one accustomed to the light, handy implements of our farmers, clumsy and bungling, but the work seems to be well and quickly done with them. I noticed a farmer mowing a short, second growth of clover with a most awkward scythe, having only one long handle, which he clutched near the top in such a way that nothing could be expected of him, but the swath he cut was clean and smooth as could be wished.

Zurich is a handsome town of 25,000 population, situated at the north end of the lake of the same name, on the river Limmat, which drains the lake into the Rhine. It is the capital of the canton of the same name, is a prosperous city with important manufactories of silk and cotton. Unless one takes pains to turn aside to get into them, he might stay here a month and see no streets not lately built up in solid and expensive styles, chiefly of excellent stone. Made a trip up the lake extending its entire length of twenty-five miles in a comfortable steamboat doing business up and down the lake, stopping at many points on the north side both in going and coming. This long, narrow, deep and winding sheet of clearest water in a rim of gradually rising hills, or rather mountains, with many an old village and single farm-house amid the green meadows and tilled fields of the more level shores, then orchards and sloping pastures, and, higher still, woodlands open to the sun. But on the north shore, with a southern exposure, miles of vines attached to short stakes in even, well-tended rows bask in the hot sun, promising fruitful clusters and a fair wine later on. The trip used up the greater part of the day, and the whole scene lay before the bodily eye like the vision of a peaceful dream. Sweet bells answered one another across the lake out of square, gray towers tipped with tall, slim spires of dull red, and, as we neared Rapperswyl, the low, rich little island of Ufnau rose fair with its Abbey of Einsiedeln, a ruin now, where intrepid Ulrich von Hutton, the stout Reformer, came for refuge from his enemies, and died in 1523. How true it is that men live in deeds, not years! He died at the age of thirty-six.

We lunched at Rapperswyl, and climbed the Lindenhof and had a wide view of great beauty from among the huge lime-trees in front of the old Schloss, now a museum of articles relating to Poland, of not much interest. We should have had the Appenzell range of the Alps in good view all day, but heavy clouds have hid the east since our arrival, and not a single peak shone on our waiting eyes until on the morning we left Zurich, as we attained the top of the Uetliberg, the northernmost point of the Albis range, 2864 feet high, we had a glorious view, sweeping from the Sentis to the Jungfrau, and just in front the Rigi and Pilatus. But for envious clouds in the north we might have seen the peaks of the Hohgau, Hohentwiel, etc. The railway up the Uetliberg, constructed in the usual way, only that the engines run behind the trains, rises about 1500 feet in five and one-half miles. A beautiful panorama is spread before the observer along the slowly winding way to the summit, Zurich town and lake, many a soft and bold valley, shining village and lofty snow-clad mountain.

*August* 17.—Came by railway to Lucerne, forty-one and one-half miles, in two and one-half hours, through pleasing mountain scenery, with many a verdant valley and narrow meadow and smiling pasture sloping to the sun, with sleek, gentle cows feeding, and narrow fields where tanned and brawny harvesters were cutting, binding and stooking the quite good wheat, or resting in tired groups, men, women and children gathered about the luncheon-baskets and big, blue water-jugs under the apple-trees, quite numerously planted here, but, unless this is an "off year," not flourishing well. The apple-trees, as well as the numerous pear-trees, look neglected, and I should think neither here nor in Germany where we have been, is much care given to the cultivation of fruit. We skirt the little lake of Zug, exquisitely set in its ring of great mountains, enter on the valley of the broad, green Reuss, which bounds joyously along to join the Rhine after its confluence with the Limmat, forming the Aare. The Reuss both feeds and empties the Lake of Lucerne, or, as it stands on Swiss maps, the Vierwaldstätter See, and Lucerne is situated at the point of its discharge.

Lucerne is a walled city of some 18,000 population, and the capital of the canton of the same name. It lies more than 1400 feet above the sea-level, and beautiful for situation it is on this emerald water, wherein most famous Alpine peaks, white with snow, look to see themselves reflected not by day only, but in the night, under the awful silence of the stars. All the world comes here to worship nature in the prescribed and fashionable way. The Hotel Schweizerhof, where we have rooms looking down the lake, shelters six hundred and fifty guests, lodges numbers in private houses, and turns many away. Looking over only two recent pages of the register, I find names from Melbourne, San Francisco, New York, Montreal, London, Paris, Russia, Roumania, Egypt, Rome, Naples, Madrid, and so on. English and Americans outnumber all others. Near at hand on the right rises the bare and jagged peak of Pilatus from its foot-hills of fair pastures, shining out from dark masses of pines, deeply serrated and gashed with frightful chasms; on the left, the Rigi, ending precipitously on the north, but sloping away southward into green pasture lands, whereon thousands of cattle find nourishment in the short, sweet grass, and still lower into tilled fields and orchards of fig, chestnut and almond trees. In front rise, rank above rank, countless peaks of the Uri range, each with its significant German name, some in cold, naked grandeur, with lofty ravines, with glaciers, and others verdurous to the very tops. There is a goodly stretch of the old town wall left on the west side, with half a dozen fine towers in perfect preservation. At some remote age a glacier tore its way through the rim of hills, cutting a deep chasm through what is now the centre of the town, leaving precipitous walls of sandstone. In the face of one of these is carved the well-known Lion of Lucerne, from a model by Thorwaldsen. The majestic lion, twenty-eight feet in length, lies dying, transfixed by a broken lance, noble and impressive, in his last agony still guarding with nerveless paw the Bourbon lily, signifying that his blood is shed not for the Swiss fatherland, but for France. The effigy commemorates the twenty-six officers and seven hundred and sixty soldiers of the Swiss Guard who fell in defence of the Tuileries, August 10th, 1792. One thinks sadly that this great monument perpetuates the memory of mercenaries who fell bravely fighting in defence of an alien despot, and would prefer that it kept before the eyes of the Swiss the heroic virtues of that earlier and better time when their fathers knew so well how to roll back from their mountain passes the tides of Burgundian and Austrian invasions, and the bare breast of Winkelried harvested so many hostile spears that liberty came in by the way he made. He too has a fine monument in a village near by, showing him in act of falling, struck through with many spears.

We sailed up the full length of the lake, including the south arm, called Urner See, or Lake of Uri. On the east bank of this lake, not far from its union with the Lake of Lucerne, stands a little chapel to William Tell, erected on the site of one built by Canton Uri in 1388, on the spot where Tell is said to have sprung from Gessler's boat. Once a year, on Friday after Ascension Day, mass is said and a sermon preached at 7 A.M., when the people assemble in gala form in boats gayly bedecked. And now come along the cold-blooded critics and say, and perhaps prove, that no William Tell ever existed, and that all his exploits are the merest fable. This is a pity, for it is a noble myth, if myth it be, dignified and worthy of the brave people who have believed it for so many years, and long will it be before it fades from the popular heart. The deep green waters of this narrow lake are closely shut in by magnificent mountains smiling to their frozen tops with pastoral scenes, sweet and tender amid the awful grandeur cast from above.

We made the ascent of Rigi from the pretty town of Vitznau on Lake Lucerne by a railway whose engines use the cogged wheels familiar to Americans on the road up Mount Washington. The road-bed is solidly laid in the conglomerate rock, the maximum grade is one foot in four, and something over an hour is used in reaching the top or kulm, where is a capital hotel, four stories high, solidly built of stone, brick and cement, a building, both in its handsome exterior and well-finished inside, which would do credit to any large town. The view from all sides is wonderfully fine, ranks of pinnacled Alps, snow-clad, stretching away interminably; a shining sea storm-tossed, delightful valleys fresh with verdure, green lakes far below, on whose edges clustering villages lift their red roofs with many a spire and tower; a broad, rich, indescribable panorama, of which no idea has or can be conveyed to a human soul except through the organs of sight. Almost under our feet lies bright Lake Lucerne; near by, an emerald gem, Lake Zug, and shining not far off, Lakes Sempach and Egeri, near which were fought the two famous battles of Sempach and Morgarten. Sentis, Glarus, the Wetterhorn, the Eiger, the Jungfrau, and many another famous Alpine peak and pinnacle are visible. I cannot speak of them in any fitting terms.

We look northward right across a most fair valley upon a prolonged mass of mingled earth and rocks, now partly covered with vegetation, reaching from the base of Rossberg far out into the narrow plain, and think with awe how on the 3d of September, 1806, this enormous and gloomy mass slid from the steep side of the mountain, leaving a vast space bare and yellow where it became detached, and in a mass a mile long, 1000 feet wide and 100 feet thick, fell on the pretty and thriving village of Goldau and buried it and more than seven hundred villagers forever out of sight, and lies there, darkly, under our eyes this sunny day, amid the stagnant pools which have formed about it; the gloomy burial-mound of a whole community. I remember when a lad reading a striking account of this great calamity written by some able pen, it being the unlikeliest notion to me, in my pioneer home on a Western prairie, that I should ever visit the scene of it.

Here at Lucerne are the very birthplace and cradle of Swiss liberty and the Swiss nation. The three forest cantons of Schwyz, Uri and Unterwalden border on the lake. Their league for mutual defence against Austria in 1291 was the nucleus of the confederacy which gradually extended through five centuries of various fortune, and now embraces twenty-two cantons, constituting the Republic of Switzerland.

I engaged Bossard, a sturdy Swiss, with his four horses to make a carriage journey over the Alps into Italy by the St. Gothard Pass. We leave Lucerne regretfully. I did not think earth had anything at once so fair and so sublime as the scenes outspread on every hand.

*August* 22. —We take leave of the excellent Hotel Schweizerhof, where we have met many American acquaintances, at 7.30 A.M., breakfast on the steamboat which conveys us to Brunnen, at the head of the lake, and at once take our hired carriage, which drove up yesterday so as to start fresh this morning, as to-day's drive is to be long and hard. The carriage is a sort of drag with a landau body, a seat in front for two, over which a hood like a buggy-top can be drawn, and in front of that still another, holding the driver and Frattini. Behind is a strong rack easily taking two big trunks, and under it a close box with a tight-fitting door, in which handbags, extra wraps, etc., are carried. The horses look strong and seasoned and are fitted out with red tassels and pleasant-jingling bells. Our plan is to make the Pass of St. Gothard so far as the Hospice on the highest ridge, then return to Hospenthal and make the Furka Pass much beyond, so that we must climb up to Andermatt to-day.

We skirt the east shore of Lake Uri on a splendid road high above the lake, built at enormous cost, and guarded at all curves by a solid stone parapet and elsewhere by heavy stone posts set in the ground about ten feet apart. Considerable distances are blasted out of the solid rock, with several tunnels and cuttings. At one point, in a long tunnel through a rocky projection, a wide opening has been made toward the lake, affording a magnificent view of the noble mountain forms which rise sharply from the opposite shore, as well as of the deep green lake far below. At ten miles Fluelen is reached, 1434 feet above the sea-level. This is the port of Uri and the starting-point of the high-road over the St. Gothard. Two miles farther is Altdorf, the capital of the canton of Uri, pleasantly nestled among the feet of the mountains. This village is the scene of many exploits of Tell, and a big statue of plaster stands in the little square on the spot where he is said to have stood when he split the apple on his son's head with his arrow. This was erected in 1861. About four hundred feet distant from the statue is a fountain with a statue to a local dignitary styled Besler. This is believed to stand on the site of the lime-tree against which the boy was placed. This tree is said to have been standing in 1567. About a mile to the right is Bürglen, another charmingly located village, where Tell is said to have been born, and we got a glimpse of a chapel erected on the site of his house in 1522. I am not familiar with the evidence by which it is sought to establish that this Swiss hero never lived nor did the deeds attributed to him, but it should be of a clear and convincing kind. It will hardly answer that certain early chroniclers did not mention his name, for that might easily be, since the early historians were a queer lot, and scarcely more likely to record what did than what did not happen.

We lunch at Amsteg, where we are 1760 feet above the sea, and at Andermatt, where we pass the night, thirty-five miles from Brunnen, 4738 feet. All day we have followed up the course of the Reuss, a turbulent Alpine stream, foamy and discolored with the grayish particles of triturated rock it is sweeping down from the glacial source of its principal branch high among the summits of the St. Gothard Alps. It sweeps roaring down, tumbling in white cascades, gliding in rapids, boiling in eddies, and fed on either hand by frequent streamlets gliding like silvery serpents down the abrupt crags lining its narrow valley. All the way up we climb by the zigzag windings of an admirable road kept in perfect order by constant attention, through scenery on either hand of the grandest and most beautiful description. The gigantic mountains which shut in the narrow valley of the Reuss, throughout its entire extent, lift their summits above the clouds, crowned with everlasting snow or bare and desolate, but their feet clothed with the richest verdure, and the eye rests on a succession of exquisite pastoral scenes, soft as the Vale of Tempe. Nor is the presence of man wanting to vivify the picture. At incredible and, so far as the eye can see, inaccessible heights stands many a châlet with its little patch of pasture and still smaller bit of tilled field clinging with steep slope to the mountain-side, or lining the depths of rocky recesses with liveliest verdure.

The weather signs were not favorable when we left Lucerne

in the morning; Pilatus had donned all his storm insignia, cap, collar and sword, the barometer threatened, while on the lake in the morning we had rough wind and a heavy rain, which moderated and ceased by fits all day, but clouds rested always on the highest peaks. Toward evening the rain grew heavier and the clouds came deeper down the sides of the mountains, and at Devil's Bridge, a little way below Andermatt, where the Reuss rushes far below, a torrent of gray foam churned by its fall of a hundred feet, the wind swirled down the deep rifts of the mountains and up the gorge of the Reuss, bearing swift-flying trails and streamers of watery vapor, deepening the natural horrors of the spot by fitfully obscuring the "Hell of waters," whose deafening roar deadened all other sounds. At a point not far below the bridge the road is covered for several rods by a heavy shed of stone to protect it from the avalanches so frequent there.

The quaint old village of Andermatt is charmingly situated on a plain made from the deposits of the Reuss, where its valley widens for nearly a mile. It is a good deal of a health resort, and the Hotel Bellevue, a large, well built and finished house, with "dependences" or smaller buildings near by, is filled with guests.

*August* 23.—Although the weather is threatening, we start at 9 A.M. to cross the St. Gothard, and follow from the hamlet of Hospenthal at the head of the Urseren-Thal—as the broad valley on which Andermatt is situated is called— the smaller of the two branches of the Reuss, rising in Lake Lucendro, a clear mountain stream, like the mountain brooks of New England, and haunted by trout, as we proved at Andermatt this morning, where we had a mess for breakfast and found them excellent, as well as the honey, these being two local products much esteemed. We mounted up by continuous zigzags, the gloom and desolation increasing, with effect heightened by the lowering sky and falling rain; yet, at the very Pass itself, 6936 feet above the sea, and all along the valley leading up to it, is such abundance of vegetation as to keep herds in pasture, and they are driven up from Italy for the summer. At a point not far below the Pass was a flock of two hundred and twenty-four big, white, handsome sheep, tranquilly resting in the care of two swarthy Italians with slouched hats and long, ample cloaks. At a quarter of a mile south of the highest point is a decent hotel, the Hotel du Mont Prosa, where we were glad to take shelter from the rain, which now came down furiously. We lunched there, and during the P.M. came back to Andermatt in a pouring rain, safely sheltered in our landau, and took rooms at the Bellevue for the night, proposing to make the Furka Pass next day. The night was cold and dreary, with heavy rain, changing to snow before morning, when the mountains and valleys were covered in a deep mantle of it, and more still falling. We decided to give up the Furka Pass and went down to Göschenen, where we took the 11.45 A.M. train on the St. Gothard road for Lugano. At Göschenen this wonderful road enters the tunnel, nine and one-quarter miles long, through the St. Gothard Mountain. We occupied twenty-three minutes in the passage, and came out on the Italian side in the warmth of summer. Two hours before, we left people shovelling snow, to find others basking under a hot sun, harvesting hay. We wind down to the level of Lake Lugano by easy, zigzag gradients with many tunnels, following the swift and clear Ticino, and leaving the beautiful valley of it at Bellinzona, are soon at the delightfully situated Hotel du Parc in Lugano, with charming views from our rooms upon the lake of that name.

This is the largest town of the Italian Swiss canton of Ticino, with 6000 population, and a delightful spot it is. Our hotel was once the monastery of Santa Maria degli Angioli, prosperous and fatly endowed, I ween, if one may judge from the big, comfortable rooms and high-arched corridors, ample cloisters and fair refectory, now changed into the good restaurant, where I am sure the wines are not better now than the befrocked cellarer could draw in the vaulted crypts below. The church of the old convent immediately adjoins the hotel, and is made famous by the frescoes of Bernardino Luini on its walls. The great space of the rood-screen is wholly covered with his picture of "The Crucifixion;" on the walls of a side-aisle is a "Last Supper," and in a chapel a "Madonna," of which I have a fine engraving at home and always greatly admired. These masterpieces were painted on the plaster of the walls early in the sixteenth century, and have lost much of their freshness by the dampness, and to save them, in the case of all except "The Crucifixion," the whole portion of the plaster containing them has been ingeniously cut out, secured upon some kind of substantial backing, framed, and replaced against the walls, but some inches removed from them.

*August* 26.—Went by a small steamboat down Lake Lugano to Ponte Tresa, thence crossed by rail to Luino on Lake Maggiore. We underwent the Italian Custom-House at Ponte Tresa, where I was compelled to pay one franc for each five ounces of a half box of cigars I had in a hand-bag. This made me feel quite at home, especially as the low-browed, black-muzzled bandits who ploughed through our luggage had manners quite like the tobacco-squirting Texans who rifled our luggage, on behalf of Uncle Sam, at El Paso, to levy toll on a few Mexican curiosities we had ventured to bring home from our tour in Mexico.

At Luino, where Garibaldi won a battle against the Austrians and is honored with a striking statue in the square fronting the lake, took steamboat down Lake Maggiore to Stresa, and passed the night at the commodious Hotel des Iles Borromées, fronting the lake at its finest part and in the midst of beautiful grounds. Most charming is the view from the balcony on which our rooms open, and it is not easy to imagine a more beautiful scene than the fair lake bordered by a great variety of wooded and pinnacled mountains and beset with shining villages. We would gladly remain here a week, but have not yet got through with the Alps. The fair Borromean Islands lie just off Stresa—Isola Madre, Isola dei Pescatori and Isola Bella—on the last of which one of the old and famous Borromeo family erected a château in the latter part of the seventeenth century and laid out fantastic grounds.

Frattini engaged Jacob Heininger with his five horses to carry us over the Simplon. Jacob produced a testimonial from an eminent New York physician beginning " My Dear Heininger," and ending with an invitation to visit him in New York as his friend, both he and his wife signing it. As it stated Jacob had driven the worthy couple for a month with great acceptance, I instructed Frattini to secure him at once, and at 8.30 A.M., the 27th of August, we set forth in great style, the plumes waving from each horse's head, the bells jingling, and the entire *personnel* of the hotel bowing and scraping. Bossard, who drove us over the St. Gothard Pass, had an idiotic way of incessantly cracking his whip to urge on his horses, they having become entirely indifferent to it, but Jacob uses the most extraordinary means to that end ever conceived of. Indeed, I cannot help thinking the doctor found it a phenomenon so interesting from a medical point of view, that he was led to value Jacob beyond his capability as a mere whip. His sole note of warning, threatening or encouragement to his horses, consists in that peculiar spasmodic eructation to which the school-boy is liable after his first cigar; that convulsive prelude to the final catastrophe uttered from the uncontrollable throat of the sensitive voyager leaning over the side of an ocean steamer in rough weather. So habitual is the use of this remarkable sound with Jacob, that whenever he has finished any sentence of the remarks he frequently indulges himself in, this sound invariably follows, as if, sickening of the ordinary forms of speech, he were about to throw up all his feelings at once. But we go merrily on with Jacob up the fertile valley of the Tosa, a swift and considerable stream which helps to feed Lake Maggiore, and note with pleasure the careful cultivation of a very considerable variety of crops, including many small patches of Indian corn. I remarked that I was amazed to see so much maize grown here, whereupon the younger members of my party very properly declared they must abandon me at the next attempt of this sort. But almost anything goes among these sombre Alps, and I have several times caused hilarity in Frattini by the production of exceedingly ancient stories which, having served their full time, have long been discharged from service. But the wily Italian well knows when he is expected to laugh, and I dare say that, could I detect it, I should find he has his revenge in the items of the weekly account he renders. Women, young and old, are at work out of doors, more numerous than men, doing the heaviest kinds of work, mowing, gathering the short cut grass into long, tapering baskets, in which they carry, strapped to their shoulders, incredible loads of the various crops, no other sort of conveyance being in use. We saw many cases of goitre in different stages of advance among these poor peasants, caused by their hard life and poor and insufficient food. Frattini says that many among them make a bread out of chestnuts to last a whole year, pounding up and soaking it into a kind of porridge.

We lunch on brook trout at the Hotel de la Ville et Poste in the quaint village of Domo d'Ossola, driving into a great court-yard round which the yellow quadrangular buildings rise four stories high, with railed balconies running along each story. Two hours before, at eleven o'clock, at Pallanzeno, Jacob had halted to give his horses a draught of a thickish meal-porridge, followed by three loaves of the black, hard bread of the country, cut into slices ; a feed, in the midst of a hard drive, to throw George, our Scotch coachman, into a sweat only to hear of it. We passed extensive quarries of rose-tinted granite at Ornavasso, and near it are the still more extensive and old marble quarries from which the Cathedral of Milan is built.

So far as Domo d'Ossola we have been accompanied by a solidly built railway which, if all things favor, is to be carried over and through the Simplon. The telegraph-wire runs from Stresa atop of solid granite pillars. Here the ascent seriously begins, the Tosa brawls more vociferously down its narrowing valley, and we climb slowly up on the road built by Napoleon I. on the highway from Milan to Paris. This road as well as that over the St. Gothard and all roads we have ridden over in Europe so far, are kept in perfect order by constant repairs, are laid out by competent engineers and built solidly in broken stone. We know little about good roads in America in comparison. We still have luxuriant vegetation in favored spots and chestnut, fig and mulberry trees and patches of corn, with lofty mountains frowning from above. At several points we noticed a stout single wire stretching from the roadside across the deep bed of the Tosa and fastened to a point on the opposite cliff, not less than a thousand feet high, on which woodmen on the narrow shelf, almost out of sight, fastened little bundles of firewood cut from the slender pines on the steep slopes. These came sliding down slowly at first, then with increasing velocity, until they landed with a crash beside the road.

We passed the night comfortably at the Hotel Posta in the little hamlet Iselle, lulled to rest by the Tosa chafing in its rocky channel. There is an Italian customs-station here, where all coming from Switzerland have strict examination, and a score of lusty fellows are kept patrolling the mountain-paths night and day on the lookout for smugglers, who nevertheless carry on a brisk trade, taking an occasional scrimmage with the revenue officers, who are backed by a small force of gendarmes and a lock-up close at hand. We calmly saw the down-coming diligence overhauled, for we, leaving Italy, were not liable to examination. The diligence is a lumbering coach-body with a glass window-front called the *coupé*. This is fully shut off by a partition from the main part called the *interieur*, and perched up behind is a covered seat for two called the *banquette*, making eight seats in all for passengers, the *coupé* holding two. They are drawn by four horses changed often, and are dreary conveyances, the only desirable part being the *banquette*.

We set out in good case next morning at 8.30, in weather which fully repaid the pains we had taken to make sure of a good day for one of the great Alpine passes. Yesterday could not be complained of, but to-day there is not a speck visible anywhere in the blue sky, the atmosphere to the very mountain-tips is clear as crystal and the sweet air charged with life. Great peace and a high serenity fill these august upper spaces as

"Tenderly the haughty day
Fills his blue urn with fire."

At two miles on the ascending road we pass a granite column on which is cut the word "Italia," marking the boundary between Italy and Switzerland, and soon reach the hamlet of Gondo, where we pass the Swiss Custom-House without examination, and are at once in the midst of the most majestic scenery conceivable. On both sides of the wild roadway tower bold cliffs 2000 feet, far below in a sunless gorge hoarsely roars the stream shrunken by distance to a line of swift-darting foam, while to the left opens the awful Ravine of Gondo, revealing the Bodmer Glacier glistening icily above. In charming contrast, on midway terraces and slopes, wherever vegetation can have got any footing, are bits of green pasture, and even patches of mowing land with grass so sweet and nutritious that Jacob says it is better than corn. It is this remarkable union of the pastoral with the savage and desolate that constitutes the inexpressible beauty of these mountains. Sleek cattle feed in sober security beside the track of the avalanche, and mowers whet their scythes on slopes overhung by everlasting snows. From the Italian lakes we saw the snowy top of the Fletschhorn rising nearly 13,000 feet, and now it towers above us close at hand.

We dine capitally at Simplon, and after resting the horses for two hours, climb up past the old Hospice at the base of the Schönhorn, rising snow-capped, and are at the highest point on the Simplon Pass, 6595 feet, 500 feet less than the corresponding point on the St. Gothard. Here is a broad, open valley of good pasture land, and all about and far as the eye can see, snowy peaks, including the towering cone of the Wetterhorn, on the right the Rossboden Glacier with its hilly moraine, and many a shining top of the long Bernese range. We called at the Hospice, a large solid stone building, were shown by a polite brother the comfortable rooms where travellers may lodge, the refectory, a long, high hall, where a table was spread with a coarse but clean linen cover, had a bottle of sourish white wine produced in the high valleys near by, peeped into the pretty chapel where services of song were going on by three of the brothers with pleasant voices and not a listener in sight, dropped into the iron-bound chest the sum which elsewhere comes to one in the form of a bill of charges. patted a handsome St. Bernard puppy and began the steep descent. On the way up we gathered by the roadside pink crocuses, blue gentians, Alpine roses, until a height was reached where only the last is found. All along on either side of the pass we saw little cascades falling as from the clouds out of their snowy sources, some gleaming deep within the narrow channels they have been for unknown ages chamfering in the solid face of the rock, others glancing in wider fall from shelf to shelf, like an endless web of unfolding lace. Those French engineers who carried this road up from the valley of the "arrowy Rhone," gleaming far down below us in the warm rays of the declining sun, surely knew their trade well, and the granite masonry of bridge and buttress and parapet stands firm and shapely. We got a view at one point of Brieg, our destination, 5000 feet below, with the green bit of the widened Rhone valley on which it stands showing in such miniature as would be produced by looking at it through an inverted telescope. We descend briskly, zigzagging down sharp gradients, one wheel sliding on a broad wooden shoe which Jacob has attached, not to be removed until we pull up in front of the Couronnes et Poste, our hotel for the night. The scenery on the way down is fully as striking as on the ascent. The Alpine snow-peaks gradually disappear for the most part, but the Rauthorn with its glacier and the shapely Fletschhorn are still shining above us; we wind under lesser but still tremendous mountains where avalanches are nursed, around craggy points where the head grows dizzy with looking down precipitous gorges a thousand feet deep, and everywhere that slope or terrace or ledge will permit tree to stand or grass to grow are signs of human existence and sylvan life.

After a comfortable night in pleasant rooms looking out on a little garden where a meek fountain plays softly, and just beyond a clear mountain stream hastens down an artificial channel of stone to mingle with the Rhone, we strolled about the little village of Brieg, remarkable for nothing but its fair situation among the mountains, and came upon a little open square among the old stone houses, where a high-rounded coffin stood on trestles in the central space, with many wreaths of evergreens and flowers on it ; a table covered with a cloth on which stood four lighted candles flaring in the warm sunlight, and another table on which stood a bowl of holy water. Two female watchers in white robes and cowls stood near, and now and then some one would advance from the little group of people in their best clothes standing about, and dipping a leafy twig in the bowl, sprinkle the coffin with drops of water. Later from our balcony we saw a long procession moving by in solemn silence, the bier borne on the shoulders of six men, and a great number of priests in white surplices carrying among them a huge cross with an image of the Saviour on it. Behind came a lengthy train of well-dressed people all on foot, and the whole filed down a long avenue of Lombardy poplars to cross the Rhone to the church on the other side.  I wondered how so many could be got together on any occasion whatever in this small community, for the cortège was nearly a third of a mile long, and was informed it was to celebrate the funeral of an estimable and well-beloved lady who had done many kind deeds here.  Frattini said the shops were mostly closed and, the funeral over, the day would be kept as a holiday and most of the people indulge in a drunken debauch.  I hope not, but am not likely to know, for at 1 P.M. we took train for Martigny, where we arrived at 4 P.M., having made the average run on the Swiss roads of forty-seven miles in three hours.

From Brieg we followed the Rhone down its pleasant mountain valley. It has its source in the Glacier du Rhone, some thirty miles above Brieg, and as it brings down in its swift current a great quantity of the powdery detritus into which the glacier grinds the rocks in its irresistible course, its color, like all glacial water, is ashen gray. It flows swiftly and deposits all along its course the earthy matter with which it is charged, forming new land, which the enterprising native of the valley enters upon at the earliest possible moment. We saw picturesque ruins at Sierre and Sion.

We lodged well at the Hotel Clerc in Martigny, and next morning took a low carriage hung like a Victoria, with two seats facing each other and another for the driver, drawn by two horses, to cross the Tête Noire on the way to Chamonix. Frattini followed in a heavier wagon with our luggage. Until within three or four years only light carriages drawn by one horse and carrying two persons could be used on this difficult road, now much improved. At first we follow the great St. Bernard road through Martigny-Bourg, Drance Bridge, La Croix; then, turning to the right, wind up slopes rich with meadows, orchards and vines, to the Col de la Forclaz, three and one half hours from our starting-point and nearly 5000 feet above the sea. All along the backward view of the Rhone valley and Martigny with its old castle has been increasingly fine, and now we enter the forest of dark firs at the base of the Tête Noire, the slender waters of the Trient murmuring nearly 2000 feet below.

We dine quite well at the Hotel de la Tête Noire, and after resting the horses two hours, proceed through scenes wilder and fully as impressive as any we have met. We descend by a road of dangerous steepness to the gloomy valley of the Eau Noire, and pass from Switzerland into Savoy, since 1860 belonging to France. At Col des Montets, 4740 feet above the sea, the Mont Blanc chain comes into view, and we descend rapidly into the valley of Chamonix by a series of bold loops and gradients, as many as five of which are in sight at once. Before this, Frattini, pointing to a dome-shaped cloud far down the valley which seemed to rest on the dimly seen tops of the great mountains at the entrance, had exclaimed, "Mont Blanc," and I had respectfully taken off my hat to this mighty monarch of European mountains, although beholding his majesty dimly and more by faith than sight. But on our immediate right, as the day is warm and clear, with not a stain on the sky, rise in their terrible majesty, stark and sharp, piercing the very heavens to the height of more than 10,000 feet, several of those granite peaks called the Aiguilles, or needles, each having its own name. We rode close by the base of the majestic one called Buet, and I have never been so impressed by a mountain form before. Soon, however, we come into full view of the great Mont Blanc range with its glistening domes and pinnacles, huge buttresses and many glaciers slanting down to the valley. We pass that of Tour, in which the Arve has its rise, next the larger one of d'Argentière, then the famous Mer de Glace, from which the Arveyron issues, soon to unite with the Arve, forming a considerable river, which rushes down the valley, on its journey to join the distant Rhone, with a mad velocity not often seen, and are soon most comfortably established in the Hotel Imperial at Chamonix, in rooms with a balcony looking directly on the mountains in front, and so near that it seems easy to stroll to the summit; so deceptive is the distance in the sunset light.

The ride to day has been long, hard and hot. After dinner we gaze from our balcony upon the heights of eternal snow gleaming spectrally under the summer stars. Down the valley of the Arve the crescent moon is glimmering through a soft haze, and just above the snow, in the gorge between the domes of Mont Blanc and du Gouter, burns with sparkling lustre the planet Jupiter, soon to be eclipsed by the Dome du Gouter and reappear again on the side of the valley.

The village of Chamonix is a point where tourists congregate, and is made up of hotels, the houses of the associated guides, shops and a few villagers besides. The valley of the same name, watered by the Arve, is some twelve miles long, about one-half mile wide, fertile, and lies 3400 feet above the sea. I have before me one of those little books of local information which I look for in places of interest, because I find them valuable, being usually written by some careful and often scholarly man in love with his subject and knowing the facts. This one, which I have had in hand for parts of two days, being pretty well confined to my rooms from the effect of the heat and fatigue of our hard ride from Martigny, is written by the pastor of a church at Vevay, and gives what may be styled the history and literature associated with Mont Blanc and the region hereabout. I might as well say that I am disappointed in Mont Blanc. In my ignorance I had expected to find an individual mountain of that name towering heavenward after the manner of great Popocatapetl from the plain of Mexico. Instead, I find Mont Blanc to be the head or nucleus of a mountain range bearing its name, over thirty miles long, and immediately surrounded by peaks and domes not greatly inferior to itself in height. These all rise from the backbone of the range, itself nearly 8000 feet high, so that the difference in altitude of the various peaks is not apparently great, seen from the base where we are. Of course, seen from a great elevation or at a distance, this difference will be more apparent; still the actual difference does not much exceed 1000 feet between the dome of Mont Blanc and several of its neighbors, the gigantic pinnacle of Aiguille Verte rising 13,500 feet, du Dru 12,500 feet, Dome du Gouter 14,200 feet, with many others not much inferior, while the height of the summit of the dome of Mont Blanc itself is 15,730 feet. The whole scene, however, is one of the highest sublimity and magnificence. Wonderful it is to see the frozen rivers of the glaciers running down between cultivated fields and green pastures, their vast masses of a hundred feet in thickness firm and unyielding in the hot summer sun. As is well known, the entire mass of billowy ice composing these glaciers moves downward at a well-ascertained rate, slower or faster during periods of years, and here averaging about five inches per day. They grind their way down the enormous gorges with irresistible power, crushing the rocks at the sides and bottom to the finest powder, and at the lower end, where they gradually yield to the solar heat, depositing the débris in a rounded heap.

Not being enough recovered to do any walking, I drove with my family to the foot of the great glacier of the Bossons, and waited in the shade of a neat white cottage with deep, projecting eaves and green balconies filled with flowers until they should have visited it. A pretty little girl of eight years came quietly out, seated herself on a bench beside the door, took from a little pocket her various colored yarns, carefully selected the shades needed, and patiently for a long time wrought quite natural flowers on a small square canvas, looking furtively out at me from under her straw hat from time to time, with large, soft eyes, and when I put a franc into her little brown hand, thanking me in a low, sweet voice, with modest blush. I waited three hours, for the young people, after climbing up to the little house of rest beside the glacier, took it into their heads to cross it, and did so, putting on woollen socks over their shoes and being helped over the crevasses and up slippery steps by two guides, Frattini following as best he could.

At my invitation, the famous mountain guide François Devouasoud, called on me in our rooms, and as he speaks English quite well, I had an interesting talk of an hour with him. He is fifty-eight years old, and has followed his trade of guide for forty years, having scaled all the mountain-peaks of importance in Switzerland and many elsewhere, notably the highest of the Caucasus, Mount Elbru, 18,500 feet. He has made the ascent of Mont Blanc twenty-seven times, and from our balcony pointed out the path pursued from the Grand Mulets across the Glacier Bossons by the Petit Plateau, the Grand Plateau, the Dome du Gouter and the Bosses du Dromadaire; or, according to the state of the weather, by the Corridor, the Mur de la Côte and the Petits Mulets, to the summit. All this route to the very top lay so plain and palpable on the vast snowy flanks of the range in the bright, clear afternoon that it seemed one might put on his rubbers and stroll up and back before supper; yet we were obliged yesterday to look through a powerful telescope to distinguish a party of six who were making the ascent, forming a string of black, spider-like specks connected by a filmy rope, as they toiled up a background of dazzling snow. The plan is to go up to the Grand Mulets—10,000 feet—the afternoon before, sleep at the comfortable station there, and a little after midnight cross the Glacier Bossons by the light of a lantern, attain the summit about 8 A.M., and descend to Chamonix the same day. François stated that with careful guides the ascent is quite safe, almost the only danger being from a sudden storm coming on when near the top, and that the difficulties are not nearly so great as in the ascent of several of the Aiguilles or abrupt granite peaks of the range.

A very interesting man is François, sincere, frank, brave, as his strong, quiet features show, and with the natural dignity, politeness and modesty of a gentleman. He is strongly built, with somewhat slouchy movements, like a farmer having a holiday, but with a quick, resolute look at times, as if obliged often to decide and act promptly. He said he himself had never experienced any alarming or very unpleasant symptoms at any height he had attained, but many whom he had conducted did so. He suffers somewhat from rheumatism, "for," said he, "weather which breaks granite is felt in the bones," and goes among the mountains less and less, and after two or three years more will cease altogether and do no more than tend his little farm and cattle a mile from the village, where he lives comfortably in a snug house and keeps with pride many presents, commendations and grateful tokens from people he has guided among these perilous heights for nearly half a century. He told in the simplest, heartiest way of his trip to Paris this summer, what wonders are in the Exposition, and, what surprised and amused me, that he would not venture to go up the Eiffel Tower, "because," he said, "you are among a lot of other people, and if anything happens to the lift there is nothing you can take hold of with your hands to save yourself." Here is a man who has climbed the precipitous crag of d'Aiguille Verte, seeking hold for hand and foot in its perpendicular wall, with 5000 dizzy feet of precipice below, who would not trust himself to ride in an elevator with a party of easy citizens. He has two younger brothers who are also famous as guides.

I learn from my little book that Mont Blanc was first climbed by Jacques Balmat in 1786, who after several trials succeeded, tempted by the inducements offered by the naturalist de Saussure, who was anxious to find a way up for himself that he might make some observations and experiments there. He did so the following year guided by Balmat, and there is in the little square in Chamonix a spirited monument representing him pointing the way up the glittering heights to his rapt companion. Since that time there have been more than one thousand ascents, of which I note sixty-four were by women, and now during the fine weather parties go up almost daily.

Chamonix is well organized for robbing tourists, some fifteen thousand of whom come here annually. The guides and muleteers are fully organized, with an exorbitant tariff of rates, and as no one can come or leave except by diligence or private conveyance, the coachmen have it all their own way, and a vile way it is.

Frattini engaged a conveyance to Geneva, but early on the morning we were to leave saw the driver of it trotting shamelessly out of town with a full carriage. Another was hired, who put on part of the luggage and then refused in the most nonchalant way to put on any more, and was driven off with ignominy by the now frantic Frattini, who, storming the town, soon returned in triumph, seated on the box beside an excellent Jehu, who, obliged to return to Geneva this morning, pulled up his four horses with a flourish, in the prospect of an unexpected fare. So at 9 o'clock, on the morning of the 3d of September, we set out in fine style for Geneva, distant forty-three miles. Our road followed the milky Arve down its swift current through the smiling valley of Chamonix, from which opens a wild ravine with fine backward views of the Mont Blanc range, which seems to grow in magnitude the farther we get from it. At the hamlet of Magland a huge spring, like the one we visited at San Philipe, near the Rio Grande in Texas, gushes out from under a great cliff by the roadside in enormous volume.

We lunch, not very well, at Bonneville, reaching it over a broad, fertile meadow-land, and note the Castle of Chatillon perched high up on a crag, seeming inaccessible. Bonneville is in the midst of a fertile and highly cultivated plain with grand mountains all about, of which the Pointe d'Andey and Mole rise 6000 feet. Two miles from Geneva we cross the French frontier, with only the formality of a question from the Swiss customs-officer by the roadside, and soon through a broad, shady avenue lined on either hand with handsome country-seats in spacious and charming grounds, enter on the steep streets of the old city of Geneva, and crossing the blue Rhone, now cleared of all impurities by its long rest in the tranquil lake, just where it issues from it, are soon installed, with the abundant care, civility and politeness characterizing the Swiss hotels, in excellent quarters in the Hotel Beaurivage, fronting the lake.

Geneva is the largest of the Swiss cities, with a population of about 70,000. It lies pleasantly at the lower end of Lake Leman, sloping down the gradual southern shore in the form of a crescent, and divided by the Rhone into halves connected by eight good bridges. It is the capital of the canton of Geneva, has nothing remarkable in its architecture, but has a prosperous, busy look and an endless number of little shops where all sorts of jewelry and ornamental goods are displayed in endless variety. It thrives on foreigners, selling them especially a prodigious number of watches, which are made here and in all the little villages among the hills. The parts of a watch so made are put together here by leading firms, and as fashion has for a long time favored these watches, pretty much everybody who comes here buys. There is a school here where watch-making is taught, and this single industry supports and enriches a vast number of people.

The legions of victorious Rome marching northward to conquer the barbarous tribes inhabiting these valleys found a town in existence here one hundred years before the Christian era and named it Genava, and for two thousand years, with stormy and varying fortunes, it has cut something of a figure in the world. Here lived and wrought and died in 1564 grim John Calvin, the artificer of the theological scheme known as Calvinism, which I believe has cast a darker shadow over more human souls during the last four hundred years than any system contrived by man since Christ was born upon the earth. With the pitiless logic of a subtle brain and an icy heart, he dared to aim at knowing the divine counsels, to formulate the methods of the Almighty, to limit His mercy, direct His vengeance, and forecast with the awful inevitableness of fate the eternal doom of the whole human race. Our pious New England forefathers strove with some success to accept his conclusions and shape their lives by his dogmas; their descendants have struggled less successfully to the same end, have grown careless and faithless, until now who of them can, or would if he could, believe in the dark predestination taught by this stern Genevan ascetic? He came here a Protestant seeking refuge from persecution because *he doubted*, and getting place and power, burned at the stake Michael Servetus, the learned Spanish physician fleeing from persecution, because *he* doubted. But Michael's doubts were not John's doubts, and could only be resolved and purged by the element of fire. Sweet, pure and loving Teacher of Nazareth, how could such fiery fruit come from the tender seeds of charity and peace and joy which Thou didst sow and water with Thy cherishing blood? "Surely an enemy hath done this," and the fagot and the axe are the tares of wickedness he sowed.

We set out to find the house in which Calvin lived, and learned, after we had started, that our driver knew nothing about it, and several citizens applied to by Frattini in a loud voice, from his seat on the box, professed themselves unable to reveal the secret; and when, at my suggestion, he addressed the question to a troop of bright boys just coming from school with satchels full of books, they seemed, by their indecorous hilarity and outcries, to think he was chaffing them. But after many hesitations and windings we came to a street named Calvin, and found a broad, substantial stone house which a melancholy butcher leaning out of a low door hard by averred to be that of Calvin, an assurance backed up by a little puckered-up old lady in a great white cap. I looked into the dusty court where were no signs of life save a cat playing with a mouse in the hot glare of the afternoon sun. We drove to the cemetery of Plainpalais to visit his grave, which the local guide-book, by J. E. Muddock, F.R.G.S.—whatever that may be—insists is in that spot; but the confident female in charge of the entrance assured us that no John Calvin is buried here. Relating this to a gentleman residing in the city, he informed me that the place of his burial is not known. So utterly are the traces of him who was so great and powerful obliterated! And as if in mockery of the dyspeptic bigot who interdicted the stage and all other forms of amusement, there rises in the fairest part of the city almost the handsomest theatre, outside and in, I have ever seen, costing nearly a million dollars!

We visited the Cathedral, which has little of interest, and the Greek church with its gilded domes and handsome sandal-wood doors, which, after thirty years, still emit a faint odor; also the well-arranged public library of one hundred thousand volumes and many interesting early manuscripts. We drove to the Villa Diodati, occupied by Byron for some time, and looked upon the scenes which fed his high thoughts and cooled his wild pulses—scenes he celebrated in verse as beautiful almost as our language can show. Also we drove to Ferney, on the opposite side of the lake, to the château built and occupied by Voltaire, where we walked in the long, close-shaded alley of dwarf beeches he planted, his favorite walk, where he barbed those arrows of scornful raillery which stung despots on their thrones and pierced through and through the dragons of superstition and mocked at holy things with reprehensible sneer. He had charming grounds here and lovely views. Many interesting relics of him are shown in some rooms of the château, now owned by a Parisian gentleman who married the daughter of the purchaser of the estate from Voltaire. Among these are portraits of the Great Frederick and Catherine II. of Russia, presented to him by themselves. He built a chapel near his house, as the inscription on it shows, and a number of manufactories, and was a sort of benefactor to the working people here gathered about him.

On the way here we visited the Musée Ariana, a collection of works of art open to the public without charge by the kindness of its owner, M. Gustavus Revilliod, one of those generous souls, not uncommon as we have found, who take pleasure in sharing the satisfaction they find in beautiful treasures of art with those less fortunate. This gentleman has built, in a spot commanding a charming view of the lake, a costly building of cream-colored stone, solid and beautiful, and in magnificent rooms within it are, among the many treasures, an endless number of exquisite specimens of the pottery of all countries and times, handsomely arranged for viewing, and labelled so as to show full particulars about them all. We saw the kindly old man walking slowly about, his benevolent-looking wife on his arm, enjoying seeing others enjoy the good things he had set forth for their happiness. Long may they both live, tranquilly happy in their noble disinterestedness!

There stands near the lake in Geneva an imposing monument, 66 feet high, to Duke Charles II. of Brunswick, who died here in 1873, leaving his property, some twenty million francs, to the city. It must have cost a great deal of money, for it is sumptuous in costly statues and carving, but is not fully pleasing.

*September* 9.—Took a steamboat to the upper end of the lake. It stretches away forty-five miles in length, with an average width of eight miles, and its shores, in the lazy tranquillity of a warm summer morning, recede hazily toward the lower mountains of the Savoy Alps on the right and the dusky ranges of the Jura on the left. Half way up the scenery begins to grow bolder. The Jura vanishes by degrees, but on the southern shore great Alpine spurs come boldly up to the lake one after another and cluster about the eastern end, where the Rhone has worn its impetuous entrance and deposited a broad alluvial tract of glacier-worn sediment. The shores are studded with costly villas and numerous villages, partly gray with age and partly span new, in curious contrast, ancient towers rising beside factory chimneys and venerable castles on neighborly terms with flaring new hotels. Most charming is the situation of Clarens, sheltered from harsh winds by the closely overhanging and picturesque mountains. Byron, who paints external nature with literal fidelity and poetic feeling, has described it as nearly as words can in the third canto of "Childe Harold."

We left the boat at Chillon, quite near the upper end of the lake, to visit the castle of that name. Byron has done a great deal for it, for it is not so formidable a structure as one expects to find, and Bonnivard's dungeon, a long hall supported by a range of great stone pillars in the centre, is not greatly worse than the rooms shown as the private apartments of the Dukes and Duchesses of Savoy, when they resided here. Bonnivard was imprisoned here for six years because he took sides with the Genevans in their contests with the Duke of Savoy, lived a long time after his discharge, and died respected in 1536, at a good old age. The most interesting room in the castle, which rises picturesquely from the lake, as much like a château as a stronghold, is the great kitchen with its well-preserved oaken ceiling and its huge chimney and fireplace, where an ox could easily be roasted entire. This would indicate good cheer, but I suppose not many cutlets found their way down into the long, high vaulted dungeon lighted by narrow slits in the wall, so high up that no peep could be had of the blue water and glorious mountains opposite, to-day half veiled in a warm, grayish mist. There is a ring in one of the pillars which looks as if it might be ten years old ; and the pillar called Bonnivard's is literally carved into names. Among them is Byron's, the letters of which are worn greatly, as if by the touch of the fingers of his pilgrim admirers. Eugene Sue, George Sand and Victor Hugo have also taken the trouble to cut their names among the thousands on these pillars, which are said to date back to about 800. The castle was improved and fortified in the thirteenth century by Count Peter of Savoy, and now stands pretty much as he left it, having been used as an arsenal for the last one hundred years.

Returning, we left our carriage at Chillon and took electric tramway, passing through an almost continuous line of villages, including Clarens, with modern houses along the lake and large, handsome hotels, where many people come to escape the heat of summer, for the " grape cure," so called, in autumn, and to be protected in the winter from the *bise*, or cold, moist north wind. We took rooms for the night in the Grand Hotel at Vevay, and it illustrates the popularity of this region that this hotel, in its construction and appointments, is fully equal to any one we have seen on the Continent, and it is not easy to imagine a more pleasing scene of blue lake and striking mountains than its beautiful grounds look out upon.

Next morning drove to the Church of St. Martin, built about 1500, with nothing interesting about it except a fine view across the lake from the terrace where it stands, an agreeable square tower, and the fact that it contains the graves of the regicides Ludlow and Broughton, who took refuge and died here, the Swiss refusing to surrender them at the demand of Charles II. Broughton read the sentence of the court, condemning Charles I. to death, and associated with him as joint clerk was John Phelps, also buried here. On the wall is a tasteful tablet with a graceful inscription placed there by his descendants " William Walter Phelps of New Jersey and Charles Phelps of Massachusetts, from across the sea." We drove up the gradual hills back of Vevay to the Château of Hauteville, two miles from the lake, and were shown through ever so fine and large gardens laid out in terraces, with endless profusion of flowers in beds of many forms, and roses such as I never saw the like of in size and hues. The château looks down upon a broad expanse sloping in gentle undulations to the lake's border, with miles of vineyards, noble copses of forest-trees—oak, chestnut, walnut—and flourishing orchards of apples, pears and plums.

On our drive to the Castle of Blonay, two miles higher up, a quaint, turreted, inhabitable structure, where the family of that name has lived for more centuries than anybody seems to know, we passed through the hamlet of La Chiesaz, where an artist, now in Paris, whose work I seem to remember in some way, A. Béguin, was born, and where he exhibited at once his youthful artistic precocity and exuberance of animal spirits by a considerable number of huge cartoons on the plaster walls of the roadside houses, stables and other outbuildings. These are mostly rollickingly facetious, rough, vigorous sketches of running horses galloping madly after having hurled their riders down fathomless abysses, and so forth, but with a female head or two of much beauty and grace.

We have come nearer to seeing the ideal Swiss châlet here than anywhere else, but have not yet seen one—I mean the châlet shown in pictures and models. The old peasant houses in the Black Forest, the shepherds' huts perched all along the mountain-sides everywhere, the little fancy houses where the comfortable *bourgeois* disports himself in his summer vacation, all present more or less of the features of the model châlet, but no one I have seen unites them all or even the greater part. The ideal châlet, the national costumes, the mountain horn and its *Ranz des Vaches* are still as far away as ever, although I have Frattini's assurance that they are still in existence somewhere.

*September* 12.—After lunch took railroad for Lausanne, an hour's ride, and passed the night at the Hotel Gibbon. In the garden sloping down toward the lake from the hotel the great historian is said to have composed much of that stalwart book which, promising at first to be a comfort and ally of Silas Wegg, finally led to his discomfiture and overthrow, "The Decline and Fall Off of the Roman Empire." Lausanne slopes sharply down a small mountain called Mont Jorat, is well built, has 30,000 population and a prosperous, bright and refined appearance, as if many refined people are among its inhabitants. We drove up to the "Signal," above the town, where we should have gained a wide view of valley, lake and mountain, if a thick haze had not shut off the distant scene of the Mont Blanc range, as it has done provokingly since we reached Geneva. The Cathedral consecrated by Gregory X. in the presence of Rudolph of Hapsburg has an interesting tower and some fine carvings, and is a good specimen of the Gothic style, but is bare and melancholy inside. No sight is more incongruous and unpleasing than an old cathedral stripped of all ornaments, its shrines desolate, its statues broken, its monuments defaced, and one end of its transept or a little space in front of the chancel "coldly furnished forth" with two dozen skimp fresh pine benches, with rows of new hymn-books atop of the railings, where a congregation of some form of Protestant Dissenters holds its stated worship. The Church of England comes so directly from the Church of Rome that its ceremonial worship in the great cathedrals of that country is nearly enough allied to the Mother Church to furnish a pomp still partly suitable to these vast interiors, but the beggarly bareness and chill austerity of these translated Swiss cathedrals are enough to freeze the very marrow of the skeleton of worship. There is a well-preserved castle here on a commanding height, but we contented ourselves with a survey of its outer walls and quaint round-towers looking threateningly down upon the town.

Took railroad P.M. to Neuchâtel (two hours), on west side of the beautiful lake of same name, and had rooms at the Bellevue, overlooking the deep green water. We part here from esteemed Brooklyn friends who had joined us at Geneva. The lake is eighteen miles long by three to four miles wide, modestly but charmingly set in its frame of gently sloping hills. Neuchâtel has a population of 16,000, is the capital of the canton of the same name, rises sharply up the slope of the Jura from the lake's edge, has a prosperous and contented look, and with its agreeable commingling of new and ancient architecture, most picturesque site and surroundings, forms almost as interesting a spot as any lake town we have visited, always excepting Lucerne, the unsurpassable. On a height above the town is a picturesque old château restored in parts and the seat of the cantonal government. We looked into the legislative chamber, with seats for one hundred and nine deputies to make the laws for a population of 100,000. Very quaint and comfortable are their quarters here, with magnificent views from the old stone balconies opening from the hall, offering all possible inducements to make legislation slow and easy. The Chamber holds four sessions a year, of two weeks each, and the members are paid eight francs per day. Suffrage is free, all citizens of the legal age being entitled to vote. There is no veto of the acts of the Chamber, but if within two months after the passage of a bill, three thousand citizens of the canton shall have signed a petition to that effect, the measure must be submitted to a vote of the whole body of citizens in the canton.

Visited the Municipal Museum and Picture Gallery, where in a handsome and commodious building is housed an interesting collection of old armor, domestic utensils, pottery, and perhaps one hundred and fifty oil paintings, of fair average merit. All this in a town of 16,000 people.

In the choir of the old Abbey church adjoining the château is an interesting Gothic monument with fifteen life-size figures, erected in 1372 by Count Louis of Neuchâtel, these being effigies, male and female, of his ancestors. The men are clad in armor, the women in white robes, with golden hair. The ladies have a modest, gentle, submissive and truly pious air, suitable to saints in peaceful rest. The artist, either from the nature of the subjects he had to deal with or from his lack of skill in expression, was not so happy with the distinguished males of that turbulent line. One of them, no doubt a tough rascal in his day, stands with praying hands and an artificial look of overdone sanctity, as if he hoped to impose on St. Peter and slip into heaven by virtue of a tardy piety, while another seems about to start off with a mincing gait and confident air, as if he fully thought he was expected above and his coming would very considerably augment the glory of the heavenly state; still another has the visor of his steel morion drawn furtively down over his eyes, as if he trusted to sneak through the celestial gate in disguise; and altogether these old mortuary images, as in almost all instances I have seen, are more comical than serious.

The guests at the Bellevue and elsewhere recently are largely English people, for the most part well-bred and undemonstrative. Occasionally an exception presents itself, and opposite us at the *table d'hôte* last evening sat a demonstrative, youngish couple, whose speech was so little like what I was accustomed to hear in England, that for some minutes I thought them to be talking in German, they so murdered the king's English in their pronunciation. When one comes to pronounce *glance* as if it were written *glons* and similarly tortures every word made use of, mystification can go no farther. I used to notice at home how much more English those English who live in America are than the English themselves; and I have met an occasional American over here of a sort I have never seen at home. It would seem as if these self-conscious tourists were fearful their nationality would not be readily discovered unless they exaggerated the national peculiarities.

*September* 12.—Came to Berne by rail, forty-one miles, following the western shore of the lake at the base of the Jura range, here nearer and more abrupt, the slopes all along smiling in vineyards, where, alas for the owners! many yellow leaves show the fatal progress of the phyloxera, whose ravages among the lakes here began, I am told, three years ago. The train leaves the Lake of Neuchâtel, and soon after reaches the pretty little Lake of Bienne, nine miles long, with gentle shores sprinkled with red-roofed villages and gemmed with the wooded island of St. Peter, where Rousseau passed the summer of 1765.

At Neuveville we enter Canton Berne, leaving the French for the German language, and changing cars at Bienne, cross the broad, green river Aare, and after twenty miles of charming scenery are set down at the Bernerhof in rooms looking down the valley of the Aare and across to the magnificent range of the Bernese Alps. We should have enjoyed a perfect view of these on our way from Neuchâtel, but the September haze interfered, and here it is the same, only, as the sun was setting, the Jungfrau, Eiger and all the range shone out quite clearly, suffused with a roseate glow. The weather here is much like the Vermont weather on the Twenty-mile stream at this time of year, and the signs of autumn in the atmosphere and vegetation much the same.

Berne is the capital of the canton of Berne as well as of Switzerland, for here the National Council meets and the President of the Republic resides, both Council and President having for their use a handsome building in the Florentine style, 400 by 165 feet. The city dates from the latter part of the twelfth century, and has undergone the many vicissitudes common to the annals of all old European towns, struggling for its rights with oppressors on every hand. It is picturesquely situated on a promontory of sandstone rock, about which the clear, green waters of the Aare wind 100 feet below, a small part of the old town lying down by the river, but the chief portion on the level heights above. It has a population of some 45,000, and while the modern portion is well built, there are more mediæval features left than is common in the Swiss towns, an especial feature being the arcades, formed by extending strong, slanting buttresses down from the second story of the compact houses on each side of a street, opening side arches between them, leaving, say, ten feet in width open into the street side of the first story and arching it overhead, so as to form continuous covered ways the entire length of the street. The shops open into these, so that the passer-by is protected from all kinds of weather. Arcades or sheltered passages for shops are not unusual in the continental cities, but not of this sort. Another feature here is the fountains, one of which, called the Ogre Fountain, has on top of a queerly decorated column the life-size figure of an ogre in act of devouring a child, and with pockets and girdle stuck full of others. Frattini says mothers here scare their children by threatening them with the ogre. The Bernese children are brought up among ample terrors, for the heraldic emblem of Berne being the bear, Bruin not only appears everywhere in effigies, realistic and grotesque, but an open den of these beasts is maintained and has been from time immemorial, at the expense of the city. The den is a deep-sunk, circular pit, some 80 feet in diameter, divided into equal parts by a high wall, the circular barrier being about 15 feet high from the bottom, and made of dressed stone rising waist-high above the terrace, from which visitors look down and are allowed to throw to the sluggish guardians of the town bread and vegetables. They have a handsome house of stone for shelter, and are well cared for. We saw six of a small brown species lazily disporting themselves and begging contributions from above as knowingly as if they wore frock and cowl and had relics to show.

The west portal of the Cathedral has elaborate sculptures, representing the "Last Judgment," of several hundred small, well-wrought figures showing throngs of the blessed and the lost going separate ways, the first placidly exultant, the second hiding their faces in confusion. The pigeons have a favorite roost atop of the inextricable heads, and whiten the crowns of saint and sinner impartially. Another portal shows life-size figures of the wise and foolish virgins, the latter much dejected, and the foolishest one of all striving to wipe away a stony tear with a great hand of stone in the most grotesque way. Inside are some old stalls of carven oak with portraits of apostles and saints of exceeding beauty, and stained glass of the fifteenth century. In one of the chapels is a Pietas in Carrara marble by Tscharner, sweetly expressive, designed in 1870. The same artist executed a statue of Berthold von Zähringen, the founder of Berne, with a bear for his standard-bearer, and bronzes in the pediment showing scenes in the building of the city, all full of spirit, as is the equestrian statue of Rudolph von Erlach, who won the battle of Laupen in 1339. At the four corners of the pediment are four bears of life size and appearance, all designed by Volmar, of this city. The unfinished Cathedral tower contains nine bells, the largest of which, according to a local guide-book, weighs twelve tons, and is the seventh largest bell in the world, and the largest which is rung by swinging.

The old city walls no longer exist, but on the east front of the tower over one of the ancient gates is a curious old clock having at one side of the great quaint dial a painted figure of a mediæval king seated in his chair of state, with a huge hour-glass resting on his knee. A little higher up, at his left hand, stands the court-jester, holding a bell-rope in his hand, with a mocking figure at his side peering across at a bear rampant, and below his majesty a circular procession of mounted men-at-arms and grotesque bears marching on their hind legs, bitted and armed. At two minutes before the hour an asthmatic cock on the right of the royal chair crows wearily, the jester sharply pulls his bell-rope and rings a clear-sounding bell hid somewhere out of sight in the tower, and on the hour the cock again crows; his majesty turns his hour-glass and extends his sceptre, the mocking figure salutes by taking off its hat, the rampant bear returns the compliment, the armed procession below wheels slowly into view, the great tower-bell strikes the hour, a minute later the weary cock crows again, and thus is each hour of the day duly honored and has been for I don't know how many changeful years.

There stands on one of the squares a large stone building (why should I write stone, when almost every structure everywhere here, as elsewhere in Europe, except the mountain châlets, is of stone?) where until a late period enough grain was kept stored to supply the city for four months. Improved means of communication render such precaution against famine needless now. Under this storehouse is a huge old vaulted wine-cellar, with venerable tuns ranged along the sides, holding, as the measures painted on the heads declare, some ten thousand gallons, some sixty-two thousand bottles. Plain tables with benches run along the centre, and wine, both white and red, is served to customers in pint decanters, "to be consumed on the premises." I tasted the white wine and found it, like all the Swiss wines, too acid for my palate. I might say that so far I have not found the quality of any wine I have ordered better than one gets in New York, nor at the hotels any cheaper.

Took train and ran out to Fribourg, twenty miles, to hear the organ in the Gothic Church of St. Nicholas, and found one of the most picturesque towns we have seen. I wonder more stress is not laid on it by those we meet. I certainly would urge any one visiting this part of Switzerland not to pass it by. It is situated, much like Berne, on a still more abrupt, rocky height, with the clear green Sarine flowing windingly by. Such quaint rows of houses on the steep hill-side, with the gray walls of an old nunnery washed by the clear stream! In a square near the handsome Rathhaus stands an exceedingly old lime-tree, fourteen feet in girth, banded with iron, its two flourishing limbs resting on a heavy frame. The story is that in 1476 a boy came running into town from the battle of Morat, breathless and bloody, and crying "Victory!" fell dead. The lime-twig he bore in his hand was stuck in the ground and became this tree.

I had supposed, in a vague sort of way, that somehow the Roeblings were the first to build cable bridges, but it seems that they only built them on a larger scale than had been known. Here at Fribourg is a *pont suspendu* built by Chaley in 1834, 810 feet long and 168 feet above the Sarine, precisely like a miniature of the great one below Niagara Falls. A little farther up is another, built in 1840, over the Vallée de Gotteron, 747 feet long and 305 feet above the water!

The organ in the Church of St. Nicholas at Fribourg, ranking as almost the finest in Europe, was built by Mooser, and has 67 stops and 7800 pipes, some of them 32 feet long. The significance of these facts I do not, in my ignorance of music, realize, but I may venture to say that I was moved and delighted by its great power and sweetness in the hands of the master who performed the following programme, which I set down as a token of our visit to Fribourg, a journey of forty miles, to be present for an hour, at 1.30 P.M., at the great organ recital:

| | | |
|---|---|---|
| 1. *Preludium*, | . | A. W. BACH. |
| 2. *Andante*, | . | HUMMEL. |
| 3. *Fuga*, . . | . | T. S. BACH. |
| 4. *Prière de Moise*, | . . | ROSSINI. |
| 5. *Invocation*, . . | . | GUILMANT. |
| 6. *Scene Pastoral*, | . . . | T. VOGT. |

In the last number a storm is described, and one rarely hears louder or grander peals of thunder than rolled from this mighty organ.

Over the west portal of the church is another "Last Judgment," represented by a great number of small figures carved with much skilful care. The damned are being driven by grinning devils to the scene of torture, where a great caldron, already full of seething bodies, is steaming over a hot fire which a little imp is fanning with a pair of bellows. Above the rim of the caldron rise faces distorted with pain, a huge monster with goggle eyes is in act of swallowing one victim out of a throng bound and lying in a pile before him, and, huger in bulk, sits Satan, high up, diabolically exultant. This horrible scene was cut in enduring stone by pious hands no doubt, from designs by pious architects, approved by holy fathers of the Church and set up in this consecrated spot for the instruction and admonition of the faithful and the profane.

I have neglected to say that the chimneys of the old houses in Berne are a curious feature. They have little sloping roofs with projecting eaves, and rows of tiny openings just below for the smoke to escape, and odd little arches and circles and windows with tiny pent-house roofs over them set on brackets. The effect of a house depends much on its chimneys. Geneva is half spoiled by the vermicular snarl of galvanized iron pipes sticking out of its chimneys.

I inquired out the best tailor here and ordered a full suit of clothes, for which the steady little German measured me to an extent beyond anything I had known and sent them home in two days. The cloth I selected out of an ample stock is of Scotch make, such as I have often worn at home, is made up with good trimmings and work, and cost one hundred francs, or twenty dollars.

We get good pears and plums, but not good apples nor often good peaches.

*September* 16.—Came to Interlaken; by rail to Thun, then up the lake of same name nine miles by boat, total distance about thirty miles, and have rooms in the Victoria, one of the very largest and best-appointed hotels in Switzerland, and always full during the season. Interlaken is a long, straggling village, made up of hotels, pensions and shops, situated in the midst of a fertile and cultivated plain formed by the deposits of two rivers, one the Lütschine, flowing into what is now the Lake of Brienz, and the Lombach, discharging its waters into Lake Thun. These rivers during an enormous period of time deposited the matter they brought down from the glaciers at two opposite points on the north and south sides of what is believed to have been one body of water, and at last cut it into two nearly equal parts, forming a plain, of something like a mile square, through which the Aare flows, connecting the two lakes, both of which it feeds and empties. Interlaken (between the lakes) has only the natural beauty of its situation to attract travellers, but that is very great, as it stands among lofty mountains and agreeable scenery near at hand. The plain is highly cultivated, with orchards and groves and avenues of great walnut and chestnut trees, meadows and tilled fields.

This is a favorite point for tourists intending pedestrian excursions. We meet various degrees of these everywhere, with more or less formidable alpenstocks, iron-pointed, and sometimes headed with a hatchet or pick. The greater number are amateurs, who do not take the mountains very seriously, while the greater part who do, present a worn appearance, something like the contestants in a " go-as-you-please" walking match on the third day. A great many in mountain costume look as if dressed to figure in the chorus of Scott's " Anne of Geierstein" done into opera. I noticed at Weggis, on Lake Lucerne, standing on the wharf as the boat touched there, a pretty French girl with a long alpenstock, from which fluttered the ends of a blue ribbon. She wore dainty Parisian shoes with high heels, well forward, and fresh kid gloves. But to render it apparent to all beholders that she considered herself doing duty among the Alps, she had donned a stout skirt, looped up so as not to interfere with the free movements of her neat ankles on the mountain-paths, and had turned back the collar from her shapely neck so as to allow the sun to impart to it a healthy brown hue, which it is permitted one to hope will attest her stories of wearisome and perilous clamberings when she shall have got safely home again. But there is a certain number of young pedestrians of quite another sort who, with stout staff and slender scrip, make light of the difficulties of these formidable mountain-peaks and passes and come in fresh and tranquil after an all-day's march. Such were a young Englishman and his two sisters who came into Andermatt in the evening of the stormy night we passed there, having walked from the Rhone Glacier, and directly appeared at the *table d'hôte* in evening costumes, showing no traces whatever of their thirty-mile tramp over muddy mountain-paths. Weighted with threescore years and two hundred pounds avoirdupois, so that I get my views from the top of a mountain carriage or some height reached by "funicular" or other sort of railroad, I try to keep myself from envying these active young climbers by thinking how much more at liberty I am in making my observations than they, who clamber up the face of these great heights through forests which shut out all views and up crags which claim their full strength and attention, to be rewarded after the toilful strain is over in a wider or grander view than the ordinary tourist is capable of attaining.

We drove up the narrow valley of the Lütschine to Lauterbrunnen, eight miles, between prodigious mountain-walls which yet nurse soft and tranquil meadows under their frowning crags, dotted thick with brown châlets and musical with the cheerful bells of sleek cattle grazing in bits of greenest pasture. At last we are favored with the *Ranz des Vaches*, not as one would prefer to have it, from the pipe of the free-born, untamed descendant of Tell, high up among the clouds, but from the long horn of a degenerate son, who by the wayside sounded its few notes clear and bright as those of a keybugle, for a small eleemosynary coin. But this was a good deal better than nothing, and the well-accented call, to which from dell and high mountain-side " 'twixt the gloaming and the mirk the kye come hame," died out in soft, far echoes most pleasingly. These Swiss cattle are fine, gentle creatures, smallish mostly, snugly built and strikingly like the Alderneys, great numbers having all the external marks, fawn color, black switch, small horns, and, I was told, black mouths. I tried several times to find out something definite about them, but could only get for answer that they are "Uri" cattle.

At a turn of the valley at Lauterbrunnen we came face to face with the Jungfrau rising in dazzling glory, with the Eiger and Monch beside her, and on our right close at hand the Staubbach falls from an abrupt wall of rock nearly 1000 feet—at first a little cascade shining high up, as if poured from the clouds, then dissolved into mist by its long descent, and at last collecting itself again in a little stream at the bottom.

In the afternoon we took steamboat up Lake Brienz to visit the Giessbach Falls, made by a considerable stream which falls abruptly a distance of 1100 feet from one of the great mountains closely shutting in the lake.

*September* 18.—Left Interlaken for Lucerne, going by steamboat up to the head of Lake Brienz, eight miles, to the brown, sleepy village of the same name, where we took the railway crossing the Brunig Pass. At Meiringen we lunched, had three hours to wait, and visited the gorge formed by the Aare, having cut its way during unknown ages sharply down through a rocky mountain-range. The cañon so formed is even more wonderful than the Black Cañon of the Gunnison. For more than half a mile the perpendicular walls on each side rise 1000 feet, and so near together that in places one, by extending his arms, can touch both sides. At the bottom of this awful chasm rushes the Aare, gray and icy from the near glaciers whence it springs, and the hard rock of the walls is worn into enormous pot-holes, whose remains present many fantastic resemblances to the architectural work of man's hand. It is made possible to see the whole extent of this surprising wonder by an admirable foot-path made, at very considerable cost and great labor, by setting iron braces into the stone wall on one side and laying planks of wood on them with a secure railing. This careful path runs the entire length of the cañon, some twenty feet above the stream.

Our train, with an engine constructed for the purpose, climbed up the Brunig through pastures, orchards and fine woods of walnut, chestnut and beech, with broad views, widening as we ascend, of the rich valley of the Aare far below, the sage-green expanse of Lake Brienz and the noble mountains around it far beyond Interlaken. At the height of Brunig Pass we are 3400 feet above the sea, and descend to Lucerne through wild and pleasing scenery, reaching that charming town at 6 P.M. to find the Schweizerhof, where we had rooms before, so full as not to be able to take us in, although Frattini had telegraphed from Interlaken the night before. The landlord had been good enough to secure us rooms at the Swan, where we were made comfortable for the night.

There are more than one thousand hotels in Switzerland, and never has any such pressure been made on them as during this season, when the best ones turn away great numbers every day. They are admirable hotels in every respect, and managed with such efficiency that they do not seem crowded, and everything goes on without friction or worry. The charges are not high for the quality of the accommodation, and the bills, of precise and, to an American, vexatiously long list of items, when footed up will be found less than those of our best hotels. The European innkeeper can afford the same accommodations as his transatlantic brother at less prices because he avoids by his methods the wasteful extravagance of the American hotel-table, where a guest is permitted to order unlimited dishes, and pays the same as if he restricted himself to one. On this side of the water the guest pays for just what he has, no more and no less, and is not allowed to waste more at table than he consumes there. The feeing of servants, when one comes to understand just what the custom is, does not go beyond what the waiters of various kinds expect at our city and watering-place hotels. The service everywhere here is excellent.

*September* 19.—Took train at 6 A.M. on the Brunig road back as far as Alpnach-Gestad, where, having joined a party of Brooklyn friends, we made the ascent of Mount Pilatus by a railway which began running last June. It is a marvel of engineering, boldly conceived and admirably executed, and not to be ventured on without a tremor, as it climbs squarely up the mountain's face on an average gradient of 40 feet in 100, bridges awful chasms, winds along dizzy depths, scales precipices, and after two hours sets the thankful passenger down a few feet from the summit of the highest peak, 6965 feet above the sea. It is not common to get a good view from Pilatus, his top being much oftener hidden in clouds than the Rigi, 1000 feet lower. But we enjoyed a day absolutely perfect, a "day of a thousand," as the manager of the resting-place on the summit informed us. During the forenoon all the vast expanse of land and water below was buried from our sight under the shining billows of a sea of clouds, out of which rose, all about the horizon, hundreds of mountain-peaks, many green and smiling, like "sunny-sided Teneriffe," while the entire range of the Appenzell, Glarner and Bernese Alps, including Sentis, Ruchen-Glarnisch, Finsteraarhorn, Wetterhorn, Monch, Eiger, Jungfrau, Blumlisalp, Stockhorn, and a hundred lesser peaks, reared their sublime heads, refulgent with everlasting snow, into a sky without stain. Below, the translucent clouds, soft as carded wool, shifted and parted, often disclosing glimpses of the green earth, blue lakes and dwarfed villages; above, in wide semicircle, the most illustrious of earth's mountains, cold, steadfast, unchangeable, the image of eternity! Later in the day the clouds at our feet slowly melted away, like the unsubstantial fabric of a vision, and the whole vast panorama revealed itself smilingly, valleys, plains, lakes and forests and mighty hills, verdure-clad, with the towers, spires and houses of Lucerne clustered at the foot of its cruciform lake. Not again may I expect to look on such a scene of mingled sublimity and loveliness.

We took the evening train to Basel and slept there, leaving by early morning train for Metz, the capital of Lorraine, where we arrived at 2 P.M., passing through Strassburg and again gaining a look at its lofty, graceful Cathedral spire. This old Roman town of Metz, plundered by Vandals and Huns in the fifth century, the capital of the kingdom of Austrasia in the sixth century, then a free city of the German Empire, was captured by the French in 1552, and incorporated with Germany in 1871. The French made it one of the most strongly fortified places in Europe, the Germans have strengthened it still more, and now it is a vast fortress, girdled with outworks, nearly fifteen miles in circumference, and swarming everywhere with soldiers, sixteen thousand of whom are stationed in the town itself, the citizen population of which numbers something over 50,000—less than before it was annexed to Germany, and it is said more than a fourth of these are German settlers.

We met soldiers everywhere, lounging on the streets and squares, marching in squads, drilling in battalions in the open spaces of the suburbs, in a bewildering confusion of uniforms, blue, green, black, red, with intermediate shades, there being as many uniforms as states comprising the Empire. Officers of various rank strut up and down, fine, proud, bold-looking men, with strong faces, broad shoulders, erect, soldiers from top to toe.

We visited the fine Gothic Cathedral, dating from the thirteenth century, with its unusually lofty nave and old stained glass, and drove to the public cemetery, where the French have erected a great monument to seven thousand of their countrymen buried here in a vast grave after the great battles of August and September, 1870, which resulted in the surrender of Metz by General Bazaine, with nearly two hundred thousand men and a prodigious amount of munitions of war. The monument is covered with wreaths and touching mementos of many kinds sent from all parts of France, and hung here in memory of a husband, son, or brother, sacrificed to the weak ambition of Napoleon III., whose star sunk in blood behind the hills of Gravelotte, now saddened by the touch of the frost of two nights ago, while the blue Moselle, then choked with the slain, flows peacefully between its vine-clad banks.

We came on to Trèves by evening train, and have good lodgings at the Hotel de Trèves.

*September* 20.—I came here mainly to see the famous Roman ruins, and am not disappointed in them. Trèves (German, Trier), on the right bank of the Moselle, with 26,000 inhabitants, is called the oldest town in Germany, was founded by the Romans soon after Cæsar had conquered the Belgic tribe of the Treveri, 56 B.C., during the fourth century was a frequent residence of the Roman emperors, and the Roman remains here are said to be the finest on this side of the Alps. Constantine introduced Christianity, and from the year 328 onward for fifteen centuries it was the residence of the bishops, archbishops and electors. All this is stated in my trusty Baedeker. The site is a noble one, on a broad plain watered by the Moselle and girdled by soft ranges of wooded hills. The vine flourishes on its banks, and the Moselle wines, ranging from one to ten marks per bottle, are among the best of the light-bodied white wines. There is now in session here what is somewhat ambitiously called the Wine Congress, consisting of representative wine-growers from all the vine districts of Germany, their object being to discuss methods of growing and marketing wines, testing the qualities of different wines for a series of years, and so forth. I have tried to pick up some information from these intelligent gentlemen, several of whom speak English well and courteously answer questions. I will keep what I think I have learned—which is not much, but seems something to me, as I knew so little before—until I have seen and located the choice regions they speak of on the Rhine.

I was astonished to see such a perfect relic of the palmy days of Rome as the Porta Nigra, a fortified gate of the old Roman wall which once surrounded the city, with its towers mostly in perfect condition. This imposing structure of red sandstone is 115 feet long, 75 to 90 feet high, and 29 feet in depth. The huge blocks of sandstone are fastened with braces of iron and copper instead of mortar. It rises in three lofty stories, with handsome pillars between the windows; the arched passage was defended by a portcullis, and an enemy passing the outer barrier found himself in an inner space where he could be assaulted on all sides and from above—a most satisfactory ruin. Another fine ruin is the Roman Palace, of great extent, one massive corner of which is 65 feet high. It must have been a regal abode in its time, with its enormous halls, courts, and spacious servants' quarters, all heated by warm air, the channels for which are visible in many places. It was built of broad, thin bricks, laid in mortar, the name of the manufacturer still legible on the edges of some. There are also the extensive remains of the public baths lately exhumed near the Moselle, which supplied the water through covered brick aqueducts; and besides the spacious swimming-pools there were tepid and hot baths; hot air to produce them being applied under the tiled floors. The arena of an amphitheatre, 228 feet in diameter from north to south and 159 feet from east to west, is distinctly shown, with its entrances for spectators, dens for the wild beasts and doors for the gladiators. It accommodated thirty thousand spectators; and here in 306, Constantine, who had then "experienced religion," caused several thousand captive Franks to be torn by wild beasts ; and seven years afterward thousands of the Bructeri were slain here for the amusement of the populace.

Four hundred years ago the monks of a monastery here began a library, which has been growing in the old vaulted rooms ever since, and is now owned by the city. Here are some of the rarest and most valuable books in the world locked away in vaults and constantly watched by a custodian who exhibits them with a great deal of proper pride—for a consideration. Among them is the Bible of Faust and Gutenberg of 1450 and the Catholicon or Dictionary of 1460, and the entire Bible written on parchment in the eighth century in a beautiful hand, but so fine that it cannot be read without a glass of very considerable magnifying power. There is a specimen dating from 950 of the art of illumination as then practised, which the librarian insists is the finest known—the "Codex Egberti." But the crown of all, which is never allowed out of its glass case, is the "Codex Aureus," containing the four gospels, presented by Ada, the sister of Charlemagne, to the Abbey of St. Maximin. It was written in the latter part of the eighth century by a monk of the monastery of Rigeneau, on the Bodensee—Lake Constance—and was bound in the fourteenth century in gold inlaid with precious stones, among them a cameo as large as the palm of my hand, engraved with a representation of the family of Constantine, done in his lifetime. The librarian stated that the city had been offered twenty-five thousand pounds for this volume. He stated that the first Napoleon, stopping here on one of his campaigns, came into the library and selected some four hundred volumes and sent them to Paris, where they are now in the National Library, and that, in concluding the peace with France in 1871, Germany would have required their restitution, but it was overlooked, and that no money which has since been offered— and he mentioned a very large amount—has been able to secure their return. On the shelves in the various recesses of this library are rows on rows of huge folios running back almost to the beginning of printing ; some of enormous thickness, bound in carved boards dark with age, boar's-hide and heavy embossed Spanish leather with enormous brass and iron clasps ; and many with chains attached to fasten them to the wall, so they might not be carried away. There is a pair of handsome globes made one hundred and fifty years ago, finely mounted and not less than four feet in diameter. On the terrestrial one California is represented as a long, narrow island.

The Leibfrauenkirche is an interesting early Gothic church, dating from the early part of the thirteenth century, with a portal ornamented with sculptures of equal date, exhibiting scenes from the Old and New Testaments. It is connected with the Cathedral of St. Peter and St. Helen by the most perfect cloisters I have yet seen, broad and arched, surrounding a cheerful, sunny court. The Cathedral itself is interesting because a part of it was a quadrangular basilica, built by the Emperor Valentinian I. about 370, and soon after changed into a Christian church and modified from time to time, so that several styles of architecture are shown in the different parts.

But the distinguishing honor of the Cathedral, and indeed of the city of Trèves, is the possession of the "Holy Coat," the seamless tunic or outer garment of our Saviour, said to have been brought from Palestine in the fourth century by that indefatigable and eminently successful relic-hunter, the Empress Helena, mother of Constantine, and by her deposited here and exhibited solemnly to the public at long intervals of time, the latest exposition having occurred in 1844, when a prodigious multitude of pilgrims from all parts of Europe gathered here to bless their eyes and hearts with the vision of it, to possess themselves of articles charged with miraculous virtue from having touched it, and to participate in the benefits of the miracles it works. As this *tunica sacrosancta* is now laid away in its costly shrine we may not see it, but as there are, I believe, twenty others in existence in various parts of Europe for which the same claims are made, we may chance to come across one yet. This one is described as smock-like in shape, with a hole for the neck and short half-sleeves. The color is a peculiar shade of brown, and the appearance like that of old Chinese silk without gloss. The history of this relic can really be traced no further back than the latter part of the twelfth century, when it was "rediscovered"—a most helpful and convenient word. It is still an object of profound reverence to the Catholic world, and doubtless the streets of this quaint old city will swarm again with visitors at the next promised exposition two years hence.

*September* 23.—The weather this morning was cold and foggy

and threatened a decidedly bad day, but our good fortune in this regard continued, for on our way by rail to Coblentz the fog soon lifted and the sun came out, not warm, but cheerful. We have had quite cool weather for a week, and in Trèves had a fire steadily in our sitting-room in one of those tall, cylindrical porcelain stoves which are found in the rooms we occupy everywhere in Germany and Switzerland as well. They are of many sizes and patterns; some a long cylinder running up to the ceiling of the room, with a fluted capital, some half as high, others square. Sometimes they are ornamented with brass bands running round them. In the shops where antiquities are sold I have seen old ones with the tiles painted in figures and landscapes, and in a room in the house of Goethe's father in Frankfort is a charmingly quaint one with excellent pictures on it. Ours at Trèves worked nicely and gave out a soft and agreeable warmth somewhat as does the freestone stove one meets with now and then in old-fashioned houses in New England. But the most astonishing contrivance for protection from cold, and one as universally in use as the porcelain stove, is the thick sack of down, a little over three feet square, used as a coverlet on the beds. It is impossible to understand how so sensible a people as the Germans got into the way of tolerating such a covering at night; for it is neither one thing nor the other, and lies on the sleeper in the centre or at either end of him like a ridiculous, huge, puffy poultice. Nothing is more comical than a human creature lying asleep with one of these down bags on his stomach, rising and falling with his breathing.

Our way to Coblentz lay along the clear, easy-flowing Moselle, whose banks, terraced high up at great expense, grow very choice grapes. There is nothing poetical about a vineyard in these districts. There may be where the vines are trellised and overrun arbors, with the dark eyes of laughing maidens peeping out from among the leaves; but a vine four feet high tied to a pole a foot higher than itself is not a specially pretty thing, either singly or by millions, and altogether less satisfactory to the æsthetic sense than a field of hops or Indian corn.

Coblentz lies pleasantly at the union of the Moselle with the Rhine. We lunched here, and drove across the bridge of boats and up to the platform of the old castle of Ehrenbreitstein, perched on a precipitous rock nearly 400 feet above the Rhine. This castle is a disappointment to me, presenting now only the long line of a modern fortification built on the scarcely visible ruins of the grim old fortress which once frowned on the smiling valley below.

At 2 P.M. took the express steamboat down the Rhine, but as it is our intention to ascend the river soon, I will defer writing my impressions until then. We reached Cologne at 6 P.M. and found excellent accommodations in the fine Hotel du Nord. This city has filled an important place in history from a very early time, and was founded by the tribes of the Ubii 38 B.C., when driven by the Romans from the right to the left bank of the Rhine, about one hundred and fifty miles above Rotterdam. In A.D. 51 Agrippina, the mother of Nero, established a colony of Roman veterans here and named the settlement Colonia Agrippina. She was born here, and Vitellius and Trajan were proclaimed emperors here. In 310 Constantine built a bridge over the Rhine here, afterward destroyed by the Normans; and his mother, St. Helena, founded the Church of St. Gereon. In 355 it was devastated by the Franks. Their kings, Dagobert and Pepin, resided here, and the wife of the latter founded the Church of St. Maria im Capitol. Charlemagne had a palace here. Then follows a long and dreary record of internal strife and outside wars, but the city prospered in spite of them, and at the end of the fifteenth century was one of the richest and most prosperous towns in Germany, with a commerce extending to all parts of the known world. Its Easter fairs were famous, it had great warehouses in London, the arts flourished, and in science and letters it could boast of Duns Scotus, Albertus Magnus and Thomas Aquinas, and many a famous painter and architect. Its prosperity waned through the change in the channels of trade consequent on the discovery of America, by the revolution caused by the Reformation, by the Thirty Years' War, and lastly by its occupation by the French in 1794, when it lost its independence and was plundered to such an extent that of its one hundred and thirty-seven churches and chapels only thirty were spared, and its population in 1807 had dwindled to 42,000. But after the overthrow of Napoleon and its annexation to Prussia, it again exhibited its strenuous vitality, and has grown with astonishing rapidity into a handsome, mostly modern town of nearly 200,000 inhabitants, the third largest city in Prussia and the sixth largest in Germany. Indeed, I have scarcely visited a city of finer buildings in its extensive modern parts.

The crowning architectural glory of Cologne, and, indeed, of all this mighty German land, so rich in architecture, is its great Cathedral, completed in 1880—six hundred and thirty-two years after the laying of the first stone. The history of this magnificent Gothic structure is very interesting, and I make a *résumé* of it from an interesting pamphlet I find here, compiled by F. T. Helmken, of this city. It stands on an artificial mound raised by the ruins of buildings dating from the Roman period, on the spot where stood the Capitol, the Forum and the Temple of Mercury. A church dedicated to St. Peter stood here in the time of Charlemagne. But when the relics of the Magi were brought from Milan to Cologne in 1163, pilgrims flocked to worship them to such an extent from all parts of Europe that it was decided to build them a more worthy shrine, and the foundation-stone of the present Cathedral was laid with great pomp on August 15th, 1248. There is a doubt about the name of the architect who prepared the designs, but it seems to have been a certain Gerard, the superintendent of the building of the choir. This part was carried on by his successor, Arnold, and completed by Arnold's son in 1330. In the year 1347 the walls of the south nave and south tower were begun, but hindered by feuds and strife, so that the work only went on by piecemeal until 1560, when it ceased altogether, and the structure remained in a ruinously unfinished state until 1833, when, at the instance of King Frederick William III. of Prussia, a subsidy was granted to restore the parts damaged by time, and gradually the enthusiasm of the German people became kindled toward its restoration, rulers of the various German states, societies and public-spirited individuals interested themselves, abundant means were supplied, and in 1842 the foundation-stone for its continuance was solemnly consecrated by Archbishop John of Geissel and laid in place by the king, in the presence of an illustrious assemblage of princes, bishops and noblemen. In the course of his speech on the occasion the King said :

"This is the work of fraternal affection among all Germans, all confessions. When I reflect on this fact, my eyes fill with tears of joy, and I thank God for having permitted me to see this day. Here, where this stone is being laid, hand in hand with yon towers, the finest gates in the world shall arise. Germany is building them, and may they, by the grace of God, be the portals through which Germany shall enter upon new, grand and good times."

I cannot trace the steps in this interesting story; how this miracle of grace and grandeur grew, as the forests grow, to its completion, until now it stands the most perfect Gothic structure, it is said, in all the world. The entire sum expended between 1842 and 1880 amounted to upward of nine hundred thousand pounds. It is a curious fact that a part of this vast sum was raised by a lottery. A huge crane which was taken down from the unfinished south tower in 1868 had stood there for four hundred years. The whole was completed according to the original designs, and in glass cases in one of the chapels are preserved two parts of these designs, supposed to be lost, one of which was found in Paris in 1816; one portion of another at Darmstadt in 1814, and the remaining portion of this also, in Paris, in 1816. No wonder devout souls looked upon their accidental recovery as a signal act of Divine Providence. It is vain for me to attempt a description of this noble edifice. I will content myself with copying the bald figures of its enormous dimensions. Unlike those cathedrals which were begun in the early Norman style and during centuries continued to grow under different architects, who used plans modified by the changing styles, until, when completed, they show parts expressive of each, this one is pure Gothic of the best period. It is built in the form of a cross, mostly of gray sandstone from the Drachenfels. The nave is flanked with double, the transept with single aisles. The total length is 444 feet; breadth, 201 feet; length of transept, 282 feet; height of the walls, 150 feet; of the roof, 201 feet; of the towers, 512 feet—the loftiest church-towers in Europe. The principal portal between the towers is 93 feet high and 31 feet wide. The interior is borne by fifty-six enormous pillars, and its area is 7400 square yards. Meagre and cold are the figures which seek to convey some idea of the dimensions of this miracle of art, this wonder of man's conception and execution, but colder still must be the human soul that does not feel moved and exalted by its sublimity and beauty. It is something as if one should find himself in a noble forest where everything incongruous and trivial had been permitted to perish; so that only the huge trunks of lofty trees in the utmost of perfection of branch and leafage, as they stood in towering, overhanging and interlacing boughs, had been touched by an angel's finger and turned to enduring stone. As the afternoon sun enters through countless windows, its light broken into all rich colors by glass wrought into holy forms of saints and confessors, archangels and the diviner forms of the Son of God and his virgin Mother, this bewildering light gleaming everywhere, intercepted only by perfect forms of pillars and tracery, far as the eye can reach, in a space so vast that he feels himself a mere atom: there is it revealed to the mind of man how nearly the truest art is allied to worship, and how veritably this vast and awful cathedral is a temple of the Most High, albeit made with hands.

In one of the chapels of the choir is the famous painting called the Dombild, a large winged picture by Stephen Lochner, representing the "Adoration of the Magi," said to be the best painting of the early German school, and, as it seems to me, a fine work. Speaking of the Magi, there is something very interesting, if one thinks upon it, of the part the "Bones of the Magi," or three wise men, Gaspar, Melchior, and Balthazar, who are reputed to be they who came from the East to worship the Infant Christ at Bethlehem, have played in the history of Cologne. They are said to have been brought to Constantinople by the Empress Helena, and afterward taken to Milan in the year 324, and in 1164 presented by Frederick Barbarossa to Archbishop Reinald von Dassel, who removed them to Cologne. The fame acquired by the city as the possessor of these holy relics is said to have greatly increased its prosperity, and the idea of the present Cathedral was conceived by Archbishop Engelbert to give a proper shrine for these illustrious remains; and in the Treasury of the Cathedral, among many rich and interesting articles, they are now enshrined in a costly reliquary of beautiful workmanship made in 1190; a silver shrine, 6 feet long, 3½ feet wide, and 4¾ feet high, gilded with pure gold and set with precious stones. In the lower portion of this shrine it is pretended that these bones now rest, and in the upper portion those of Sts. Nabor, and Gregory of Spoleto, whoever these last may be—a strange belief, or pretence of belief, to have lasted so firmly and actively from an early period in the spread of Christianity. The remains of St. Engelbert, the canonized archbishop, are also enshrined here in a large, costly reliquary, wrought in this city in 1663, of solid silver gilt with gold; a magnificent example of goldsmith's work, weighing one hundred and sixty-seven pounds. The upper portion of St. Peter's staff is also shown, consisting of an ivory knob resting on twelve inches of old hollow brass, such as might serve for a cane-handle. That I might correctly understand, I asked the sacristan if it formed a part of the staff St. Peter the Apostle used to carry. He said, "Certainly; do you not see how old and black the ivory is?" By the miraculous power inherent in it, St. Maternas, the first bishop of Cologne, is said to have been raised to life forty days after his death. There is also a rich Gothic reliquary of the fifteenth century containing two links of the chain of St. Peter—that is, of the chain with which he was bound in prison at Rome. There is also in the Treasury great store of crucifixes, croziers, staffs, monstrances, mitres, and so on, of prodigious intrinsic value, in gold and precious stones and ivory wrought with wonderful skill, all being presents from mighty dignitaries in Church and State during many centuries.

In the third story of the south tower hangs the peal of bells, five in number. The largest of these, the "Emperor's Bell" (Gloriosa), cast in 1875, weighs twenty-seven tons, the largest and heaviest bell in Europe, the bell of Toulouse coming next, then the bell of St. Stephen's Tower in Vienna, then Big Ben of Westminster. The tongue or hammer is eleven feet long and weighs sixteen hundred pounds, and requires the force of twenty-eight men to strike it. This bell was cast from cannon taken from the French in the Franco-Prussian war, and bears, among other inscriptions in German, the following as it is translated:

> "I'm called the Emperor's bell,
> The Emperor's praise I tell.
> On holy guard I stand,
> And for the German land
> Beseech that God may please
> To grant it peace and ease."

In the Gurzenich, built in 1440 by the city as a house in

which to entertain distinguished guests, is a noble banqueting hall 174 feet long by 72 feet wide, with a gallery, whose lofty ceiling of carved oak is sustained by twenty-two finely carved wooden pillars.

The Church of St. Gereon is interesting in several respects. The original structure was circular and of Roman origin, having been built by the Empress Helena, mother of Constantine the Great, and later changes have converted this portion into a decagonal nave 153 feet high, with a groined vault. This church is dedicated to St. Gereon, who with three hundred and eighteen Christian soldiers is said to have suffered death here during the persecution of the Christians under Diocletian. Stone sarcophagi arranged around a gallery along the chapels surrounding the nave are said to contain the bones of these martyrs, whose skulls are set in rows under gilded arabesques about the choir.

The Church of St. Maria im Capitol, consecrated in 1049 by Pope Leo X., has an ambulatory around the semicircular ends of the choir and transepts, giving the east end a trefoil shape. The original structure is said to have been founded by Plectrudis, wife of Pepin of Héristal and mother of Charles Martel. Her tomb, with a recumbent effigy of well-carved stone, in excellent preservation, and dating from the twelfth century, is in the large and handsome crypt sometimes used as a place of worship.

There is a Romish legend that an English princess named Ursula, on her return from Rome, whither she had gone on a pilgrimage, was intercepted here by the Huns, and with eleven thousand virgins of her train barbarously murdered. She was canonized, and we visited the old Church of St. Ursula, where thousands of bones, said to be those of these spotless maidens, are arranged in open cases, in all sorts of fantastic patterns, in the neatest and strangest way. Great stone coffins stand ranged about the chapels, said to be full of the same osseous fragments, while row upon row of smooth brown skulls are arranged on shelves, each dressed in a wide embroidered band, the work of generations of pious nuns. The priest who showed them, in answer to my question said they had recovered all the bones of the whole eleven thousand, including those of Ursula herself, which are choicely kept in a costly reliquary in the Treasury, only the skeleton of the right foot and an arm-bone mounted in silver being shown in separate shrines. Herein, too, is matter for reflection, if one will consider it. I should add that the burial-place of these martyrs was indicated by a dove, whose figure is shown in many places in the church, in painting and sculpture.

We ran down to Aix-la-Chapelle—German, Aachen—by rail, forty-four miles, over a broad, fertile plain—passing through Stolberg, a very important manufacturing town of 11,000 population, founded by French Protestant refugees who set up foundries here in the seventeenth century—and went directly to the Cathedral, an interesting structure of two distinct parts, in different styles of architecture ; one, built by Charlemagne in 800, in the Byzantine style, in octagon form, copied from St. Vitale in Ravenna, the remaining portion in the Gothic styles of different periods. The interior of the original octagon is supported by eight great columns, the upper story being relieved by a double row of pillars, some of marble brought from Rome, Trèves, and Ravenna. Napoleon carried the marble ones to Paris in 1794, but they were restored in 1815. In the dome is a huge mosaic on a gold ground, and below hangs an enormous circular candelabrum of gilded iron, presented by Frederick Barbarossa in 1168. There stands in the choir a reading-desk of great beauty cast in copper in the fifteenth century—an eagle, said to be of Roman work, on a copper stand. The pulpit, richly carved and stuck with precious stones and carved ivory, is a present from Henry II. of Germany in the year 1000. From it St. Bernard preached the second Crusade. In the gallery of the octagon stands a settle or chair made of marble slabs joined with iron clamps, a rude piece of furniture, in which, as the story is, Charlemagne was found seated in his tomb when it was opened by Otho III. in the year 1000, dressed in his imperial robes, bearing the insignia of the empire, his sword by his side, on his knees a copy of the Evangels bound in gold, and on his head a fragment of the Holy Cross. Frederick Barbarossa opened the tomb a second time in 1164 and put the remains in a beautiful, well-preserved Roman sarcophagus of Parian marble with the "Rape of Proserpine" finely cut in relief on the sides, and placed it in the gallery where it now stands. The chair was used for the coronation of the emperors.

This city was a favorite residence of Charlemagne, who

raised it to the second city of his empire, and died here in 814. All the German emperors from his time down to 1531 were crowned here, and it was specially designated the Free City of the Holy Roman Empire and Seat of Royalty. The insignia of the Empire were kept here until 1793, when they were transferred to the Imperial Treasury at Vienna. Many important treaties of peace have been concluded here, among them that of 1668 between Louis XIV. and Spain. It now has a population of 95,000 and is as modern a city as possible, with almost no remains of mediæval times except its churches, and is mainly, I should say, a dull and uninteresting town.

When one considers the wealth of the Cathedral Treasury in relics, one is not surprised to be informed, as I am by a curious little pamphlet sold me by a sacristan who made a great show of doing it stealthily, that during several centuries, beginning with the eleventh, pilgrims flocked here in prodigious numbers to witness the exposition of these relics, so that my veracious description states that in one day, in the year 1496, only four years after America became known to the world, one hundred and forty-two thousand were gathered in and about the city. Indeed, there seems to have been a sharp rivalry between Aix-la-Chapelle and Cologne as to whose prosperity should be most enhanced through the possession of relics superior in number and sanctity. The tide of popularity, gifts from rich pilgrims and the "offering-penny" from the poor, flowed to one and the other of these cities and cathedrals, according to the alternate rumors of new miracle-working relics acquired by each; and as the rivalry went on an enormous number were aggregated in the treasuries of their cathedrals, and their accumulation from time to time, to counteract each other's successful acquisitions, must have greatly taxed the ingenuity of the pious ecclesiastics charged with the duty of enhancing the revenues of their respective churches. The strange and wonderful subject of sacred relics and miracles has here in this state of things a lively and striking illustration. I have given a list of a few exhibited in Cologne. I copy at some length from the authenticated list of those in Aix-la-Chapelle.

In the Treasury of the Cathedral, in a great shrine of the thirteenth century, adorned with twelve hundred precious stones, are the "superior" or, as popularly known, "great" relics. These were during many centuries shown only once in seven years, except to crowned heads, on their special demand. They are:

> The yellow white garment of the mother of our Lord.
> The swathing-clothes of our Saviour.
> The cloth in which was laid the body of St. John the Baptist after his decapitation.
> The cloth which our Saviour wore around his loins in the dreadful hour of his death for our salvation.

Besides these is a long list of the inferior relics, from which I select only a few:

> The woven linen girdle of the holy Virgin, in a reliquary of the fourteenth century.
> The girdle of Jesus, made of leather, in a precious vessel of the fourteenth century.
> Part of the rope with which our Saviour was tied in his passion, in a vessel of the fifteenth century.

Joined in a reliquary:

> A fragment of the sponge that served to refresh our dying Lord upon the cross.
> A particle of the holy cross.
> Some hair of the Apostle St. Bartholomew.
> A bone of Zachary, father to St. John the Baptist.
> Two teeth of the Apostle St. Thomas.

In a shrine, richly enamelled and adorned with pearls and precious stones, given by Philip II., King of Spain:

> A fragment of the reed that served to make a mock of our Saviour.
> A part of the linen cloth which was spread over the holy face of our Lord in the grave.
> Some hair of St. John the Baptist.
> A rib of the first martyr, St. Stephen.
> A golden cross of Charlemagne, containing a particle of the holy cross.
> A statue of St. Peter the Apostle, showing in his hand a ring from the chain with which this man of God, who had suffered so many persecutions and trials, was chained in the prison.

A vessel containing little pieces of the bones of the twelve apostles.

A silver vessel containing bones of St. John the Baptist and of St. Nicolas.

Also in the Church of St. Adalbert here:

A shoulder-bone and a leg-bone of St. Mary Magdalen.

Two small particles of the sponge with which our Lord was refreshed upon the cross.

A fragment of the crib in which our Lord was laid at his birth.

Also in the parish Church of St. John the Baptist near the city:

A cross containing two particles of the holy cross, particles of the clothes of Jesus Christ, of the pillar and the whip serving at the scourging of our Lord, of the garment of the Holy Virgin and bones of St. Paul and St. James the younger, and finally a particle of the rod of Aaron and Moses.

In a small vial some blood of St. John the Baptist.

A particle of the bones of the innocent children.

Also in the Free Abbey of Cornelimuenster:

The linen cloth with which our Saviour girded himself and dried his disciples' feet at the Lord's Supper.

A large piece of the cloth that covered the Lord's face while in the grave.

The reason for this vast accumulation of relics as seen by us here is plainly to advance the prosperity of these two cities and aid in building their cathedrals, and is it not fully probable that they were invented and named and sanctified by the Church to further these ends? Could their motives have been honest? Were they sincere? How far at this time can these questions be answered? Certainly all the civilized world easily believed in them for centuries, as do devout Catholics now, and came to reverence and to worship. Nor in these very years were our English ancestors at all behind in relic-worship, for the shrine of St. Edward the Confessor in Westminster Abbey contained a no less holy relic than the crystalline vessel of our Saviour's blood. This precious relic was presented to King Edward, and is thus mentioned by Brayley in his history of the Abbey: "In 1247, on the day of the translation of Edward the Confessor, a vessel of blood which in the preceding year had been sent to the king by the Knights Templars and Hospitallers in the Holy Land, and was attested by Robert the Patriarch of Jerusalem to have trickled from our Saviour's wounds at the time of his crucifixion, was presented with great ceremony to this church," and conveyed in solemn procession by King Henry III in his own hands on foot from St. Paul's to the Abbey. The Bishop of Norwich that same day preached before the king in commendation of the relic, furnished the proofs of its genuineness, and the bishops there present pronounced one year and one hundred and sixteen days' pardon to all who should come and reverence it. Besides this vessel there was in this shrine, the stone marked by the impression of Christ's foot at his Ascension, a thorn of Christ's crown and a large piece of the true cross.

Returned to Cologne, and September 27th, at 7.30 A.M., took steamboat up the Rhine as far as Bingen, where we left the boat and passed the night at the Victoria Hotel. We had already descended the river by boat from Coblentz, sixty miles. For the first twenty miles between Cologne and Bonn the scenery along the river has only the interest belonging to a flat, well-cultivated region. At Bonn the banks rise in gently sloping hills, growing more and more abrupt, the river narrows, and soon the bold crag of the Drachenfels with its picturesque ruined castle rises on our left 900 feet above the river, all the circumstances agreeing to make an impressive picture. The Seven Mountains, being seven peaks of volcanic origin, rise grandly from the long range of which the Drachenfels is the head. The view up and backward on either hand unites beauty and a tender grandeur well portrayed by Byron with his masterly touch:

>  "The castled crag of Drachenfels
>   Frowns o'er the wide and winding Rhine,
>  Whose breast of waters broadly swells
>    Between the banks which bear the vine,
>  And hills all rich with blossomed trees
>    And fields which promise corn and wine,
>  And scatter'd cities crowning these
>    Whose far white walls along them shine."

Only now the tints of autumn are on the trees, and the promise of the vine is realized in the ripened clusters. One might feel disappointed in the Rhine who should not see it above Coblentz, but certainly not above that city, where it is lessened by the very considerable volume of the Moselle, and as far up as Bingen flows in many windings between lofty banks, precipitous in many places, abruptly sloping elsewhere, often intersected by narrow and dark ravines, bearing terrace upon terrace of vines, bright with the white walls of many an ancient village with its quaint towers and spires, lifted into the region of poetry by its ruined castle frowning down upon it, as if still affording a haughty protection ; and mediæval strongholds whose names abound in a wide realm of tradition and song and story. Stolzenfels, Marksburg, Sterrenberg, Liebenstein, Deurenburg, Rheinfels, Schönburg, Gutenfels, Stahleck, Fürstenberg, Nollich, Hoheneck, Sooneck, Falkenburg, Rheinstein, Ehrenfels, Mouse Tower, who is not more or less familiar with these from his boyhood? Very notable, wonderfully fair, were all these to me, seen in the hazy light of this September afternoon, the breath of Autumn in the air, and her many-hued mantle flung wide over all the stately landscape, as the boat passed slowly up the strong brown current of the classic Rhine.

At Bingen the river suddenly expands, its southern bank quickly sinks into the level of a broad plain, only at infrequent intervals presenting a rounded elevation of no especial interest. On the other hand, the bank slopes roundly up to the southern sun, and for the next twelve miles, with the special name of the Reingau, contains the famous vineyards of the Rhine in this order as we ascend the river : Rüdesheim, Geisenheim, Schloss Johannisberg, Marcobrunner, Steinberg. These vineyards are small in extent. That of Schloss Johannisberg consists of forty acres, in perfect cultivation, lying about the old yellow château standing on a rounded knoll, the site of an old Benedictine monastery. It is the property of Prince Richard Metternich, who once a year sells the product in the cask at auction on the premises. Near by are vineyards yielding the Johannisberg Klaus, next in value to the true Johannisberg, and besides there are vineyards about the village of Johannisberg, whose vintage is called by the general name of Johannisberger. These last are the wines we get in New York and other cities at home, when we get anything at all entitled to be called genuine. The Steinberg vineyard, sixty acres in extent, belongs to the government and is esteemed equally precious with the Schloss Johannisberg. It belonged to the rich Cistercian Abbey of Eberbach, seen dimly, by the aid of a glass, nestled in a narrow valley two miles away, and for more than six hundred years the good monks tended these precious vines, whose produce is also sold at auction every spring, the sale attracting the great wine merchants of a wide region. It is easy to see how limited is the quantity of these famous wines and what a prodigious amount of the ordinary wine of the country is bottled and sold under their titles.

The village of Bingen lies pleasantly on the sloping southern bank, and is picturesque and quaint with its surviving towers and bits of ancient wall. Very naturally would the "soldier of the Legion" who, in Mrs. Norton's fine poem, "lay dying in Algiers," turn his longing heart to his birthplace in "Bingen, fair Bingen on the Rhine." Just opposite, on the crest of a fair eminence, rises the great German National Monument, raised to perpetuate the rising of the German people and the foundation of the German Empire in 1870. The base is 78 feet high, and the grand figure of Germania with her sublime and serene and beautiful face, looking across the river, rises from it to the height of more than 30 feet.

The fifty-nine miles of river from Bingen to Mayence has little to interest, and we do no more in this latter city than visit an interesting museum of Roman and mediæval antiquities, the Cathedral, the house where Gutenberg was born, another where he set up the first printing-office ever known, and his noble statue in one of the squares, designed by Thorwaldsen, and by the afternoon train come to Heidelberg, a somewhat weary party, to find good welcome, and a grateful fire in the tall German stove, in pleasant rooms of the Hotel de l'Europe, where we propose to rest quietly over Sunday.

*September* 30.—Yesterday was a decidedly stormy day and, with its unseasonable cold, quite the worst we have encountered since leaving home, where we should call the weather of the last few days a magnified equinoctial storm ; but we feed the odd stove with sound beech-wood, read the packet of letters from home awaiting us here, and succeed very well in creating something of a home atmosphere in the heart of this old foreign city. To-day brings some improvement in the weather, and we have used it in a long visit to the Castle, the most famous in all the German land. The Castle or Château of Heidelberg is a fortified residence of huge extent, standing, a well-preserved ruin, on a wooded point projecting from the abrupt range of the Königsstuhl, which ends precipitously at the Neckar, just above the city, on which it looks down from the height of more than 300 feet. The oldest part was built by the Count Palatine Rudolph I. in 1294, was extended by several successors and strongly fortified, and in the sixteenth century palatial parts were added by several of the Electors who resided in it, among them Frederick V., King of Bohemia, who married Elizabeth, daughter of James I. of England. It stood intact until after its capitulation to Count Mélac, a French general, in the war Louis XIV. was waging against the Rhenish Palatinate, who dismantled it, destroyed its fortifications, and tried with only partial success to blow it up with gunpowder, leaving it a magnificent ruin of vast extent. It covered with its outer enclosures some forty acres, and its towers and the long line of palatial walls of red sandstone, richly carved and embellished with many heroic effigies of valiant mediæval knights and warriors of renown, its great halls, all desolate now, where feasting and revelry went on in royal fashion, its huge kitchens with hearths so prodigious that whole oxen were easily roasted below the enormous funnelled chimneys, its arched cellars below stored with wines, its halls of audience, its throne-room, its armory, its defensive walls, twenty feet thick, its deep moat, supplied from a reservoir up among the hills, its battlemented gates, all attest the strength and extent of this palatial fortress, and bring back the romance of the middle ages more vividly than the pictured pages of Froissart or Scott. Ivy festoons its outer walls and long weeds flaunt from its lonely battlements. Still, it is not to me so picturesque nor striking as several of those ruder keeps perched on the crags of the Rhine nor so impressive as Stirling Castle, which realized to my mind the ideal of a structure of this kind. In the cellar stands, sound and good, the great tun or cask, 30 by 25 feet, capable of holding forty-nine thousand gallons of wine—or rather it does not stand, but lies on huge beams, as it has done since 1751, when it was built to take the place of one made by Charles Philip in 1728, it in turn supplying the place of one built by Charles Lewis in 1662, and this succeeding the first one constructed by the Count Palatine Casimir in 1591. Huge as it is, it has frequently been filled, but not in these later years. There stands near it a wooden figure, in the style of a tobacco-shop sign, of Perkeo, court-jester of Elector Charles Philip, and fastened to the wall beside him a merry jest of his contrivance—one rings a bell, the handle of which depends from the bottom of a cupboard, the door of which flies open and a fox-tail is whisked into one's face—a bit of facetious coarseness worthy of a court-fool.

Heidelberg is a pleasant little city of nearly 30,000 souls, about one-quarter Catholic, and is crowded between the mountain-range on which the castle stands and the Neckar, a considerable stream, joining the Rhine some fifteen miles below, with sunny banks which furnish the Hock wines. I am told that the wines made into "sparkling" Hock and Moselle are usually of an inferior sort. There are factories at several points for manufacturing the sparkling German wines. The university here is the chief light of Southern Germany, and celebrated its five hundredth anniversary in 1886. It boasts of nearly one thousand students. The buildings are plain and simple, and the students' rooms mean, bare and dirty to an astonishing degree, but there is a fine new hall, which we were kindly permitted to see, together with other parts, although the winter semester is not yet begun.

*October* 1.—Left Heidelberg for Nuremberg at 8.30 A.M. by rail, following the windings of the turbid Neckar for two hours, its steep wooded banks glowing in the dyes of autumn and fringed with narrow margins of verdurous meadows and beset with many a brown old village overlooked by its ruined stronghold ; a continuously pleasing scene in the grateful sunlight. Leaving the valley of the Neckar, the road crosses to that of the Main, and at Wurzburg, a distance of one hundred miles, we lunch at the Russischer Hof, and give three hours to this very ancient and interesting city of 55,000 inhabitants, about one sixth of whom are Protestants. The capital of the district of Lower Franconia, it was formerly the seat of a prince-bishop and has been under ecclesiastical rule almost from its foundation. Its first bishop, Burcardus, was consecrated by St. Boniface in 741, and from that time until incorporated with Bavaria in 1803 it was ruled by an unbroken line of eighty-two bishops, who were made Dukes of Franconia in 1120. This well illustrates the kind of government these cities and adjacent regions, from Cologne up the course of the Rhine, were subject to until the power of Rome was broken by the Reformation. Haughty prelates lorded it over all this land, putting on armor oftener than the cassock, and wielding a mightier sway than mere secular princes were able to do. In the old Cathedral here stands a double row of them in well-wrought effigies of stone, and this cold material scarcely suffices for the arrogance and pride in which they stare forever from above the worn brasses whereon their praises are sounded in lying eulogy. At least one should be excepted; the good Bishop Echter von Mespelbrunn, who in the latter part of the sixteenth century founded a great hospital, whose extensive buildings we visited, where six hundred persons are fed and lodged and tended, the property belonging to it having an estimated value of four hundred and fifty thousand pounds.

We took a peep at the Royal Palace, one of the residences of the King of Bavaria, built in the style of the Palace of Versailles, with an imposing front of five hundred feet, a great stone staircase, a gaudy chapel, a theatre, and two hundred and eighty rooms, many richly furnished. And this is only one of the residences of a king of a nation unable to stand alone and forming only a component part of the German Empire! The cellars are said to be the most spacious in Germany, and to have in them some two hundred casks of good wine from the royal vineyards.

Near the Cathedral is a small ancient church, several times restored in its different parts, with cloisters now effaced, in one of which the famous mediæval Minnesinger or minstrel, Walther von der Vogelweide, was buried in 1230. There is a tablet to his memory on the exterior wall of the choir, erected in 1848, with inscriptions, and at the top a carved nest of young birds in act of being fed. The minstrel, as the story is, left a sum of money to be used for all time to feed the birds, but soon the priests attached to the church appropriated it, and it was seen no more. May the malison of all good singers rest heavily on their memory!

There is a fine old bridge over the Main, 650 feet long, built in 1474, with rows of saintly stone statues of heroic size on either parapet. The city has many interesting ancient buildings; a Rathhaus with a fine old square tower, and a ruined castle on a crag above the river, now restored and occupied as a citadel, and is altogether a town of attractions. But we hurry on at 5 P.M. to Nuremberg, where we have taught ourselves to expect the perfect expression of the mediæval period, and reaching it at 7 P.M. after dark, see, for a beginning, a horse railroad in the light of glaring electric lamps on poles thirty feet high. Only these we note on the way to the comfortable Bavarian Hotel, where we await the morrow.

*October 2.*—We awake to find ourselves in a huge, rambling hotel consisting of several connecting houses, one side running along the Pegnitz, which flows midway of the city, with two courts enclosed, overhung by old balconies, the whole dating from the fifteenth century. Its long, winding passages, numerous stairways and irregular rooms and general monastic air prepare one for antiquity outside.

Nuremberg, or Nürnberg, as the Germans spell and pronounce it, has a population of 114,000, and until 1806 was an independent imperial town, but has since belonged to Bavaria. It dates back to the early part of the eleventh century, when its castle was begun by the Emperor Conrad II., extended by Frederick Barbarossa in 1158, and fitted up as a royal residence in 1854 in the Gothic style. The city grew to great prosperity, in spite of the feuds, dissensions and frequent change of rulers common to all towns through the dreary middle ages, and in the beginning of the sixteenth century ranked next to Augsburg as the chief seat of trade between Germany, Venice and the East. Its citizens were rich and liberal, and built fine private residences in the best style of the times, and lavished their wealth in embellishing them. By a happy coincidence, there arose here at this period artists whose lives were given to beautifying the city in their respective provinces of art—Adam Krafft in sculpture, Veit Stoss in wood-carving, Peter Vischer and his sons, the brass-founders, Ludwig Krug and Peter Flötner, the die-cutters, the goldsmiths Wengel Jannitzer and Valentin Maler. Here lived and wrought the great painter Albrecht Dürer, and here the merry cobbler Hans Sachs sang his joyful songs. All kindly arts flourished in these fostering circumstances of easy opulence, treasures of art accumulated here, and although the prosperity of the city fell off after the new sea-route to India was found, and was abated still more by the Thirty Years' War, these treasures continued, and the old town stands less changed from its mediæval state by the modern prosperity come to it from its incorporation with Bavaria than any city we have visited on this side the Atlantic, quaint Bruges perhaps excepted.

The walls surrounding the early city date from the middle ages and are intact, except where they have been opened at several points to afford communication with the newer parts growing up outside, and with the covered ways extending along their tops, interrupted at intervals by noble and picturesque towers various in form and built with an eye to beauty as well as to safety, forming a fitting frame to the lofty, red-tiled houses rising from narrow, sinuous streets, topped with steep roofs as tall as themselves; broken from foundation to ridge with openings for doors ; and windows, square, round, oval, lozenge, ornamented with the quaintest, most fanciful and graceful, even when grotesque embellishments of carved stone balconies, copings, tiny pent-house sheds rising into tiled pinnacles—fifty forms, in short, of curious device, to impart a charming variety to the ancient roofs and gables. It seems as if each builder exercised his individual taste and invented his own peculiar dwelling, making it an expression of his own sentiments and character, not even paying regard to the line of the street in placing it ; so that the houses stand not in rows, but at all sorts of angles to the streets ; and the narrow footways are obliged to conform as well as they can, running along the front of one, in width scarcely enough for a single pedestrian, widening in front of the next, turning a sharp angle to a third, and so on, with admirable differences and picturesqueness, presenting something rare and strange at every turn. Time has softened and enriched the grays, reds and yellows of walls and roofs, so that viewed from a high point, like the platform of the castle, the whole presents a harmonious and agreeable picture.

The castle is one of the most interesting we have seen ; indeed, one's ideal of an antique stronghold is fully realized when one stands in the court-yard with square towers and round, connected by battlemented walls shutting him in—here the low entrance through an iron door which has swung on its worn hinges for five hundred years; there a worn flight of stone steps leading down to a half-subterranean chapel, now bare, but in perfect preservation, where Christ and the Virgin were worshipped seven hundred years ago, and on every hand perfect remains of ages before the land we live in was even conjectured to exist. In the centre of this court stands the huge trunk of a lime-tree, now well denuded of its branches, but still sound and able to show some tufts of foliage, believed to have been planted by the fair hand of the Empress Cunigunde, wife of Emperor Henry II., in the year 1000—a thing probable enough when we consider the prodigious age attributed by the botanists to the big sequoias of California. In some of the ancient rooms are several old tiled German stoves of patterns and decoration which make them delightful works of art, and from a balcony looking out from the queen's apartments is a broad and beautiful view across the great plain to the blue Franconian hills and down upon the picturesque city; its steep, dull-red roofs surmounted with a hundred antique domes and towers and spires; on the broad moat, now grown with great trees and laid out in little garden-plats; on odd-shaped little parks scattered among the streets, enlivened with noble statues of famous men, artists and poets who lived and worked here; and fountains in stone and bronze, works of old art and beautiful exceedingly.

Near one of the towers in the court is a famous well, dug down through the solid rock more than 300 feet some centuries ago, and still furnishing excellent water. Half way down this well begin two opposite subterranean passages, one leading to the centre of the city, the other to a point beyond the walls. We are shown, in a sort of dungeon of one of the towers, a great collection of instruments of torture, comprising all sorts needful to agonize and mutilate God's image—long pincers with wooden handles to be heated red in the brazier standing by and used in tearing away the quivering flesh; iron caps which could be forced into the brain by tightening; iron boots for crushing the leg; a notched blade fitting into another by a hinge for cutting out the tongue; many forms of thumb-screws; a cradle set with iron nails; the wheel, the rack—indeed, the walls are hung full of the devilish enginery by which their High Mightinesses, lay and ecclesiastical, terrorized and held in abject submission the bodies and souls of the toiling masses subject to their tyranny.

In a gloomy chamber of massive stone, in another tower, stands, where it is said to have stood for centuries, an instrument of death called the Jungfrau—" Young Maiden "—the heavy cast iron statue of a girl with smiling face, but opening in two ponderous, longitudinal parts, hinged at the back, with the concave inner sides of face and breast stuck full of long, sharp spikes. The destined victim, who has passed his last night on earth in a rough stone crib set in a dark angle of the walls, is led before it, the body opens, he is thrust backward, still erect, within its dreadful hollow, it resumes its form, the iron face smiling in cruel mockery, and there only remains a ghastly mass of quivering flesh to be dropped down through the trap-door opening below the feet of the statue. One deems it incredible that these dreadful instruments could actually have been used by man on man, and that an age has ever been when so much cruelty and diabolical savagery existed in the world; for have I not just seen in the great Gothic church of St. Lawrence, whose beautiful and pious walls grew through these same centuries at the foot of this stronghold of cruelty ; illumined with windows where saints and angels shine in the many-dyed glory of old glass, and rich with rows of holy men in well-carven stone, the ciborium or tabernacle for the sacred Host by Adam Krafft, under whose patient and pious hands the stone figures of it grew to life, amid rarest forms of carven flowers, the whole graceful and airy as a dream of the night ? And in those same ages can it be that Peter Vischer consecrated thirteen years of devout toil to the wonderful bronze tomb wherein, in the Church of St. Sebaldus, are enshrined the bones of that holy personage ? Was Dürer giving to immortal canvas then, the sweet, pitiful face of the Virgin and her divine Son ; and could merry Hans Sachs tune a gleeful lay—could all these masterful and tender souls labor here, with wails of prisoners moaning on the rack, falling on their ears from the castle on the hill ? Strange and incongruous is this mingling of the savage and the refined ; this barbarism with enlightened art !

In the interesting museum of antiquities admirably arranged in the halls and cloisters of an old Carthusian monastery, among a great store of mediæval relics, is an ancient guillotine, which has evidently done service, of the precise pattern used in France for capital punishment, except that it lacks the plank to which the victim is lashed; showing plainly, since it is not less than three hundred years old by the arrangement of the collection, which is most exactly made by learned German antiquarians, that Dr. Guillotin, of the Reign of Terror epoch, did not invent the instrument to which he gave his name. Perhaps he improved it in some respects, and so got the reputation of an inventor; as Colonel Colt of Hartford did in the article of the revolver; a form of which, dating back not less than two hundred years, is to be found in many collections of old arms I have seen. There is in this museum a pistol with seven barrels, all fired by one lock.

The several bridges over the Pegnitz, of quite individual styles, are interesting features of the city—one covered, one in imitation of the Ponte Rialto in Venice, one set with statues, and among them a suspension foot-bridge built in 1824.

We part reluctantly from this most interesting city, and at 7 P.M. take train for Ratisbon—German, Regensburg—a ride of two and one-half hours. We passed the night here in the Goldenes Kreuz, or Golden Cross Hotel, built more than four hundred years ago, having a massive tower, on one side of which is a medallion of Don John of Austria, the famous general, a natural son of Charles V., and a pretty girl here, Barbara Blumberger. The Emperor lodged at the Golden Cross when attending a Diet here in 1546, and Don John followed as one of the consequences in 1547.

*October* 5.—We came to this old city of Ratisbon chiefly to visit the Walhalla—" Hall of the Chosen"—erected on a hill 320 feet high, six miles from the town, to which we drove in the bright autumn weather, over a pleasant level country, meeting many peasants on foot carrying huge panniers filled with vegetables and fruits, and queer carts drawn by cows harnessed to them by the horns, trudging to market; with many more men, women and children at work gathering the late crops in the fields on either hand. The season is advanced, much the same as in southern Vermont at this time of year, and the forests and patches of woodland, distant and near, show pretty nearly the same variety and depth of colors in the foliage of the oaks, maples, lindens, chestnuts, walnuts and the lesser shrubbery.

This Walhalla was designed by the famous architect Klenze for King Louis, who founded it in 1830 for a German "Temple of Fame," wherein to place the busts of such Germans of renown as he should think worthy—a royal conception royally carried out at a cost of more than a million pounds sterling. The edifice is in the pure Doric style, in close imitation of the Parthenon at Athens, built of unpolished gray marble, is 246 feet long and 115 feet broad, and surrounded by a colonnade of fifty-two fluted columns nearly 60 feet high. The interior consists of one vast hall in the Ionic style, lighted from above. The ceiling, richly ornamented and gilded, is supported by fourteen painted Walkyries (warrior virgins of the ancient German Paradise), the sides and the floor are of beautiful marble-mosaic—everything of stone. The most eminent German artists were employed in its construction and decoration. The Walkyries are by Schwanthaler. The magnificent marble frieze running all around the hall, depicting the life of the Germanic nation from the earliest times to the introduction of Christianity, is by Wagner, the six beautiful marble statues of Victory are by Rauch. In this grand, cold, silent hall are one hundred finely executed marble busts arranged along the walls, and for them the massive pile was builded. The king showed a catholic taste in his choice of candidates for his "Temple of Fame;" and Frederick Barbarossa, Gutenberg, Frederick the Great, Luther, Blücher and Mozart stare at each other with steady eyes of stone across the vast, empty spaces. A strange thing under the sun is this shining Greek temple standing here in the lonely country-side, dedicated to such a purpose! The views from the porticoes are sublime and beautiful, including the winding sweep of the blue Danube past the gray walls of towered Ratisbon, its broad shining tributary, the Regen, and the dark line of the Bavarian forests in the far western horizon.

There are in Ratisbon some fine mediæval houses with peculiar towers of defence, and a cathedral with long, high aisles, like those of Strassburg, and handsome open towers and charming old cloisters with richly carved window-frames, and floors fully paved with tombstones of canons and patricians of the church and city; but it is a dull and rather gloomy town, whose 36,000 inhabitants do not seem to prosper overmuch. We had *table d'hôte* dinner in the great musty dining-hall at one o'clock, the German hour, the landlord sitting, in the good old way, at the head of his table, as did mine host at Nuremberg, and rising and bowing ceremoniously to the guests as they left the room. The table manners of the average German seem to fall something short of the standard prevailing in other countries. A well-dressed, highly respectable and intelligent-looking neighbor at table leaned forward so as to bring his face close down to his plate, and emptied it into his mouth with both knife and fork impartially. Here and elsewhere I observed both ladies and gentlemen take toothpicks from the stands containing this useful article set all along the tables, and beginning after the first course, use them freely and openly; laying them down on the cloth, and resuming them at each change of cover. With the dessert, lighted candles were set along the tables with alcoholic dips for smokers, who lighted up and puffed away regardless of the ladies around them.

We took train for Munich at 5 P.M., and in four hours were enjoying an open wood fire in cheerful rooms in the Four Seasons, well fagged with a hard week's work.

*October 6, Sunday.*—A cheerless, cold, rainy day, passed around the fire and over books. Monday—not much better—we passed in the old Pinakothek, a Greek name given to the admirable building containing the pictures of the old masters. This famous gallery—on the whole the best, I think, we have seen—contains some fourteen hundred pictures, arranged chronologically and according to schools, with a catalogue, which is a model of its kind, giving a few clear items about each painter and a description of each picture, translated from the German of Dr. Franz v. Reber into English of most felicitous expression by Mr. Joseph Thacher Clarke. The introduction gives a very interesting account of the sources of this collection, and sets forth how, under a succession of wise and liberal rulers who spared no pains or money in gathering paintings from all countries, this great gallery grew during three hundred years to its present excellence. ·The perseverance with which these royal enthusiasts hunted for individual works of fame, the diplomacy they used in the pursuit, the checks, delays, disappointments and triumphs they experienced in their acquisitions, and the perils to which these treasures were many times exposed by the shifting fortunes of war and the rivalries of other royal collectors, make a romantic story, but I cannot enter upon it. Let it suffice that here they are to-day, royally housed and open without charge to all the world. Nor can I undertake to give particulars of the treasures on the walls of the twelve great saloons, lighted from above, with twenty-four adjoining cabinets. Here are eighty-nine pictures of Rubens, including many of the finest works of this most fertile master, who exhibits in this one collection a prodigious range of imaginative power, extending from his awful "Last Judgment" through all grades of the savage and the tender, the wild and the graceful, to the "Children with Garlands." Many of these are not fully pleasing to me, but wonderful richness pervades them all. There are many by Rembrandt, but with the exception of his "Descent from the Cross" and two or three of his wonderful portraits, nothing to be compared with those I have seen elsewhere, especially at Amsterdam. There are some fine examples of Dürer and a few of Titian, his "Christ Crowned with Thorns" and his portrait of Charles V. among them. Here are Raphael's Madonnas, *di Tempi* and *della Tenda*, and his "Holy Family" from the House of Canigiani. Here is the original of Andrea del Sarto's "Holy Family," of which many "repetitions" are to be found elsewhere. But I cannot enlarge. Nearly all the great painters of all lands and times before the middle of the last century are represented here. The charm and perfection of the collection to me, however, are not so much in the merit of particular pictures as in the great number of excellent painters of each school ; so that the eye goes with delight over a wide range of the works of the best painters of every age and school, including those of the Dutch, Flemish, Upper German, Italian, Spanish and French. I must mention Murillo's "Beggar Boys." What a painter he was ! I have not seen a poor Murillo ; not one but is most natural and admirable.

I love to linger in these spacious continental galleries, so quiet and orderly, picking out what most pleases me in design or form or color, and if often weary of the interminable array of themes from Biblical story and the legends of the saints, still find something to admire and be thankful for in the tender piety and graceful love which sought in dark and untaught times to shadow forth a mystery or record a miracle for the comfort and instruction of the people. What visions of grace and beauty, what dreams of terror, what grotesque fancies haunted the minds of these early workers in the world of art ; from the dying and dead Saviour and tender Madonna to the emaciated saint and demons belching flames ; and how they struggled with touch upon touch and color upon color to depict them adequately ; great bands of gold and wealth of purple and crimson and blue and green, and how well, in some one respect at least, each one has succeeded ! The motive may be unnatural or grotesque, the drawing at fault, the grouping absurd, the personages and costumes archaic ; but one is sure to find some beautiful, tender or noble sentiment, or some bit of delightful execution, which lifts the work of even the earliest painters from the mean and trivial, and invests it with a certain sacred dignity and beauty. At least so it seems to me, as day after day, now for months, I go about in gallery after gallery and church after church, in these old continental cities.

There is a collection of modern pictures in a noble building designed by Voit, called the New Pinakothek. This numbers several hundred pictures by the leading German artists who have painted in the present century, including examples by Achenbach, Becker, Braekeler, Camphausen, Defregger, Diday, Dietz, Feuerbach, Hasenclever, Kaulbach, Lenbach, Max, Piloty, Rottmann, Verboeckhoven, Zimmermann, etc. With few exceptions, I was not much interested in these, but returned again and again to the old collection with renewed satisfaction. We also passed a day in two great collections contributed by the painters who send their works in to be sold. These are very interesting and contain many fine pictures, which seem to me to show and indicate a greater variety and exuberance of talent than the more stately New Pinakothek.

Munich is one of the great centres of the fine arts, and the agreeable evidences of it are visible on every hand. I think, if forced into exile, I should be as well content to wear away some years here as in any spot we have found. The streets are wide and broken by frequent bits of squares and angles, giving place to many noble statues and fountains, the shops are bright and rich with all sorts of artistic handiwork, the houses are large, commodious and of agreeable exterior. The people have a comfortable and refined air which seems to be in some sort imparted from their elevating surroundings. Munich is situated on a vast plain watered by "Iser, rolling rapidly," and has something over 250,000 inhabitants. It spreads over a good deal of space, and although an old city, has become so modernized that scarcely more remains of its mediæval features than suffices to give it picturesqueness. A long line of Bavarian rulers of wealth and taste and liberality have found their pleasure and pride in enriching their capital with noble architecture.

We visited the Old Palace, or Alte Residenz, erected by Elector Maximilian in 1600, and passed through a long series of magnificent apartments, and in the Festsaalbau, a modern building in the later Italian Renaissance style by Klenze, examined the large frescoes by Schnorr, illustrating the poem of the Nibelungen. These quite cover the walls of five large rooms on the ground floor. This poem is the source of the plots of Wagner's operas. In the Glyptothek, or Repository of Sculptures, we found many interesting and beautiful things. I was specially pleased with a statue of "Venus of Cnidos," after Praxiteles, and an original Greek torso of a child of Niobe.

A charming feature of Munich are the plantations of fine trees in all quarters, disposed in many natural and agreeable forms, which impart a secluded and sylvan aspect to the residential portion.

The beer brewed here under government control is famous all over Germany, and also goes largely abroad under the general name of Bavarian beer. 'Tis a capital beer, but should be drunk here, because, as is said, it is not sent long distances without being reinforced with a greater proportion of alcohol to preserve it. I went to the Bräuhaus, expecting, from the glowing accounts I had heard, to find a notable, spacious and elegant Trinkhalle where the burghers meet with their families, in a sort of half elegance, to drain the foaming brown-amber brew and indulge in social amenities to the inspiring sounds of choice music. I passed by a broad doorway through a dingy, gray-walled building of enormous extent with iron-barred windows, into a gloomy, rough court, on one side of which opened a long, low, badly lighted hall crowded with plain tables, with wooden settles before each one, these filled with the commonest sort of working people, not many women, drinking the royal beer from earthen, pewter-lidded mugs, in a stifling atmosphere of tobacco-smoke rolling from five hundred pipes, and a prodigious clatter of tongues. The mugs hold a quart, and each consumer, on entering, goes to a tier of long shelves, takes one down, rinses it under a running faucet, carries it to a long counter, where it is filled from a huge cask; the brown, mellow girths of a whole brotherhood of which loom out of the haze in the background. The romance of the Trinkhalle of the Hof Bräuhaus was rudely dissipated, and one more illusion vanished. But I took down a mug, laid on the bar fifteen pfennings, equal to three and three-quarter cents, and took a seat opposite a dull but cleanly enough gentleman, who might be by profession, let us say, a stonemason, deliberately intent on slicing a sausage which lay on the table before him in a wrapping of newspaper, and had likely come from his pocket. I noticed all about me, that each drinker, when he had finished a draught, carefully shut down the lid of his mug, fearful, it would seem, of losing some of the finer essence or aroma of the wonderful concoction, studiously brought to its perfection during three hundred years of learned experiments. When I had lifted the lid of my great flagon and taken a deliberate and thoughtful pull at it, I set it down with a feeling that the lot of the poor man in Munich is very considerably ameliorated by the possibility of such beer—if he only fully realizes the blessing of it. Quart mugs would seem to imply that he lives up to his privileges; but there seemed to be no intoxication going forward—indeed, I would say one might get overloaded and oppressed with the bulk of this beverage, but not drunken; as the frequenters of English and American bars do on spirits. I noticed one or two vaguely hilarious tables, as if, after several hours of potation, a low grade of fuddle had ensued, but the beer of Munich does not send its consumer home to brain his wife or beat his children. But my observation is that the average German is too much made up of beer and is the worse for it; still, it is not easy to say, for this is a nation of mighty people in brain and brawn. I also visited what passes for a more fashionable Trinkhalle, handsome enough in itself, with its gaudy frescoes; but stuck full of little dingy tables and crowded with drinkers of all degrees in the social scale, except the few uppermost rounds, and stifling with heated tobacco-smoke.

As in all German cities, soldiers are met everywhere, in the handsome blue uniform of Bavaria. It seems to an American, whose country is so fortunately placed by nature that its borders are peaceful and safe from menace or danger from foreign foes, a great burden and strain upon these continental nations to keep themselves constantly on a war-footing and to be compelled to maintain enormous armies simply to overawe hostile neighbors who would strike if they dared. It is a heavy burden, no doubt ; but if one may credit what intelligent Germans tell him, and what the superficial observations of one visiting a good many important points seem to confirm, there are some redeeming features and some offsetting advantages in putting the population, as it were, under arms. In the first place, it is a necessity calling for sacrifice and self-denial, and out of these grow naturally, fortitude, independence and an heroic, manly and high spirit. All the young men of the German Empire are under obligation to go into the army at the age of twenty for a term of three years, and afterward are variously enrolled in the reserves ; so that all males between the ages of twenty and sixty are drilled soldiers, and liable to serve in some capacity in the armies of the Empire in case of war, although their actual service in time of peace is limited to certain reviews, somewhat like the exercises of our State militia, occupying about two weeks of each year. The young men who serve for three years undergo an admirable system of physical training, and as they are sent away from their native districts and moved about from time to time into the different states of the Empire, and as the sons of the rich and educated and the better sort of the middle classes mingle with those of the poor and ignorant, the latter obtain an education of the mind not of the worst sort, and at the comparatively early age of twenty-three are at liberty to go about their own pursuits, none the worse fitted for them from having been so exercised and drilled and disciplined as to begin life with a sound body, erect carriage, and a manly self-respect, united with regular habits and orderly obedience to rule. Then, too, the spirit of the whole nation is stirred, active and resolute, and kept in that mood where great things are always possible. Certain it is that this German land is full of life and energy in all directions of activity, and steadily prospering. I like the Germans ;

they are a sincere, hearty, kindly people, of deep natures and a trusty, firm strength of character. Their race is not yet run either, and they will certainly continue to play an increasing part in the world's affairs.

*October* 12.—Took the train from Paris for Vienna at twelve noon and made the distance of about three hundred miles in eight and one-quarter hours. This astonishing rate of speed for a Continental train is due to ours being a special one, called the Orient-Express, made up of sleeping-cars and running, with very few stops, from Paris to Constantinople, doing the whole distance in little more than seventy hours. There is a dining-car attached, where we had *table d'hôte*, at one dollar and twenty cents each, but the meal in quality or abundance or service does not compare with those on the Pullman cars at home. But the train is an excellent one, well-appointed cars, with an easy motion over an admirable road-bed.

The road from Munich to Vienna is over an agreeable, level country watered by the Danube, and spreading away in a verdure of turf rich as that of England in June, with all the marks of prosperity in its fields, villages and towns. Linz, one hundred and seventeen miles from Vienna, is an important city on the Danube, of 40,000 population, and here we get a view of the Salzburg and Styrian Alps, stretching southward in a lofty, broken line of blue, and a little farther on, of the quaint town of Enns, whose walls were built with the ransom paid by the English to redeem King Richard Cœur de Lion from the dungeons of Leopold, Duke of Austria—a sum, as the historians say, equal to one-quarter the income of all the people of England; which would show that the combined incomes of the English people in the latter part of the twelfth century were ridiculously small, or that the walls of Enns were prodigiously costly, or that most of the money raised was stolen somewhere along the line, the last supposition being exceedingly probable. The sun set in rosy glory, and we finished our ride in darkness, arriving at the extensive and luxurious Grand Hotel in Vienna at 8.15 P.M.

The first thing that struck me when I looked out of the window Sunday morning, the 13th inst., was the grandeur of the buildings within view, both public and private. This impression increases as I become acquainted with this magnificent modern city of some 800,000 souls. I have driven and walked very considerably about it, and have as yet seen very few ancient buildings, although it dates almost from the Christian era, when it bore the Roman name of Vindobona. The Roman Emperor Marcus Aurelius died here in 180. Its fortunes rose and fell through the centuries, being high during the Crusades by reason of the trade flowing through it, and falling into the hands of Rudolph of Hapsburg in 1276, it was made the seat of the dynasty of that house. It was twice besieged by the Turks, first under Soliman II. in 1529, and again under Mohammed IV. in 1683, when they were defeated under its walls by John Sobieski, King of Poland, with an allied army of Poles, Austrians, Saxons, Bavarians and Franks. After the battles of Austerlitz, 1805, and Wagram, 1809, the city was occupied for a time by the French. Until 1809 it was surrounded by a double girdle of fortifications, of which scarcely any traces remain. In 1858 the inner line was levelled to give place to the Ringstrasse, a wide street running round the city, with sub-names for different sections of it, and to this broad avenue streets radiate from the centre. On this wide, circular avenue and on others, as well as on the numerous public squares, are a vast number of grand and beautiful public buildings, palaces and private residences, revealing the wealth and public and private spirit of this modern city, which looks as new and fresh as Chicago and grander than London or Berlin. The fashionable streets are lined with cafés, so filled with well-dressed and bright-looking people that one would think the citizens lived in them, and the footways are thronged with elegant, vivacious passengers, the women especially showing more beauty than I have noticed elsewhere, and now and then a face flashes out such as painters love to copy, but more often imagine than meet in real life. I have never seen finer horses, better formed or of better action, than swiftly draw the private carriages; even the hackney-coaches go at a great pace behind horses fit for any use. In brief, this is a beautiful and splendid city.

There is a large, airy vault, reached by descending a dozen steps, under the old church of the Capuchins, where in huge sarcophagi of copper, heavily embossed with funereal shapes, repose the remains of Maria Theresa and her husband Francis, Joseph II., Francis II., Marie Louise Napoleon's second wife; and their son the Duke of Reichstadt, who died here in 1832. Here, too, rests ill-starred Maximilian, for so brief a time Emperor of Mexico (whose place of execution at Queretaro in Mexico we visited, now more than two years ago), with a vacant place at his side for poor, distraught Carlotta, wearing her life away in Brussels. We were shown about by a gentle-voiced monk, who reverently rehearsed the titles of his sleeping charge, and showed us out into the welcome sunlight with a look of such peace that it seemed a benediction.

The Imperial Hofburg, or Old Palace, usually called the Burg, the residence of the Austrian princes since the thirteenth century, is a huge, irregular pile of buildings surrounding a court. We visited the rich Imperial Treasury in one of the wings and saw a great number of exceeding rich and exquisite articles; among them the celebrated salt-cellar made by Benvenuto Cellini for Francis I. of France, of which the artist says in his autobiography, after minutely describing it, "When I showed the king this piece of work he burst into an exclamation of surprise and could never sufficiently admire it." Also a great oval dish of silver-gilt by the delightful metalworker, Jannitzer of Nuremberg, in the sixteenth century. There are two hundred and seventy-six articles in the cases, and the catalogue, with particular descriptions, is interesting reading. The jewels, the private property of the Imperial Family, are also shown; including the imperial crown of Austria, the imperial orb and sceptre, the diamond crown of the reigning Empress, whose value exceeds seven hundred and fifty thousand dollars, with diamonds once forming a part of the jewels of the Empress Maria Theresa; a set of rubies forming a complete parure, including a tiara, girdle, necklace, pair of earrings and watch. The greater part of these articles formed a part of the bridal jewels of poor Marie Antoinette, Queen of France, and having been hid during the Revolution, were bought from her daughter, the Princess Maria Theresa, by Francis II., Emperor of Germany. Also a set of emeralds, the principal of which were taken from a stomacher belonging to the Empress Maria Theresa. Also the brilliant diadem with the Frankfort solitaire in the centre, a stone of purest water, weighing forty-two and one-half carats, bought by the German Emperor Francis I. in Frankfort-on-the-Main for twenty-eight thousand golden Louis in 1764, and worn by him as a hat-button. Also a diamond necklace, called the rose-necklace, consisting of thirteen rows of brilliants, which formed part of the bridal set called "the Esclarage," received by the Empress Maria Theresa at her marriage from her mother-in-law, the Duchess Elizabeth Caroline of Lorraine, who had them from her mother-in-law, Eleanor, Queen Dowager of Poland, daughter of the Emperor Leopold I., who afterward married Charles V., Duke of Lorraine. Also the "Florentine," a great diamond of a yellowish cast, forming part of a hat-button, and weighing one hundred and thirty-three and one-third carats, making it one of the largest in the world. It was once the property of Charles the Bold, Duke of Burgundy, who always carried it with him on the battle-field to have the benefit of the mysterious power then attributed to precious stones. He lost it at the battle of Granson in 1476. A Swiss soldier picked it up on the road, and thinking it a piece of glass sold it to the parish priest of Montigny for a florin; from whom a Bernese got it for three francs. Some years after, a Bernese merchant, one Bartholomew May, bought it for five thousand florins, and sold it for seven thousand florins to a Genoese, who in turn sold it to Duke Ludovico Moro Sforga, of Milan. Through the mediation of the great bankers, the Fuggers, it was bought for twenty thousand ducats for Pope Julius II., of the house of Medici, and remained in that family until its extinction in 1737, and later, by a series of marriages, came into possession of Francis of Lorraine, the husband of Maria Theresa, and through her into the Treasury.

It pleases me to dwell for a little on the strange history and romantic adventures of these precious things, so interwoven with the lives and shifting fortunes of mighty personages; and in their flashing radiance one seems to see the great scenes of royal olden pomp in which they bore their part, flaming on the heads of proud kings and adding lustre to the white necks of fair young queens, to be laid aside by some of their unhappy wearers after a life of sorrow, tragically ending. There are fifty-six of these rare articles in this most interesting collection. There are also the regalia of the Emperor Napoleon I. as King of Italy, the regalia and sacred relics of the holy Roman Empire; but I cannot dwell on them at further length. It is with an odd feeling of incongruity that one finds among these secular treasures, and equally guarded and honored with equal precision of date and authentic history, "a piece of the holy table-cloth which covered the table at the Last Supper of our Lord," "a piece of the holy cross," "a chip of the manger of Christ," "a bone of the arm of St. Anne," "three links of the iron chains by which the Apostles Peter, Paul and John were fettered," "a piece of the garment of St. John the Evangelist," and "a tooth of St. John the Baptist."

There is an excellent gallery of pictures, not well accommodated, in the Château of Belvidere, once the residence of Prince Eugene of Savoy, but to have place soon in the magnificent halls of one of the two museums now completing. In this gallery is choice store of Rubens' best works in great numbers, of Dürer, Titian, Rembrandt, Van Dyck, and a long line of fine examples in all the continental schools. I passed two days in this most interesting collection of some eighteen hundred pictures, pretty nearly all good and many notably fine. We saw many interesting incunabula, or books printed before the year 1500, among them a Psalter of 1457, printed by Schöffer and Faust, in the Imperial Library, occupying a grand half-monkish hall, erected in 1722, with fine ceiling paintings by Daniel Gran, and in the palace of the Archduke Albert a notable collection of drawings by the old masters, Raphael, Dürer, Rembrandt, and so on, to the number of more than one hundred thousand, many of which I saw with curious interest.

In the pleasant grounds of the Volksgarten is a Temple of Theseus, containing Canova's group of the "Victory of Theseus over the Centaurs," in white marble; as grand as his monument to the Archduchess Maria Christina, daughter of Maria Theresa, in the nave of the Augustan Church, is tender and beautiful. Such delicacy of carving in the figures of the mourning group on their way to the tomb, such anguish and sorrow expressed in the cold, mute marble, which seems to have melted in grief under this master's hand!

At the corner of the Graben and Kärtner streets is an odd relic in what is said to be the stump of a pine-tree; so entirely overlaid with the heads of iron nails driven into it since 1575 by believers in its sanctity, who sought by this customary act to obtain some spiritual benefit, as to present the appearance of a column of solid iron roughened on the surface. This memento is protected by standing in a hollowed space in the corner of a massive building with a padlocked grate in front.

The Prater is a park and forest of over four thousand acres in extent, belonging from 1570 to 1766 to the Imperial Family, who used it as a hunting park, but the Emperor Joseph II. opened it as a public resort. The principal avenue through this fine wood has a double row of handsome chestnut-trees on each side and runs in a straight line three miles, much like the Coney Island Boulevard ; where the fine world disports itself in the afternoons.

Passed an hour in the Stock Exchange ; a handsome building, with about the same number of brokers in the Pit as in the New York Exchange, fully as much Bedlamite vociferation and a vast deal more grimacing and fiery gesticulation.

I am informed that this stately city does not fulfil its business promise of twenty years ago, and that from various causes, some of them political, its prosperity is becoming divided with Buda-Pesth and Prague.  One would not suspect any eclipse, however, when visiting the imperial stables, where four hundred picked horses, for the different uses of His Majesty's self and household, stand in stall in a vast circuit of stables covering more than a full Brooklyn block. On one of the upper floors is His Majesty's gun-room, where more than a thousand pieces, I should say, chiefly for hunting, are kept in perfect order and readiness ; also the gorgeous carriages of state, new and old, the panels of one of the latter painted by Rubens, it is said. There are stately coaches and catafalques for funeral occasions and black caparisons of woe for the horses drawing them ; significant of a sorrow deeper than ordinary mortals can be supposed to feel or be able to manifest.

We attended a performance of Verdi's opera of " Un Ballo in Maschera " in the gorgeous Imperial Opera House, the part of Amelia taken by Materna, now obese and showing marks of age in person and voice. The auditorium seats twenty-five hundred luxuriously, with its five tiers of gilded boxes. The great stage was richly and fittingly set for the various scenes, the orchestra excellent, the individual parts and the choruses well sung by thoroughly trained voices; as it seemed to me, an incapable judge of matters musical ; the effort being, it would seem, to produce an artistic *ensemble* rather than particularly striking effects. From what I had heard of the ballet here, I looked for something better than was shown in the incidental dancing in the ball-room scene, but very likely this was kept subordinated to the general effect. The audience would certainly be considered a refined, bright and handsome one anywhere, with many fine faces and toilets in the boxes, and no display at all of shoulders, busts and arms, so lavishly made in the boxes and stalls of Her Majesty's Opera House, Covent Garden, London.

*October* 21.—Took Oriental Express-train of " Wagon-Lits " —sleeping-cars—for Constantinople at 9 P.M. Each single compartment makes up into two berths at right angles to the side of the car; and quite good they are too. The lavatories and other accommodations are not at all equal to the Pullman sleepers, but answer very well. This train left Paris at 5 P.M. yesterday, and is due at Constantinople the day after to-morrow at 4 P.M. My married daughter, Mrs. Van Deusen, joined us yesterday for a month's travel in company, thus increasing my party to five.

*October* 22.—Woke on a vast plain in Eastern Hungary, with great fields of Indian corn on either hand and the general appearance of our large Western prairies. At 11 A.M. reached Belgrade, on a height overlooking the Danube, the capital of Servia, with 35,000 population, and appearing fully modern. The railway from here is said to coincide with the old Roman road built by Trajan and used in the first Crusade by the hordes pouring into Asia to recover Jerusalem from the Mohammedans. We pass through Palanka, follow the valley of the Morava—the ancient Margus—cross a mountain-spur to Ratcha, on a branch of the Morava, along a mountain-slope to ancient Oromago in a defile on a small stream; through several towns with unpronounceable names, over a ridge with good scenery, to Alexinatz--ancient Rappiana—to Nisch or Nissa—ancient Naissos, founded by Philip of Macedon, the birthplace of Constantine the Great, A.D. 272. We enter upon Bulgaria, pass through Sofia, its capital, with scarcely a glimpse of its low yellow buildings, traverse the Balkan Mountains—ancient Hæmus—through an ancient pass with rocky sides like a Colorado cañon. The Balkan range is some

4500 feet high, and the peak of Mount Scarpus, in our sight for many hours, nearly 10,000 feet.

The country we have been traversing now since leaving Hungary is flat for the most part, treeless, poorly watered, not unlike the broad alkaline plains of the West, if we think of these as somewhat more fertile and capable of crops. The brown monotonous expanse of dusty plain is enlivened rarely with petticoated peasants ploughing in the cheerless fields, with great white oxen yoked four to five feet apart—but more sensibly than in Germany and elsewhere on the Continent, because the draught is from the shoulder—flocks of large, coarse-wooled sheep, white and black ; squalid villages of low clay houses or huts, thatched with straw loosely laid—why they do not burn up daily is a marvel. At the stations gather groups of natives, barbaric in form, feature and costume ; among them fierce, wild, handsome horsemen on magnificent horses, with long guns strapped to their shoulders and belts stuck full of pistols and daggers ; each one a walking armory.

Early in the afternoon of Monday a narrow line of blue water gleams between low brown shores, extending southward, where the sky, clear and warm, shows more soft than elsewhere over the Sea of Marmora ; whose waters, except in this bright bay, are as yet invisible, but continue to reappear in its many little indentations on our right. Villages of strange aspect grow more frequent on the dusty plain, the blue sea itself appears, the misty hills of Princes' Island rising between us and the Asiatic shore—a long line of lofty gray walls with battlemented towers of Roman construction rises on our left ; we are whirled through a breach in them, skirt the shore of the Sea of Marmora, whose transparent wavelets almost wash the base of the railway, roll with scarcely diminished speed through a confusion of flowing robes, bare brown legs, swarthy faces capped with red fezzes swarming in the narrow streets ; and all at once are in the depot of Constantinople and take carriage among a Babel of crowding, hoarse-throated Oriental cabbies, to be driven over a long bridge across the Golden Horn, up a steep, narrow street to the Royal Hotel, where we have spacious rooms on the first floor and on the sunny side. From our balcony the configuration of the city is apparent.

Except for the carpets and rugs and some few articles of furniture and ornament in our rooms and elsewhere about the house, one might suppose one's self in any one of a score of the hotels we have had entertainment in since coming to the Continent, and we went to a *table d'hôte* at 7 P.M., of the usual French *menu*. The guests at table bore a cosmopolitan character. A quiet-looking gentleman whom I had noticed on the train proved to be the president of the Imperial Bank in London and a director of the Imperial Ottoman Bank here; come to look into its affairs as he told me, and seeming quite able to do so, with his strong Scotch face. Beside him were seated two young English gentlemen, also our fellow-passengers, in full dress, as if they felt it incumbent on them to maintain the English table fashions under whatever sky; the pleasant family of a New York gentleman whose acquaintance we had made on the train; a German gentleman, in business here; a Frenchman ditto; a solitary lady of undisclosed nationality, and one or two others—all, ourselves included, feeling more than usually curious perhaps, and drawn toward one another from the fact of our remoteness from familiar conditions.

We had noticed a great number of ill-conditioned, mongrel curs all along our way from the depot, and Betty had mourned over the sudden demise of one in the street before our balcony, occasioned by its Oriental indifference to fate in allowing a carriage to be driven over itself without the slightest movement on its own part to prevent it. As night came on after a glorious sunset, in whose glow the tranquil waters of the Golden Horn shone in roseate light, such maddening, incessant and discordant din of barks, howls, yelps and canine cries of rage and anguish came in at our windows and were continued with scarcely an interval of cessation all the night long, that I heartily wished that all the rickety vehicles of the entire city could be set in fatal motion over their vile carcasses. To add to the horrors of the night, a resounding clang began under our windows early in the evening, stroke upon stroke, lasting a full half minute, and renewed at regular intervals of a quarter of an hour, all night long. At first I took it to be the noise of a paver's rammer pounding the flagging into place, but came to understand that it was the customary signal of the watchman to make it known to all whom it might concern that he had completed his round without shirking.

*October* 24.—A warm, bright day. Crossed the Bosphorus in a small steamer to Scutari, a quarter of Constantinople on the Asiatic side, taking the boat from the middle of one of the two wooden drawbridges connecting Pera and Galata with Stamboul. We landed at the foot of a dirty, narrow street broadening into a little square near the quay, and then rising steeply along a causeway of rough stones whose irregularities reminded me of Brooklyn's side-streets, lined with shabby little wooden houses and swarming all about with clamorous vagabond human and animal life. It required all the efforts of our dragoman, Joseph Jacob, and the use of the eleven languages he claimed to be master of when I engaged him last evening, to prevent our being thrust bodily into the many rickety, dirty landaus lying in wait for fares. At length, after a deal of shrill hubbub of voices and wild gesticulation and swaying backward and forward of a river of red fezzes, we got deposited in two of these vehicles, and with Joseph on the box beside the driver on one and Frattini on the other, forced our way through the mob with loud cries of warning; our rawboned and worn horses warmed to their work under the whip and constant jerks at the bits, and we pounded along up the rocky ascent with an expectation which possessed me all day, that the rattling carriages would break in pieces the next moment. But they did not, and we rolled on, jolting and swaying from side to side in a cloud of hot dust, and entered upon a lonesome avenue, passing through the vast burying-ground of Scutari, used as such, Joseph said, for a thousand years.

It would not be easy to imagine anything more desolate and mournful than this dusty city of the dead, where no objects meet the eye but plain, narrow stone slabs, not less than seven feet high, set as thickly as they can be planted on their narrow bases in the dismal shade of tall cypresses. Not a patch of green earth anywhere, scarcely a glimpse of the sky, only a wilderness of dusty gray stones standing ghost-like in the gloomy silence. Passing through this Golgotha and over a stretch of dull country we reached the well-planted and kept English cemetery, where on a promontory, laved on one side by the blue waters of the Sea of Marmora, sleep some ten thousand soldiers of the English armies, slain in the battles of the

Crimea and wasted in the hospitals of Scutari; the yellow walls of that one where noble Florence Nightingale toiled in deeds of mercy standing in plain sight a little lower down on the gradually sloping Asiatic shore. On the horizontal gravestones are many titled names, and Inkerman and Balaklava are often repeated. The loving care of their far-distant friends and countrymen has made a beautiful spot of this one piece of sacred earth. To the south the blue and tranquil Sea of Marmora stretches away beyond the sight, broken only by the high, undulating profile of Princes' Island, to-day half veiled in violet mist; to the westward, on its many hills, domed and minareted Stamboul, gleaming in the abounding light; and running northward the shining line of the Bosphorus dividing Asia from Europe, the Orient from the Occident.

From the cemetery we drove to an eminence on the north of Scutari, Mount Boulgourlou, whence, after a short climb on foot, we beheld a wide panorama extending twelve miles around and including a glimpse of the Black Sea. On the way we met, walking along a suburban road, three ladies of the harem of a court dignitary having a country palace here, not so closely veiled that we might not easily see that two were old and ugly and one young and pretty. But the striking figure of the little party was a tall, robust, handsome Nubian, with a proud step, swarthy, but not to the point of blackness, whom Joseph informed me in a whisper belonged to that mutilated class fitted to be the custodian of an Oriental harem.

Our main purpose in Scutari to-day is to witness the exercises of the howling dervishes, these occurring only on Thursday of each week and in this quarter of the city. We were shown into a hall some 30 by 50 feet, overhung by a latticed gallery, under which and behind a railing running round an area some 20 by 30 feet a row of turbaned devotees squatted on carpets, and within the railing, likewise in sitting groups and rows, a score of dervishes praying in a low, monotonous, not unpleasing sing-song. Their ages are all along from twenty to seventy years, the last being about that of the chief, who, sitting at the upper end, looking toward the sacred city of Mecca, led rather than directed the exercises. There was one full-blooded negro in the number.

Their flowing robes of many pleasing shades of color, their swarthy faces surmounted with white turbans, their picturesque groupings, so that these colors harmonized, the afternoon light cautiously admitted through small windows and directed so as to fall most effectively, the grave dignity and introspection evident on all the faces, formed a scene strange and impressive. The salutations and obeisances they used were graceful and reverential movements. When the droning chants had continued so long as to begin to grow wearisome, by an easy change of positions, during which several recruits entered the enclosed space, all except the old men, who continued to sit cross-legged on their carpets, rose, and forming a compact line across the lower end of the arena, began gradually to sing in a higher tone and increasing volume of voice, accompanied with rapid and violent movements of the head and body, carried to an amazing pitch. The prayerful ejaculation of "*Allah hou!*" seemed to explode from their throats like bullets, in deafening puffs; and the principal participants rolled their heads with prodigious velocity, as if gaining impetus to throw them into each other's faces. The young Ethiopian worshipper was especially remarkable, and with incredible swiftness and without a second's intermission for more than an hour threw his body forward, as did the others, until his face nearly touched his knees, and erected it again as if it were flung into place by a powerful steel spring running along his spine. Rivulets of perspiration glistened in their channels down his dark hide, until, when human nature would seem to find it impossible to endure longer, his movements were checked by some order secretly conveyed, and he was apparently advanced in rank by removal from the end of the line, where he had performed his meritorious gymnastics, to a position midway between two older athletes of maturer sanctity, where he stood quiescent during the remaining exercises.

While this extraordinary worship was at its height, a pretty boy not more than six years old, habited in a green turban and brown robe descending to his naked feet, whom Joseph, when we drove up, had pointed out, playing outside among other lads, as a young dervish, entered the enclosed space and, extending his arms, began whirling on the spot where he stood, and without moving six inches from it, with such rapidity that his features became almost indistinguishable, making, as nearly as I could count, more than one hundred revolutions per minute; and this dizzy spinning he maintained for twenty-six minutes by my watch, and then walked away and out of the hall quite as fresh-looking as when he entered, having attracted no notice at any time from his older brethren. A little later a number of children of both sexes came in singly and in groups and ranged themselves in a row near the chief, who had risen and sought to take into his arms from its father a mere babe, who screamed in such terror that it was borne out, while the older children—the oldest might have been eight years—laid themselves down on their faces side by side closely in a row. The chief, a tall, spare man, then walked across the children, stepping somewhat carefully, but resting his whole weight on the one nearest him, then on the next, and so on, until he had literally stepped on each one; placing his foot on the upper part of their thighs, and returning to his place in the same manner. They did not seem at all hurt by the pressure of his weight, and when the ceremony was over jumped up, gathered about him, kissed his hands and ran out. As near as I could learn—it seems quite impossible to ascertain the significance of this ancient worship—this treading upon the children is a form of blessing, and is supposed to ward off and cure diseases.

We drove down to the landing and dismissed the carriages in the same hubbub in which we took them, and returned across the smiling Bosphorus, amid a shoal of the long, slender, canoe-like boats called caiques, and the shorter, broader and safer row-boats known under the general name of barques. The westering sun flooded with glorious light the close ranks of low white walls rising from the water rank above rank to the high crest of the promontory, to whose sides the old city of Stamboul clings on the extreme point of the ridge, its gray walls washed by the sea and strait; the imposing buildings of the old Seraglio, now unoccupied, stately and mysterious in their spacious enclosure, above which tall trees whispering no secrets, and gilded domes and pinnacles rise as they have done through many dark centuries; and although some of the inland parts were destroyed by the fire of 1865, to me the most fascinating spot in the city.

*October* 25.—Drove northward through Pera to Yildiz, the

palace of the present Sultan Abdul Hamed II., to see him go to mosque. This takes place at noon of Friday, the Mohammedan Sabbath, when he, as Caliph of the Mussulman world, attends official religious service. This ceremony called the *salemlik*, has been regularly observed since 1361, and is a pompous, theatrical scene. By the courtesy of our *chargé d'affaires* here, Pendleton King, Esq., we received a permit from the Grand Marshal of the palace to occupy with others an apartment in a building appertaining to the palace, but outside its walls, looking upon the wide avenue leading down from the gate in the lower side of the palace-walls, through which the cortège descends to the beautiful modern white marble Mosque of Hamidiéa, diagonally opposite. From the windows we had a full view up to the palace, across to the mosque and down upon the picturesque masses of troops guarding the lower end of the street, behind whom the people, in variegated and picturesque crowds, pressed for a view. The palace stands on the brow of a considerable hill in the northern suburb of Pera, its isolated position and extensive pleasure-grounds enclosed in lofty walls, making of it really a country residence. The Sultan is said not to leave his palace here except to make this weekly official ceremonial. The whole distance from the gate to the mosque is not more than forty rods; the way is lined with soldiers and all avenues of approach are strongly guarded. Ordinarily some four to five thousand troops are in attendance ; but as the German Emperor is to make a visit here next week, arriving in his steam-yacht, the "Hohenzollern," from Athens, there is to-day a sort of preliminary display, and some twenty thousand various troops are present.

The side of the street toward the mosque is open, and only an iron railing separates it from the small square in which the mosque stands. At noon the muezzin from one of the minarets calls to prayer, and in a hush of expectation, signs of the coming of the "Commander of two continents and Ruler of two seas" began to appear along the freshly sprinkled roadway. First came a close coach drawn by four led horses richly caparisoned, containing the Sultan's mother, followed by another bearing the Sultana, these ladies looking, through the open coach-windows, to be heaps of Oriental silks and other rich stuffs, so closely were they wrapped and veiled. In a third rode a princess some sixteen years old, and in a fourth another princess, a child of perhaps eight years. These daughters of the Sultan had uncovered faces, pretty and pale and childish, and looked like those beautiful great dolls luxuriously arrayed by the lavish taste of the Parisian manufacturers. Then came the young prince, also in a coach, wearing a military suit of dark blue, his regular, smooth, waxen features relieved by a slight black mustache and large, soft black eyes. He looked to be a youth of twenty years, and quite harmless. Then followed two led horses of the Sultan, one black, the other an Arabian, both of beautiful form and handsome action, bearing rich saddles; then a light, empty phaëton drawn by a pair of gentle, cream-colored horses, and lastly an open landau with the Sultan by himself on the back seat and two high officers, one military and one civil, facing him on the front seat. He wore a black frock-coat buttoned in front, with several orders on his breast, and a red fez on his head. This he always wears, and it is a rule that all Turks shall do the same, while his other subjects may exercise a choice of headgear. Before he had reached the entrance to the mosque, the preceding carriages had been stationed on either hand and the horses detached; their occupants remaining inside them, as the Sultan enters and worships alone. So he rode along slowly, amid the blare of many bands playing wild, martial music, and plentiful cries of welcome, to the marble steps of the mosque, descended and walked alone on the carpet spread for the purpose, up into the interior; where he remained for nearly an hour, during which all waited patiently, the troops being served with water from long, conical leathern cans strapped to the backs of carriers. When he reappeared and had descended the steps, still unaccompanied, he got into the phaëton and by himself drove the cream-colored horses slowly back to the palace-gate, his cortège following in the order it used before.

The Sultan is forty-nine years old, and fully looks it. He has a mild, thoughtful face, an erect bearing, and firm step—not a greatly remarkable man to look at. From some point of observation, either on or within the palace-walls, out of sight of our station, he now reviewed the troops, who occupied nearly two hours in marching past. These were from various parts of his vast dominions in Europe, Asia and Africa, and in their striking national garbs formed a strange and magnificent spectacle in the midst of these Oriental surroundings : regiments of Albanians in the dress now become the national costume of the Greeks, their belts stuck full of pistols, daggers and yataghans ; Egyptians, tall, bronzed, sad-faced men in white turbans wound round with coils of dull green cloth like serpents, mingled with regiments of the Turks proper, wearing the fez. The cavalry were mounted on fine horses, two regiments of lancers especially so. These soldiers seemed to me capital material, but not altogether well drilled. Some companies marched with the German step exaggerated almost to burlesque, evidently under the training of officers who carried it much further than the model they had adopted. Some of these, in addition to a great backward bend of the spine and a dancing-master pace, sought to heighten their warlike appearance by a scowling visage and a martial fierceness of the eye, and glared along the lines as if they would make nothing of charging a battery single-handed. If the young German Emperor has a sense of humor it must certainly be tickled at the review next week to see the neat, clean, firm step of his German officers at home so travestied.

By immemorial custom nothing must hinder the Sultan from performing this weekly ceremony of the *salemlik*, if he be alive. Not hail, rain, or any tempest ; pestilence, earthquake or his own sickness must keep the Caliph of the Faith from these official prayers, which cannot be made for him by any one else.

On the 26th we made an excursion, in company with our New York acquaintances, extending the whole length of the Bosphorus, from Seraglio Point to the Black Sea, twenty miles, or rather to a point where the view extends into the opening of that sea, following the European shore as far as Rouméli-Kavak. We pass on the water's edge or on the hill-side the handsome and substantial palaces or summer residences of the ambassadors of Sweden, Russia, Holland, France, Germany, and, farther up, England and that of the United States Minister. These European powers are a watchful and fatal presence here, gathered like eagles to the prey, waiting, and perhaps willing, to aggravate the disorders of the sick man, impatiently looking for his demise and ready enough to seize upon his effects before the breath leaves his body, if not restrained by mutual jealousy, wherein lies the safety of the Turk in Europe.

The shore is gently undulating, sloping upward to a considerable ridge, the scanty herbage dead and brown, as it is ten months in the year, for lack of rain. The villages are single streets along the water, where small, mean and dirty houses show now and then the variety of long, beautiful palace fronts of white marble, with rarely the dull walls of an old mosque lifting its slender minaret in air, and often terraced gardens climbing the slope with graceful trees and an attempt at verdure. Four miles up from the city is a little village where Medea is said to have joined Jason on his return from Colchis, and a mile farther on is Bébek village and bay, the ancient Chéfæ, where the Greeks built a temple to Diana, and near by on a prominence the college founded in 1863 by Mr. Robert, of New York, and spoken of by all as an institution doing much good in the cause of education.

In the almost continuous line of villages beyond the upper arm of the bay are some cemeteries greatly venerated by the Turks, because here lie buried the Ottomans who first crossed over from Asia with Mohammed II., and just beyond stand the grand ruins of the Rouméli-Hissar—the Château of Europe—a prodigious series of stone towers with massive connecting walls, built by that Sultan in 1452 to command the Bosphorus before his capture of Constantinople. Here is the narrowest part of the strait—about one-quarter of a mile wide—where Darius built a bridge, over which he passed an army from Asia of seven hundred thousand men, where the Crusaders crossed, and lastly the Turks, who still remain. On the Asiatic shore opposite, at Anatoli-Hissar, are the ruins of less extensive but greatly impressive towers. A mile above opens a deep bay whose shores are prettily studded with good houses amid considerable verdure at the upper end, where a small stream comes in; with Thérapia on the northern arm, where we had a fairly good dinner on shore at the Hotel d'Angleterre on the quay. This spot is the old Pharmakia—poisons—taking its name from some one of the many legends of Medea and her necromancy, what time she

> " Gathered the enchanted herbs
> That did renew old Æson,"

and these shores are the scenes of the exploits, perils and deliverances of Jason and his Argonauts in search of the Golden Fleece; told fully and with wonderfully strange and poetical beauty by William Morris in his poem of "Jason."

At Rouméli-Kavak the seventeenth and final landing on the European side is reached, and the boat crosses to the Asiatic shore of the Bosphorus and follows it down on its return, with frequent landings at Turkish villages not dissimilar to those on the opposite shore, and presenting the same sharp contrasts of opulence and squalor.

To read the heated accounts of travellers, especially of the French nation, who seem to have adopted the Oriental habit of exaggeration as soon as they set foot on these historical shores flushed with the romance of so many centuries, one would suppose the whole scene to be of enchanting beauty; but I take the liberty of assuring those of more temperate and sober minds that the descriptions of Theophile Gautier and all his class are as rose-tinted as those of Moore's "Lalla Rookh."

We pass in sight of a dome-like hill rising from the tawny ridge of the monotonous Asiatic coast, called Giant's Mountain, or Mount of Joshua, of classic interest, where, according to an old legend, Amycus, King of the Bébryces, was killed by Pollux in a boxing-match and buried on its top. The coast lower down is indented by frequent shallow bays, and on the little promontory of Hiéron once stood a temple to the "Twelve Gods," endowed by Jason on his return from Colchis; and near by a temple to Jupiter Favoring, built by the Chalcedonians, changed afterward by Justinian into a church dedicated to the Archangel St. Michael. This promontory is the termination of the Bithynian range of mountains and confronts the limit of the range of the Balkans—the ancient Hæmus—on the European side.

Our dragoman, Joseph, is of himself an interesting study. His pretence is that he is a German. One cannot question this, perhaps, but one would not suspect it, so fully has the stoical fatalism of the Orient subdued the original Teutonic features of his nature. Whether he is arranging the terms of the contract by which he serves us during the brief sojourn we propose in the city of his adoption, or guiding us, in carriage or by boat or on foot, among the objects of interest in this marvellous agglomeration of polyglot humanity, stolidly awaiting our movements, humoring our wishes, indulging our whims, he is the same always, imperturbable, unruffled, inscrutable, all commands and desires of ours being to him alike important, or rather alike indifferent, and fulfilled on his part with the same tranquil and heavy complaisance, not without intelligence showing in his dull face, and prompt and easy acquiescence, as if he were born under Moslem rule and in the Moslem faith, with *Kismet* as the ruling fact of his life. He has lived here for forty years, is married—how much he did not state, nor did I venture to inquire—and declares himself the father of eleven young children depending on his earnings as dragoman; perhaps stating the number of the pledges of his multitudinous affection high enough and not too high to interest the more susceptible members of our little party in the pecuniary success of his services while in our employ.

He guided me on Sunday—the only possible day—down an ancient, jagged, stony street, leading from our hotel so precipitously as to make foothold difficult, to the balconied hall where the dancing dervishes hold their weekly religious exercises. These were not of the wild, grotesque and resilient nature I had been led to expect from the accounts I have read in the books of excited travellers. At least they were not so on this day, but were rhythmic, graceful and dreamy; almost languorous. Some twenty or thirty slender, gentle-featured youngish men in dark robes and cylindrical head-dresses, after prescribed prayers, such as we observe the imams or priests to make in the mosques, rose in a large circle, with much courtly and refined salutation of each other, somewhat as partners make to each other in the opening of a cotillon, only more prolonged and continued into an interchange of places; with frequent kissing of hands and graceful gestures of significant acts of prayer not understood by me. All this was long continued and repeated over and over, to the low and melodious notes of an orchestra of flutes and long, softly-breathing horns; and finally several, laying aside their robes and space being made for them, extended their arms and spun rapidly about, but neither so rapidly nor so long as the little boy whose wonderful movements I have tried to describe in our visit to the so-called howling dervishes. Altogether a most graceful, almost tender ceremony in that plain and not unpicturesque hall with its latticed galleries and sedate, calm-eyed, many-colored Mohammedans squatting in rows all about ; the light falling from the high, narrow windows in varying distinctness here and there on the clean floor, relieved all about with richly hued rugs.

On our toilsome way back, at the corner of a very narrow lane intersecting the street we were climbing, stands one of the houses common here ; a small two-story structure of unpainted wood with the invariable projecting latticed window. As we approached it I noticed a masculine Turk standing under the window in an attitude expressive of the most abject humility and contrition, while through the lattice from an unseen female issued the unmistakable sounds of high and termagant scolding, falling in a scalding torrent on the abject son of Islam, who made no reply, save a deprecatory gesture expressing much, and intended to excuse and conciliate. Joseph could not or would not explain why this evident householder should stand at his own door unable or unwilling to enter, so lashed by the unseen voice from his ill-regulated harem. Plainly trials of a domestic sort are not confined to the Western world.

Of wonderful interest are the bazars or markets of Stamboul. The Grand Bazar is an enormous covered space vaulted and lighted by little domes rising from the vast flat roofs, a city within a city, an inextricable labyrinth of winding avenues, streets and lanes, lined with countless little shops stuck close together on either hand, open spaces at the crossings, small squares here and there enlivened with fountains, thronged with an innumerable multitude of buyers, crowding, pushing, chattering, bargaining—confusing beyond conception. The little shops, or rather booths, have their fronts quite open, the interior being reached by two or three steps up from the rough stone-paved passage-way, and on a sort of low counter running along the front sits the imperturbable merchant cross-legged, dignified, taciturn, picturesque in his red fez, blue jacket, broad parti-colored girdle, baggy trousers, and red morocco slippers. His more showy goods, whatever he may deal in, are ostentatiously scattered about the entrance, and hang suspended to the supporting posts and along the walls of the flimsy structure. Usually there is behind this a closed and dusky room whence can be produced for serious buyers out of presses and chests and other hiding-places, much richer goods than are in sight. Although our mercantile friend appears so unconcerned, he has really not neglected to take measures to obtain his fair share of custom, for as we advance along the crowded ways we are constantly importuned by eager salesmen or drummers, who in quite sufficient English seek to draw attention to the shops they represent, often lying in wait for a considerable distance in advance; and near at hand in the front shop is always a smiling, handy and shrewd clerk, acting under the eye of the proprietor as he sits calmly smoking, who will exhibit the stock with tireless patience, putting to the various articles not less than ten times the price he will finally accept. The goods exposed for sale are of Eastern form and fabric, silks of rich colors, cloth of gold, beautiful embroideries, all novel and pleasing, but of no great variety, as it seems to me.

The mosques of this city are reckoned at four hundred and eighty, of which ninety were made such from the ancient Byzantine churches. Most interesting structures they are, lifting their tall, slender, graceful, balconied minarets into the intense blue of the sky, like admonishing fingers. Only within a comparatively short time have unbelievers been allowed to visit them, but now, under strict guidance, one may freely do so, all save the peculiarly sacred one of Eyoub, into which no one, not even ambassadors of foreign nations, is permitted to penetrate. It was erected by Mohammed, the conqueror of Constantinople, in 1460, in honor of Eyoub, the standard-bearer of the Prophet, slain in the siege of Constantinople A.D. 668. In its court is the tomb of the companion of the prophet, whose sword, the highest and most sacred symbol of Mohammedan power, and the green banner of the Prophet are preserved here. The mosque with its two minarets stands in a grove of stately trees, and about the tomb of Eyoub burn unceasingly a great number of lamps.

Specially interesting is the Ahmédié or Mosque of Ahmet, situated in a vast enclosure, amid lofty trees, on the great open space called At-Meidan, the ancient Byzantine Hippodrome, existing as such before the time of Constantine. Six lofty minarets rise from it, a greater number than any mosque possessed when Ahmet I. built it in 1610, except the Kaaba of Mecca, to which, in consequence, was added a seventh. After the Mosque of St. Sophia this is the principal one in Constantinople, and the richest in revenues. The great commemorative festivals are celebrated here. The sun was near its setting as we emerged from it and took places in our carriage in the great space of the Hippodrome; a roseate glory suffused the motionless air, when there rose, clear, high and vibrant, the voice of the white-robed muezzin standing on one of the upper balconies of a minaret, his bronze features strongly contrasting with his white turban, as in the magical light pouring full upon him he issued the call to prayer, which is thus translated: "Most High! There is no God but the one God! Mohammed is the Prophet of God. Come to prayer! Come to the Temple of Life!" I wish I might complete the picture with pious devotees suspending all avocations to prostrate themselves at the call in the direction of Mecca, for then I should be in agreement with the accounts I have read, but am constrained to say that I saw no notice taken of the summons by the scattered groups upon the amphitheatre or by the rows of dusty idlers squatting in the shadow of the walls. This charming mosque rises from the third of the ridges on which Stamboul is situated, counting from the Bosphorus; and looking from the paved space on the summit to the east of the mosque, I saw a great smoke lighted up with broad sheets of flame in Scutari, on the Asiatic side. This spread rapidly, and while we watched seemed to involve a great space.

Most sumptuous and fairest of situation of the mosques in Stamboul is that of Solyman the Magnificent, called Suleimanié, constructed in 1550 by Sinan, of the highest fame as an architect. Like all original mosques—by which I mean those not converted from early Christian churches—its interior is nearly a square, with sides 290 feet in extent, surmounted by a lofty, hemispherical dome. Four minarets rise above it. Behind stands the tomb of Sultan Solyman the Magnificent, exquisitely wrought of white marble, into which one passes through a vestibule where four pillars of verd antique support a cupola, while the inner one rests upon four columns of white marble and as many of red porphyry. Under this dome, enclosed by a balustrade of costly wood incrusted with mother-of-pearl, rests the coffin of the great Sultan, covered with magnificent shawls, each worth a king's ransom. Splendid arabesques adorn the walls, also beautiful plaques of white and blue pottery of Persian manufacture. The dome is beset with huge lumps of unpolished crystal, and from it hang lamps thickly adorned with precious stones. Near by and only less magnificent is the tomb of his wife, the beautiful Sultana Roxolana, the seductive, accomplished and cruel Russian slave whom the infatuated Sultan raised to the throne and allowed to lead him by her evil inspiration.

Memorable is our visit to the great Mosque of St. Sophia, converted from the Christian church of the same name built on the site of an earlier one by the Emperor Constantine the Great in 326, and destroyed by fire in 531. As it now stands it is the work of the Emperor Justinian, who laid the cornerstone in 532 and gathered from all parts of his vast empire an amazing richness of material in costly marbles, works of art and treasures of all sorts. In its vast and majestic interior, rising in arch above arch of beautiful and impressive proportions, twenty-five thousand worshippers may gather, and the cost is computed at seventy million dollars of our money. Of course the altar and all insignia of Christian worship have been removed, as Mohammedanism permits no shrines or images of saints in its mosques; and as all worship is in the direction of Mecca, the matting covering the floor is so laid that the seams run in that direction, so as to indicate to the faithful their true position in the act of prayer.

Until somewhat recently, as I have said, unbelievers were not admitted to the mosques, but this is now freely permitted under certain easy restrictions; one being that all must enter with uncovered feet. Even this has been so far modified, in deference to the stubborn foot-gear of Western infidels, as to permit of putting on over one's shoes a sort of loose slipper, in which the visitor shambles awkwardly along the matted floor. I had the misfortune to don an uncommonly ill-fitting and perverse pair, of which one or the other would now and then become detached; and whenever this occurred a half dozen white-turbaned Kaims, a lower order of clergy having in charge the order and regulation of the mosque, gathered about to see that the delinquent foot did not touch the ground until the awkward slipper was restored to its place. Here and there in the majestic and solemn space, their forms dwarfed by distance, crouched robed and turbaned figures reading in a singsong tone from volumes of the Koran lying open on cushions before them, rocking their bodies to and fro in regular, unceasing motion; and cuddled together under the great dome, all prostrate, a group of some thirty about one in priestly garb with full beard, who, sitting cross-legged, seemed to be expounding with an air of authority the contents of an open book, and listened to with eager and reverential attention by the younger, bright faces upturned to his. I asked Joseph what might be the nature of this absorbing discourse, and he, cautiously moving within earshot, returned to say that the grave and learned teacher was enforcing from the Koran the steps in due order of the ablution required before attending religious services in the mosque, and that many days would be given to instruction on that point of ceremonial. One can hardly conceive a more grandly impressive interior than this noble mosque, beautiful in its sublimity.

Before leaving Stamboul to day, it occurred to me to count as many of the dogs as possible, seen on the way to our hotel, a distance of perhaps two miles. I do not understand it to have been a particularly good day for dogs, but was able to reckon very nearly four hundred in sight from our carriage. These dogs, the scavengers of the city, are mongrel curs, mostly of smallish size and a dirty brown color, rather intelligent-looking and not bad-tempered. I incline to think, from what I saw and heard, that there is truth in what is said of their having their own quarters of the city, from which they are not allowed to stray, being set upon and driven back by their canine neighbors whenever they attempt to change domicile.

After dinner walked out into the gathering night to a point looking across to Scutari, where the conflagration is still raging and seeming to be an ocean of flame, lighting up the sky and gleaming luridly on the blue Bosphorus. Next morning we learned that two hundred and fifty houses, two mosques and one Greek church had been fully consumed and many hundreds of poor people made houseless and beggared. Such a conflagration is not at all uncommon, as the small, unpainted wooden houses set close together are in the long dry season like tinder-boxes, and the only apparatus for extinguishing fires ridiculous portable squirt-guns, carried to the scene on the shoulders of brawny, bare-legged firemen in a disorderly rush, with loud outcries and frantic and well-nigh imbecile efforts, so that a fire ceases only when there is a lack of combustibles to feed on.

Fair, too, are the white marble palace-walls gleaming from plantations of stately trees and the ornate fountains in the little squares. Of the former, no one has for me the interest of the old Seraglio in its air of seclusion and mystery, standing conspicuously on the point of the promontory overlooking at once the Sea of Marmora, the Bosphorus and the Golden Horn; now tenantless and silent, but thronged with sinister memories of intrigues, poisonings, assassinations, through many dark and bloody centuries. Whenever in sight of it, by an irresistible fascination my mind calls up its history and the romances associated with it: Sultanas shining on perfumed divans, their blazing gems not brighter than the lustrous eyes of the wearers, laughing odalisques whose fair necks shall come to the bowstring on the least suspicion, truculent eunuchs with scimitars ready in their golden belts, hushed mutes gliding along dim corridors bearing fatal messages; the scenes of Oriental voluptuousness, distrust, faithlessness and revenge, all ceased now; the dumb walls standing silent in the purple atmosphere, the blue water smiling below, the solemn cypresses murmurous only of the sounds of modern life.

The really beautiful structures in this city, the palaces, mosques, tombs and fountains, are painfully in contrast with the generally mean aspect of the city, and the pleasing impression derived from a distant view is changed to one of disgust as the visitor finds himself involved in the vile, narrow streets, swarming with dirty life, squalid and reeking with nauseating stenches. The anticipated visit of the German Emperor and Empress next week is made the occasion of scraping off the upper layer of filth from the streets along which the procession of honor is to pass, and these are still further distinguished by daubs of red and green on an occasional shop-front. Among the many fruits exposed for sale are delicious melons of a flavor combining the best tastes of the watermelon and cantaloupe.

We passed some hours in the extensive warehouse and showrooms of the firm of Souhamie Sadullah & Co., and were shown innumerable Eastern carpets and rugs and rare and costly embroidered and woven stuffs, a good deal of which comes to our country through private purchasers. The venerable Turk who met us at the entrance and conducted us to a member of the firm came to us later with a copy of Mark Twain's "Innocents Abroad," and stating himself to be the Holy Moses therein described, stood by while we gravely read the page devoted to him, beaming with satisfaction at the facetiously extravagant portrait drawn of him by that renowned humorist, and plainly taking pride in it as a sincere and cordial recommendation. The partner who showed us about with much civility, although of full Turkish blood, had married a wife from Connecticut, and—she coming in to call upon him—politely introduced us to her and two pretty little girls, their children, both dark of skin, with black hair and eyes fully Oriental; and to complete the picture, her gray-haired, slouchy father lounged about in baggy trousers, jacket and fez, a transmogrified Yankee, quite at home in his Turkish garb and well illustrating the cosmopolitan nature of that ubiquitous race. We were shown a ladies' sleeping apartment completely fitted up in the Turkish manner, with a beautiful carpet, charming hangings, divan, and articles of Oriental ornament and bric-à-brac, including a rare tea service. The German Empress will visit this establishment and be shown into this room, and if—as surely she will—she express admiration of it, will be informed that its contents are hers, and all will be sent to Berlin—and the bill to the Sultan. We were served in a cool apartment of the establishment with little cups of coffee made in the Turkish way; this being a refreshment to its customers in which the house prides itself as being superior to what can be had almost anywhere else in the city. The coarsely ground berries of the coffee are put in the cup, boiling water poured on, and when seasoned to taste drank off directly.

   The evening spectacle from the balcony of our apartments in the Royal Hotel—the same as were occupied by the Hon. Samuel S. Cox when Minister here—is strangely enchanting. The eye follows the declining street running down sharply past our hotel to the Golden Horn, its lights throwing into relief the motley and fantastic passengers; the slim, tall cypresses of the ancient cemetery below us on the right rising solemnly against the deep blue sky, whose constellations glow and sparkle with a lustre I have never seen before; beyond the gleaming line of the Golden Horn, Stamboul rising steep above steep, its domes and minarets faintly showing in the faint lights; and beyond the Bosphorus, the dim outlines of the undulating Asiatic hills and the twinkling lamps of Scutari; and coming to the ea'r from all directions, a confusion of sounds alien and barbaric, not unsuited to the unfamiliar surroundings.

Nowhere is the outdoor life of this cosmopolitan city to be seen to such advantage as on the long wooden bridge connecting Pera with Stamboul. In the hurrying processions which pass and repass all through the day are mingled all nationalities, types and costumes of the Eastern world. The Italian traveller De Amicis has sketched this with so attractive a pencil, albeit in heightened colors, such as all tourists seem to use freely in the Orient, that I will transcribe it bodily; and allow my reason, whenever I turn to these imperfect notes that I may refresh my imperfect memory, to make the proper allowance for the ardor of the Italian's vivid nature:

"The crowd passes in great waves, each one of which is of a hundred colors, and every group of persons represents a new type of people. Whatever can be imagined that is most extravagant in type, costume and social class may there be seen within the space of twenty paces and ten minutes of time. Behind a throng of Turkish porters who pass, running and bending under enormous burdens, advances a sedan-chair inlaid with ivory and mother-of-pearl, and bearing an Armenian lady; and at either side of it a Bedouin wrapped in a white mantle and a Turk in muslin turban and sky-blue caftan, beside whom canters a young Greek gentleman followed by his dragoman in embroidered vest, and a dervish with his tall, conical hat and tunic of camel's-hair, who makes way for the carriage of a European ambassador, preceded by his running footman in gorgeous livery. All this is only seen in a glimpse, and the next moment you find yourself in the midst of a crowd of Persians in pyramidal bonnets of Astrakhan fur, who are followed by a Hebrew in a long yellow coat open at the sides; a frowzy-headed gypsy woman with her child in a bag at her back; a Catholic priest with breviary and staff; while in the midst of a confused throng of Greeks, Turks and Armenians comes a big eunuch on horseback, crying out "Larya!" ("Make way!"), and preceding a Turkish carriage painted with flowers and birds, and filled with the ladies of a harem, dressed in green and violet, and wrapped in large white veils; behind, a Sister of Charity from the hospital at Pera, an African slave carrying a monkey, and a professional story-teller in a necromancer's habit; and what is quite natural, but appears strange to the new-comer, all these diverse people pass one another without a look, like a crowd in London, and not one single countenance wears a smile. The Albanian, in his white petticoat and with pistols in his sash, beside the Tartar dressed in sheepskins; the Turk, astride his caparisoned ass, threads pompously two long strings of camels; behind the adjutant of an imperial prince, mounted upon his Arab steed, clatters a cart filled with all the odd domestic rubbish of a Turkish household; the Mohammedan woman afoot, the veiled slave woman, the Greek with her red cap and her hair on her shoulders, the Maltese hooded in her black *faldetta*, the Hebrew woman dressed in the antique costume of India, the negress wrapped in a many-colored shawl from Cairo, the Armenian from Trebizond, all veiled in black like a funeral apparition, are seen in single file, as if placed there on purpose to be contrasted.

"It is a changing mosaic of races and religions, that is composed and scattered continually with a rapidity that the eye can scarcely follow. It is amusing only to look at the passing feet and see all the foot-coverings in the world go by, from that of Adam up to the last fashion in Parisian boots—yellow Turkish babouches, red Armenian, blue Greek, and black Jewish shoes; sandals, great boots from Turkestan, Albanian gaiters, low-cut slippers, leg-pieces of many colors, belonging to horsemen from Asia Minor, gold-embroidered shoes, Spanish *alporgatos*, shoes of satin, of twine, of rags, of wood—so many that while you look at one you catch a glimpse of a hundred more. One must be on the alert not to be jostled and overthrown at every step. Now it is a water-carrier with a colored jar upon his back; now a Russian lady on horseback; now a squad of imperial soldiers in Zouave dress, and stepping as if to an assault; now a crew of Armenian porters, two and two, carrying on their shoulders immense bars, from which are suspended great bales of merchandise; and now a throng of Turks, who dart from left to right of the bridge to embark in the steamers that lie there. There is a tread of many feet, a murmuring, a sound of voices, guttural notes, aspirations interjectional, incomprehensible and strange, among which the few French or Italian words that reach the ear seem like luminous points upon a black darkness.

"The figures that most attract the eye in all this crowd are the Circassians, who go in groups of three and five together, with slow steps; big-bearded men of a terrible countenance, wearing bear-skin caps like the old Napoleonic guard, long black caftans, daggers at their girdles, and silver cartridge-boxes on their breasts; real figures of banditti, who look as if they had come to Constantinople to sell a daughter or a sister, with their hands imbrued in Russian blood. Then the Syrians, with robes in the form of Byzantine dalmatic and their heads enveloped in gold-striped handkerchiefs; Bulgarians dressed in coarse serge, and caps encircled with fur; Georgians in hats of varnished leather, their tunics bound round the waist with metal girdles; Greeks from the Archipelago, covered from head to foot with embroidery, tassels and shining buttons.

"From time to time the crowd slackens a little, but instantly other groups advance, waving with red caps and white turbans, amid which the cylindrical hats, umbrellas, and pyramidal head-dresses of Europeans, male and female, seem to float, borne onward by that Mussulman torrent.

"It is amazing even to note the variety of religions. The shining bald head of the Capuchin friar, the towering Janizary turban of an Ulema, alternate with the black veil of an Armenian priest; imaums with white tunics; veiled nuns; chaplains of the Turkish army, dressed in green, with sabres at their sides; Dominican friars; pilgrims returned from Mecca with a talisman hanging at their necks; Jesuits; dervishes—and this is very strange—dervishes that tear their own flesh in expiation of their sins, and cross the bridge under a sun-umbrella—all pass by.

"If you are attentive, you may notice in the throng a thousand amusing incidents. Here is a eunuch showing the white of his eye at a Christian exquisite who has glanced too curiously into the carriage of his mistress; there is a French *cocotte*, dressed after the last fashion-plate, leading by the hand the beloved and bejewelled son of a pasha; or a lady of Stamboul feigning to adjust her veil that she may peer more easily at the train of a lady of Pera; or a sergeant of cavalry, in full uniform, stopping in the middle of the bridge to blow his nose with his fingers in a way to give one a cold chill ; or a quack taking his last sous from some poor devil, and making a cabalistic gesture over his face to cure him of sore eyes ; or a family of travellers arrived that day and lost in the midst of a throng of Asiatic ruffians, while the mother searches for her crying children, and the men make way for them by dint of squaring their shoulders. Camels, horses, sedan-chairs, oxen, carts, casks on wheels, bleeding donkeys, mangy dogs, form a long file that divides the crowd in half.

"Sometimes there passes a mighty pasha with three tails, lounging in a splendid carriage, followed by his pipe-bearer on foot, his guard and one black slave, and then all the Turks salute, touching the forehead and breast, and the mendicant women, horrible witches, with muffled faces and naked breasts, run after the carriage, crying for charity. Eunuchs not on service pass in twos and threes and fives together, cigarette in mouth, and are recognized by their corpulence, their long arms and their black habits. Little Turkish girls dressed like boys, in green full trousers and rose or yellow vests, run and jump with feline agility, making way for themselves with their henna-tinted hands. Bootblacks with gilded boxes, barbers with bench and basin in hand, sellers of water and sweetmeats, cleave the press in every direction, screaming in Greek and Turkish. At every step comes glittering a military division, officers in fez and scarlet trousers, their breasts constellated with medals ; grooms from the seraglio, looking like generals of the army ; gendarmes with a whole arsenal at their belts ; zebecks, or free soldiers, with those enormous baggy trousers that make them resemble in profile the Hottentot Venus ; imperial guards with long white plumes upon their casques and gold-bedizened breasts ; city guards of Constantinople, as one might say required to keep back the waves of the Atlantic Ocean. The contrasts between all this gold and all those rags, between people loaded down with garments, looking like walking bazars, and people almost naked, are most extraordinary. The spectacle of so much nudity is alone a wonder. Here are to be seen all shades of skin-colors, from the milky whiteness of Albania to the crow blackness of Central Africa and the bluish blackness of Darfur ; chests that if you struck upon them would resound like a huge bass or rattle like pottery; backs, oily, stony, full of wrinkles, and hairy like the back of a wild boar; arms embossed with red and blue and decorated with designs of flowers and inscriptions from the Koran.

"But it is not possible to observe all this in one's first passage over the bridge. While you are examining the tattoo on an arm, your guide warns you that a Wallachian, a Servian, a Montenegrin, a Cossack of the Don, a Cossack of Ukraine, an Egyptian, a native of Tunis, a prince of Imerezia, is passing by. It seems that Constantinople is the same as it always was —the capital of three continents and the queen of twenty vice-realms. But even this idea is insufficient to account for the spectacle, and one fancies a tide of emigration produced by some enormous cataclysm that has overturned the antique continent. An experienced eye discerns still among the waves of that great sea the faces and costumes of Caramania and Anatolia, of Cyprus and Candia, of Damascus and Jerusalem, the Druse, the Kurd, the Maronite, the Croat, and others— innumerable varieties of all the anarchical confederations which extend from the Nile to the Danube and from the Euphrates to the Adriatic. Seekers after the beautiful or the horrible will here find their most audacious desires fulfilled; Raphael would be in ecstasies and Rembrandt would tear his hair. The purest types of Greek and Caucasian beauty are mingled with flat noses and woolly heads; queens and fairies pass beside you; lovely faces and faces deformed by disease and wounds; monstrous feet and tiny Circassian feet no longer than your hand; gigantic porters, enormously corpulent Turks, and black sticks of skeleton shadows of men that fill you with pity and disgust—every strangest aspect in which can be presented the ascetic life, the abuse of pleasure, extreme fatigue, the excess of opulence and the misery that kills.

"Who loves colors may here have his fill. No two figures are dressed alike. Here are shawls twisted around the heads, savage fillets, coronets of rags, skirts and undervests in stripes and squares like harlequins, girdles stuck full of knives that reach to the arm-pits, Mameluke trousers, short drawers, skirts, togas, trailing sheets, coats trimmed with ermine, vests like golden cuirasses, sleeves puffed and slashed, habits monkish and habits covered with gold lace, men dressed like women and women that look like men, beggars with the port of princes—a ragged elegance, a profusion of colors, of fringes, tags, and fluttering ends of childish and theatrical decorations, that remind one of a masquerade in a madhouse, for which all the old-clothes dealers in the universe have emptied their stores.

"Above the hollow murmur that comes from this multitude are heard the shrill cries of the sellers of newspapers in every tongue, the stentorian shout of the porters, the giggling laugh of Turkish women, the squeaking voices of eunuchs, the falsetto trill of blind men chanting verses of the Koran, the noise of the bridge as it moves upon the water, the whistles and bells of a hundred steamers, whose dense smoke is often beaten down by the wind, so that you can see nothing at all. All this masquerade of people embarks in the small steamboats that leave every moment for Scutari, for the villages of the Bosphorus and the suburbs of the Golden Horn; they spread through Stamboul, in the bazars, in the mosques, in the suburbs of Fanar and Galata, to the most distant quarters on the Sea of Marmora; they swarm upon the Frankish shore, to the right toward the Sultan's palace, to the left toward the higher quarters of Pera, whence they fall again upon the bridge by the innumerable lanes that wind about the sides of the hills; and thus they bind together Asia and Europe, ten cities and a hundred suburbs, in one mighty net of labor, intrigue and mystery, before which the mind becomes bewildered."

I am sorry to be obliged to add a prosaic note to the effect that I have never seen a more ungraceful gait than the female pedestrians practice as they waddle awkwardly along, "hen-toed," their ankles encased in slouchy stockings, their feet thrust into loose yellow or red slippers without heels, and only kept in place by a world of practice. Nor are handsome faces at all frequent. The Turkish women go abroad apparently with perfect freedom, the wealthy in close carriages, the poorer sort with their forms covered with the *feridjie*, or long loose robe or mantle of white cloth or silk, their faces covered with the *yashmak*, or light, thin veil, which leaves only the eyes exposed, but, as managed almost universally by its wearers, quite plainly revealing all the features, unless one seeks for some special reason to conceal the face, and I should say this is far from common.

There is prevailing here and in other Eastern cities, as we are informed, an epidemic of the *dangue*, a short-lived fever, with great pains in the limbs, not often fatal, and, as the *chargé d'affaires* here, Mr. King, who is from North Carolina, informs me, is very like what is known in our Southern States as break-bone fever. Fortunately none of our little party are affected by it. We have prolonged our visit sufficiently, for although very much has of course been imperfectly seen, we carry away a tolerably fair impression of this strange and wonderful city founded by Constantine the Great in the fourth century of our era on the older Greek city of Byzantium, itself dating from the seventh century before Christ, and now numbering nearly a million of the most heterogeneous population of any city in the world.

We take our last dinner at the good table of the comfortable Royal Hotel, but may not finish until Betty, whose heart is pitiful to all, the least of the creatures God has made, has abundantly supplied with her own hands an exhausted canine mother lying exposed under the window in the midst of her numerous blind litter; and under the charge of the constant dragoman, Joseph, and the agile Frattini, reach the station of the Oriental Express in the early evening, where we have a long wait, while 'mid infinite hubbub the train is got ready. I passed a half hour walking with Betty in a little dusty garden connected with the station, and sought to answer her eager questions about the stars shining overhead in marvellous splendor. The whistle screams, the rush and hubbub redouble, we take our compartment, and with effusive salaams and hand-kissings on the part of Joseph Jacob, slowly roll out into the night under the shadow of the mighty walls which have borne bravely the sieges and assaults of nigh twenty centuries, and are on our way back to the better civilizations of the Western World.

*October* 31.—Left Constantinople at 7.30 P.M. in a sleeper of the Oriental Express-train, and woke next morning on the boundless plain which, watered by the Danube, stretches from western Hungary to the Black Sea, broken only by the Balkan chain of mountains, and in its western portion, so far as one can judge, of great fertility, but for want of rain becoming in its eastern expanse an arid, undulating desert. Almost the whole of Servia and all of Hungary we traversed are like an

Iowa prairie, and would seem capable of yielding enormous crops of cereals and fruits. While along the line of the road a good deal of the soil is under cultivation, one sees very few farmsteads, so that the land must be in the hands of large proprietors, or its owners live in the villages at inconvenient distances away. Certainly the soil is capable of sustaining a great population under favorable circumstances. On the morning of November 2d we left the train at Buda-Pesth, the capital of Hungary, after two most uncomfortable nights in a close, ill-ventilated and ill-accommodated sleeping-car, bad to a degree unknown on any road I have travelled over at home in the last twenty years.

Buda-Pesth is a quite modern city in all its aspects, beautifully situated on the Danube, here a broad, noble river, with Buda on its right bank and Pesth on its left, the two cities being connected by a handsome suspension-bridge. Their united population is something over 400,000, and I should say that, with the exception of Vienna, we have not visited on the Continent a more handsome, well-built, bright and fine city. One might fancy himself in New York or Chicago when driving along its wide streets, thronged with well-dressed people and lined with fine shops all in modern guise, until one would recall that neither American city is as well-paved nor can show so fine public buildings. Here again my ignorant prepossessions got another rude correction. I had thought of the Hungarians as a half-wild, intractable nation, full of fire and a noble spirit, but unpractical and half Oriental in costume, manners and way of life, and here I am in their principal city, to find it more modern than London, with all the marks and aspects of high civilization and refinement. Quite likely there are not many so poorly informed as I have been in this matter.

We called on a niece of Louis Kossuth, who was educated at the same school with my wife in New York, and is now married to a Hungarian gentleman here. It was pleasant to learn from her that her uncle, now eighty-nine years old, is living in Turin, Italy, in good health and activity of mind, passing his time among his books and the flowers he loves to cultivate, and able to speak last summer for more than an hour in the open air to a great company of students who called upon him. I referred to the surprising skill he showed in the use of the English language in the eloquent speeches he made in America on the occasion of his visit to the United States in 1852. She said he learned English in the prison where he was confined for two years, and had as his only books the Bible, Shakespeare and an English dictionary. She said of the brilliant painter Munkacsy that he was the son of an upholsterer in a little village near Buda-Pesth, and attracted attention to himself by the wonderful way in which, when a lad, he painted pictures on the trunks or chests his father made for the country people.

Came on to Vienna and took night train for Venice, three hundred and ninety-eight miles, arriving at our rooms in the Royal Hotel Danieli at 3 P.M. on November 5th. Awoke this morning, after a poor night in a hot, cramped sleeper, to find ourselves near Villach on the Drave, two hundred and thirty miles from Vienna, and still among the Tyrolean Alps, in a cold rain. We had fine mountain scenery to Pontebba and a hasty cup of coffee there, after a slight examination of our luggage by the Italian Custom-House. Passed through Udine, the capital of the Venetian province of Friuli, a town of importance, with 28,000 inhabitants. The country along the way grew more level and then marshy, like parts of the New Jersey coast near Long Branch, with oozy channels among the coarse grass worn by the tides of the Adriatic, the shallow bays of which deeply indent and overspread the land. We crossed a solid bridge more than a mile long, resting on handsome brick arches, and rolled into a railway station with solid earth all about and nowise differing in the character of its location, so far as one would notice, from any other on good, solid earth, and Frattini, opening the door of our compartment, called out " Venice !"

I was not at all satisfied with this humdrum introduction to the Bride of the Adriatic. I might as well have been in the dépôt at Rochester and have heard the magic name of Venice spoken under its smoky vault. Nor was the case improved when, after walking under cover of the prosaic roof, we emerged on a platform to be solicited by a crowd of dirty fellows in ready-made clothing of material and fashion like unto that which greets the eye of the stunned traveller when he steps outside the Grand Central Depot in our well-regulated metropolis and is invited to have a cab—solicited, I say, and vehemently urged to come without loss of time into a long, narrow, black and dirty boat floating among twenty others alongside the platform in water of a dirty sage-green, stretching away to right and left between rows of grim old houses rising from it on either side. "What is this?" I asked Frattini as soon as we floated from the wharf, and being answered, "The Grand Canal," sank back on my seat, the most disenchanted of men. The sky was leaden, the air cold, we had had little sleep and no breakfast, and in a resigned and apathetic state of chilled enthusiasm hardly knew or cared by what devious watery ways we came to the hotel on the Riva degli Schiavoni, out on which and the broad lagoon to the south our cheerful rooms look from the second floor. A bright sitting-room, made more so by the blaze of a handful of fagots laid on the tiniest of andirons, a bath, a change of dress, an excellent dinner, disposed me to look kindlier on the external world. Vainly does any man imagine that he is the same being before and after dinner. If, as we are taught, the soul is a spiritual entity capable of an independent existence in other and higher states of being, it is certainly true that in its present sojourn it is fast-bound to a material associate, and until the clamorous and vulgar wants of its partner are satisfied, it is nowise at liberty to find comfort in exercising its own functions, but is obstructed and fretted and unfit for enjoyment. This by way of preface to saying that, cheered and fortified as indicated above, I went forth from the portal of the Hotel Danieli, built by the blind old Doge Dandolo more than four hundred years ago wherein to entertain the ambassadors to the Republic, and turning to the right, a few steps took me to the bridge connecting the Riva with the Molo across the Canal Paglia, and stopping on the arch of it, looked up to the Bridge of Sighs and along the frowning wall of the old prison to my right and the bright façade of the Palace of the Doges on my left, and then passing along the southern front of it, stood before the superb columns of polished granite with their exquisite capitals on one of which rests the winged lion of St. Mark and on the other St. Theodore atop of his crocodile. These front the water at the opening of the Piazzetta, or broad paved space leading into the Piazza of St. Mark, to the centre of which I at once betook me, and looked with strained and delighted attention on the marvels of architecture all around, objects familiar to my mind through pictures and books, seen a thousand times in fancy and longed for from boyhood. Here they all are more grand, more beautiful, "more moving-delicate and full of life" than my imagination had painted them: the Church of St. Mark with the four bronze horses over its glorious portal, the clock-tower, the imposing Campanile with its sculptured vestibule, the long line of massive marble palaces on three sides of the square, the red flag-staffs rising from their exquisite bronze pedestals—all are here; and this indeed is Venice the wonderful.

The following day was cool enough to make a blaze on our hearth desirable; leaden clouds kept their places sullenly, with fits of rain; but hiring a gondola, I set out to find our consul here, taking his address from the directory, and gliding along the Grand Canal amid old palaces, reached it to find him removed elsewhere. Getting another address after much inquiry, the porter at the old one being ignorant of his whereabouts, we came in sight of the American flag-staff rearing itself obliquely from the third story of a lonely house on the Grand Canal. We found he had again removed, no one whom we found within knowing where, and only after much inquiry among watermen and market people, up and down, did we come upon his modest rooms on a little square on a side canal. The young gentleman who upholds the honor of our nation here is holding over from Mr. Cleveland's term, this being his fifth year, and his frequent change of residence would seem to be explained by the statement he made when dining with me at our hotel the next day, that his salary, no fees or other perquisites attaching, is one thousand dollars per annum, from which he pays all expenses, including the rent of his premises. This would seem to be a rather shabby stipend, and one would think him not likely to be disturbed, though why an able-bodied and energetic enough young man, to look at him, should continue in it I did not learn.

In the afternoon again admired the glorious structures surrounding the Piazza and passed an hour in the church, or, as it is now in fact, the Cathedral of St. Mark. This consummate flower of architecture is not imposing by reason of its size, and more resembles one of the mosques of Constantinople in its outward form than a Christian church, having, indeed, been remodelled in the Byzantine style from an earlier Romanesque form in the twelfth century. Some Gothic features, too, were added, but such is the richness and beauty of its adornments, or rather of its intrinsic structure, that the mind refuses to see any incongruity in its parts, and dwells with satisfied delight on the endless variety and completeness, the marvellous tints and the softened harmonies which everywhere meet the eye in bewildering and sumptuous profusion. The mosaics cover an area of 46,000 square feet, and date all the way from the tenth to the sixteenth century; without and within are five hundred columns of marble, mostly from the Orient, with capitals of exquisite carving in all styles conceivable, and everywhere is profusion of gilding, bronze and the richest marbles; so that the whole interior, and, for the matter of that, the exterior of the walls as well, might be cut into small parts, framed and hung on the walls of a room one wished to beautify with choice ornaments. I am quite incapable of describing this gem of the earth, this pride of Italy, whose builders and decorators fairly revelled in the construction of it, and as if, in an ecstasy of the imagination, they had quite forgotten or abandoned the formal rules of art, and, with a strange and profuse freshness of creative power poured the prodigal richness of the East upon this shrine of the Occident. Time has softened the hues of the costly marbles and blent all into a more perfect harmony of color. The rich floor has become so uneven by the irregular giving way of the foundation that in nave and transept and under the great central dome it fluctuates like the swell of the ocean arrested and frozen into stone, but by a careful process of restoration all is fixed and continuous, so that the effect is even heightened by this peculiarity.

The gondola grows in favor as one becomes more familiar with it. The commonest sort are no more pleasing objects than any other black, weather-worn boats, but the better ones, with their bright steel prows, carved sides and tops, brass decorations, stuffed leathern seats and fringed cloth canopies or *felzes*, are graceful, convenient and picturesque. They carry six persons, besides two gondoliers, one in the body of the boat forward, the other perched on the high stern, where he presents a pleasing figure as he guides his long, narrow craft with singular dexterity, using only one oar against a rowing-post set some four feet from the bow on the left side. All gondolas are painted black, and the cloth covering of the little cabin, which is easily removable and left ashore in fair weather, is of the same sombre color. This fashion continues as the result of a sumptuary law enacted in the fifteenth century to check the extravagant outlay practised by the citizens in the ornament of these indispensable vehicles, which here take the place of carriages, there being not a horse nor anything on wheels in the city, I believe. As the gondolier has so far given way to the spirit of the age as to rig himself out generally in nondescript ready-made garments, which are as fatal to romance as a steam-engine, I engaged a handsome gondola by the day for our use, with the condition that the gondoliers should put on the uniform the better sort of them have for occasions.

The next morning the sun rose in a sky of soft blue, warming the pure sea air with a feel of September; our gondola floated in the narrow canal at the side entrance to the hotel, with two brawny, bronze rowers in dark blue suits faced with white and girt round the waist with colored sashes, and we set forth on the Grand Canal, gliding by time-stained, silent palaces of various and massive architecture, beautiful in their decay, the fair vestiges of noble and wealthy families whose names shine in the annals of the last five centuries. From the Grand Canal, frequent narrow ones open on either side, no streets being visible; the houses everywhere rise from the water, as if a well-built and populous city should be inundated and its streets flooded up to the very thresholds of the houses. The tide rises something above two feet in the city, and at its full the gondolas set their passengers down on the very topmost steps of the landings. Families who maintain private gondolas indicate their residences by tall posts planted in the water in front, bearing their coats-of-arms in colors.

Very many of these palaces which line the Grand Canal along its length of two miles are not less than one hundred feet in front, with four lofty stories, of elaborately carved stone, sometimes faced with richly colored marbles. Not many of them are fully occupied, and very few by descendants of the old families who built them. Many are let out in flats, many are closed altogether, quite a number are used for business purposes and a few are owned or rented by foreigners, and these have an appearance of being really human homes. One of the finest is now being renovated by Mr. Browning, son of the poet Browning, who married Miss Coddington, of New York. This rich stone pile, of enormous size and cost, certainly could not be built or purchased on Manhattan Island for less than a quarter of a million dollars ; and as an illustration of the condition of the real-estate market here, I might mention that I was informed that this cost Mr. Browning forty-five thousand dollars. Fine and grand as these old houses are, one would think it a dreary thing, after the novelty had worn off, to live on the water and have no way of leaving one's house except by boat. We pass the pretty balconied house said, by I know not what fantastic tradition, to be that of Desdemona what time she was wooed by the Moor, the Contarini Palace, the Cavalli, the Foscari, and a plain house built on a grand foundation, begun by Francisco Sforza, the traitor, but ordered by the Republic to be left unfinished, the Palace Balbi, Pisani, Dandolo, Bembo, Ca d'Oro, Pesaro, Vendramin, Calergi, and many another one famous in old-time annals.

Half way up the Grand Canal is the famous Rialto Bridge, "where merchants most do congregate," and until the iron bridge was built some distance below the only one spanning the Grand Canal and connecting the eastern and western quarters of the city. This noble structure consists of a single marble arch of 74 feet span and is 158 feet long, 46 wide and 32 high, resting upon twelve thousand piles. It was built in 1588 by Antonio da Ponte, and has a row of shops along each side. One would not think it ever a likely place for a meeting of the merchants, but conditions have changed since this was the rich mart of Eastern commerce, and very likely precious wares were then stored in the huge decaying warehouses near the Rialto, and merchants from both sides of the canal met on its broad and spacious arch to effect their sales and exchanges. We passed into many narrow side canals overhung by lofty mouldering houses, penetrated the old Jewish quarter—the Ghetto—where these people, once proscribed, still dwell, not exclusively, but did not recognize the "gentle Jessica" among the frowzy maidens leaning over the decrepit balconies, half screened by the picturesque tatters of probable underclothing waving from the walls.

The tide was ebbing as we glided among these sinuous channels and the receding water left unromantic stenches behind, not noticeable at high tide, and we were glad to issue forth upon the blue lagoon to the northward, viewing with pleasure the long, graceful yellow line of the cemetery-wall; stopping to see the Church of San Michele, built in 1466, with some good sculptures on its façade. Here and at every landing we encountered the most adhesive of the beggar tribe in the form—always—of a tatterdemalion, shaky, watery-eyed old man who is lying in wait with a hooked pole to hold one's boat to the landing-steps. He and his function are useless, but he fastens upon the boat as if he were a government official with full powers, and no extent of prohibition or volume of objurgation has the least effect upon him; he takes all as a matter of course and never relaxes his hold until, yielding to his imperturbable impudence, you slip a small gratuity into his relaxing palm.

As we returned homeward the declining sun flooded the intervening tract of tranquil water with a flow of opalescent light far to the eastward, and in the unreal radiance of it, floated or seemed to float, rising and falling in the slight pulsations radiating from the gondola's noiseless prow, the low lines of islands white with churches, to the left of us the blue Alps veiled in mist, and on the right, more silent and weird than any other thing, the strange, unreal city, in whose streets no sound of wheels is heard, hoary with centuries, beautiful in decaying grandeur, lifting, as if in mournful supplication, its graceful domes and campaniles to the pitiful heavens, their sad bells sobbing over the friendly sea.

We were early afloat next morning under the sky of a perfect day, again gliding along the Grand Canal as in a dream, finding new beauties of form and color everywhere, the commonest things so altered by the "sea change" that nothing seemed "common or unclean," the comfortless, crumbling palaces shining like the work of enchantment; and the imagination in the easiest and most natural way restored them to their pristine beauty and filled the pillared galleries with jewelled ladies whose dark eyes outshine the sun, waving white hands of welcome to gleaming knights below, sweeping with swift oars to greet them, fresh home from brave wars and rich with the spoils of the East; precious jewels, costly silks, cloth of gold, spices and perfumes. What feasting followed! what revelry! These empty halls blazing with light shining out from these pointed windows, now dead to light, across the gleaming water; these mournful walls flaunting with many colored streamers and hung with embroidered cloths of velvet fringed with gold! I count him less than man whose blood does not stir in this scene of antique glory.

All day long we floated and glided about, threading passages so narrow that two boats could scarcely meet, between ranks of houses so tall and near together that only a long strip of azure sky showed above. At each of the frequent turns the gondolier utters a peculiar cry of warning to any boat likely to emerge from the hidden turn of the channel. From the wider canals, indeed from the narrowest, rise frequently the worn fronts of dilapidated palaces rich with patches of glorious colors, their sculptured water-gates still surmounted with grave, bearded heads of well-wrought stone, empty, forlorn and desolate beyond words.

The young people of my party desired to be photographed in our gondola, and so after lunch we had the *felze* or canopy put on, and were rowed across to the little island of San Giorgio Maggiore, where, on the landing in front of the wall of the old Benedictine Monastery, we found the camera of Signor Salviati awaiting us, and making fast the boat to a post, with a background of the Ducal Palace and the Piazzetta, we got what proved to be a good picture, the chief features in it being Frattini in proud attitude on the prow and the graceful gondolier poising his idle oar astern. Afterward we were rowed past the Giardini Pubblici—the principal, indeed the only public garden, made by Napoleon in 1807, who demolished several old monasteries at the southern end of the long crescent of the Riva degli Schiavoni—to the Lido, the largest of the islands of the lagoons, with summer cottages among trees fronting the Adriatic, bluest and tranquillest of seas, as we looked on it from the sands much frequented by bathers in the season. A tramway with positively live horses crosses the island to the sea, and we regard these sorry hacks with something of curiosity born of abstinence. Thence to the yellow walls of the Armenian Monastery on the island of San Lazzaro, the peaceful home of a body of learned Armenian scholars engaged in printing and diffusing literature, sectarian and other, among the Eastern peoples of their faith.

Nothing more tranquil and winning to the mind tired of the

18

world and seeking pious solitude can be imagined than these dim cloisters and arched halls, full of silence, rising from the blue water, where no breath of heated outer life with its jars and turmoils can penetrate. I said to the kindly, placid father who had shown us the library where Lord Byron, in one of his many moods, had studied Armenian, residing here some weeks among the fathers, the dim, silent chapel where they worship, the great stone refectory where they sit at table on stone benches against the walls, and the many retired apartments, severely simple, yet elegant from their fine proportions and utter cleanliness, that I almost envied him this learned seclusion. His smile was touched with sadness, I thought, as he only said in his pleasant voice and in the English he spoke brokenly well, "You would find it monotonous, I fear." He took us through the little garden in the court, looked out upon by the cloisters, well planted with many choice varieties of exotic plants, and sending for a gardener, had him cut from a prosperous catalpa-tree in the centre, a huge green cone bursting with rich red seeds and handed it to us with an unworldly kindliness graceful beyond art.

The brothers have a large plat of land outside the walls where they grow fruits and vegetables for their simple table, and also have possessions on the mainland near Padua, and are altogether a prosperous brotherhood, for which I for one am thankful. We visited their printing-office, an orderly, well-arranged establishment, where all the various work is done by hand in a slow, restful way, indicating no anxious waiting on the part of the reading world outside. We bought a copy of "Uncle Tom's Cabin" in Armenian and a volume of prayers in thirty-seven languages, and, infected with the silence, glided homeward through oozy channels among hundreds of little black islets of mud exposed by the receding tide.

We passed the entire evening in our boat rowing under the golden radiance of a full moon. The air breathed soft, and a barge laden with a company of singers and hung with colored lanterns floated down the Grand Canal, where a great number of boats flocked to it and surrounded it. There were two or three good voices in the company, and with these for solos and duets and the rest for chorus, we had very satisfactory music, since "soft stillness and the night become the touches of sweet harmony." One song by the best voice, a clear baritone, had much dramatic variety in it and was supposed, as Frattini explained, to express the varying emotions of a crew of fishermen at Chioggia, a fishing village at the mouth of the lagoons, who, having landed with empty nets, go to a drinking-shop much cast down, lamenting their ill-luck, but soon recovering, bid each other cheer up and seek the comfort there is in a cup of wine. Extricating our boat from the floating mass, we stole into the small canals and roved about their dim, mysterious channels; all the stories I had ever read of stealthy bravos and dark intrigues coming back as we darted among the shadows. We emerged at last, by way of the Canal Paglia under the Bridge of Sighs—the soft wash of the gondola murmuring along the walls of the Ducal Palace and the gloomy foundation of the old prison—into the shimmering blue of the broad water in front of the Riva degli Schiavoni.

I pass all my spare half hours either in the Church of St. Mark or on the Piazza among the incomparable works surrounding it. The interior of St. Mark grows in beauty as one becomes more familiar with it and able to separate one charm from the rest and consider it singly. Such extravagance of beauty, such opulence of charms, such accumulations of wealth and lavish adornments! At the grand mass on Sunday I noticed how well fitted the church is for worship, receiving its thronging devotees in a royal way, rich and poor alike welcomed to such a temple as is not on earth for costliness. Among the objects of especial richness, where all is rich and rare, I will note the high altar canopied with verd-antique, with an altar-piece of enamels on gold and silver thickly set with precious stones and of inestimable value, wrought in Constantinople early in the twelfth century. This is securely hidden behind thick sliding doors, and only shown to the general public on high festivals. Also the altar behind the high altar, with its four spiral pillars of alabaster, reputed to have belonged to the Temple of Solomon; two of them so transparent that, although some eight inches in diameter, the light from an ignited match held behind them is seen as a spot of creamy light.

But why begin to catalogue the marvels of beauty and grace on every hand in this church? In the Treasury, among many precious things, are two candelabra by Cellini exceeding in grace and delicacy anything I have seen in bronze. I asked the significance of a huge, coarse, rusty knife carefully placed on a rest within a glass case, and was informed that St. Mark, whose remains, brought from Alexandria by Venetian citizens in 828 repose beneath the high altar, was done to death with it. It is not conceivable that so notable a church should be without the relics of an evangelist at least. In the Baptistery is a fine bronze font of the middle of the fifteenth century. There, too, is the fair-carven monument to the Doge Dandolo, and here we are shown a broad granite stone from Mount Tabor, on whose level face the Transfiguration occurred! Nor does the wonder stop here, for below the head of John the Baptist on the wall is the stone on which his decapitation took place.

We visited several other churches in Venice: the Gli Scalzi, scarcely less rich in its variety of costly marbles than San Marco itself; San Giorgio Maggiore, with its beautifully carven choir-stalls; San Maria della Salute, erected in 1631 by Longhena, a successor of Palladio, in commemoration of the plague of 1630, with its ceiling-pieces of "Cain and Abel," "Abraham and Isaac," "David and Goliath," by Titian; the Frari, where many eminent men repose. Here is Titian's monument, completed in 1852, elaborate and rich, from a design by Longhena in the seventeenth century—a noble tomb. A statue of St. Jerome there, by Alessandro Vittoria, is said to delineate the features and face of Titian in his ninety-eighth year. There is in this church a sweet Madonna by Giovanni Bellini, and another, strong and grand, by Bernardino Licinio da Pordenone. The Doges Francisco Foscari and Niccolo Tron and Giovanni Pesaro have mausoleums here, and very grand they are, as well as Canova's mausoleum, erected in 1827, from his own design for that of Titian, done by his pupils, Martini, Ferrari, Fabris and others. But the crown of all is Titian's altar-piece, "The Madonna of the Pesaro Family;" or, as it is called here, "The Madonna di Casa Pesaro," reputed almost the finest of his works. I should not rank it so high, but my opinion of a picture I constantly feel is of no consequence to any one but myself. This is a painting of great majesty and beauty.

The Church of San Giovanni e Paolo has an imposing interior, and even more than the Frari contains the monuments of famous men, especially the burial-vaults of the doges whose funeral services were always held here. We note the imposing tombs of Doges Pietro Mocenigo, who died in 1476; Michele Morosini, died 1382; Antonio Venier, died 1400; Pasquale Malipiero, died 1462; Michael Steno, died 1413; Tommaso Mocenigo, died 1423; Niccolo Marcello, died 1474; Giovanni Mocenigo, died 1485; Giovanni Bembo, died 1618, and many another of less distinguished title but great in Venetian annals, notably that of Marc Antonio Bragadino, died in 1571, flayed alive by the barbarous Turks, as shown in a painting above his tomb. He it was who so stoutly defended "famed Famagosta" in Cyprus against the Turks, who, after his surrender, put him to so cruel a death. Beautiful exceedingly is the one to Andrea Vendramin, who died in 1478, by Alessandro Leopardo. A chapel of this fine church—Cappella del Rosario—founded in 1571 to commemorate the battle of Lepanto, was as clean burned out by a fire in 1867 as if it were only pine-wood. I have been surprised where we have been, both in Great Britain and on the Continent, at the number of castles, churches and palaces of massive stone whose records show them to have been destroyed and ruined by fire, sometimes over and over again. In this chapel remain only some beautiful marble reliefs on a portion of one wall, mutilated and blackened.

Visited the little church of Maria Formosa on purpose to see the queenly St. Barbara of Palma Vecchio, and found there besides that worshipful creation, a "Madonna and Child" by Sassoferrato, and I am not sure if it does not please me almost beyond any of the endless Madonnas after those of Raphael.

The Academy of Fine Arts is poorly located in the halls of a suppressed monastery, where the light is difficult and trying, and the gallery contains pictures of Venetian painters almost altogether. There are fine works of Bellini, Tintoretto, Paul Veronese, Palma Vecchio, and among many of note and fame, two whose pictures I felt much interest in, Bonifacio and Carpaccio. I should say I had not seen anything by Paul Veronese to compare with his "Jesus in the House of Levi." Titian is here numerously, of course, and his "John the Baptist" and his "Assumption"—in a bad light by the way—are creations of wonderful sublimity and beauty. What abounding and redundant life was in the blood and brain of many of these great old painters! Here is the great canvas of "The Entombment," on which Titian was working when death not unkindly took the brush from his hand at the age of ninety-nine years, leaving the unfinished picture to be finished by Palma the Younger.

I was much interested in the Arsenal, where, within handsome old brick walls, the Republic during the centuries of its power built the redoubtable galleys and forged the warlike implements which spread its triumphs into distant lands and over many seas. This is the "Sagittary" mentioned in Shakespere's "Othello." There is a magnificent gateway of 1460 at the outer entrance, in front of which crouch four huge lions brought from Greece in 1687. It is said that in the height of her power the Republic employed sixteen thousand workmen here, but now only a small force is used. We found an admirable museum here, especially rich in Oriental arms and costly spoils of the Turk. There are exact models of the Venetian galleys and a rich one of the Bucentaur, the great, many oared boat from whose deck the Doge annually, on Ascension Day, threw a ring into the Adriatic, in symbol of the marriage of Venice with the sea. The Bucentaur, which was so utterly destroyed by the French Vandals in 1796 that only a small portion of the richly decorated sides remains in the museum here, is thus described : " It was in the form of a galley and two hundred feet long, with two decks. The first of these was occupied by one hundred and sixty rowers, the handsomest and strongest of the fleet, who sat four men to each oar and there awaited orders ; forty other sailors completed the crew. The upper deck was divided lengthwise by a partition pierced with arched doorways, ornamented with gilded figures and covered with a roof supported by caryatides, the whole surmounted by a canopy of crimson velvet embroidered with gold. Under this were ninety seats, and at the stern a still richer chamber for the Doge's throne, over which drooped the banner of St. Mark. The prow was double-beaked and the sides of the vessel were enriched with figures of Justice, Peace, Sea, Land, and other allegories and ornaments."

It must not be supposed that because Venice is permeated with water-ways that it has no streets. It is honeycombed, as it were, with an intricate network of them, all the way from three to ten feet wide ; and as one might think, when on the water, there are no streets, from anything he can see, so, when losing himself in these noiseless alleys, he might well believe them to be the only channels of communication between the different sections of the city, except for the frequent stone bridges by which these streets cross the many canals. As there are no wheeled vehicles of any sort, these narrow alleys —for the widest of the streets are scarcely more—quite suffice for the domestic traffic, and at frequent intervals all over the city these open into little courts or squares, called *campos*, in the centre of which stands always the handsome stone curb of a well, from which the neighborhood gets its supply of fresh water—even now when there is a supply brought in by pipes from the main-land. These courts are the centres of the many parishes into which the city is divided, and besides the church there will be found in each the trades and shops needed for the regular supply of the wants of the poorer families crowded into the stories of the lofty old houses elbowing each other on every hand.

We visited several of the large palaces on the Grand Canal and saw how dreary and unhomelike they are, with great rooms of stone, chilly, cheerless, dismal. When renovated, divided into smaller apartments, wainscoted, floored, and made comfortable by modern appliances for heating and lighting, they will do very well for summer, but, I should say, dreary enough in the main, and I cannot well imagine a more cheerless city for a steady residence than Venice, with water and stone below, above and around. Baron Franchetti is now thoroughly making over the grand Palace Cavalli, and we were permitted to see his new staircase of white marble, rich with statues and frescoes, said to have cost two hundred thousand dollars of our money. He has a pretty garden with good trees at the side and rear and access to one of the narrow streets, so that he will have a homelike residence after an enormous outlay ; but there are not many Baron Franchettis, and Venice is a poverty-stricken city. While its material prosperity seems to have sunk to its lowest point after its dissolution as an independent state by Napoleon in 1797, when its population dwindled from 200,000 to 96,000, it continued to languish under the hated Austrian rule. Since 1866 it has been reunited with Italy, and in a languidly improving way is feeling the quickened current of the new Italian life. The population in 1881 is reported at 129,000, but with the sad comment that one-quarter are paupers. The Italian government has interested itself in the revival of several of the arts and crafts for which Venice was once famous, and beautiful articles are made in carved woods, lace and glass. We visited a manufactory of laces where in the factory itself and the training-school connected with it, the latter being aided by the government, some four thousand persons, mostly women, are employed.

We climbed the inclined plane, mounting easily up the inside of the Campanile of St. Mark, some 300 feet, to "assist" at the sunset of an afternoon not less perfect—and I cannot give it higher praise—than some I recall of the Indian-summer time on Prairie Ronde in the early years of the State of Michigan. But there the opulent and gorgeous Western sky shed its glory of crimson and purple, gold and blue upon scenes of unsophisticated nature sadly attendant upon the dying year; here it flooded, through the soft autumnal mist, the most enchanting works of time-worn art, and dome and tower and gilded pinnacle, many a one, flashed and shone above the dull-red roofs of the silent city far below, in heavenly dyes, richer than Venetian galley ever fetched from the Orient. A memorable scene, this city rising from the broad lagoon, flashing all around it in the sunset. A numerous flock of pigeons has its "procreant cradle," likewise its roosting-places, on every "coign of vantage" of the façades of St. Mark and the Procuratie. There are at least two accounts of how they come to be here, where they have remained immemorial years. One is that Admiral Dandolo, while laying siege to Candia, early in the thirteenth century, received intelligence of value through carrier-pigeons. He sent them home with the news of his conquest, and the race of them has been tended with reverent care by the citizens ever since. Another is that as far back as the erection of St. Mark, in the tenth century, the sacristans of the church used to let loose pigeons on Palm Sunday for the people to scramble for in the Piazza. Some escaped and took refuge in the roof of the church, and gradually taking on a sort of sacred character, increased and multiplied, and became the pets we now behold them. Whichever account of their origin may be true or not true, here the pigeons are in great force, crop-full, tame, plump and impudent burghers, living on the plentiful grain and polenta fed them daily by visitors like ourselves and also from a fund left by a pious lady for their maintenance. The oily rascals are like the world in general: they fawn and cluster around and on you until your bag is empty, and then all flutter and waddle away to the fresh supplies.

In the evenings an excellent band plays in the well-lighted Piazza with sweetness and vivacity, and a numerous concourse of citizens of all degrees throngs the arcades of the Procuratie, promenading slowly and in silent decorum in the glare of the bright shop-windows or in the freer spaces of the Piazza, or standing in mildly chatting groups, or seated before little tables in front of the Café Florian over little cups of coffee. The only color and picturesqueness is furnished by the lively uniforms of the handsome officers here and there, all others, men and women, old and young, being clothed in dull, ill-fitting garments of styles originated in Paris or London, and getting a well-defined but scarcely describable derangement and unshapeliness in the translation from the art centres to the backs of people who in the article of dress are in the transition state. The movement of the beaux and dandies would seem to be of the most aimless and vapid nature, and milder or more inoffensive young men to look at I have never seen than these gilded youths of Venice, with their pointed shoes, little canes and ill-fitting trousers, as they stroll aimlessly up and down in couples or sit at coffee with a far-away look of gentle imbecility. I see few handsome or even pretty faces among the women. Once in a while a maid or young matron moves by, of free, graceful step, and olive features lighted by glorious dark eyes of dangerous sparkle, with hair raven in darkness or of that peculiar rich auburn once an attribute of the best Venetian beauty; but these visions are rare, and certainly on the streets and watery ways of Venice, by daylight or gaslight, one sees very few attractive women.

The Ducal Palace, so beautifully conspicuous at the corner of the Riva and Piazzetta, still preserves within its lofty and imposing walls the magnificent apartments where the affairs of the government were transacted during those centuries of the Republic's highest pride and power. The Senate Chamber, with its dull-red raised seats on two sides and the Doge's gilded chair at one end, its lofty ceilings heavy with gold and alive with the frescoes of Tintoretto, is a most noble chamber, and realizes one's conception of a hall fit for such an assemblage. So of the other famous rooms related to this—that of the Council of Ten, the Great Council Hall, the room of the three inquisitors of the Republic, into the antechamber of which is an opening from the hall at the head of the staircase where in the old time a bronze lion's head was set, into whose open jaws any one might thrust anonymous charges against whomsoever he saw fit; such secret accusation being received and acted on in the same mysterious manner, the victim never knowing his accuser. The chamber of the Council of Ten is connected with some cells by way of a narrow passage; these cells or dungeons, as they are called, being large, dry chambers—well enough as dungeons, except for an almost total lack of light. Apart from this—and certainly it is a drawback to lie and sit and stand in darkness—these cells are more roomy and comfortable than those of our prisons, and vastly more so than the dens shown us as used for a like purpose in Ireland, Scotland, England, and elsewhere on the Continent, in the strongholds of four hundred years ago. This narrow passage is continued to the Bridge of Sighs, where it is divided into two passages crossing this bridge to the prison on the other side of the Canal Paglia. This covered stone way from the palace to the prison is some 15 feet long, and connects the upper stories of these structures about 30 feet above the water. It was built much later than these, for the convenience, no doubt, of bringing prisoners before the judicial tribunals in the Doge's Palace for trial, whence they were returned by the same way; and there is no doubt that the pitiful and tragical notions connected with it are largely the sentimental creations of poetical romancers.

One morning the thunder of a salute from an Italian man-of-war lying just off the Riva, to the left of our hotel, shook the windows, advising us that the Emperor and Empress of Germany, who were in Constantinople the week after we left that city, were approaching Venice, where the Emperor is to land and proceed by rail to Mensa, to hunt with the King of Italy for a day; and shortly before noon the royal yacht "Hohenzollern" steamed grandly up the tortuous channel and cast anchor just in front of our balcony, some thirty rods away. We took to our gondola, and in a minute were in the midst of a swarm of like craft lying in wait for a glimpse of the royal couple. Our desires were soon gratified, as they appeared in company on the promenade-deck in full view, and bringing to bear on their august features the excellent field-glass purchased in Edinburgh, I surveyed them long and well with the unconstraint of a proud native of a land where all are born to the purple. The Empress is shown handsome and fair in the photographs one sees of her everywhere, and so she may have been in girlhood and in the earlier years of her wedded life, but now the lines of face and form have coarsened, and she has the heavy German countenance, and can no longer be called more than a comfortable, pleasant-looking matron without distinction in look or bearing. The Emperor was in a jovial mood, and frequently taking his cigar from his lips, laughed heartily at remarks addressed to him by the little group of officers near by, or haply at his own wit, as great kings are said to do. He has strong, cold features, bold, clear, earnest eyes, and a bearing of mingled dignity and haughtiness which he does not find it easy to repress—altogether a young man of power and clear intelligence and a strong will, a young man of mark and consequence, likely to be heard from in this world's business. After their majesties had dined and recreated themselves down below out of the sight of men for a good hour or more, with tall, fine veterans and young officers pacing the decks in watchful attendance, and the world of us below paddling round and round the steamer, fearful something would transpire without our knowledge, the State gondolas under direction of the city authorities appeared, and a procession was arranged for the Grand Canal, down which the Emperor was to pass to the railway-station. The largest of these is a long, gilded barge, built to succeed the Bucentaur, with high prow and a platform astern enclosed in curtains of colored silks, forming a pavilion carpeted with red cloth, where two gilded chairs are placed, and manned by twenty rowers. The three other State boats are large gondolas covered with gilding, and, like the barge, richly carved, all manned by gondoliers in the costumes of four centuries ago, each crew in different colors of blue and red and gold, charmingly picturesque.

We moved out of the wilderness of boats and rowed down the Grand Canal in advance of the cortège, and taking a position by one of the posts at the side of the Palace Foscari, waited for the procession, which swept by us in a torrent of swift confusion, the great barge towed by a steam-launch, so that the long white oars of the idle rowers of it were held upright, ten on each side, and under the canopy the Emperor and Empress sat side by side, the splendid gondolas of State, urged by the utmost graceful exertions of picked rowers, close following in its wake, all shining like burnished gold in the westering sun, the oars dripping silver, the swaying forms of the rowers gleaming in their liveries of antique fashion and gorgeous dyes, contrasting richly with the low, black gondolas of the people pressing onward beside and behind them ; the hurrying pageant of a dream. We took a narrow canal cutting off a bend in the Grand Canal, emerging again to see the procession sweep by once more and land the Emperor at the steps of the railway-station. The Rialto and the banks of the canal, wherever a human foot could be set, were crowded with spectators, and it seemed to me, as I looked upon the sea of faces turned to the spectacle, that nowhere had I ever seen countenances wearing in the mass an expression so squalid, worn and despairing.

In the evening the Piazza was illuminated by increasing the number of gas-jets on the handsome branching lamp-posts in and around the Piazza, and to the music of two excellent bands, playing alternately, the people moved up and down as on other evenings, but more numerously, and in the same politely gentle, quiet way. They seem to have gone to decay and mournful hopelessness, like the crumbling, tattered, beautiful city wherein they survive like reminiscences of the past, ghosts of ancient reality. Repairs have been going on for a quarter of a century about the Palace of the Doges, chiefly in its substructure, which had given tokens of weakening, and during that time a high board fence had concealed a very considerable portion of the south façade. The restoration being well-nigh complete, the Emperor's visit was made the occasion of removing this barrier, so that we had the satisfaction of seeing this unrivalled building in its full beauty of outline.

The Empress returned to the steamer after setting her imperial consort down at the railway-station, and on the second night of her stay here the long crescent line of the waterfront from the entrance of the Grand Canal to the Public

Gardens was illuminated at intervals with Bengal lights of red, green and white—the national colors—flashing weirdly upon the fastastic architecture of the shore and dying away into darkness far out upon the lagoon ; the tall campanile of San Giorgio on the island opposite glowing redly from its bell-tower, as if a conflagration raged within its massive walls. But the finest effect of the illumination was furnished by the royal yacht of the imperial guests, which blazed with a line of close-set electric lights from stem to stern and from these upward to the top of the mainmast, flooding all the distance between itself and the shore with liquid gold, across which the dark gondolas glided silently, like pleasing phantoms. Near midnight the Empress was rowed to the station with the blare of a military band and a sea of flaring torches, and next day the "Hohenzollern" quietly put to sea, Venice resumed its customary ways, and on the following day, November 15th, at 2 P.M., we regretfully left this strange and beautiful city for Florence, two hundred miles distant, where we arrived at 10 P.M. to find spacious and comfortable rooms, cheerful with open fires, in the Hotel New York.

Our way from Venice lay over a pleasant country, level and fertile, but much of it subject to destructive overflow from several very considerable mountain-streams, which bring down a vast quantity of sand and spread it over large tracts of plain, to the great loss of the farmers between Venice and Ferrara. We pass through Padua, Rovigo, Bologna and many villages with picturesque remains of many centuries, all showing fair in such autumnal sunshine as used to fill the air and tinge with the vague and undefinable tints of romance the silent aspect of Prairie Ronde and its grandly solemn surrounding forests.

We dined at Bologna, where Frattini urged us to try the celebrated sausages which take their name from this city, where they have for a long period borne a high reputation. We found them excellent, and of fine and delicate flavor. We were sorry to cross the Apennines after dark and miss the scenery of them. The highest point attained by the road is at Molina del Pallone, a little more than 2000 feet above the sea-level. Five miles on, a little this side of the village of Pracchia, the train crosses the water-shed of the Adriatic and that broad indentation of the Mediterranean called by the ancient Romans the Tyrrhenium Mare, through a tunnel nearly two miles long, and entering the valley of the Ombrone, crosses that stream by a lofty viaduct and passes through no less than twenty tunnels before reaching Pistoja, a distance of only ten miles. This little village is said to have given its name to the pistol. Near Prato, ten miles from Florence, is the quarry of serpentine known as "Marmo verde di Prato."

I had intended to pass not less than three weeks on the lakes and among the old towns in the north of Italy before coming to Florence, but the season is so far advanced that the nights are cold, and we did not care to expose ourselves to the chances of frequent changes of hotels, which are in Italy of massive stone, and unless one's apartments are well warmed beforehand—something the Italian in the towns off the regular lines of travel very poorly comprehends—are chilly and cheerless to a degree that not only affects one's pleasure and comfort, but even subjects the health to risk; so, as we wish to see the lakes, of which we had a charming bit of experience last summer when we came over from Switzerland to Lugano and Maggiore, at their best, and to walk the solemn streets of dozing old cities like Mantua and Ravenna when they shall have all the advantage they may derive from blue skies flooded with sunshine and the flowery earth smiling under them, we must pass them by, trusting a more convenient season may occur to us before we leave for home, and for the winter limit ourselves to the larger cities, journeying southward and along the Riviera as the winter grows more rigorous.

*November 6.*—We have now been three weeks in Florence, during which time I have not made an entry in my note-book, having given myself over to the luxury of idleness and indolent sight-seeing, and enjoying careless rest after more than half a year of constant travel and observation, until the very vision became benumbed and unreceptive. Indeed, it seemed to me clear that I would at least ease myself to the extent of discontinuing these fragmentary and thoroughly unsatisfactory memoranda of travel, necessarily made in snatches of time when weariness demanded rest or agreeable distractions invited attention. But as this is my first and likely to be my only visit to foreign lands, and my memory, never greatly to be depended on, is not likely to improve with age, as I begin to be aware already, I would like to record so much of my impressions as in such years as may remain to me will help recall in part the scenes and objects which I have enjoyed with such relish when among them. Therefore I will keep on, after my poor fashion, and set down in a hasty, desultory and ill-informed way what I can of the novel abundance on every hand in these lands of the old world—nowhere of higher interest to a citizen of the new than in this fair city of Tuscany.

Florence has a population of some 150,000. This was never greater, and during those centuries when its splendor was brightest the number of its inhabitants probably did not reach 100,000, and in 1864, when it supplanted Turin as the capital of Italy—an honor it held for four years, when the seat of government was removed to Rome—its population was nearly 120,000, so that the prodigious debt it incurred for improvements consequent on the brief honor of being the capital has not hindered its proper growth, and it is prosperous even in the modern sense. Although it was founded in the century before Christ and became a place of importance under Roman rule, since it lay in the track of the barbarian hordes from the north it was often laid waste by them in their incursions into Italy during the dark ages, so that only very scanty traces remain of its early existence, and the Florence known in history really dates from the early years of the eleventh century, when the city began to emerge from obscurity and directly entered upon that renowed career which raised it to the foremost position in political affairs, in the sciences and arts, a position it kept more continuously and with more brilliant results than any city with whose history I am at all acquainted. No other city can show a list of so distinguished names in the provinces of art, and by a singular good fortune the works they wrought have been largely spared by the changes of time and the spoliations of conquest and are still here to be seen and admired. I shall not try to follow its history during those turbulent ages when war was the business of nations and the powerful preyed on the weak, nor speak of those internal factions of Guelph and Ghibelline, White and Black, led by powerful rival houses and stained by dark and bloody deeds of brawls and intrigues and poisonings and banishments, as either party gained the upper hand. All these belong to the history of every city in Europe during many centuries after the decay of the Roman Empire. But the peculiar good fortune of Florence was that its rulers, conspicuously those of the family of the Medici, fostered learning and art and preserved their fruits, so that it is now a vast storehouse of the most beautiful and precious things.

The city lies pleasantly on both sides of the Arno, ordinarily flowing languidly between high walls of solid masonry, and here some 300 feet wide. Four old stone bridges cross it at short intervals, the most important and picturesque being the Ponte Vecchio, or Jeweller's Bridge, lined on both sides by little shops, chiefly of jewelry, clinging to its sides like irregular rows of marten-houses built by some kindly proprietor and stuck under the eaves of an old barn in New England. The Arno is easily swollen by sudden and heavy rains, and after a day during which considerable had fallen I heard at midnight, in our apartment fronting the Lungarno, close by the entrance to the Ponte alla Carraja—the bridge lowest down the stream—a heavy, sullen roar of water, and in the morning looked out on a full, swift current yellow with earthy matter. It soon spent its force and resumed its languid shallowness, even exposing patches of its sandy bed in places, its surface of a dull blue or green in the varying light.

The level valley of the Arno is not of great width, and on the southern side a long, broken continuation of a lesser range of the Apennines runs almost parallel to it near at hand, furnishing, in its intersecting valleys and gentle slopes and sharp projections, most charming suburbs studded with old villas enclosed in high yellow walls, above which rise ancient trees, long ranges of monastic enclosures, and high up little clustering villages, with many an old tower and gray campanile contrasting with the green of many a tall cypress grove and harmonizing with the olive and the vine.

Architecturally Florence presents a more uniform appearance in its ancient and modern houses than the cities we have visited elsewhere, because the buildings erected for a century back and those now building are in the same simple, massive style as those of the early Renaissance, when the Roman style of palaces and private dwellings began to be modified by the native architects and forms introduced which still continue, so that the old and new blend harmoniously and the city seems built after one plan. The new palaces, as all the great houses of the wealthy are called along the Lungarno, are pretty much the same in external form as those built four hundred years ago. The ordinary houses are lofty, with heavy walls of granite or painted stucco on brick, mostly in dull yellow or gray, and with fronts so plain as to present an almost gloomy aspect under skies less bright, in air less transparent than exist here.

The city is thoroughly well built, and would be thoroughly cheerful except for the very narrow streets of the old and principal portions. These, as in all ancient towns, seem to have been planned with a view to defence from invasions, as before the invention of artillery they could be held by a small force opposing and by hurling missiles from the lofty upper stories. There are no sideways in most of these old streets, a stone pavement extends from wall to wall, with little more than room for two carriages to meet, foot-passengers being obliged to save themselves as they can by standing against the walls or dodging into doorways. The houses on such streets—and a good part of the city is occupied by them—do not satisfy modern notions of comfortable dwellings with the light so greatly shut out.

The number of palaces built by the ruling and influential families during the middle ages is something prodigious. These are really castles, although built in the form of a square and mostly without towers. A famous one among many is the Pitti, designed and begun in 1440 by Brunelleschi, the famous architect who built the dome of the Cathedral. Luca Pitti, who ordered this work, was the powerful rival of the Medici family, whom he proposed to surpass by erecting the grandest palace yet built by a private citizen. He conspired against Piero de' Medici in 1466, lost his power and influence, and the palace stood unfinished until the middle of the next century, when it came into the possession of the Medici family through Eleanora, wife of Duke Cosimo I., who completed it. It is of extraordinary size, massiveness and interior magnificence. The huge unfinished blocks of stone in the lower story give it a grim aspect, but its just proportions and noble simplicity are very striking. The central part is 350 feet long, the whole façade 660 feet long, and the height 121 feet. The lofty wings enclose a grand court. It is connected with the charming

Boboli Gardens extending up the hill-side in terraces, at the entrance a singular grotto designed by Michael Angelo, and in the middle an open space surrounded by stone seats, where the gay Medician Court was wont to hold its festivities. There is a handsome fountain, an Egyptian obelisk brought from Rome, an ancient basin of gray granite 21 by 15 feet, and at the top of the ascent a Basin of Neptune with a statue of that god by Lorenzi, and a statue of Abundance by John of Bologna. There are well planted and kept walks and points where charming views are seen of the city below, and the whole spot is exceedingly lovely.

The Pitti Palace has been the residence of the reigning sovereign since the sixteenth century, and is that of King Humbert when in Florence, and the royal apartments are filled with exquisite furniture and works of art. We have not found so stately and magnificent apartments in any palace in any country as in this, not only those used by the sovereign, but also those which constitute the great and far-famed Picture Gallery of the Pitti, where the works of the great masters are shown on walls and under ceilings vying with themselves in sumptuousness of form and color. In the Silver Chamber of the palace among the royal plate are a dozen gold platters with exquisite designs in relief by Benvenuto Cellini, and a bronze crucifix by John of Bologna, whereon the face of the dying Christ is inexpressibly tender. Another adversary of the Medici, Filippo Strozzi, built a little later another of these enormous palatial strongholds near the Piazza San Trinita, an imposing structure of stone in the perfected Florentine style, 105 feet high. It has on the corners wrought-iron lanterns finely chased, and around the sides are rings for supporting banners and torch-holders similarly wrought by Caparra, and a fine court. I mention these out of a vast number not much less imposing, whose founders, long since in dust and their families extinct, ranged in opposing factions as Guelph and Ghibelline, filled these narrow streets with brawl and revel. I must note the imposing Palazzo Vecchio, built in 1300 by the great architect Arnolfo, with its battlements and tower 308 feet high, originally the seat of the Signoria or Government of Florence, later the residence of Cosimo I., and now used as a town hall. It has a fine court, in the centre of which is a basin of porphyry with an exquisite figure of a boy with a fish by Verrochio.

We have passed all the hours of daylight for a week in the two great picture galleries of the Uffizi and Pitti, which are really one, as they are connected by a covered passage crossing the Arno above the Ponte Vecchio. I cannot undertake a description of the treasures of art gathered here, begun by the Medici and augmented by subsequent rulers and magnates of the city until the collection in rank and value stands as one of the first in the world. In one beautiful room of the Uffizi known as the Tribuna, for instance, are to be seen with ever-growing admiration these objects in sculpture :

"The Venus of Medici," by the Athenian Cleomenes, found in Hadrian's villa at Tivoli, called the most perfect specimen of the sculptor's art in existence, and lauded to the skies by a long line of poets and novelists and admiring critics. Hawthorne says of it, " A being that lives to gladden the world, incapable of decay or death ;" the poet Rogers styles it, " Venus herself, who when she left the skies came hither ;" and the all too susceptible Byron wrote,

> "The goddess loves in stone, and fills
> The air around with beauty ; we inhale
> The ambrosial aspect, which, beheld, instils
> Part of its immortality ; the veil
> Of heaven is half undrawn ; . . .
>
> We gaze and turn away, and know not where,
> Dazzled and drunk with beauty, till the heart
> Reels with its fulness. . . ."

While I cannot feel swayed to any such extent, I am sufficiently susceptible and appreciative to recognize the charming presence of a form of perfect womanhood, and nothing more. Its height is four feet and seven inches. The right arm and lower half of the left are modern and inferior to the rest.

"The Wrestlers." A group of two athletes, one of whom has thrown the other, and in the struggle to keep him down the muscles of both are in such wonderful representation of activity and strain as to cause this to be ranked as one of the best specimens of ancient Greek sculpture.

"The Dancing Faun," with head and arms renewed by Michael Angelo, the nude figure showing such perfection of anatomy as to place it in the best epoch of ancient sculpture, and cause it to be attributed to Praxiteles.

"The Little Apollo," so called to distinguish it from the Apollo Belvedere in Rome, exceedingly fine and graceful, and so analogous in style to the Venus as to cause it to be thought the work of Cleomenes.

"The Arrotino" ("The Whetter"), found at Rome in the fourteenth century and brought to Florence in 1677. It is the nude figure of a man bent over a stone on which he is whetting a hooked knife, with his strong face looking up in earnest attention. There are several conjectures as to who is intended by this statue, one of which is that it is the slave who discovered the plot of Brutus' sons in respect to Tarquin; another that he revealed the conspiracy of Catiline against the Roman Republic; but the best opinion is said by the curator of the gallery to be that it is the Scythian to whom Apollo gave the order to flay Marsyas for his temerity in boasting that he rivalled that god in music. Whoever he may be, this statue is to me the most remarkable and perfect in form and expression of the famous marbles in the Tribuna.

In painting, omitting several which do not appeal to my feelings, there are in this one room these:

Titian's "Venus," the world-known figure of that goddess lying naked on a bed. There is certainly nothing of the celestial about her, and I fail to recognize in this quite earthly form the perfection of female beauty, but the coloring is such as few but Titian can give to the human flesh.

"Madonna," by Andrea del Sarto, whose pictures I always admire, and this one of his best.

"The Holy Virgin," by Guido Reni.

"The Samian Sibyl," by Guercino, called Barbieri.

"Jean de Monfort," by Van Dyck.

Another "Venus" by Titian, much like the other more famous one in position and execution.

"After the Flight into Egypt," by Correggio, not a great picture as it seems to me, and so inferior to his famous and beautiful one, also here, of the "Holy Virgin Adoring her Child," that I do not wonder its authenticity is questioned.

"Portrait of a Young Woman," by Raphael, a sweet picture.

"The Holy Virgin and Two Saints," by Perugino, a noble picture.

The well-known "Fornarina" of Raphael. I return to this wonderful face over and over again. I have never seen or expect to see again such an expression of deep, subtle, glowing, tempting, consuming sensuality as glows far within those dark eyes, whose steadfast gaze burns into the soul. And beside her, attributed to the same unrivalled master, the sweet and pure "Virgin of the Well," who is depicted sitting and holding her Divine Child, while the young St. John, standing at her right side, is holding before them a paper on which are the words "Ecce Agnus," etc. Near by also is the same painter's "The Virgin of the Goldfinch," so named from the bird which the young St. John is offering Jesus to caress; and his great picture of "St. John in the Desert," a full figure, and said to be the only painting by Raphael on canvas, all the others being on wood. The bold, enthusiastic prophet is here shown as a fiery youth of say fourteen years, vigorous and glowing with health, standing in a desert country, pointing with his right hand to a slender cross fastened to a tree close by. Full-length figures of the prophets Isaiah and Job, noble and impressive.

Raphael's portrait of Pope Julius II., most vigorous, clear and rich in color.

"Holy Family and St. Catharine," by Paul Veronese.

"The Holy Family," by Michael Angelo. This painting is held most precious, but it does not please me either in composition or color. This is heresy, and will at once dispose of me in the opinion of all true lovers of art.

"Hercules between Virtue and Vice," by Rubens.

"The Adoration of the Kings," by Albrecht Dürer.

"The Holy Virgin and Child," by Giulio Romano—sweet and graceful.

"Eleazar and Rebecca," by Caracci.

To what good end do I catalogue the treasures in this one room with feeble comment when seven miles of stately apartments with their connecting passages are opulent with canvases almost equally famous with those I mention? There are many of wonderful beauty signed with such names as Albrecht Dürer, Salvator Rosa, Tintoretto, Titian, Fra Bartolommeo, Frans Porbus, Rubens, Rembrandt, Cigoli, Del Sarto, Van Dyck, Palma Vecchio, Bronzino, Perugino, Guido

Reni, Pordenone, Carlo Dolci, Murillo, Raphael, whose Holy Family, styled "Impannata," lights up the Salle de Mars in the Pitti with an expression composed of that of the Virgin in the Tribuna and that of the Virgin seated in the Salle de Saturne, known to all the world by its reproduction in all known forms of copying. The Virgin wears the same aspect as in the "Madonna del Sisto" in the Dresden Gallery. Let me add the names of Michael Angelo, represented by his "Fates," a strange and powerful picture showing the three Parcæ spinning and clipping the thread of human life; Ribera, Leonardo da Vinci, Giorgione, Dossi, Domenichino, Bassano del Piombo, Pontormo, Velasquez, Baroccio, Holbein, Filippo Lippi, Sir Peter Lely, who is represented by a portrait of Oliver Cromwell. This portrait, the story is, was sent to the then Grand Duke of Tuscany with a protest against the persecution of the Protestants in his dominions, and an intimation that he whose portrait went with the protest was alive and able and of a disposition to avenge the wrongs of his co-religionists. I must note that other beautiful and sweet Virgin of Raphael known as the "Madonna del Gran-Duca," and the so sweet "Virgin in Sorrow" by Sassoferrato, one of the most exquisite conceptions of the Mater Dolorosa ever given to canvas.

In the great corridors of the Uffizi, whose ceilings are enriched with arabesques by Poccetti in 1581, of so exquisite patterns that artists come to take bits of it for precious studies, are rare objects of antiquity, busts and statues, sarcophagi and beautiful Roman urns and altars. Among these are authentic busts of Julius and Augustus Cæsar, Livia, Marcus Agrippa, Julia, daughter of Augustus; Tiberius, Antonia, mother of Claudius and daughter of Marc Antony, and Octavia, sister of Augustus; Agrippina, wife of Germanicus and mother of Caligula; Caligula himself, bearing all the marks of the beast he was; Messalina, Claudius, Nero and his wife Poppæa, of much beauty; another of Nero in his innocent and fair childhood; Galba, Otho, Vitellius, Vespasianus, Titus—a noble marble showing the greatness of his soul; Domitian, Nerva, Trajan—three of him, all fine—Plotina, his wife; Adrian—Sabina, his wife; Antoninus Pius—Faustina, his mother, Galerius, his young son; Marcus Aurelius, his wife Faustina and their young son, Annius Verus, who died at seven years, and equally beautiful with that of the young Nero, Commodus, whose busts are said to be rare, because the Senate ordered them all to be destroyed that his memory might be effaced; Crispena, his wife; Severus; Caracalla—Plautilla, his wife; Heliogabalus, Maximinus, the giant emperor whom the historians state to have been 8 feet 2 inches in height; Gallienus, Constantine the Great. These are vouched for as authentic by the directors of the Uffizi, and I am careful to enumerate them, as they afforded me a pleasure I have craved from my school-days—that of seeing contemporaneous portrait busts of the long line of Roman emperors. I had not supposed so many of these to be in existence as I find here.

Deeply interesting are the marble sarcophagi carved all over into pictures in relief of scenes from the Greek and Roman mythology and fable. There is one of the "Rape of Proserpine," full of figures incident to the scene; another of Hippolytus hunting a wild boar; and divided from this by the pillar of a gate a scene delineating his temptation, with Phædra, and her attendant maidens and young Cupid before her with torch and quiver. Still another shows the labors of Hercules, crowded with eight stirring scenes of them, the killing of the Nemean lion, the fight with the hydra of Leona. In the third he bears the wild boar of Erymanthus on his shoulder; in the fourth the naked hero grasps the horns of the Arcadian hind; in the fifth he darts his arrows against the Stymphalides; in the sixth, naked and with his club, he is in the act of taking away her girdle from the waist of Hippolyte, the queen of the Amazons. Next he is seen clad in his lion-skin, his right hand raised and his left grasping his club. Above his left shoulder a spring of water is falling from a rock. This represents the cleansing of the Augean stables. The last group represents the hero vanquishing the Marathonean bull. Another represents the triumphs of Bacchus, a throng of chained slaves, Ariadne's chariot drawn by tigers, that of Bacchus by centaurs, Victory preceding, and cupids, fauns and mænades following. Still another depicts the fall of Phaëton from the chariot of the Sun headlong into the Eridanus, with his sisters, the Heliades, changed into poplars. On the back of this sarcophagus in shallow bas-relief is shown a race in a circus, with the names of the charioteers taking part in it: Liber, Polyphemus, Trofimion, Entyones, and the names of their chariots, Libyo, Jubilatore, Dicatesyne, Engranmo. The marble altars too, of exquisite forms, and sides sculptured in scenes from the old mythology, interested me greatly.

On fine afternoons we drive in the Cascine, a handsome park below the city lying along the Arno, well laid out in avenues planted with large trees, agreeable but not remarkable, nor equal in picturesqueness to many other drives in the neighborhood. Far more interesting is the drive up to Fiesole on a road winding among fair villa grounds enclosed in high yellowish walls, on whose tops flourish grass and violets and roses, to the Cathedral on the height, with its campanile dominating the spacious Piazza, with a fragment of the ancient Etruscan wall near by, and an ancient theatre with its sixteen tiers of semicircular stone seats and marks of the old stage facing them. A little below the Franciscan Monastery, which occupies the site of the old Acropolis of Fæsulæ from a plateau in front of a venerable church on the spot where a heathen temple once stood, is an extensive view of the valley of the Arno, with distant mountains and many white villages far and near and Florence itself below, its dull red roofs and domes and belfries and towers showing fair in the slant afternoon sunshine. Descending, we pass the attractive pile of Badia di Fiesole, a monastic structure by Brunelleschi, and lower down still another, that of the Monastery St. Salvi, of the order of Vallombrosa, dating back to 1080. Among the charming villas is to be noted that of Palmieri, where Boccaccio laid the scene of the "Decameron," and that company of gallants and fair ladies passed the time, when the plague raged in the city below, in telling merry tales "good against infection"— high-bosomed dames with kindling eyes of lustrous fire, whose descendants still walk the streets of Florence with more modest mien, but with free, elastic step and dignity of manner, so that watching them on the promenades, matrons and maids, one finds beauty of person the rule and ugliness so much the exception that in no city, unless possibly in Vienna, have I noticed so many handsome women. The grounds of the old Boccaccio Villa are still extremely beautiful—terrace above terrace, where fountains play, and a green enamelled meadow beset with pleasant trees sloping softly down to a pretty babbling brook.

Once afternoon we crossed the Arno and drove up to the old square tower, in excellent preservation, where Galileo first observed the heavens with his so-called telescope, still preserved among other interesting mementos of him in an upper room of the tower. The instrument he found sufficient to enable him to demonstrate that the earth moves about the sun is no more than we call a spy-glass, and with its four lengths shut together is about a foot long. On the wall is hung a copy of an "Index Expurgatorius" issued by the Inquisition, forbidding his little book announcing his discovery to be printed or read under heavy pains and penalties. Did not Joshua command the sun to stand still? Then it must be the sun which moves, and the prison stands open to the blasphemer who shall gainsay it.

I often walk from my hotel up the Lungarno to the Ponte Vecchio, admiring along the way the singular irregularity of the houses on the opposite bank of the river. Nowhere, not even in Nuremberg, does one see such a picturesque variety of front and roof in faded parti-colors, especially between the bridges of Trinita and Vecchio. Turning sharply to the left there one strolls along a noble colonnade set on each side with statues of men who have made Florence famous, and through it to the Piazza della Signoria, the old Forum of the Republic, the centre of its eager activity, and still one of the busiest and most interesting spots in the city. Here the excitable populace used to run tumultuously together when the "cow lowed," as the tolling of the bell *La Vacca*, or "the cow," was called ; and from a stone platform on the north side of the Palazzo Vecchio della Signoria, now removed, the prior and judges sat to witness the burning of Savonarola, May 23d, 1498. At one angle of this platform stands the famous "Marzocco" of Donatello, a marble lion with a name of unknown origin, and near by is the great fountain of Neptune by Bartolommeo Ammanati (1571), whose design was preferred to that of John of Bologna, who made the equestrian statue of Cosimo I., close by, in 1594. On the south side of the Piazza is the beautiful Loggia di Lanzi, consisting of three open arches with three pillars enclosing a platform reached by six steps. In this open loggia, begun in 1336, are placed many noble statues in marble and bronze, and among the latter the "Perseus" of Benvenuto Cellini, cast in 1545, and I think the most beautiful and impressive of all the statues I have seen. I admire all the work in various kinds I have seen of this wonderful artist, and this ranks as his masterpiece. Such radiance in the face of Perseus, such calm beauty in that of the Medusa, whose head, freshly dissevered, he holds extended in his left hand. The pedestal on which the statue stands, whereon this great sculptor has told the story of Andromeda in lifelike and touching pictures, is exquisite and fully worthy of the statue itself.

Many times by different routes, coming on objects of delightful interest whichever way one takes—for in this fascinating city one is among marvels of art so soon as one sets foot out of doors—we betake ourselves to the square of the Cathedral, where the glories of Florentine art culminate in the Baptistery with its bronze gates, the Campanile and fairy dome of the Cathedral conspicuous objects from whatever point the city is viewed and full of grandeur and grace seen from afar or near at hand. The Cathedral, Santa Maria del Fiore, was begun in 1298 by Arnolfo del Cambio, who was instructed to build "the loftiest, most sumptuous edifice that human invention could devise or human labor execute." In 1331 the work begun by Arnolfo was entrusted to Giotto, who erected the tower and continued to work on the original design. Soon after his death a beautiful façade was built by the most famous sculptors of the time, but this was destroyed in 1575, and has been recently replaced after the church had stood without a façade for three hundred years, when in 1860 Victor Emmanuel laid the foundation of the new one, selecting from the competitive designs that by De Fabris. This new front seems to me well worthy of the church and to harmonize in richness of its colored marbles and exquisite workmanship with the other portions and with the Campanile close by.

I was informed by a gentleman who resides here a good part of the time, as illustrating the keen interest felt by the entire Florentine population in matters of art, that when a question arose among the authorities as to the better of two methods of finishing the upper surface of the new front, books were opened for signatures of the partisans of either method, and that boys ranged themselves and fought in the square in behalf of one and the other. In 1418 occurred the public competition of models for the dome; gained by Brunelleschi, who was fourteen years in building it, the lantern after his design being added in 1462. This airy structure rises to the height of 300 feet, with the lantern 352 feet, and is of such grace that it is reported that when Michael Angelo, a century later, was summoned to Rome to surpass this work of Brunelleschi in building St. Peter's, he replied, " I will make its sister larger, but not more beautiful." The Cathedral, of the style known as Italian Gothic, is 556 feet long, 342 feet wide across the transepts, is encrusted with precious marbles, and altogether, inside and out, rich to a degree, but not so imposing to my mind as the great Gothic cathedrals I have seen elsewhere, nor so impressive as the vast interior of the Mosque of St. Sophia in Constantinople. The Campanile or Bell-Tower close beside the façade of the Cathedral is a square structure rising in four stories to the height of 292 feet, and is regarded as one of the finest existing works of the kind. Certainly a more pleasing object cannot be imagined rising grandly in colored marbles, with graceful windows enriched with exquisite tracery, and set with row upon row of statues by famous masters. It was designed and begun by Giotto in 1334 in the style of the Cathedral, and after his death completed by Taddeo Gaddi in 1387. In its adornment assisted such renowned workers as Donatello, Bartolo, Rosso, Niccolo d'Arezzo, Andrea Pisano, and that most charming master Luca della Robbia, whose colored terra-cotta reliefs are to be seen here in many places, and always with pleasure. It was the original intention, I believe, to place some terminal structure at top of this square tower ; but in all the centuries no one has had the audacity to venture to think himself capable, or the well-instructed city has refused to sanction any attempt.

The Baptistery stands in the square in front of the Cathedral, and its modest proportions are at first, or rather to me at first, were disappointing, and only after several visits did I realize the charm of its octagonal exterior, the low tones of its harmonious parts, its well-proportioned stories, marble ornamentation and fine cornices. It was once the Cathedral, its date is uncertain, it was encrusted with marble by Arnolfo, but thought to have been once a temple to Mars. The interior is so dark at any time of day that it is with difficulty one can see the not numerous works of interest under its dome 90 feet high, the circular space below being set round with pillars of Oriental marble. In its marble font all children born in Florence are baptized, and whenever I visited the interior the rite was going on, robed priests, with faces dull and often sensual, gathered round little mewling atomies not four hours old, the lamp-light showing their tiny heads protruding redly from the costliest wrappings the family means can furnish, and drenched with holy water to such extent as made its survival a miracle. But oftener I got no farther than the glorious bronze doors, whose storied reliefs would stand forth clearly in the abundant light but for the dirt accumulated on them and never removed for fear of wearing away the sharp features of the countless figures wrought on them. There are three of these precious doors, or gates as they are styled, each with double valves and deep bronze borders. That on the south is the oldest, and was completed in 1330 by Andrea Pisano, after twenty-two years' labor, and its reliefs comprise scenes from the life of John the Baptist. The door on the north side is by Lorenzo Ghiberti, done between the years 1403 and 1424, and the reliefs show forth, in twenty-eight sections, the history of Christ, the Apostles and Fathers down to St. Augustine. The third, facing the Cathedral, is by Ghiberti also, and executed between the years 1425 and 1452, and represents ten scenes from Scripture history of the Old Testament. This is the gate Michael Angelo pronounced worthy to form the entrance to Paradise. These noble doors were originally gilded with gold, now worn away except in some deep portions, and even in their dusty coverings show such figures of dignity and grace, such life and beauty, as one could not believe possible. Nor less exquisite are the frames of these doors, with their deep, faithful portraiture of flowers and foliage sheltering various birds, the whole with the scenes they enclose needing only to be awakened from the sleep of ages by the touch of some gentle enchantment to glow before us with perfect life. Well may these doors, to which I go over and over again, be reckoned among the marvels of art.

Gathering from the scrappy information which filters through various irregular channels from beyond the sea, that the 28th of November has been set apart for a day of Thanksgiving by the ruler of 65,000,000 of people flourishing and free on a continent undreamed of by patient Ghiberti in all those years he was working on the gates of the Baptistery; we resolve, in company of some agreeable friends we have made here, also from the States, to celebrate our most homelike festival as nearly in the orthodox Yankee fashion as the circumstances of our voluntary banishment will allow. Our large private parlor, in the New York Hotel, once rejoicing in the title of palace, the last forgotten owner of which for some reason failed to marry an American heiress, and so retain the vast rooms frescoed with chilly cupids wearing no raiment in this cold season but scanty wings and little bows and arrows, was chosen as the scene of our memorial festivities, and our combined faculties proved competent to a *menu* satisfactory under any sky; but at once, on attempting to realize it, we came on obstacles which threatened to be insurmountable. The intelligent and obliging head-waiter, who, from his intimate knowledge of "English as she is spoke," was our medium of communication with the Italian *chef*, was painfully obliged to report, after a prolonged conference with that awful functionary, that the accomplishment of cranberry-sauce and a pumpkin-pie were impossible, for the excellent reason that he had no knowledge whatever of those indispensable elements of a Thanksgiving dinner—indeed, could not imagine what these esculents might be. We strove to enlighten the mind of our interpreter, and with such success that, for his part, he felt quite sure of the pumpkin, having, he remembered, seen it growing once on a sort of a tree in Sicily. As to the cranberry, he would advise himself, and later in the day brought a thin volume, opened to a page whereon stood a list of various vegetables, fruits and berries in the English tongue, and placing his finger triumphantly on "cornel-berry," declared the problem solved. Not content with this, we sent out foraging parties, myself being detailed to address me with all diligence to the "English Bakery," no great distance away. Going forth under an umbrella, I came upon that manufactory of Anglican bread and pastry, and found behind the counter of it a plump and merry Italian lady; and inquiring if I were quite correct in supposing this to be the establishment known to the citizens of Florence as the "English Bakery," was told, in very much broken English, that it was indeed that same, but that the English lady who formerly inhabited here had returned to Ireland, and when, with drooping expectation, I ventured to inquire if pumpkin-pie constituted one of the delicacies of her stock, she showed her white teeth and broke into great mirth at the uncouth name; and I left her, hands on sides, enjoying a repetition of the sound as she tried to pronounce, with halting and difficult effort, struggling long with the first syllable, "pump-kin pie, pump-kin pie." But the inspiration of the *chef* was not yet exhausted. He sent us word that on the morrow he would send in with our luncheon his realized conception of the national pie, which duly appeared, smoking hot, between two crusts, and opening with all the outward signs and inward tokens of a mince-pie without meat. Endeavoring to fathom on what ground the *chef* rested his claim that his production should be recognized as pumpkin, we found among the ingredients some scanty slices of citron, and were no longer hopeful of anything but the turkey, that "tame villatic fowl" being well domesticated in all the lands we have yet found. But on the eve of the eventful day Frattini, revealing a new depth in his resourceful nature, paid us a visit, and in a calm and confident manner which carried conviction assured us that all would be well on the morrow; that he had now taken the matter seriously in hand himself; that at the proper time not only would the turkey have its garnish of cranberries, but the pie should present itself of due form and elements. And of a truth when we were set down to a table handsomely spread, flowers blooming about our cheerful parlor, converted for the occasion into a bit of Uncle Sam's domain by the protective folds of two American flags, Frattini hovering about in the capacity of major-domo wrapped in an air of mystery, there appeared among the well-cooked dishes of an abounding dinner excellent cranberry-sauce and a better pumpkin-pie than many a New England home could boast. We sat long at table, with many thoughts of home, and over the wine and walnuts, when the mind is most disposed to make allowance, I ventured to read these lines, made for "this occasion only," to the eight uncritical partakers of the feast:

### THANKSGIVING-DAY IN FLORENCE, 1889.

We changed our sky but not our hearts,
  Crossing the wide Atlantic Sea,
From the far land we proudly claim,
  To this sweet town of Tuscany;

Through which the classic Arno glides
  Past Brunelleschi's airy dome,
Grand palaces and hoary towers
  And snowy walls of many a home,

Soft-gliding, as it fain would pause,
   And feel its watery pulses glow
In light divine from David's face
   Kindled by Michael Angelo.

Fair are the scenes of this fair spot :
   Gray olive-trees festooned with vines,
Gleams of time-mellowed convent-walls,
   And sad slopes of the Apennines.

We love this peopled world of art,
   Trophies august of antique times ;
Ghiberti's gates, whose conscious saints
   Listen the Campanile's chimes,

Marbles that breathe and burn to tell
   Of the dead hands which gave them birth,
Paintings that stir and raise the soul
   Till heaven is nearer us than earth.

So rest we here in full content ;
   And yet upon this festal day
Our hearts return o'er land and wave
   To homes of kindred far away,

Where shine the hospitable fires
   On forms belovéd, gathered near
The feastful tables crowned with thanks
   For blessings of the ripened year.

And though our softening eyes must miss
   Dear faces that once smiled and shone
Above the feast in other years,
   And we are left still more alone ;

Let us be thankful, nor forget
   What loving mercies crown our way,
And bow our heads with grateful hearts
   Upon this glad Thanksgiving-day.

We drove, on a bright morning, across the Arno and through groves of olives with vines running from tree to tree and well-tilled fields studded with noble trees, past villas and old gray walls of palaces to the famed monastery of Certosa di Val d'Ema, two and one-half miles from the city. The huge walls rise from a commanding height like those of a fortress and overlook a beautiful expanse of varied hill, valley and plain, once the possessions of the monks here and tilled by them for five hundred years. Within the walls are a rich church and handsome chapels with fine pictures and tombs ; a veritably impressive place, with its ample cloisters and dim, silent corridors. The numerous fraternity of Benedictines who lived here, each one in a small cell, the door furnished with an opening for handing in the meals, have all been turned out by the government, which has appropriated this and all similar property in the most high-handed manner, leaving some score of them to be "care-takers," as the pleasant monk who showed us about said with a natural touch of bitterness, "of our own property." The good fathers make a chartreuse and perfumes, which one can buy in their quaint old pharmacy, from whose clean and well-ordered shelves the poor are supplied with remedies free of charge. A spot well worth visiting. Returning we meet, as always in our drives, little two-wheeled carts laden with vegetables and wicker bottles of wine, the smaller kinds of pretty shape with long, slender necks, said to be a graceful form peculiar to Tuscany, the same as are served at the *table-d'hôte* of our hotel, holding a red wine called "Chienti," a sort I prefer, and resembling a fair claret. These little carts are drawn by mules or donkeys, the long shafts fastened high above their sides to cumbersome harness ornamented with heavy brasses and parti-colored tassels, until the little creatures are almost hidden and overladen with their needless equipments. The larger carts employ two and sometimes three animals, and I have seen a horse, a mule and a donkey working together abreast.

There are several American painters and sculptors with studios here, among them Mr. Longworth Powers, son of Hiram Powers, quite a number of whose best statues and all his models are on exhibition in the *atelier* of the son. To my untaught eye the "Eve Tempted" of the elder Powers is a marble figure as pure and beautiful in its naked innocence as the "Venus de' Medici," but this I must not say, I suppose. Mr. Powers was engaged, on the occasion of one of my visits, in modelling a striking portrait bust—a form of art in which he excels—from the same clay his father used in modelling the "Greek Slave" forty years ago. He uses it over and over, and says it still improves with using. At a reception at Mrs. Powers' villa we met the widow of Hiram Powers, a well-preserved and agreeable old lady. I was shown there a literary bit which so interested me that I begged a copy and give it place here. Who ever knew of Charles Francis Adams "dropping into poetry," or, if that were possible, that the "Iceberg," as his grateful countrymen called him when, after his noble work for the nation during the civil war, he stood for their suffrage, ever melted into such a bit of fun as this? We don't know our fellow-men very well, and often better knowledge would give kindlier judgment, I fancy.

### A TALE OF A NOSE.

#### BY CHARLES FRANCIS ADAMS.

'Twas a hard case that which happened in Lynn !
Haven't heard of it, eh? Well, then, to begin.
There's a Jew down there whom they call "Old Mose,"
Who travels about and buys old clothes.

Now Mose—which the same is short for Moses—
Had one of the biggest kind of noses;
It had a sort of an instep in it,
And he fed it with snuff about once a minute.

One day he got in a bit of a row
With a German chap who had kissed his frau,
And, trying to punch him, *à la Mace*,
Had his nose cut off close up to his face.

He picked it up from off the ground
And quickly back in its place 'twas bound,
Keeping the bandage upon his face
Until it had fairly healed in place.

Alas for Mose! 'Twas a sad mistake
Which he in his haste that day did make;
For, to add still more to his bitter cup,
He found he had placed it wrong side up.

" There's no great loss without some gain,"
And Moses says in a jocular vein,
He arranged it so for taking snuff,
As he never before could get enough.

One thing, by the way, he forgets to add,
Which makes the arrangement rather bad :
Although he can take his snuff with ease,
He has to stand on his head to sneeze.

The sculptor Mead has in progress a colossal work symbolizing the Mississippi River, intended for a public park in Chicago, and next door to him Mr. Turner is doing a colossal female figure, nine feet high, for the front of the building of an insurance company in St. Paul. This is to be in bronze, and

Mr. Turner tried to explain to me that it would be cast in Florence by a method revived from that of Benvenuto Cellini, who filled the mould with wax, which, keeping the form in place, melted and was displaced by the molten bronze.

I see no way of dealing with the great number of interesting churches here. Were I capable, a whole volume would be needed to describe them. They are full of treasures, and so is all Florence for that matter. But I must call to mind and help my future recollection with meagre mention of a few of those we saw with so much pleasure. After the Cathedral and Baptistery, the Church of Santa Croce, on the spacious Piazza of that name, naturally attracts attention as the Pantheon of modern Italy, where are many fine monuments to celebrated men, and interesting frescoes brought to light under a coating of whitewash said to have been spread over them by the envious dislike of Visari in 1566. These were by Giotto and his successors, Taddeo Gaddi, Maso di Banco, Giovanni da Milano, Agnolo Gaddi and other masters of note, with bas-reliefs by the Robbias, whose work in terra-cotta one always sees with increasing pleasure. Especially beautiful are the paintings of Giotto discovered not many years ago in the chapels of Peruzzi and the Bardi. The church is cruciform, and begun in 1294 from a design by Arnolfo di Bambio, with a modern façade from the old design by Cronaca. The interior is impressive from its size, and the nave has no side chapels. There is a charming rose-window over the west door by Ghiberti. Ranged round the interior walls of the nave are the monuments, among them one to Daniel Manin, the Venetian patriot, and the tomb of Michael Angelo, who died in Rome in 1563, but is buried here. This tomb was erected after Vasari's design, with a bust above it by Battista Lorenzi. Here, also, is the monument to Dante, who is buried at Ravenna, where he died on September 14th, 1321, at the age of fifty-six. This fine monument, by Stefano Ricci, was erected in 1829, and bears the proud inscription, "*Onorate l'altissimo poeta!*" which those who only read him in translations and do read Shakespere in the original may very well question. There is an exquisite monument to the poet Alfieri, who died 1810, by Canova, ordered by the Countess of Albany; the tombs of Macchiavelli, died 1527; Prince Neri Corsini; the Countess of Albany, widow of the young Pretender, died in 1824; Galileo, died 1642 ; the engraver, Raphael Morghen, died 1833; the composer, L. Cherubini, died 1842 ; a chapel belonging to the Bonaparte family, with monuments, by Bartolini, to Carlotta and Julia Clary Bonaparte, who died respectively in 1839 and 1845.

One of the most beautiful tombs I have seen—and there are many of these—is that of Carlo Marsuppini, Chancellor of Florence, Secretary to Pope Eugenius IV., who died in 1455, by Desiderio da Settignano, and there are many others which I must pass without even a mention. One realizes, in looking at the names on these grand and costly monuments, what an illustrious roll of men Florence possessed, and how their power and genius exerted here through many centuries have made her the famous city she has been and must continue to be so long as the arts and sciences are honored among men. At the end of the corridor leading to the sacristy is the Medici chapel, where is a sweet and tender picture of the " Coronation of the Virgin," by Giotto. The sacristy is a charming room, of admirable proportions, with old inlaid cabinets around the walls for keeping the priestly robes, an exquisite font, interesting frescoes by Niccolo, and, most beautiful of all, five great missals with miniatures, some of them from the hand of Fra Angelico. There are noble cloisters by Arnolfo and Brunelleschi, and in the old refectory opening from them a fresco of a " Last Supper," fast fading from damp, but beautiful to a degree, by Giotto. In this portion of the old convent, now suppressed, are the rooms in which the Inquisition held its tribunals from 1284 to 1782. Church and cloisters and tombs and monasteries and frescoes and all else here, are of exceeding interest.

I allude to the Church of Or San Michele to indicate how the love of art in the middle ages had penetrated all ranks of the citizens here. When this church was completed in 1412, the twelve guilds of the city undertook to decorate the outside walls with statues, and here they stand in handsome niches. The judges and notaries placed one of St. Luke, by John of Bologna ; the merchants, one of Christ and St. Thomas, by Andrea del Verrocchio, in a niche designed for them by Donatello ; the cloth-dealers, John the Baptist—perhaps to indicate the need of more clothing than that prophet was used to wear—by Ghiberti ; the silk-weavers, one of St. John, by Montelupo ; the physicians and apothecaries a Madonna—possibly with a consciousness that none needed pity and celestial succor so much as their patients—by Mino da Fiesole. This has been removed to the interior of the church and its place filled by a noble figure by Donatello made originally for the armorers. The furriers set up a statue of St. James, by Nanni di Banco ; the joiners, one of St. Mark, by Donatello—a grand, simple, honest face ; the farriers, one of St. Eligius, also by Nanni di Banco ; the woollen-weavers, one of St. Stephen, by Ghiberti ; the money-changers, one of St. Matthew, by Ghiberti and Michelozzo ; the bricklayers, carpenters, smiths and masons set up in their niches four saints also by Nanni di Banco ; the shoemakers, one of St. Philip by the same, and the butchers, one of St. Peter, by Donatello. What a pleasant and instructive light gleams from those remote times here, when the very humblest craftsmen united to set up these fair works of art, and cast about them for the greatest masters money or influence could command to honor their trades and adorn the city wherein they practised them ! Think of the butchers of New York, to say nothing of the merchants, and Wall Street "money-changers," seeking for some best sculptor—where would they look ?—to make some noble work for their own satisfaction and that of their fellow-citizens ! In the interior is an exquisite high altar, by Andrea Orcagna, in marble and precious stones, with beautiful reliefs, completed, as the inscription states, in 1359, and set up over the miracle-working image of the Virgin. In the Piazza before the church stands an imposing statue of Dante, in white marble, 19 feet high, on a pedestal 23 feet, erected May 14th, 1865, on the six hundredth anniversary of the poet's birth.

San Lorenzo is one of the oldest churches in Italy, having been consecrated by St. Ambrose in 393, burned down in 1423, and rebuilt in 1425, from designs by Brunelleschi. Before the high altar is a slab in the pavement marking the simple grave of Cosimo de' Medici, with the inscription "*Pater Patriæ.*" He died August, 1464, the founder of the illustrious house of Medici, several of whom sleep here. Donatello is buried in the same vault. This noble artist has much good work here, a marble monument to the parents of Cosimo, a bust of St. Lawrence, bronze doors and a reading-desk or ambo being among them. Cosimo founded the Laurentian Library adjacent to the church, subsequently enlarged by the succeeding Medici, where are a great many rare and valuable manuscripts, of which I examined with pleasure one of Virgil of the fifth century, one of Tacitus of the tenth, brought from Germany, and said to be the only copy containing the first five books of the "Annals," a copy of Petrarch's Sonnets, with exquisite miniature portraits of himself and Laura, Boccaccio's "Decameron," etc. The library building, with the portico and staircase, were designed by Michael Angelo, and to me are crude and sombre. He also built the new Sacristy as a tomb for the Medici, containing the mausoleum of Giuliano de' Medici, surmounted with a statue of him as the General of the Church. The sarcophagus below is adorned by the statues of "Day" and "Night," and opposite is the statue of Lorenzo de' Medici above his tomb, on which recline the statues of "Evening" and "Dawn." This is the famous tomb of the Medici, and these are the statues, all by Michael Angelo, of which I had read and heard so much, and on which writers of fame have gushed in bathos as they have done over the "Venus de' Medici." The effigies of the Medici are indeed strikingly life-like figures, but the other marbles convey little meaning to me, and I might stand before the bepraised figures of "Evening" and "Dawn," "Night" and "Day" till Doomsday and see no more than huge sprawling forms in stone, with the meaning intended so obscure as to be confusingly undiscoverable to me. The room itself with its dome is suitably majestic, as it could not well fail to be, having been copied, as to its form, from the old one designed by Brunelleschi. The Chapel of the Princes, connected with the tomb by a passage, was built as a burial-chapel of the Grand-Dukes of the Medici family, and, begun in 1604, is not yet completed. This octagonal room, rising into a lofty dome, and I should think 50 feet in diameter, has walls encrusted with precious marbles and mosaics, whose richness may be inferred from the fact that the Medici expended from their own private fortunes about four and one-half million dollars in our money in its construction and ornament. Think, too, how much greater than now the purchasing power of money was during the two hundred and fifty years the work has been going on!

In the Piazza di Santa Maria Novella stand two obelisks of marble resting on brazen tortoises. These served as the goals of chariot-races instituted in the reign of Cosimo I. in 1563. The Church of Santa Maria Novella is in a style uniting the Gothic with the Tuscan, with pleasing effect. It is mentioned in the "Decameron." The façade of red and white marble and the portal strike me very agreeably, and the spacious interior is helped by the pointed Gothic arches to be more impressive than I find the Romanesque churches are as a rule. The most notable of the frescoes with which this church abounds are those which cover great spaces in the choir by Domenico Ghirlandajo, done in 1490, and called the finest specimens of Florentine art before Leonardo, Michael Angelo and Raphael. They contain a great many portraits, but I care little for them, nor for the much-bepraised "Madonna" by Cimabue. There is exquisite stained glass in some windows as old as these frescoes after designs by Filippino Lippi, and in the sacristy such a delightful fountain by Giovanni della Robbia, and the ancient cloisters are rich in frescoes, some of them by Orcagna. A little way off one enters through a handsome gateway the laboratory of the old monastery, where a liqueur special to Florence, "Alkermes," and perfumes are distilled, and a suite of the charming old arched rooms are kept up in a simple and befitting style, ornamented with old faïence of great value.

The Church of San Spirito, on the left bank of the Arno, has a noble interior, and is attractive with its thirty-eight altars designed by Filippo Brunelleschi in 1433. This church was built for the Augustinians, and Martin Luther, who was a monk of that order, preached in it on his way to Rome. Very stately is the sacristy, to which a beautiful covered passage leads. On the left bank, too, are the church and convent of Carmine, where, in the Cappella Brancacci, are the famous frescoes of Masaccio done in 1423, mingled with others by Masolino and Filippino Lippi. The adjoining cloisters of the Carmelite Monastery are very attractive, and in the old refectory is a fresco of a "Last Supper," by Allori, in which the face of Christ is of exceeding sweetness.

These churches, as well as the galleries, museums and all public buildings, are very cold, the massive stone walls and floors emitting a peculiarly penetrating chilliness hard to bear. The only apparatus for heating, where anything at all is used, as in the galleries, is an upright cylinder of brass forming a brazier, in which smoulder a quantity of live coals and hot ashes, giving out just enough heat to make one more sensible of the cold. Priests and monks go shivering about with red hands and sandalled feet blotchy with chilblains, and poor women come in to pray hugging a little earthen dish of coals called *scaldino*, as if it were a precious baby. As elsewhere, these churches are dedicated to saints whose lives and deeds and miracles they respectively commemorate, and although among the enlightened Florentines the body of relics and pious legends does not seem to have grown to such bulk as one finds in many other great cities, still it is respectable in quantity and quality. Take as a specimen the Florentine legend of St. Minias or Miniato, in whose honor the beautiful church of San Miniato was built, as related by Mrs. Jameson. The same grotesque puerility is found in most of the legends of the church. "San Miniato was an Armenian prince serving in the Roman army under Decius. Being denounced as a Christian, he was brought before the emperor, who was then encamped upon a hill outside the gates of Florence, and who ordered him to be thrown to the beasts in the amphitheatre. A panther was let loose upon him, but when he called upon our Lord he was delivered; he then suffered the usual torments, being cast into a boiling caldron and afterward suspended to a gallows, stoned, and shot with javelins, but in his agony an angel descended to comfort him and clothed him in a garment of light; finally he was beheaded." He held out well, and to him stands the church bearing his name, with a façade exquisitely wrought in colored marbles, subdued and softened by time.

From church to monastery is an easy step. That of San Marco, on the Piazza of that name, is not only interesting as a complete and well-preserved monastic pile, but famous from its associations with the Dominican monk Savonarola, its prior. Fra Angelico came here from his convent at Fiesole and profusely adorned the walls of the cloister and cells with the most beautiful of his works. Here he lived and wrought through many gentle and peaceful years, never taking up his brush without a prayer nor altering anything once expressed of his tender fancies on canvas, because it was the will of God they should appear as first painted. He died here in 1455, at the ripe age of sixty-eight. The long range of monastic cells opening into a corridor ceiled with wood dates from 1436, as do almost all parts of the present pile. The cells are as large as the hall bedrooms of our Brooklyn twenty-five-feet houses, well lighted by pleasant windows, floored with dull red brick, and now untenanted, as the monastery has been suppressed by the government, save by Fra Angelico's glorious saints and angels shining in gold from the walls. At the upper end of the corridor are the two small cells of the prior Savonarola, burned at the stake on the Piazza della Signoria in 1498. Here are shown among other relics of him his crucifix, hair-shirt, an old picture representing his execution, and a bust showing the coarse, strong features of an ecstatic bigot, as I fancy him to have been. Fra Bartolommeo was also a brother here, and has left fine frescoes; so was the beneficent San Antonio, founder and promoter of many charities here. A cell adjoining the church has a plain inner room reached by steps built, as an inscription shows, by Cosimo de' Medici, that he might have a quiet place for converse with Fra Angelico and other brothers. In the pleasant old library are shown as many as eighty great choral-books of parchment-leaves exquisitely illuminated, some done by Fra Benedetto, a brother of Fra Angelico, and the rest by celebrated artists of the fifteenth century, gems of patient, loving labor, the miniatures set in broad margins of gold. This library is the old Scriptorium too, and one fancies the gentle monks, in the soft light of the high narrow windows, bending devoutly over this pious work. In the monastery are the rooms of the Della Cruscan Academy, founded in the latter part of the sixteenth century to preserve the purity of the Italian language. The Academy is putting through the press a large dictionary of the language.

We often meet bands of the "Brothers of Mercy" from the Hospital of the Misericordia, founded here in 1240, and since maintained to afford succor to sick or wounded people. At a summons from the Campanile—their hospital is on the Cathedral square and connected with the Bigallo, a lovely little Gothic loggia, by Orcagna, for the exhibition of foundlings to the charitable public—those on duty for the day come forth in long black robes with hoods so enveloping face and form as to leave only the eyes visible, making recognition impossible. Four of the party bear a litter on their shoulders covered with a black pall, and they hasten to any scene of accident or sickness to which they may be summoned, their services being quite gratuitous. All ranks of society are represented in the brotherhood, and when Dickens was here forty years ago he writes that the Grand-Duke was a member and did duty with the rest.

The old palace of the Bargello, built in 1255 from designs of Arnolfo di Lapo, and for several centuries the residence of the Podestà or chief magistrate, then and to 1859 serving as prison and seat of the head of police, is now occupied by the National Museum. There is a fine but not numerous collection of weapons here, once owned by the Medici, and a beautiful great bronze cannon cast in 1638 by Cosimo Cenni. The great court, with its grand staircase by Agnolo Gaddi and charming upper loggia by Orcagna, most quaint and rich in color everywhere, make a most impressive picture of the circumstances of lordly life in the middle ages. There is a series of reliefs carven upon white marble slabs by Luca della Robbia representing the execution of various forms of music, vocal and instrumental, intended for the organ gallery of the Cathedral, so simply quaint in their naturalness that I declare I fell in love with them at sight and think them almost the charmingest objects I have seen. These reliefs are so fittingly described by a writer in the *Church Quarterly Review*, quoted by Hare, that I repeat it here:

"These happy children standing or sitting in careless ease with their varied instruments in their hands, these fair-faced boys and maidens blowing long trumpets, sounding their harp and lyre, and clashing their symbols as they go, singing all the while for gladness of heart, breathe the very spirit of music. Not a detail is left out, not a touch forgotten. We see the motion of their hands beating time as they bend over each other's shoulders to read the notes, the rhythmic measure of their feet as they circle hand in hand to the tune of their own music, the very swelling of their throats, as, with heads thrown back and parted lips, they pour forth their whole soul in song. Never was the innocent beauty, the unconscious grace of childhood more perfectly rendered than in these lovely bands of curly-headed children thrilled through and through with the power and the joy of their melody."

There are others intended for the same purpose by Donatello, but one cannot see even the work of so great a master in the presence of those others by della Robbia. But this comparison, unfavorable in this instance to Donatello, will not prevent one's pleasure at sight of his bronze statue of David with the head of Goliath at his feet, a figure and face and attitude realizing the idea of the young shepherd victorious, more naturally and fully, by far than Michael Angelo's "David," whose face is noble and full of the triumphant ardor of a hero of classical antiquity. There is a rich collection of Majolica and Urbino ware and some good tapestries, and many other fair and pleasing objects in many kinds, and notable among them to me the walls of a room where are hung many glazed terra-cotta reliefs by Luca and Andrea della Robbia.

More of these beautiful works greet our entrance into the Academy of Fine Arts, where are many pictures of interest and a "Tribune," where in 1882 the "David" of Michael Angelo was brought from its old position, chosen by him at the gate of the Palazzo Vecchio, and placed along with casts from a number of his other most famous works. The "David" is a noble figure truly, vital with power, but it is the form of a giant and not a shepherd-boy. Among the pictures I most liked some by Fra Bartolommeo, Fillipino Lippi, Ghirlandajo and Perugino, Raphael's master, his "Mount of Olives" and "Assumption" being more admirable than any work of his we have met elsewhere.

The Protestant Cemetery is a pleasant spot, grassy and well shaded with old trees, and now no longer permitted to be used as a burial-place. Once it stood in the fields outside the town, which has overtaken and enveloped it in dusty streets. Here I went one pleasant Sunday afternoon and looked on the graves of Elizabeth Barrett-Browning, Arthur Clough, Walter Savage Landor and Theodore Parker. I was surprised to see the flat stone above the grave of the last named quite covered with bunches of flowers, separate offerings in various stages of decay, showing that his grave is frequently visited by affectionate admirers, of whom I have always been one. As I stood by his grave in this foreign clime, I recalled some lines I wrote on hearing of his death in 1860, and I insert them here as my poor offering on his grave:

### ON THE DEATH OF THEODORE PARKER.

Striving at longest life for noblest ends,
He fled from Death to meet him under skies
Stellar and grand with old-world memories,
To which his name an added lustre gives.

The True, the Beautiful, the Good were met
And full insphered in his ample soul ;
His scornful eye withered Tradition's scroll
Where cunning lies and hoary shams are set.
Grasping the sword of Truth in mailèd hand,
He lopped the Time's abuses as they rose,
And smote steadfastly with his dreadful blows
Full on the Giant curse of this fair land.
Yet was he meek and gentle, loved all, but the best
Earth's suffering ones, despised of the rest.

Amerigo Vespucci, whose name, to the neglect of Columbus, was undeservedly bestowed on the Western continent, was a Florentine, and a large handsome palace bears a tablet to the effect that he was the owner and occupant.

I took a box at the opera, filling it with friends, to witness a performance of "Roberto el Diabolo." The popular tenor, Spagno, has a good voice and fine presence, and the well-filled house lavished on his singing abundant and, it seemed to me, discriminating applause. The boxes rise impressively above each other in six tiers, and were filled with handsome ladies and fine-looking men. The ladies were well, even elegantly dressed, but in quiet taste, and I did not see one instance of that style of "full-dress"—more correctly named undress—which was universal in the boxes of Her Majesty's Opera House in London. The incidental ballet was well danced by graceful and pretty girls, but, as with us, seems to be less and less regarded.

Florence is, of course, largely supplied with churches, and the churches are well supplied with bells, and as these are well-attended upon, the city is musical with them, striking the hours in clocks, or rung in peals, or tolled on occasions frequent throughout the twenty-four hours. They are bells of refined characters, too, and exchange soft Tuscan responses with their near and remote neighbors from Arno side to the far-away declivities on which gray chapels or low-walled convents cling. The bells of the Campanile especially, utter rich, dripping tones, as if half smothered in honey, and are singularly sweet, whether heard as one lies dreamily awake in the advancing dawn or in the crowded street at midday. But whether at dawn or midday or eventide, their tones will cease to vibrate in my ears, for we must leave this charming city, full storehouse of delightful art, growing each day more delightful to us. Adieu, fair Florence !

*December* 14.—We left Florence for Rome by rail at 7 A.M., just as the dawn had fully overspread the sky with a roseate light changing to purple, the mist lying like a veil carelessly flung along the valley of the Arno, but violet on the long, broken spurs of the Apennines, their crests powdered with snow. The valley narrows rapidly and grows more picturesque, and thirteen miles down is intersected by the Sieve, of whose beautiful valley we have a glimpse. Twenty-five miles from Florence, near Figline, is a region made widely known by the fossil remains found there of the elephant, rhinoceros, mastodon, hippopotamus, hyena, tiger, bear, etc. At the distance of fifty-four miles lies the pleasant town of Arezzo, the ancient Arretium, one of the twelve confederate cities of Etruria, and more distinguished as the birthplace of many noted men, among them Mæcenas, patron of Horace and Virgil and friend of Augustus Cæsar, who died at Rome A.D. 9 ; the Benedictine monk, Guido Monaco, who invented the present system of musical notation, dying in 1050 ; Petrarch, the poet, born here of Florentine parents in 1304 ; and many others less noted, among them Vasari, the painter, architect and biographer of artists.

We leave the valley of the Arno for that of the Chiana. High up above its fertile plains rises the walled city of Cortona, one of the oldest cities in Italy and the principal stronghold of the Etruscans. It clings to the side of the steep rim of the valley like a heap of enormous rocks worn by time and storm into fantastic resemblances to human habitations, gray and sombre as the rocky hills themselves. How a population of say 10,000 manage to live up there can only be known to themselves. Near by is Lago Trasimeno, the ancient Lacus Trasimenus, where 217 B.C. Carthaginian Hannibal defeated with great slaughter the Romans under the Consul Flaminius, who perished there. It is a handsome sheet of blue water, some thirty miles in diameter, rimmed round with a deep setting of oak and olive woods. At ninety-three miles is Chiusi, the ancient Clusium, one of the twelve Etruscan capitals, and the seat of Lars Porsena,

> " Lars Porsena of Clusium,
> By the nine gods he swore
> That the great house of Tarquin
> Should suffer wrong no more,"

as Macaulay hath said in his ballad of Horatius. At one hundred and eighteen miles lies Orvieto on an isolated tufa rock —for we are now in a volcanic district, the centre of which is the Lake of Bolsena, or Lacus Vulsiniensis, occupying the huge crater of an extinct volcano—at an elevation of 700 feet, with precipitous natural walls, making it a place of such strength that in the middle ages it afforded a refuge to the popes. Our way is now along the valley of the Tiber, here a stream where we first meet it some 50 feet wide, but with a broad, sandy margin, indicating that it is liable to wide overflows. It winds its way with many folds and convolutions along a widening valley of much fertility, like a huge tawny serpent, augmented in volume all along by frequent tributaries, yellow as itself and charged with earthy material brought from the mountains where they take their rise.

We should have made a stop at Orvieto to see the fine Cathedral there, said to be one of the most interesting structures in Italy, a noble example of the Italian-Gothic, and unusually rich in precious marbles, sculptures and mosaics; but the peculiar chill of the weather, to which we feel unaccountably susceptible, makes me desirous of the comfort to be had only in the large cities, and we reluctantly pass it by. There is something inexplicable in the effects of this winter climate upon all the members of my party. Although roses are in bloom out of doors, we are chilled to the bone, in spite of wraps and extra precautions, and have symptoms of influenzas and aches —observable, too, everywhere among the Americans we meet.

A little below Orvieto lie two as picturesque villages as one may expect to see, Baschi and Bomargo. We soon have in full view the strikingly picturesque Mount Soracte, sung by Horace in the ninth ode of the First Book, " *Vides ut alta stet nive candidum Soracte*," one of his most charming poems, and I could have wished to see Soracte "*candidum nive*." It rises precipitously about 2500 feet, its summit cleft into three peaks, on the highest of which stands the Church of San Silvestro, with a monastery of the same name lower down. In Horace's time a famous temple to Apollo stood on the site of this church, and the peaks of the mountain rising abruptly from the plain would lie on the very northern horizon of the poet's view from the Sabine hills. A translation I made of this ode runs in my mind all the way along in sight of this classic mountain, and I give myself quiet by inserting it here :

*Horace, Ode IX., Book I.*

## AD THALIARCHUM.

See how the wintry snow is piled
    High on Soracte's brow,
And whitens wide the forest-tops,
    Low bending every bough ;
And frozen to their inmost depths
    The streams are silent now.

Drive out the cold with logs high-piled
    Upon the blazing hearth ;
And, Thaliarchus, freely draw
    From jar of Sabine earth,
The mellow wine, whose ripened cheer
    Four autumns since had birth.

Leave to the gods all things beside ;
    Lo ! at their high command,
The winds late battling with the waves
    Breathe soft o'er sea and land ;
The cypress and the aged ash
    In unvexed quiet stand.

Enjoy each fleeting hour, dear boy,
    Free from foreboding care ;
Mix with the dance, and, warm of blood,
    In love's fond transports share ;
For crabbed age comes on apace,
    Age with his silver hair.

Freely perform in camp and field
    All deeds of skill and might ;
But fail not the appointed tryst,
    When, midst the silent night,
Faint whispers stealing through the dark
    Confess the maid's delight.

And when at length a merry laugh
    Her hiding-place betrays,
And to surrender she is fain,
    With many coy delays,
A ring or bracelet fondly snatched
    The long chase well repays.

We run along the left bank of the Tiber through the high

region of the Sabina, and twenty-three miles from Rome are at the village of Passo di Correse, derived from the ancient Curos, the old Sabine town where Numa Pompilius was born, and within five miles of the city, on a hill to the right, note the site of ancient Fidenæ, cross the Anio near its confluence with the Tiber, two miles above the city, and making a wide circuit in the broad and desolate Campagna, with picturesque ruins everywhere, roll into a large, handsome depot, having made the distance of one hundred and ninety-six miles from Florence in just seven hours. The lofty dome of St. Peter's had been in view a half hour before, almost the only visible object from the car-windows to remind one of the near presence of the Eternal City ; and now, entering one of a long line of omnibuses drawn up before the station, we are driven through broad modern streets, whose aspect chased away the sentiments natural to one whose thoughts of Rome are of her as she was nigh two thousand years ago, in that period when "the mightiest Julius fell." We have a pleasant suite of rooms in the Quirinale Hotel, looking south and west, on the Quirinal Hill, a thoroughly modern quarter. This hotel, kept by a Swiss landlord, is fully modern, and there are a large number of Americans here, among whom we find several friends and acquaintances.

The first sound to greet my ears on coming out of a prolonged sleep at ten o'clock on our first morning in Rome was "There is a Happy Land," rung out from a chime of pleasant bells in the belfry of the American Church. In the afternoon, with that profound and imaginative antiquarian, Signor Frattini, at this present, and for some months heretofore, consenting, for a quite unworthy stipend, to sweep me along with him, as it were, through the civilizations of the old world, in the character of guide, philosopher and friend, I strolled forth to see if, perchance, I might happen on anything dating back beyond the time of Victor Emmanuel. At the distance of a few steps from the hotel I was rewarded, for in a crossway below the wall of the Villa Aldobrandini lies, quite apart from any other structure, a few short courses of a wall of huge blocks of black stone, a fragment of the ancient walls, dating from the time of the kings and put in place centuries before Christ.

A few minutes' walk brings one to the Piazza of the Monte

Cavallo, on which fronts the huge, ugly Palace of the Quirinal, the residence of the popes, until Pius IX. made his escape from it in 1848, after which it remained unoccupied until Victor Emmanuel took possession in 1871, since which time it has been the Royal Palace. In the centre of the Piazza stands a red granite obelisk, with its base 95 feet high, brought from Egypt by Claudius, A.D. 57, and placed before the mausoleum of Augustus, and removed to its present site in 1781. At its base and close by a fountain playing into a handsome basin of Egyptian granite brought here from the Forum, where it had long been used as a watering-trough, tower the majestic statues of Castor and Pollux reining in their horses. They once stood in front of the baths of Constantine, and Hare states that by an old tradition they are said to have been a present from Tiridates to Nero. On their bases are the names of those greatest of the Greek sculptors, Phidias and Praxiteles. I do not know the grounds of imputing these works to such hands, and from what little I know of the matter, the presumption would be that they are from the hand of a pupil of the former. They have certainly come down from a remote time as the work of these greatest sculptors of the best age of Greece, and by whomsoever wrought, they greatly impress me, the heroic forms of the twins rising in godlike proportions, the clear profiles of their beautiful faces serene in resistless power, in glorious relief on the stainless blue of the western sky.

A walk of a few minutes took us to the summit of the Pincian Hill, the northernmost of the seven hills of Rome, the ancient "Collis hortorum," or "hill of gardens," so named because the rich and luxurious Lucullus had his famous grounds and villa here, where he gave those feasts which have made his name the symbol of costly living. Later, the infamous Messalina, the fifth wife of the Emperor Claudius, compassed the death of Valerius Asiaticus, the owner in her time, in order to possess them, and held high revel here until her debaucheries so enraged her husband that she was murdered in the gardens, which had a bad name afterward and fell into decay, being during the middle ages no more than desolate fields, where the ghost of Nero was believed to walk, and later a vineyard belonging to the monastery of Santa Maria at the foot of the hill. During the French occupation under the third Napoleon it was laid out in a public drive and pleasure-ground approached by a broad, fine, winding avenue, with statues and basins and fountains bordering it. The whole summit is not more than ten acres, I should say, but is laid out with such art, and its scanty proportions are so screened by rows and clumps of handsome trees, cypresses, sycamores, live-oaks and a variety of flowering shrubs, and the drives and walks are so artfully prolonged and doubled on each other, that one feels himself in a spacious park. Here all the world of Rome comes in carriages and on foot, and a sprinkling of the gilded youth on horseback, every afternoon between four and six, to listen to a good band playing sparkling music, to see and be seen. The crowd is picturesquely made up of all sorts of people, princes and fine ladies, friars of many an order, priests, and strong, brown nurses in the only national costumes visible, giving a bright air to the moving panorama, as they thread the throng in blue and gold and red, carrying, as if they did not feel the weight, their young charges swathed in long, trailing white robes. These nurses, so full-throated, striking and even noble of feature and expression and carriage, come nearer to realizing my previous idea of the ancient Roman type of form and face than do any other of the people, high or low. They are from the country round about. The approaches and walks all about are set thickly with ancient statues and fountains and busts of eminent Italians to the number of several hundred, giving the grounds a noble and inhabited look. A terrace on the west side 150 feet above the valley of the Tiber affords a magnificent view in all directions, including the lofty dome of St. Peter's and the Vatican buildings, the long, low line of the Janiculan hills on the opposite side of the Tiber, with the huge bulk of St. Angelo, the Pantheon, and a world of domes, belfries and towers, rising above the close, narrow streets on the hither side, and beyond all, stretching away to the blue line of the sea, the vast and solemn Campagna.

Returning, I stopped for half an hour in the chapel of S. Trinità de' Monti, to hear the sweet-voiced nuns sing the Benediction. They are invisible behind a screen in the gallery, and one would like to think them as fair and pure as the notes which float down into the silence of the hushed nave like the tones of silver bells. An organ accompanied them, and before the altar a handsome priest sang the responses in a rich baritone voice.

For ten days now I have made no further entry, and have done little more than endeavor to get some partially clear idea of the topography of the Eternal City. The city of Rome lies in a vast plain beginning among the recesses of the Apennines and stretching away southwest nearly to the Mediterranean, some eighty-five miles long by twenty-five wide. This plain, called by the general name of the Campagna, was once the bed of the sea, raised into broken undulations by volcanic forces, remains of which exist in numerous extinct craters all about, in the lava and peperino often met with and the red tufa found everywhere. On the east lie the Sabine Mountains, a chain of the Apennines, and to the south of these, and separated from them by a level interval of four miles, the short, detached range of the Alban Hills, also of volcanic origin. Through this vast plain flows the Tiber, some two hundred miles in length, having its rise far up among the Apennines, and joining the Mediterranean some fourteen miles below the city, through which it flows, having been increased by the Anio just above the walls. The famous seven hills of Rome are a detached range of volcanic hills on the eastern or left bank of the river, between which and the bases of the range lies a considerable plain, broadened at one point by a curve of the river into the classical Campus Martius. These seven hills are now not very clearly distinguishable from one another, as their elevation above the range is slight, having been diminished through the centuries by cutting down and filling up. Looked at from the low range of the Janiculan on the opposite bank, these hills seem no more than a low, even range, some 200 feet high, sloping up from the river and covered with buildings. But sufficient differences still exist to mark the designations by which the inequalities have long been known, although these are not the names in all cases used by the Romans in the earliest times, when some subdivisions of the principal heights had special names now no longer used and counted to make up the "Septimontium," or seven hills. But after the earliest times, stated roughly, the designations were made as they now stand; and leaving the archæologists and antiquaries to contend over minor particulars, I will name the hills in order from north to south, and speak particularly of each later on as I visit them. The seven hills of Rome, then, are the Quirinal, Viminal, Capitoline, Esquiline, Palatine, Cœline, Aventine, of which the Capitoline, Palatine and Quirinal are historically the most important. On a portion of these hills and on the plains on both sides the Tiber, in the palmy days of the imperial rule, dwelt a population of from one and a half to two million people, where now is less than one-fifth of that number. In the fourteenth century it had fallen as low as 20,000. The vast and melancholy Campagna, marshy, malarial, deserted, with not a tenth of its surface under cultivation, was then densely populated and covered with prosperous towns. This sad change began when the small farmers who owned and tilled the soil were gradually displaced by large landed proprietors and the great plain converted into vast estates and pastures. As cultivation diminished the malaria increased and has reduced the inhabitants to a scanty race of herdsmen, who with their cattle go to the mountains during the summer months, so plague-stricken is all this surrounding country. It is estimated that only one-sixth of the land of the Campagna belongs to the working owners, one-third to the nobility and about one-half to ecclesiastical corporations. These large properties are let out to wholesale contractors, of whom there are only some fifty altogether; and although the government is taking some feeble steps to reform and improve this inadequate cultivation, but little progress has been made, so that this capital of Italy, well situated of itself, with an excellent water supply, has surroundings more unhealthy than an old-time Indiana marsh.

I shall say nothing of the history of this marvellous city, "mother of nations," mistress of the world through so many ages, first by the power of arms and after by that of religion, so that the heart beats faster at the very mention of the name of Rome. Every school boy and girl knows the wonderful story from the legends of the mythical time of Romulus and Remus and their foster-mother, the tameless but nourishing wolf, which

> "Gave them of her own fierce milk,
> Rich with raw flesh and gore,"

perhaps more than a thousand years before our era, all along down through the periods of the kings, the Republic and the

Empire, followed by the long sway of the Papal See. What wealth of conquest, what magnificence of art, what glories of all time were gathered here to be despoiled by barbarian nor less by Christian hands, consumed by fire and the tooth of time and the wasteful passions of man through eighteen centuries, yet presenting enough still of glorious remains and tokens of her former greatness to enchain the affection and rouse the admiration and sensibility of cultivated souls over all the earth! No one knows how many times the city has been rebuilt since the time of Christ. The remains of that time and the two or three centuries following—and these, although pitiably few, are yet more than I had supposed—are mostly from fifteen to twenty-five feet below the present surface, and have been largely revealed by excavations chiefly made in the last twenty-five years. Just what treasures of architecture and art have perished in all the ages is not known, but a record published by Cardinal Mai even so late as 540, when the destruction had been going on for two centuries, mentions as existing at that time 324 streets, two Capitols—the Tarpeian and that on the Quirinal—80 gilt statues of the gods—only that of Hercules remains—66 ivory statues of the gods, 46,608 houses, 17,097 palaces, 13,052 fountains, 3785 statues of emperors and generals in bronze, 22 great equestrian statues of bronze—only Marcus Aurelius remains—9026 baths, 31 theatres, and 8 amphitheatres. That even so many relics now remain is in good part due, it is said, to Raphael, who in the early part of the sixteenth century implored Pope Julius II. to "protect the few relics left to testify to the power and greatness of that divine love of antiquity whose memory was inspiration to all who were capable of higher things."

Very much of the Rome of to-day is quite modern, wide streets lined with huge lofty buildings of stone, mostly stuccoed and painted yellow, the principal parts of the older portion lying along the low line of the Tiber and including that large level tract known in classical times as the Campus Martius. Only the ancient remains and the great and rich churches of the middle and later centuries and the galleries of ancient and more modern art are of interest to me, and these have been made so familiar to all the world by such a great number of scholars and most capable writers in all styles and reproduced by famous engravers that I need not dwell upon them even to effect the purpose of these notes—that of aiding my imperfect memory and seeking to fix the fleeting impressions made upon my mind in its state of lively exaltation when finding myself after so many years of longing in the midst of these glorious objects. Here is the seat and heart of that venerable church whose wide arms embrace the world, and although its aged head, Pope Leo XIII., now eighty years old, no longer wields any temporal power and is a voluntary prisoner in his huge palace of the Vatican, still his spiritual sway over 200,000,000 souls is, when allowance is made for the altered condition of the time, almost as complete as that enjoyed by the most absolute of his predecessors ; and, as a consequence, here in the sacred city the influence of the Catholic Church is everywhere apparent, and religion in its prescribed and ancient forms seems in this Christmas week to be predominant in all the life of the city. Ecclesiastics of all degrees, from the well-kept cardinal of high and serious face down to the barefoot monk, are met everywhere on the streets, and the great churches, hung in the Christmas-time with red draperies, are thronged with worshippers.

St. Peter's, where we attended services on Christmas day, surpasses in grandeur and magnificence all my anticipations, high as these had been raised. One experiences a momentary feeling of disappointment when, crossing the great court between high gleaming fountains and the noble curved colonnades, the eye notices that the not altogether pleasing front hides the majestic dome ; but once the heavy double leathern curtain is pushed aside and one stands upon the marble floor of the interior, all is one vast and overwhelming scene of light and splendor, and the soul is only conscious of admiring awe. I had an impression, from some reading or other, that the interior was dusky and in parts gloomy with shade ; on the contrary, everywhere is a flood of mellow light from the great dome, so vast, so lofty that it seems a part of the sky itself. The floor, the walls, the massy and countless pillars are of costly and many-colored marbles ; the roof is vaulted and gilded ; not an inch of space but is adorned with gold and precious marbles. Colossal statues and winged angels, their size lessened by the greatness of the space, shine everywhere above and around, gloriously bewildering, but harmonious, symmetrical and beautiful. On both sides of nave and transept open broad chapels, themselves as large as most modern churches, rich with gilding, pictures, mosaics, costly altars and the tombs and monuments of popes, kings, princes and many noble and distinguished dead, with confessionals, it is said, for every language spoken among Christian men. Naked figures give but a cold impression of this the most imposing church reared by the hand of man, but they may assist the mind by furnishing some data for comparison with structures within our knowledge. The length of St. Peter's is 613½ feet; St. Paul's in London, 520½ feet; Milan Cathedral, 443 feet; St. Sophia, Constantinople, 360½ feet. These comparative sizes are marked on a line in the pavement of St. Peter's, whose dome rises on the interior 405 and on the exterior to the height of 448 feet. The size is more effectively shown by contrasting its area as follows: St. Peter's, 18,000 square yards; Milan Cathedral, 10,000; St. Paul's, 9350; St. Sophia, 8150; Cologne Cathedral, 7400. The four enormous piers supporting the dome enclose the shrines of the four great relics of the church—the lance of St. Longinus, the soldier who pierced the side of our Saviour, presented to Innocent VIII. by Pierre d'Aubusson, Grand-Master of the Knights of Rhodes, who had it from Sultan Bajazet; the head of St. Andrew, said to have been brought from Achaia in 1460; a portion of the true cross brought by St. Helena; the napkin of St. Veronica or her handkerchief which wiped the brow of our Saviour on his way to Calvary and bears the impress of his countenance. These renowned relics are exhibited from a balcony above the statue of St. Veronica on Holy Thursday, Good Friday and Easter Sunday, but at such a great height surely nothing can be distinguished with any clearness. Beneath the dome rises the imposing gilded canopy nearly a hundred feet above the high altar, at which only the Pope may officiate. This altar stands over the tomb of St. Peter, one half of whose body is believed to lie enshrined here in a sarcophagus brought from the Catacomb near St. Sebastian, the other portion being at the Lateran. Also one portion of the body of St. Paul is supposed to be enshrined here with Peter, the rest being preserved in the Church of S. Paolo fuori le Mura. The descent to this confessio or shrine, one of the most sacred spots on earth to the Catholic mind, is by a short flight of broad marble steps, and on the heavy balustrade surrounding these, eighty-nine lamps burn perpetually, day and night. Not far away against the last pier on the right of the nave is seated in a chair, some four feet from the pavement, a rude, life-like bronze statue of St. Peter, its naked right foot extended within easy reach of the lips of the throng of worshippers, chiefly of the lower sort, including low-browed and debased-looking herdsmen and peasants from the Campagna, who kiss the big toe reverently, press it to their foreheads and prostrate themselves with a passionate fervor I have seen nowhere, save in the great Cathedral of the City of Mexico. This statue is said to have been cast from the old one of Jupiter Capitolinus.

In one of the great chapels to-day is wondrous music, and among the voices one known as the "angel voice of Rome," that of an old man, high, pure and sweet. The means used to secure tenor voices some time ago are no longer used, I am informed, and this one is a survival of a cruel practice. After mass a procession of cardinals, prelates, canons and minor dignitaries shining in vestments of white and red, gold and purple and violet, paced along the aisles, the clouds of perfumed incense from the swinging censers slowly dissolving in the vast upper spaces in faint fragrance ; a pageant of picturesque beauty.

St. Peter's and the adjoining palace of the Vatican stand in a hollow of the low range of the Janiculan Hills on the right bank of the Tiber, where Agrippina, the mother of Caligula, possessed gardens, and he, a circus in whose arena in the reign of Nero, when it took his name, many martyrdoms of Christians occurred from A.D. 54 to 68, watched by him from the adjoining grounds, and where, according to Tacitus, he used their living bodies wrapped in pitch and set on fire as torches in the night. St. Peter, according to the traditions of the church, was buried in the circus of Nero, and to mark the spot and perpetuate the memory of the early martyrs who suffered here, an oratory was founded on the site of the present edifice in A.D. 90 by Anacletus, Bishop of Rome, who is believed to have been ordained by St. Peter himself, whose crucifixion is said to have taken place on the hill-side near by, A.D. 67. In 306 Constantine the Great began a church on the site of the old oratory, which, although only half the size of St. Peter's, was larger, says Hare, than any mediæval cathedral except the equally large ones of Milan and Seville. It was 395 feet long by 212 feet wide and was extremely rich in relics and works of art, nearly all of which were lost or wilfully destroyed when it was pulled down by Pope Julius II., who in 1506 began the present St. Peter's from designs by the great architect Bramante, although several changes were made by different hands during the one hundred and seventy-six years it was completing in its present form. The squatty, low and heavy dome designed by Michael Angelo was not built, but instead the present wonderful one planned and built by Giacomo della Porta. The cost of the main building of the church alone has been estimated at fifty million dollars, and to raise this enormous sum Julius II. and Leo X. resorted to the sale of indulgences, the immediate cause of the Reformation. The annual expense for repairs exceeds thirty thousand dollars. The temperature of the vast interior scarcely varies the year round from that of a pleasant spring day.

Directly beside St. Peter's and connected with it is the Vatican Palace, the largest in the world, built in the fifth century for a dwelling-house for the popes, but enlarged from time to time, until now it embraces an area of some twenty acres and comprises twenty courts, eleven thousand halls, chapels, saloons and private apartments. Here the Pope resides with a household in various sorts, numbering in the time of Pius IX. more than two thousand persons, probably now reduced. The Pope no longer exercises temporal authority even in the city of Rome, but by a law passed by the Italian Parliament in 1871 this palace of the Vatican, that of the Lateran and the papal villa at Castel Gandolfo are secured the "privilege of exterritoriality," so that they are under exclusive papal control. Only a few apartments here are made use of by the Pope, who is said to live in a very simple manner, the greater number being occupied by the priceless collections of works of art, and open to the public with slight restrictions. We first enter the Sistine Chapel, a beautiful hall 133 feet long by 45 wide, the upper portion of the walls decorated with frescoes by Florentine masters, Perugino, Botticelli, Ghirlandajo, etc. The lower portions of the wall are left naked, it being usual on festival occasions to cover these with Raphael's tapestry. The entire ceiling is covered with frescoes by Michael Angelo representing in nine sections the creation of the world and man, the Temptation and Fall, the Deluge and the story of Noah. So far as one can see by bending the head backward to a right angle with the spine and staring upward in a state of half strangulation, these frescoes, with the prophets and sibyls at their base, are grand and nobly executed compositions. Thirty years later, in 1541, the same master, the three pictures by Perugino which then occupied the space, having been erased, painted on the altar-wall the vast fresco of "The Last Judgment," of which I will only say and take the consequences, that to me it is a confused and horrible nightmare. Lady Eastlake writes in her "History of Our Lord" that the art of Michael Angelo is "not always sympathetic nor comprehensible to the average mind." I am well enough content with this explanation of my want of enjoyment in almost everything in architecture, sculpture and painting from his hand.

On the floor above—the second floor of the palace—are three apartments or stanze, whose ceilings and walls are adorned with the famous and delightful frescoes of Raphael, the king of painters, of which I most enjoyed the "Parnassus" on one of the walls of the Stanza della Segnatura, in which grouped about Apollo are the Nine Muses and on either hand Dante, Virgil, Petrarch, Sappho, Pindar and Horace. Besides these the third loggia or corridor of this floor is decorated with the still more famous frescoes of Raphael and his pupils, fifty-two in number, from the Old and New Testaments. Also in the Gallery of Arras we see with admiration the wonderful tapestry executed early in the fifteenth century in the looms of Brussels from cartoons drawn by Raphael. They are beautifully wrought in wool, silk and gold; the scenes are from the New Testament and have been made familiar everywhere by countless reproductions. Many pieces are sadly faded, but the eye rests on them in their rich borders with ever-increasing pleasure. Seven of the original number were purchased by Charles I. of England, and are now shown in the South Kensington Museum. The following have been copied many times in tapestry in famous looms, and we saw them in Dresden and Vienna and elsewhere: "Paul Preaching," "Death of Ananias," "Conversion of St. Paul," "St Peter Healing the Lame Man in the Temple," "Miraculous Draught of Fishes," "Stoning of Stephen." Eleven great halls contain the collection of antiquities, said to be the richest in the world, where among the noblest trophies of all time we see admiringly the busts of Zeus from Otricoli ; of Hadrian, found in his mausoleum ; of Antinous ; the sitting statue of Nerva ; bust of Pericles ; of Aspasia—the only known representation of her ; statue of Commodus on horseback ; statue called " The Genius of the Vatican," supposed to be a copy from a cupid by Praxiteles ; Apollo Sauroctonos, also a copy of a work of this master ; a fine bust of Augustus ; the Laocoön ; the Apollo Belvedere ; Daughter of Niobe ; Venus Anadyomene ; Sleeping Ariadne ; the Antinous (now called Mercury), and esteemed by many the most beautiful statue in the world ; the Torso Belvedere ; statue of Demosthenes ; Apoxyomenos, a replica of the celebrated bronze of Lysippus. The latter represents an athlete after exercise scraping his arm with a strigil to remove the oil. Pliny describes it and states that it was brought from Greece by Agrippa to adorn the baths he had built for the people, and that Tiberius so admired it that he carried it off to his palace, but was forced to restore it by the loud outcries of the populace the next time he appeared in public. So says Hare. We note, too, the curious colossal group of the Nile, and the Minerva Medica, and do not visit the Etruscan Museum or the library.

On the third floor is the Pinacoteca or Gallery of Pictures, a not large collection, but exceedingly fine and almost all worthy of notice, but I can only mention in bare terms as we come upon them, the "Annunciation," "Adoration of the Magi" and "Presentation in the Temple" by Raphael, Murillo's "Marriage of St. Catherine," Domenichino's "Communion of St. Jerome," reckoned the greatest work of this master, Raphael's "Transfiguration," esteemed by many good judges the grandest picture in the world. It was scarcely finished when the painter died at the untimely age of thirty-seven years ; it hung over his death-bed as he lay in state and was carried in his funeral procession. Here is his beautiful "Madonna di Foligno," not so impressive, perhaps, as many of his numerous Madonnas, but a work of such charm as no other painter, it seems to me, could execute.

In the third room is Titian's "Madonna and Saints ;" Perugino's "Resurrection" and "Virgin and Child ;" and in the fourth room Andrea Sacchi's "St. Romualdo." I must not omit to mention the little Cappella de Niccolò V. near the

Stanze of Raphael, whose walls are decorated with frescoes from the lives of Sts. Lawrence and Stephen by Fra Angelico, tender, pure and holy, as are all emanations of that beautiful soul; nor the marvellous Barberini candelabra with reliefs on one of Jupiter, Juno and Mercury; on the other Mars, Minerva and Venus. Curious is it, too, that the striking portrait statues of the Greek comic dramatists Posidippus and Menander, said to have been wrought by Cephisodotus, son of Praxiteles, found here in Rome under Sixtus V., had long been revered as saints.

Even more venerable and historically more interesting than St. Peter's is the great church of St. John Lateran, facing the Piazza di San Giovanni on the Cœlian Hill, which bears on its west front the proud inscription, "*Omnium urbis et orbis Ecclesiarum Mater et Caput,*" whose Chapter takes precedence even over that of St. Peter's, and where every newly elected pope comes for his coronation. It is a vast edifice crowded beyond my describing with tombs, monuments, relics, rich with sculpture and gilding—oppressively so—and containing many objects of exceeding interest. Here is the pontifical throne, bearing the words, "*Hæc est papalis sedes et pontificalis,*" and among the many relics enshrined under the canopy in the centre of the transept are said to be the skulls of Sts. Peter and Paul, while enclosed in the altar is the famous wooden table supposed to be that on which St. Peter celebrated mass in the house of Pudens, with whom St. Paul lodged A.D. 41 to 50, whose family were that saint's first converts, and who is said to have himself suffered martyrdom under Nero. Sts. Peter and Paul are found constantly in intimate association everywhere in Rome. Above the arch of the Tribune is a noble head of the Saviour in mosaic of the fourth century, commemorating the vision of the Redeemer, who is said to have appeared here on the day of the consecration of the earlier church on this spot by Pope Sylvester and the Emperor Constantine, A.D. 324, looking down upon the people and hallowing the work with his visible presence—a face grand and sad in expression. From one of the chapels a door opens into the beautiful twelfth-century cloister of the monastery, whose surrounding arcades are supported by exquisite inlaid and twisted pillars with a fine frieze of colored marbles. The court thus enclosed is a garden of roses, and in the centre is a rich well of the tenth century, called the "Well of the Woman of Samaria."

There are many curious traditional relics preserved in this delightful cloister, among them a porphyry slab upon which the Roman soldiers are said to have cast lots for the Saviour's seamless robe, columns rent by the earthquake of the Crucifixion, and a slab resting on pillars, shown as a measure of our Saviour's height, which I made to be 5 feet 11 inches.

Fair and grand and wide-sweeping is the view from the broad and noble portico of St. John Lateran, including the Alban Hills, blue in the morning, purple in the evening light, sprinkled with white villages of old-time fame, the Sabine Mountains to the north tipped with snow, the long lines of the aqueducts lost in the hazy distance, and in the nearer view picturesque ruins and rugged fragments dotting the melancholy Campagna ; and under our feet the glorious old walls of the city and the white road of the Via Appia Nuova stretching interminably away in the direction of Naples.

Adjoining the Church of St. John Lateran is the Lateran Palace, the residence of the popes for nearly a thousand years from the time of Constantine until their migration to Avignon. The old palace was considerably larger than the present one built on its site by Pope Sixtus V., 1585, and only the ancient Triclinium remains, while the newer erection was converted into a museum by Pope Gregory XVI. in 1843. In a building behind the old Triclinium, attached to a convent of Passionist monks and erected by Sixtus V., is preserved the Scala Santa, a marble staircase of twenty-eight steps, supposed to be that of the house of Pilate, which the Saviour mounted and descended at the time of his trial. It is said to have been brought from Jerusalem by Helena, the mother of Constantine the Great, A.D. 326, and for fifteen hundred years has been the object of peculiar reverence in the Roman Church. So sacred is it that it can only be traversed kneeling ; no footstep is permitted to profane it. Pope Clement XII. in 1730 caused the steps to be covered with a wooden casing, repeatedly renewed since, because worn out by the knees of pilgrims. There are openings through the wood permitting the marble steps to be seen ; two of them are said to be stained with the Saviour's blood. Pilgrims and devotees only ascend on the knees ; all return by a corresponding stairway on the left, and visitors go up by a similar one on the right of the Scala Santa. We were present on a festival day, and when in the atrium or entrance-room, I heard a pounding noise, such as might be made by a drove of cattle crossing a wooden bridge, and found it to come from the thuds of the knees of a crowd of devotees swarming upward on the stairway, only halting now and then to kiss with effusion the wooden covering. Having reached the top they clattered down the lateral stairway and departed to make room for still other throngs in uninterrupted succession. It was when toiling painfully up these steps that the monk, Martin Luther, seemed to hear a voice from heaven saying, "The just shall live by faith," and returning home began that divergence from the doctrines of the Mother Church which resulted in the Reformation and the great variety of Protestant sects.

At the top of the Scala Santa is an exceedingly old chapel rebuilt by Nicholas III. in 1216 from one whose origin is lost in the night of time and certainly existing in A.D. 578, and so sacred that none but the Pope can officiate at its altar, and never open to others save on the morning before Palm Sunday, when the canons of the Lateran come in solemn procession to worship, with torches and a veiled crucifix, and even then none but the clergy are allowed to cross its threshold. Above the altar is the inscription, "*Non est in tota sanctior urbe locus.*" We look through gratings into the relic chamber, containing the reputed sandals of our Saviour, fragments of the true cross, and above the altar a beautiful silver tabernacle made to contain the surpassing relic whence comes the peculiar sanctity of this chapel. This is a portrait of our Saviour placed here by Pope Innocent III. in the year 1200, held by the Roman Church to be authentic, the painting of which, begun by St. Luke, was finished by an angel, whence comes its name, "Acheiropoeton," or the "picture made without hands." In the dusky light within nothing is visible with any distinctness, and we can only stare through the gratings into a gloom where these objects are suggested rather than seen. In the centre of the square before St. John Lateran stands an obelisk, the oldest object in the city, erected 1740 B.C. in the Temple of the Sun at Heliopolis in Egypt and brought by Constantine the Great to Alexandria, and thence by his son Constantius to Rome to ornament the Circus

Maximus, and afterward in 1588 moved to its present position. At this time it was broken, so that a portion had to be cut off, but it is still 150 feet high. The old Romans seem to have made nothing of transporting these huge monoliths from Egypt to ornament the city, more than half a score being still erect in the different squares.

Each of the seven hills of Rome was surrounded by a wall from a time antecedent to history, but more than five hundred years before Christ, in the reign of Servius Tullius, as the tradition is, that king included the whole within one massive wall which bears his name and is known as the Servian Wall, only a few portions of which remain. As the power of the city grew and its empire extended, since it had no enemies at hand to fear, it less and less needed the protection of walls, and they were pulled down; but toward the close of the second century after Christ its decline had well begun, its foes grew threatening, and so for more complete protection from the invasion of the Germans and other northern races, the Emperor Aurelianus, A.D. 270, began, and his successor, Probus, A.D. 280, completed, the wonderfully massive circuit of gigantic masonry, twelve miles in length, the greater part of which now exists, a striking monument of Roman power and architectural skill, enclosing the city on both sides the Tiber. The Aurelian wall is some 12 feet thick and from 20 to 40 feet high, built of tufa concrete mixed with broken brick and faced with triangular bricks one and one-half inches thick. A sentinel's passage runs all around formed in the thickness of the wall, and at regular intervals of about 45 feet tall square towers containing three stories of chambers rose, lighted by windows on the city side, and on the outer side pierced with small slits for shooting through. This wall suffered much injury from the repeated attacks of the Goths and was several times restored, especially by Theodoric, about A.D. 500, and by Belisarius, A.D. 560, and throughout the middle ages by the popes. A writer in the ninth century reckons fourteen gates in all and three hundred and eighty-three towers; the fourteen gates still exist, but a great many of the towers have disappeared. For ages, until the completion of the railway from the North, the greater number of travellers and pilgrims to Rome entered the city at the northern gate, called Porta del Popolo, leading into the square of that name, looked down upon from the Pincian Hill, of which I have spoken above. This Piazza del Popolo is itself a spot of exceeding interest, surrounded as it is by buildings of historic and sacred fame ; among them the Augustine Convent adjoining the fine church of St. Maria del Popolo, where Luther resided when in Rome, celebrating mass here on his arrival after he had prostrated himself on the earth, saying, "Hail, sacred Rome ! thrice sacred for the blood of the martyrs shed here," and where he also celebrated mass for the last time before departing for Wittenberg.

In the centre of the Piazza stands an obelisk brought to Rome and set up in honor of Apollo, of which Merivale says : " Apollo was the patron of the spot which had given a name to the great victory of Actium ; Apollo himself, it was proclaimed, had fought for Rome and for Octavius on that auspicious day : the same Apollo, the Sun-god, had shuddered in his bright career at the murder of the Dictator, and terrified the nations by the eclipse of his divine countenance." Therefore, "besides building a temple to Apollo on the Palatine Hill, the Emperor Augustus sought to honor him by transplanting to the Circus Maximus an obelisk from Heliopolis in Egypt. This flame-shaped column was a symbol of the sun, and originally bore a blazing orb upon its summit. It is interesting to trace an intelligible motive for the first introduction into Europe of these grotesque and unsightly monuments of Eastern superstition."

The Corso, upward of a mile in length, and the handsomest street in Rome, begins at the Piazza del Popolo and ends at the steps of the Capitol ; it is narrow, but lined with the best shops, palaces, and private houses, and sometimes opens into a broad piazza. It lies in the neighborhood of the Tiber, following the ancient Via Flaminia, with the Campus Martius on the right, now occupied thickly with mean mediæval houses. The tall houses lining the Corso are crowded with balconies, story above story, for watching the sports of the Carnival which occur here, including the races, now discontinued, whence its name is derived. Horses without riders dashed along its full length, stimulated by spurs fastened to their shoulders by loose thongs, and were brought to a stand at the lower end by large curtains of heavy drapery let down across the street.

A little way out of the Piazza del Popolo, a cross-street to the right leads to the imposing Palazzo Borghese, where we visited its picture gallery, said to be the finest private gallery in Rome, and saw among other delightful pictures Raphael's "Entombment," Dosso Dossi's "The Sorceress Circe," Correggio's "Danäe," Sebastian del Piombo's "The Flagellation," the beautiful and joyous "Four Seasons" by Fr. Albani, and, chief of all, the glorious "Sacred and Profane Love" of Titian. Still further on the right, on the small piazza of that name, is the little church of St. Lorenzo in Lucina, made memorable by the noble painting of the "Crucifixion," by Guido Reni, over its high altar, of which Browning says :

"... beneath the piece
Of Master Guido Reni, Christ on cross,
Second to naught observable in Rome."

A little farther on a narrow street soon leads, on the left of the Corso to the wonderful Fountain of Trevi, occupying one end of the gigantic Palazzo Poli, from which it seems to pour its enormous volume of water, called Aqua Virgo, brought from a source fourteen miles distant, by Agrippa to supply his baths at the Pantheon 27 B.C. The subterranean channel supplying this gigantic fountain also supplies the great fountains of the Piazzas di Spagna, Navona and Farnese, and the spring yields daily upward of thirteen million cubic feet of clear sparkling water said to be the best in Rome. Here, too, is the shop of the famous jeweller Castellani, where we saw a fine collection of ancient Etruscan works of art on which he models his own beautiful work. I purchased of him a pin of Etruscan design as a Christmas present to Betty. Well along the Corso on the right is the interesting Church of St. Maria in Via Lata, where a little chapel is shown, in which, says Mrs. Jameson, the tradition has been handed down from the first ages, St. Luke the Evangelist wrote, and painted the effigy of the Virgin Mother of God. The basement of this church is shown as the actual house in which St. Paul lodged when in Rome. It belonged, says Hare, "to Martialis, whom a beautiful tradition indentifies with the child who was especially blessed by the Divine Master when he said, 'Suffer little children to come unto me,' and who, ever after a faithful follower of Christ, bore the basket of bread and fishes in the wilderness, and served at table during the Last Supper." A fountain is shown in the crypt as having miraculously sprung up in answer to St. Paul's prayers that he might have water to baptize his disciples. There extends along on the right the vast Palazza Doria, where in handsome rooms, ornamented with many valuable and deeply interesting relics, we see among a great many poorish pictures the fine ones of an "Annunciation" by Filippo Lippi, "Holy Family" by Sassoferrato, "Madonna" by Guido Reni, "Landscape with Temple of Apollo," by Claude Lorraine, and "The Misers," by Quentin Matsys. Near by is the huge palace of the famous old Roman family of the Colonna, built near the site of the ancient fortress so celebrated in the middle ages, in the warfare the Colonnas carried on with the stout race of the Orsini. One tower of the old structure still remains. Farther on to the right is the Palazzo Bonaparte, where Lætitia Bonaparte, the mother of Napoleon I., died in 1836; then the castellated palace of the Republic of Venice, now the residence of the Austrian ambassador; and opposite, the palace of Torlonia, the ennobled Roman banker. Behind the palace of the Republic of Venice is the large and sumptuous church of Il Gesù, its magnificent altar of St. Ignatius, with a group of the Trinity; the Almighty holding in his hand a globe of lapis-lazuli, said to be the largest piece in existence. A "Te Deum" is sung in this church on December 31st for the mercies of the closing year, which I attended, and was greatly impressed, not only with the music, but with the gradual lighting of the three thousand wax candles; those high above the lofty altar and under the roof, reached by men crawling far out on ladders and by long poles supporting torches. This is the Church of the Jesuits, as its name implies, and adjoining is the Convent of the Gesù, the residence of the General of their order and the centre of its religious life. The four rooms in which St. Ignatius Loyola lived and died are here, and his body lies beneath the altar in the church bearing his name, in an urn of gilt bronze adorned with precious stones; and a great ceremony takes place here on the day of his feast, July 31st. In one of the rooms he occupied in the convent, now a chapel, is the autograph engagement to live under the same laws of obedience, poverty and chastity signed Laynez Francis Xavier and Ignatius Loyola.

We are now near the southern end of the Corso, and turning into a narrow street on the right, soon find ourselves in a bright, open space whence a broad flight of one hundred and twenty-four steps leads up to the Piazza del Campidoglio, or Square of the Capitol, which occupies the very summit of the Capitoline Hill, where stood the great temple of Jupiter Capitolinus, to which the long triumphal processions were wont to climb from the Forum below. Here stood in the early ages of Rome many another temple to the several gods, superb in richest adornments; indeed, all this summit was crowded with the noblest buildings man could raise in honor of the supernal powers. This hill was known in very early times as the Mons Tarpeius, from the familiar legend of the treachery of Tarpeia, but later the name Rupe Tarpeia was only applied to a cliff on the western slope. In the hollow between the two low peaks of which the Capitol consists, now raised and levelled to make the Square of the Capitol, Brutus addressed the people after the murder of Julius Cæsar, and on the site of the exceedingly interesting Church of Ara-Cœli on the side of this Square, Romulus in the beginning of Rome reared the Temple of Jupiter Feretrius, the goal of the triumphal procession and the depository of the *spolia opima*, and up the steps now leading to this church, nigh two thousand years ago, great Julius Cæsar climbed on his knees after his first triumph.

This is Christmas week, and so we are able to witness in the Church of Ara-Cœli the exercises connected with the exhibition of the Bambino or holy infant, "Santissimo Bambino d'Ara-Cœli," during this season shown in the "Presepio," a word meaning simply, manger, but used by the Church to signify the birth of Christ. In one of the chapels a scene is shown as on the stage of a little theatre, and on it, in life size and due perspective, as if in a grotto with a skilful pastoral landscape behind it, "we see in the foreground the Virgin Mary seated with Joseph at her side and the miraculous Bambino—a fresh-colored doll, crowned, wrapt closely in cloth of gold and silver and sparkling with jewels; behind, an ox and an ass. At one side kneel the shepherds and Eastern kings in worship, and far in the background are seen shepherds guarding their flocks lying under palm-trees or feeding on green hillocks bright in the sunlight. Midway in the scene is a crystal fountain wrought of glass, with figures of sheep made of real wool, and women carrying baskets of real oranges and other fruits on their heads. Overhead looks down God the Father, well-pleased, with cherubs and angels playing on instruments"— altogether a most pleasing scene and witnessed by great throngs of people. To-day a platform is erected, some feet from the entrance to this chapel, from which children declaim short pieces in verse and prose addressed to the Bambino or in explanation of the scene, these having been written for them by the priests or some friend, and I saw many kind-faced priests wrought into mild excitement and smilingly approving when tone and gesture were apt, tender and graceful, as they often were. A pretty sight altogether. When not thus publicly exhibited on festival days the Bambino is shut up in the sacristy, where it is attended by servants of its own, who accompany it when it goes out in its own carriage to visit the sick, with whom it used to be left for a while that it might work a miracle of healing. This is no longer permitted, because it is said a bold, bad woman made another doll of the size of the Santissimo, and feigning sickness, got permission to have it left with her, put its clothes on the false image and sent it back to Ara-Cœli. But see how the devices of naughty people, including women, are brought to naught! That very night, in a howling storm, the good monks were awakened by a tremendous ringing and knocking at the west door, and hastening found the naked, cold figure of the true baby, who is not allowed out alone any more.

On a wall of the church are hung hundreds of small votive tablets bearing pictures of persons rescued from imminent dangers by the intercession of some saint or other to whom prayer for succor had been made. Those in the most frightful circumstances of danger are shown in the attitude of rescue. For instance, a gentleman of a red face, staring eyes and wildly sprawling limbs is shown arrested in mid-air on his way down from the top of a lofty building, from a window of which the Virgin Mary, whose help he had implored, looks calmly and modestly, as if she regarded arresting the power of gravitation a very small matter indeed. Noticing a fine, handsome Italian boy looking earnestly on the picture of an unfortunate under the wheel of a prodigious cart, with St. Paul looking on, I bade Frattini ask him if this exceedingly imperilled individual was saved alive. "Si, Signor," he answered, with a beautiful trust shining in his dark eyes. The remains of St. Helena are said to repose in the chapel in the east transept called from her name, and enclosed within the present altar is one with the inscription "*Ara Primogeniti Dei,*" said to have been erected by Augustus in the twelfth century. The legend is, that the Sibyl of Tibur here appeared to that emperor, whom the senate proposed to raise to the rank of a god, and revealed to him a vision of the Virgin and her Son. Hence the name of the church, "Church of the Altar of Heaven."

To-day on the broad flight of steps leading up to the Square is a multitude of vendors of all sorts of little articles of a religious kind, especially such as relate to the Madonna; the cheapest quality of colored prints, crosses and medals of pewter, little wax dolls and sheep, etc., all sold at the uniform price of one *baiocco*, equal to three-fourths of an English penny. At the left of the stairway, half way up in a sort of little garden, is a cage in which two wolves are kept in memory of the foster-nurse of Romulus and Remus, and at the top the colossal statues of Castor and Pollux, ordered to be wrought to commemorate the battle of Lake Regillus, where they fought for Rome, and after riding to the city to give tidings of the victory and watering their horses at the spring of Aqua Argentina by the Temple of Vesta in the Forum, spurred their horses heavenward and disappeared from the sight of man. At either end of the parapet is an ancient milliarium, or milestone, being the first and seventh on the Appian Way, and since the first was found in position it showed that the distance on the various roads was reckoned from the gates and not from the centre of the city, as had been supposed.

In the centre of the Square stands in noble majesty the famous equestrian statue of the Emperor Marcus Aurelius, preserved from destruction at the hands of the Church during the middle ages, it is said, because it was thought to be that of Constantine. He sits his warlike charger with a warrior's ease and confidence, clad in the antique Roman garb, his right hand extended in command, his countenance grand, high and serene, like the noble soul within. Interesting, too, is the porphyry statue of Rome in the form of Minerva wearing the Phrygian cap of liberty, and the Tower of the Capitol with its great bell of Viterbo, rung only to announce the death

Fifth line on this page should read:
said, since the twelfth century, to have been erected by Augustus.

of a sovereign or the opening of the Carnival, events apparently of equal importance in the Roman mind.

On the east side of the Square of the Capitol stands the Museum of the Capitol, where we saw many famous objects of ancient art, dwelling with admiration on the Greek statues of the Venus of the Capitol, Cupid and Psyche, the Antinous of the Capitol, the Faun of Praxiteles—the marble faun of Hawthorne's story—the Amazon, the Apollo, the Juno, the bust of M. Junius Brutus, the assassin of Julius Cæsar, the Dying Gladiator, now called the Wounded Gaul, who, preferring death to slavery, has fatally wounded himself in the breast, the two life-like Centaurs, and in one of the Halls of the Conservators the bronze Wolf of the Capitol, dedicated B.C. 299, bearing the marks of a stroke of lightning inflicted in the time of Cicero.

Let us now descend to the Forum by the stairway at the northeast of the Square of the Capitol, stopping at the foot of the stairs and entering the low church of St. Pietro in Carcere on the left, to see the old Mamertine Prisons, excavated centuries before Christ in the solid rock. They consist of two dungeons, one above the other; and anciently prisoners were let down through a hole into the upper one, a villainous chamber 16 feet high, 30 long and 22 wide, and from it through a similar opening, into the still viler den below. This prison plays an important part in Roman history far back into the years of the Republic, and is thought to be the oldest structure in the city. A modern staircase and door now admit visitors to both chambers, and there are remains of a still earlier flight of steps, called the *Scalæ Gemoniæ*—named so from the groans of prisoners—up which the bodies were dragged to be exposed to the insults of the populace or thrown into the Tiber. By these steps Cicero came forth to announce to the throng in the Forum the execution of the Catiline conspirators in the one word *vixerunt*. The lower dungeon where these executions occurred was called *robur*, and in it the decemvirs Appius Claudius and Oppius committed suicide B.C. 449, and here Jugurtha was starved to death by Marius. It was customary for the victorious general, to whom a triumph had been decreed, as he moved up the slope to the Temple of Jupiter on the Capitol, to pause in the portico of the Temple before entering, until word should be brought to him that such of his captives as he had selected had been executed in the Mamertine Prison. Thus the brave Vercingetorix was executed by Julius Cæsar in his triumph for the conquest of Gaul, and Simon Bar Gioras, the last brave defender of Jerusalem, during the triumph of Titus. The further interest attaches to this prison of being the one in which Sts. Peter and Paul are believed to have been confined for nine months to a pillar still shown. The fountain of pure water beneath the floor is attributed to the prayers of St. Peter for water in which to baptize his jailers, but Plutarch speaks of it as existing in the time of Jugurtha, nearly two hundred years before. The Roman Catholic Church believes that Peter and Paul addressed their farewell letters to the Christian world from this prison, that of the former being 2d St. Peter and that of Paul 2d Timothy. A few steps to the right and we are standing in the Roman Forum on the Via Sacra in front of the Arch of Septimius Severus, and all about are the more or less distinguishable ruins of the successive religions and civilizations of nearly three thousand years.

\* \* \* \* \* \* \* \*

My pen here falls from my hand; I can write no more.

---

Died at the Hotel Quirinale, Rome, January 5th, 1890, of typhoid fever, Elizabeth Graham, only remaining child of James Hale and Mary Field Bates, aged sixteen years.

---

Although after this bereavement we travelled far in many lands—not returning home until the following September—so thick a cloud of sorrow darkened the way that I had no courage for anything, not even these poor notes.

# INDEX.

Abbotsford, the Home of Scott, 68.

Aix-la-Chapelle, 210—its Cathedral, 210; the Cathedral Treasury, 211—its Relics, 212; Relics in the Churches of St. Adalbert and St. John the Baptist and in the Free Abbey of Cornelimuenster, 213.

Amsterdam, 130; Royal Palace, 132; Ryks Museum, 132—the Rembrandt Room, 133.

Andermatt, 167; St. Gothard Pass, 168.

Antwerp, 121; Cathedral of Nôtre Dame, 121; Museum of Paintings, 122; the Bourse, 122; Church of St. Jacques, 123; Rubens' House, 123; National Bank Building, 123; Musée Plantin-Moretus, 123; the Steen, 124; Churches of St. Andrew and St. Paul—their Works of Art, 125.

Ayr, 30; Burns' Cottage, 30; Alloway Kirk, 31; Burns' Monument, 32; Tam o' Shanter Inn, 33.

Belfast, 21; Attend a Presbyterian Church, 24; the Museum, 25.

Berlin, 137; "Unter den Linden," 138; Royal Palace, 138; the Old Museum, 139.

Berne, 189; the Ogre Fountain, 190; the Cathedral, 190; a Curious Old Clock, 191.

Bingen, 215; the Famous Vineyards of the Rhine, 215; German National Monument, 216.

Black Forest, 156.

Brieg, 174; a Funeral Procession, 174.

Bruges, 119; Cathedral of St. Sauveur, 119; Hospital of St. John, 120; Church of St. Basile, 120.

Brussels, 111; Palais de Justice, 111; Hotel de Ville, 112; Palais des Beaux Arts, 112; Place Royale, 114; Church of St. Jacques sur Caudenberg, 114; the Manikin Fountain, 114; Battle-Field of Waterloo, 114; Mound of the Belgian Lion, 115.

Buda-Pesth, 265; Call on a Niece of Louis Kossuth, 265.

Carrickfergus Castle, 25.

Chamonix, 176; Mont Blanc, 177; François Devouasoud, the Famous Mountain Guide, 178; Jacques Balmat, 179.

Charlottenburg, 139; Royal Palace, 139; Hohenzollern Museum, 140.

Cheviot Hills, 73.

Chillon Castle, 184—Bonnivard's Dungeon, 184.

Clachan of Aberfoyle, 38.

Coblentz, 203; Castle of Ehrenbreitstein, 204.

Cologne, 204—its Cathedral, 205 ; Bones of the Magi, 207 ; the Cathedral's Relics, 208—its Peal of Bells, 208 ; the Gurzenich, 208 ; Churches of St. Gereon, St. Maria im Capitol, and St. Ursula, 209.
Constance, 159—its Cathedral, 159.
Constantinople, 239 ; a Night of Discordant Sounds, 240 ; Scutari—its Golgotha, 241 ; the Howling Dervishes, 242 ; Sultan Abdul Hamed II., 245 ; the *Salemlik*, 245 ; Cortège of the Sultan, 246 ; the Sultan Reviews his Troops, 247 ; Classical Ground, 248 ; Exaggeration of Travellers, 249 ; the Dancing Dervishes, 250 ; Grand Bazar, 251 ; Mosques of Ahmet, Solyman the Magnificent and St. Sophia, 252-254 ; Expounders of the Koran, 255 ; the Dogs of the City, 255 ; the Old Seraglio, 256 ; a Turkish Warehouse and " Holy Moses," 257 ; De Amicis' Description of the Passing Crowd of People on the Bridge, 258-263.
Cork, 8 ; "The Shandon Bells," 9 ; Blarney Castle, 9 ; the Blarney-Stone, 10 ; "The Groves of Blarney," 11 ; a Drive to St. Ann's, 12.
Coventry, 90 ; the Three Tall Spires of Coventry, 91 ; St. Mary's Guildhall, 91 ; a Drive to Rosehill, 92.

Darmstadt, 152 ; the Bergstrasse, 152.
Delft, 129 ; Monuments to William of Orange and Admirals Tromp and Piet Hein, 129.
Derby, 88 ; All Saints' Church, 88.
Doune Castle, 43—" Keek into the Draw-well, Janet," 43.
Drachenfels, 214.
Dresden, 143—its Palace, 144 ; the Roman Catholic Court Church, 144 ; Picture Gallery, 145 ; Dresden Porcelains, 146.
Dryburgh Abbey, 70.
Dublin, 16 ; Phœnix Park, 16 ; Nelson Monument, 17 ; Bank of Ireland, 17 ; House of Lords, 17 ; Trinity College, 17 ; Brewery of Guinness & Co., 18 ; the Castle, 19 ; St. Patrick's Cathedral, 19 ; Christ Church Cathedral, 20.
Dumbarton Castle, 34.
Dumfries, 28 ; Statue of Burns, 28—House where he Died, 28—his Tomb, 29 ; Globe Hotel, 29 ; Some Objects of Interest in the Town, 30.
Dunblane Cathedral, 43.
Dunluce Castle, 23.
Durham Cathedral, 75.

Ecclefechan, 26 ; Carlyle Cottage, 26 ; the Carlyles, 27 ; Carlyle's Grave, 27.
Edinburgh, 44 ; General View of the City, 45 ; John Knox's House, 46 ; Holyrood Palace, 47—Picture Gallery and Queen Mary's Rooms, 48—the Murder of Rizzio, 49 ; the Chapel Royal, 49 ; Funeral of the Earl of Caithness, 50 ; National Museum of Antiquities, 51; Visit the Castle, 51—Crown Room and Queen Mary's Room, 52 ; "Mons Meg," 53 ; a Drive to Calton Hill, 53 ; Arthur's Seat, 53 ; the "Queen's Drive," 53 ; Muschett's Cairn, 53 ; Craigmillar Castle, 54 ; an Article on the Late Earl of Caithness, 54-59 ; Attend Morning Session of the General Assembly of the Church of Scotland, 59 ; National Picture Gallery, 60 ; Rosslyn

Chapel, 61; Rosslyn Castle, 61; a Ramble Over the Grounds of Sir James Drummond, 62; Dalkeith House, 62; Morning Service at St. Giles' Church, 63; a Walk through the Old Parts of the City, 64; Advocates' Library, 66.

Florence, 286; a Brief History of the City, 287—its Architecture, 288; the New Palaces Along the Lungarno, 289; Pitti Palace, 289—its Silver Chamber, 290; Palazzo Vecchio, 290; Statuary in the Tribuna of the Uffizi, 291—Some of the Paintings, 292—Famous Masters, 293—Rare Objects of Antiquity, 294—the Marble Sarcophagi, 295; the Cascine, 296; the Drive to Fiesole, 296; Boccaccio Villa, 296; Galileo, 296; Piazza della Signoria, 297; Loggia di Lanzi, 297; the Cathedral Santa Maria del Fiore, 298; the Bell Tower, 299; the Baptistery, 299—its Bronze Doors, 300; a Reminder of Thanksgiving-Day, 300—Preparations, 301—Difficulties in Obtaining Cranberry Sauce and Pumpkin-Pie, 301—Success at Last, and a Bounteous Dinner, 302—" For this Occasion Only," 303; Monastery of Certosa di Val d'Ema, 303; Son of Hiram Powers the Sculptor, 304—Reception at Mrs. Powers' Villa, 304—"A Tale of a Nose," 305; Church of Santa Croce, 306—its Frescoes and Monuments, 306; Church of Or San Michele, 307—its Statues, 307; Church of San Lorenzo, 308—the Laurentian Library, 309—Chapel of the Princes, 309; Churches of Santa Maria Novella, San Spirito and Carmine, 310; Legend of San Miniato, 311; Monastery of San Marco, 311—the "Brothers of Mercy," 312; National Museum, 313; Academy of Fine Arts, 314; Protestant Cemetery, 314; Lines on the Death of Theodore Parker, 314; a Performance of "Roberto el Diabolo" at the Opera House, 315.

Frankfort-on-the-Main, 149; Gutenberg Monument, 149; Visit the House of Goethe's Father, 149; Römerberg Market-Place, 149; Jews' Street, 150.

Fribourg, 192; the Organ in the Church of St. Nicholas, 192—an Organ Recital, 193.

Geneva, 180—its Watch-making Industry, 181; House of John Calvin, 182—a Vain Search for his Grave, 182; Villa Diodati, 182; Voltaire's Château, 182; Musée Ariana, 183; Monument to Duke Charles II. of Brunswick, 183.

Ghent, 116; the Bell Roland, 116; Cathedral of St. Bavon, 116—its Paintings, 117; Hotel de Ville, 118; Statue of Jacques van Artevelde, 118; "Mad Meg," 118; the "Beguinages," 118.

Giant's Causeway, 22.

Glasgow, 34—its Cathedral, 34.

Hague, The, 127; the Mauritshuis and its Picture Gallery, 128; Baron Steengracht's Collection of Paintings, 128; a Noble Park, 129—the "House in the Wood," 130.

Heidelberg, 216—its Castle, 217; the Great Tun, 217; Wines, 218; the University, 218.

Homburg, 150—its Springs, 150; the Cursaal, 151; the Saalburg, 152.

Interlaken, 194; Amateur Tourists, 194.

Jedburgh, 71—its Abbey, 72.

Kenilworth Castle, 92.
Killarney, 13; Muckross Abbey, 14; Lakes of Killarney, 15, Innisfallen, 15; Ross Island, 15.

Lausanne, 186—its Cathedral, 186.
Lauterbrunnen, 195; the *Ranz des Vaches*, 195; the Jungfrau, 196; Staubbach Falls, 196; Giessbach Falls, 196; a Wonderful Cañon, 196.
Leeds, 85.
Lichfield, 88—its Cathedral, 89; House of Dr. Johnson, 89; Three Crowns Inn, 90.
Loch Katrine, 37.
Loch Leven, 64—its Castle, 65; Priory of Port St. Mary, 65.
Loch Lomond, 35.
London, 101; "Macbeth" at the Lyceum Theatre, 101; House in which Carlyle Died, 101; Westminster Abbey, 102; "Lohengrin" at the Royal Italian Opera House, 103; Hear Mr. Spurgeon Preach, 103—Description of the Great Preacher, 104; National Gallery, 105; Hyde Park, 105; Henley Regattas, 105; Tower of London, 108.
Lucerne, 162; the Lion of Lucerne, 163; Chapel to William Tell, 163; View from the Summit of the Rigi, 164.
Lugano, 168; the Church of the Old Monastery of Santa Maria degli Angioli, 168—its Frescoes, 168.

Marburg, 148—its Castle, 148.
Marken, 133; Quaint Customs and Costumes, 135.
Melrose Abbey, 67.
Metz, 198—its Cathedral, 199; the Public Cemetery, 199.
Mont Blanc, 175.
Mount Pilatus—Scene from its Summit, 197.
Mount Soracte, 317—"Ad Thaliarchum," 318.
Munich, 226; the Old Pinakothek, 226; the New Pinakothek, 228; the Old Palace, 229; the Bräuhaus, 229; Training of the Young Men of the German Empire, 231.

Napoleon's Great Road, 171.
Neuchâtel, 187; Legislation in a Château, 187; Municipal Museum and Picture Gallery, 188; Ancestors of Count Louis, 188.
Neuhausen—Falls of the Rhine, 157.
Newcastle-on-the-Tyne, 74; Church of St. Nicholas, 74.
Nuremberg, 220; the Castle, 222—its Instruments of Torture, 222; an Ancient Guillotine, 224.

Old Coach Roads, 86.
On a Coach-Top, 78.

## Index. 347

Potsdam, 140—its Palace, 140—Rooms of Frederick the Great, 140—his Tomb, 141 ; Park and Palace of San Souci, 141 ; the Orangery, 142.

Queenstown, 7.

Ratisbon, 224 ; the Walhalla, 224.
Ravine of Gondo, 172.
Rome, 319 ; Piazza of the Monte Cavallo, 320 ; Pincian Hill, 320 ; View of the Surroundings of Rome, 321 ; Seven Hills of Rome, 322—their Names, 323 ; the Past of the Eternal City, 324 ; St. Peter's, 325—its Size, 326—its Shrines, 326 ; Statue of St. Peter, 327 ; Vatican Palace, 328—Sistine Chapel, 328—Gallery of Arras, 329—the Pinacoteca, 330 ; Church of St. John Lateran, 331 ; Lateran Palace, 332 ; the Scala Santa, 332 ; Portrait of the Saviour, 333 ; the Servian and Aurelian Walls of Rome, 334 ; Piazza del Popolo, 335 ; the Corso, 335 ; Palazzo Borghese, 336 ; Church of St. Lorenzo in Lucina, 336 ; Fountain of Trevi, 336 ; Church of St. Maria in Via Lata, 336 ; Palazza Doria, 337 ; Palazzo Bonaparte, 337 ; Church of Il Gesù, 337 ; Piazza del Campidoglio, 338 ; Church of Ara-Cœli, 338—Exhibition of the Bambino, 339 ; Statues in the Square of the Capitol, 340 ; Museum of the Capitol, 341 ; the Mamertine Prisons, 341 ; the Forum, 342.

Schaffhausen, 158—its Cathedral's Big Bell, 158 ; Castle of Munot, 158.
Scheveningen, 129.
Sheffield, 86.
Simplon Pass, 173 ; the Hospice, 173.
Stirling, 38—its Castle, 39 ; Argyle's Lodging, 41 ; "Mar's Work," 41 ; Statue of Robert Bruce, 41 ; the Bore Stone, 41 ; Gillies Hill, 42 ; Ruins of Cambus-Kenneth Abbey, 42 ; Monument to William Wallace, 42.
Strassburg, 153 ; the Cathedral, 153—its Famous Clock, 154 ; Monument to Marshal Saxe, 154 ; Pâté de foie gras, 155.
Stratford-on-Avon, 95 ; Attend Morning Service at the Church of the Holy Trinity, 96 ; Site of New Place, the House of Shakespere, 96—his Statue, 98—Grave, 98—Bust, 98—Birthplace, 99—the Stratford Portrait, 99 ; Anne Hathaway's Cottage, 100.
Stresa, 169 ; Our Eccentric Coachman, 170.

Trèves, 199 ; Remains of the Porta Nigra, Roman Palace and Public Baths, 200 ; a Library of Rare and Valuable Books, 201 ; Cathedral of St. Peter and St. Helen, 202 ; the Holy Coat, 202 ; Porcelain Stoves, 203 ; a Bed-Poultice, 203.
Trossachs, The, 37.

Venice, 266 ; the Grand Canal, 267 ; Piazza of St. Mark, 267 ; Search for the American Consul, 268 ; Cathedral of St. Mark, 268 ; the Gondolas, 270 ; Rialto Bridge, 271 ; the Ghetto, 271 ; Scenes Along the Grand Canal, 272 ; Frattini in Proud Attitude, 273 ; the Armenian Monastery, 273—the Brotherhod, 274 ; Interior of St. Mark, 275 ; Churches of Gli Scalzi, San Giorgio Maggiore, and San Maria della Salute, 276—their Works of Art,

276; Church of San Giovanni e Paolo, 276--its Monuments of Famous Men, 277; Academy of Fine Arts, 277; the Arsenal, 278—a Model of the Bucentaur, 278; Visit Several Palaces on the Grand Canal, 279; the Pigeons of St. Mark, 280; the Piazza at Night, 281; the Ducal Palace, 281—its Senate Chamber, 281—Great Council Hall. 282—Chamber of the Council of Ten, 282; Arrival of the German Emperor and Empress, 283; an Imposing Pageant, 284.

Vevay, 185; Church of St. Martin, 185; Château de Hauteville, 185; Castle of Blonay, 185.

Vienna, 232; Description of the City, 233; the Imperial Hofburg, 234; the Jewels in the Imperial Treasury, 235; Château of Belvidere, 236; Temple of Theseus, 236; the Prater, 237; Stock Exchange, 237; Imperial Stables, 237; a Performance of " Un Ballo in Maschera" at the Imperial Opera House, 237.

Warwick, 93; Hospital of Robert Dudley, 93; the " Twelve Poor Brothers," 93; the Castle and its Treasures, 94; Church of St. Mary, 95.

Würzburg, 218; the Royal Palace, 219; Walther von der Vogelweide, 219.

York, 78—its History, 79; Yorkshire Philosophical Society's Museum of Antiquities, 80; The Cathedral, 80—a Pompous Verger, 81—the Chapter-House. 82—the Choir, 83; its Stained-Glass Windows, 84; the Curfew-bell, 85.

Zurich, 160; a Trip up the Lake, 161; View from the Top of the Uetliberg, 161.

www.ingramcontent.com/pod-product-compliance
Lightning Source LLC
Chambersburg PA
CBHW030313240426
43673CB00040B/1154